praise for CHOOSING RAW

"Gena's easy-to-digest nutrition information and foolproof food preparation techniques will let you explore the world of vegan and raw foods with complete confidence."

—Virginia Messina, MPH, RD, author of *Vegan for Her* and *Never Too Late to Go Vegan*

"A breath of fresh air—and whiff of fresh cuisine—*Choosing Raw* is a delightful take on food as is should be: colorful, beautiful, delicious. The recipes are a joy (they work!) and the informational portions of the book are Gena Hamshaw at her smart and friendly best, replacing the confusion that so often surrounds nutrition with good sense and great food."

—Victoria Moran, author of *Main Street Vegan* and director, Main Street Vegan Academy

"With menus that make meal-planning a breeze and recipes that fit easily into a busy schedule, *Choosing Raw* is *the* go-to cookbook and guide for anyone interested in incorporating more raw and vegan meals into their daily routine."

—Kathy Patalsky, author of *365 Vegan Smoothies* and creator of Lunchboxbunch.com

Choosing Raw

Choosing Raw

making RAW FOODS
part of the way you eat

by Gena Hamshaw

Da Capo
LIFE
LONG

A MEMBER OF THE PERSEUS BOOKS GROUP

Designed by Lisa Diercks
Set in 9.5 point Tisa Sans

Cataloging-in-Publication data for this book is available from the Library of Congress.

First Da Capo Press edition 2014
ISBN: 978-0-7382-1687-4 (paperback)
ISBN: 978-0-7372-1688-1 (e-book)

Published by Da Capo Press
A Member of the Perseus Books Group
www.dacapopress.com

NOTE: The information in this book is true and complete to the best of our knowledge. This book is intended only as an informative guide for those wishing
to know more about health issues. In no way is this
book intended to replace, countermand, or conflict
with the advice given to you by your own physician.
The ultimate decision concerning care should be
made between you and your doctor. We strongly
recommend you follow his or her advice. Information
in this book is general and is offered with no guaran-
tees on the part of the authors or Da Capo Press. The
authors and publisher disclaim all liability in connection with the use of this book.

Da Capo Press books are available at special discounts
for bulk purchases in the U.S. by corporations, insti-
tutions, and other organizations. For more information, please contact the Special Markets Department
at the Perseus Books Group, 2300 Chestnut
Street, Suite 200, Philadelphia, PA, 19103, or call
(800) 810-4145, ext. 5000, or e-mail special.markets
@perseusbooks.com.

10 9 8 7 6 5 4 3 2 1

For my Mom

Contents

Preface

OVER THE PAST DECADE, I'VE HELPED to guide thousands of women and men on their path to greater health and fulfillment through diet and lifestyle. As a wellness activist, best-selling author, and cancer thriver, I've witnessed and experienced the powerful ways in which whole plant foods can reignite your energy, strengthen your immunity, and support the healing process. I also know that the road to dietary transformation isn't always straight and narrow. Sometimes it's twisting, turning, and treacherous. It can be full of potholes: confusion, culinary experiments gone wrong, protocols that are either too strict or too strange. Change is powerful, but it can be daunting too.

Today, we're armed with so much information about the way certain foods—especially whole, plant-based foods—can help us to fight chronic disease, inflammation, pain, and aging. But amid all of that information, there's also a lot of confusion. There are contradictory and competing theories about what you should eat, how much you should eat, and when you should eat. Foods that are advertised as lifesaving one day are demonized the next. Advice you get from one guru is countered by another. With all of the bickering out there in the nutrition world, it's hard to know whom to trust. It's difficult to feel confident about your food choices, even when you're trying to do everything "right."

This is where Gena Hamshaw swoops in and soulfully saves the day. A certified clinical nutritionist with a brilliant head on her shoulders, Gena is determined to take the guesswork and confusion out of eating raw and vegan food. She's on a mission to help you make raw foods a part of your life without letting them *take over* your life. Gena knows how amazing green, clean, plant-based foods can be, but she also knows that there's more to life than nutrition, that healthy food isn't worth much if it doesn't taste great, and that no amount of kale salad will help you if you're constantly stressing out about what you eat.

I met Gena Hamshaw in 2009. At the time,

she was a fledgling blogger with a small but growing nutrition practice. I was immediately struck by the depth of her knowledge, her intense curiosity about the workings of the human body, and her ability to bring critical insight to the raw food world. I appreciated the fact that she could savor her green juice along with her coffee, and that her passion for raw food was met with an equally strong sense of practicality. When she told me she was considering making wellness work her full-time career. I told her without skipping a beat that she had to do it. This is her calling, and I know she's going to make a difference.

Throughout our friendship and our professional acquaintance, I've watched Gena refine her understanding of health, wellness, and diet. I've admired her ability to reassess her opinions, even when it means calling her previous ideas into question. I've always known that I could count on her for a balanced perspective, and she's on my speed dial for reliable answers to burning health questions. In fact, Gena was one of a select handful of trusted nutrition advisers who I turned to when I wrote my first *New York Times* bestseller, *Crazy Sexy Diet*. That's how much I trust this fabulous woman!

Gena's intellect, energy, and sass have finally come together in this incredible book. Here you'll find 125 of her characteristically easy, no-fuss, and delicious recipes (along with mouthwatering photos). You'll get a healthy serving of Gena's hilarious, no-nonsense approach to nutrition science and health advice. You'll smile at her savvy (and spot on!) responses to some of the biggest myths and misconceptions surrounding vegan and raw food. Many of the questions she addresses are the same ones I'm asked about every day from readers around the world. With good humor, insight, and authority, Gena separates fact from fiction.

Most of all, you'll be inspired by Gena's energy, and by the delight she takes in the vegan lifestyle. You may not be vegan, raw, or even a veggie lover. But no matter who you are and how you like to eat, I promise you that you'll find something to savor in this book. Maybe you'll want to try a meatless dinner now and then. Maybe you'll discover a couple of new ingredients. Maybe you'll be convinced that eating raw food doesn't have to be scary or weird or a hassle: It can be fun and refreshing. And if you've been wondering about plant-based diet but are worried about meeting your nutrient needs, let Gena walk you through a safe, realistic road map for making the transition.

Even with a growing body of evidence that points to the vital benefits of whole, plant-based food, too few people are able to make the connection between the foods they eat and the way they feel. If you've just started to realize that your diet has the power to harm or heal, then this is the moment for you to discover *Choosing Raw*. I know you'll be informed, empowered, and transformed by what you learn.

Cheers to your magnificent health and happiness!

—KRIS CARR
New York Times bestselling author,
Crazy Sexy Diet and *Crazy Sexy Kitchen*

Introduction: My Story

Welcome to Choosing Raw

EARLY IN MY CAREER AS A NUTRITION-ist, I realized that I often had a lot in common with my clients, many of whom were exploring veganism for the first time. When I asked what they were hoping to accomplish, they said that they wanted to heal digestive issues, experience abundant energy, and make peace with their bodies. They wanted to find freedom from dieting and regimentation. They wanted to eat in a way that would be sustainable long term, not endure yet another six-week reboot or a four-week fat blast or a seven-day slim-down. They were overwhelmed by all of the conflicting nutrition advice out there on the Internet: clashing dietary theories, grandiose promises from health gurus, and frightening declarations that this or that food is "the devil." I could recognize their exasperation instantly; I had known it intimately for over thirteen years myself.

Our collective interest in wholesome nutrition has boomed in the last decade.

Americans are shifting their focus away from diets and dieting and toward food choices that are sustainable, socially responsible, and nourishing. With this shift comes a widespread interest in plant-based diets: diets that are centered around fruits, vegetables, nuts, seeds, legumes, and grains.

In this book, I'll describe how a vegan diet—which excludes all animal foods—can be healthful, environmentally conscious, compassionate, and, most important, enjoyable. I'll also introduce you to a particular kind of vegan dining that is near and dear to my heart: raw food. Raw food dishes haven't undergone any cooking; they're prepared by slicing, dicing, chopping, and arranging vegetables, fruits, nuts, and seeds in ingenious ways. While these uncooked dishes might sound foreign at first, I hope to show you that they can breathe new life into your culinary routine, help you to become less reliant on processed ingredients, and even encourage you connect more intimately your food. Vibrant raw food dishes, coupled with a steady foundation of cooked vegan staples, can supercharge your diet with vitamins, minerals, antioxidants, color, and flavor.

As I introduce you to this fresh way of eating, I'll also try to steer you away from some of the alarmism and bad information that pervades the health food realm (raw and vegan camps included). It can be hard to ignore the voices of health personalities who are encouraging you to "detox," "cleanse," rush into elimination diets, or take a very rigid approach to what you eat. In my experience, those sorts of extremist attitudes do nothing to promote a truly healthful and joyous relationship with food. While I'm all for encouraging you to make wholesome choices, I won't ask you to give up pleasures (such as your cup of morning coffee, the odd convenience meal when you're in a rush, or every gram of sugar). Nor will I tell you that you have to become a strict raw foodist in order to be healthy: I don't think that's true, and, as you'll see, I think that a diet that's inspired by raw food techniques but inclusive of cooked foods is actually healthier than a fully raw paradigm. I'll never tell you that a particular food is evil or suggest that one morsel of some suspect ingredient will lead to your demise. The body is resilient and strong, and we have wiggle room to enjoy indulgences or less-than-ideal choices every now and then. This flexibility should be celebrated, not feared.

While I hope that this book will inspire you to consider the many benefits of a vegan lifestyle, I also welcome you to explore veganism one meal at a time. Move at a pace that will be realistic, sustainable, and enjoyable for you. Be gentle to yourself, and don't get paralyzed by the idea of perfection (whatever that means). Vegan activist Colleen Patrick-Goudreau has a saying I love: "Don't do nothing because you can't do everything. Do something. Anything." Try one recipe, and then try two. See where your journey takes you.

My Journey

I grew up in a Greek American home, eating a pretty regular diet. There were family dinners full of fresh vegetables and rice, and there were also buttery bowls of spaghetti, Stouffer's chicken à la king, Entenmann's coffee cakes, and plenty of Häagen-Dazs in the freezer. Contrary to what you've heard about the Mediterranean diet, Greek home cooking is not all salmon and legumes and tomatoes and olive oil; it is also hunks of lamb, plenty of beef, and a lot of kasseri cheese.

When I was about eight, I saw *Bambi* for the first time. I watched, horrified, as Bambi's mother was killed by hunters. It just so happened that red meat—steak—was on the menu that evening. I stared down at the red "jus" swimming around my plate, and my stomach turned. Later that night, I asked my mother if we could eat less meat. By the time I turned thirteen, I had consciously cut red meat from my diet; between that time and the time I went vegan over a decade later, I ate it only a handful of times.

I had an enormous appetite growing up (still do) and loved to eat. Like a lot of young girls, I found myself entering an awkward phase between childhood and puberty. I gained some weight, which became an easy source of teasing. I became self-conscious about my big appetite. The summer I turned eleven, my pediatrician suggested that I lose some weight, and my previously carefree relationship with food took a dramatic turn.

All throughout that summer and into the fall, I learned how to diet. I began hiding part of my breakfast and disposing of it when I left the house. I ate as little as I could during the day so that I could eat dinner at night and avoid raising eyebrows. It didn't take long for me to lose a significant amount of weight. By the time my pediatrician voiced his concern, I had also lost the enthusiasm and joy I'd once brought to food. I dutifully gained back the necessary pounds but remained obsessed with calorie counting, monitoring my fat intake, and skipping meals when I could. These habits followed me through the remainder of middle school and high school. Little changed when I went to college, except that I had less parental guidance, so it became easier to skip meals and fuel myself on skim lattes, cigarettes, and fat-free candy.

At some point in the middle of my junior year of college, I relapsed into the worst of my former habits. My clothes started sagging, my period stopped, and I became increasingly isolated from my friends. I was hungry all the time, and cold; stomach rumblings kept me awake at night. Concern from my friends, coupled with a family crisis, compelled me to get better for a while, but it was an uneasy truce, and I relapsed again in my early twenties. This time, I had discovered healthier eating habits—whole foods, green smoothies—but instead of using this knowledge constructively, I got sucked into

a new kind of restriction. Whereas I'd once counted calories, I now started to obsess over whether or not my food was "healthy" enough. My weight plummeted once again, my period stopped, and I found myself older, but no wiser than I had been a few years before.

The fortunate thing about this relapse was that I had more to lose, and more responsibility for my losses, than I had as a teen. I was a young assistant editor at a publishing house—a career I had always dreamed of. I was an adult, building a life of my own, and I didn't want to jeopardize my future. I began talking about food with a therapist. Eventually I was able to use the words "eating disorder" and confront the depth of the problem. I began gaining weight, pound by pound. I was lucky, all things considered, but the disorder left me with a number of health challenges, including osteopenia (premature bone thinning) and damage to my already-delicate GI system. I'd always struggled with digestive problems, but, at some point in my teenage years, I started to have strange episodes of cramping and bloating. They were intensely painful, came on suddenly, and would retreat just as mysteriously as they had arrived. For days after an "attack," which is what I called them, I'd feel sore, as though someone had punched me in the gut. My physician said it was IBS, also known as irritable bowel syndrome. I was told that it was related to stress, that there wasn't too much I could do about it, and that I should take muscle relaxants when the symptoms got really bad.

IBS is the name given to a wide smattering of symptoms, ranging from diarrhea and bloating to constipation and cramping, that effect 10 to 15 percent of the population (though some studies put the number as high as 20 percent). Women are twice as susceptible as men. IBS doesn't cause long-term inflammation or damage, but it can dramatically impact one's quality of life, and it certainly complicates one's relationship with food. It's hard to say how much my IBS was spurred on by my years of irregular eating, or whether my history of bloating was actually a factor in my body dysmorphia, but each problem tended to intensify the other.

All throughout college and early in my career, I lived in fear of flare-ups: the anxiety, the extraordinary bloating, the pain. At one point, the cramping was so bad that I went to the emergency room thinking it might be my appendix. Rather than seeking out wholesome solutions, I tried liquid diets and "cleanses," which would only make me more irregular and miserable. I asked my physician what I should be eating to feel better, but he insisted that dietary changes probably wouldn't help, that it was all stress. I was stressed alright, but I knew that what I was experiencing wasn't all in my head. I decided to take matters into my own hands. I went shopping around for a doctor who would listen to me, and hopefully give me some dietary solutions.

After a lot of hunting, I came upon an unconventional gastroenterologist who was enrolling some of his patients in an experimental hypnotherapy protocol. I quickly offered to sign up for the study. It helped, but not as much as a few simple pieces of advice the doctor gave me: don't chew sugarless gum. Don't drink carbonated beverages. And if you've never tried it before, see whether or not cutting out dairy gives you any relief.

This was a daunting prospect at first; fat-free Greek yogurt, skim milk lattes, and goat cheese salads were all staples in my diet. Like a lot of people, I used to say such things as "I could never live without cheese." But I was willing to try anything, so long as it would make me feel better. I bought a bunch of soy yogurts, a container of almond milk, and a package of almond cheese, and I decided to see what life without dairy was like. Much to my surprise, it was easier than I expected it to be, and, more important, the improvement I experienced was immediate and profound: more energy, better digestion, and fewer seasonal colds.

I began to wonder if veganism was a possibility for me. Now that I wasn't eating dairy, and since I didn't care much for poultry, my diet wasn't too far from vegan already. I had read about the vegan lifestyle online, and I was intrigued both by the healing narratives and by the environmental arguments. I wasn't quite ready to consider the ethics of plant-based food—like a lot of folks, I was scared by the stereotype of the "angry vegan"—but I knew there was something to the idea of forgoing foods that came at the expense of other creatures' lives. I decided to give veganism a try, and I told myself that I could always change my mind if it turned out to be too hard.

Making the jump to a vegan diet was surprisingly painless. I kept it simple: lots of salad, fruit smoothies, rice, beans, tofu stir-fries, and avocado, hummus, and tomato sandwiches. I ate soy yogurt parfaits or oatmeal for breakfast, and I often made whole wheat pasta with steamed veggies at night. Sometimes I ate Amy's burritos or Dr. Praeger's veggie burgers. Like a lot of folks, I was worried about whether I was getting enough of this or that nutrient, but these fears faded as I grew more energetic and strong. I hadn't expected so much health improvement, but the benefits of my dietary shift were undeniable. And as I learned to consider animals and the environment more prominently in my choices, I was able to break free of some of the isolation and obsession that had defined my relationship with food for so long.

The one piece of the puzzle that I couldn't quite make fit was my digestion. I was better than I had been, but even after going vegan I struggled with bloating and irregularity. It was at this point that I started to read about raw foodism, a particular kind of diet that included no cooked food at all. Raw foodists constantly raved about their perfect digestion, their newfound energy, their deep sleep, and their robust immunity. I was intrigued, if intimidated. I decided to explore raw foods with the same attitude I'd brought to my vegan experiment: I'd try a couple of recipes, see how I liked them, and refuse to label myself as anything other than "curious."

Raw foods changed my life. They turned me into a better, more creative cook. They boosted my energy. They introduced me to textures, tastes, and preparation methods I'd never tried before. My digestion continued to improve, incrementally at first and then dramatically as time went on. The discomfort to which I'd grown so accustomed started to feel like a thing of the past.

More important, exploring raw helped to transform my relationship with food. I had taken great strides forward in my recovery, but I was still prone to anxiety at mealtime and fearful of certain foods. Going raw helped me to get comfortable with avocados, nut butters, desserts, and other foods that I'd historically deemed too caloric or fattening to enjoy. As I explored raw cuisine, I learned to trust that wholesome ingredients would nourish me, and that numbers mattered less than the quality of what I put in my body. After so many years of assessing a meal numerically, in macronutrients and calories and grams of this or that, raw foodism allowed me to pay attention to the beauty and value of my food.

That summer, I made smoothies with many different and brilliant hues. I put together artful, gigantic, and exquisite looking salads; I chopped, minced, sliced, and chiffonaded my way to a vast array of bright new dishes. I didn't set out to become a "raw foodist," but, as the weeks went by, I hardly noticed the fact that I wasn't eating much cooked food at all. I remember this "raw honeymoon" as one of the happiest times in my life. Like all honeymoon periods, though, it wasn't destined to last forever. After a year of enthusiastic raw foodism, I started to miss my cooked vegan favorites (brown rice and vegetables with tahini dressing, baked sweet potatoes with coconut butter, vegetables roasted with olive oil and sea salt). On top of that, my body was still delicate from my last eating disorder relapse, and I was having a hard time gaining the weight I needed.

Most important, I was starting to doubt some of the fundamental assumptions of the raw foods movement. A central tenet of raw foodism is that foods cooked above a certain temperature (115°F, according to some; 105°F, according to others) lose their naturally occurring enzymes. If you eat raw food, the logic goes, the enzymes in the food will aid in the digestive process, sparing your body effort that can be directed toward healing and regeneration instead. It's a very compelling idea, but the more research I did, the more flaws I uncovered (we'll talk more about enzyme theory on page 43). I was also developing discomfort with the raw food community's emphasis on "detox," juice fasting, and other extreme diets. I'd gotten into raw food because it felt celebratory and joyous. This culture of abstinence and restriction was anything but, and it reminded me of the disordered thinking I'd worked so hard to overcome.

I took a step back—and for me, a step forward. Rather than adhering to strict raw foodism for the sake of it, I decided to refine my relationship with raw foods in a way that would make sense for me. I continued to create and savor a lot of raw meals and recipes, but I stopped identifying as a "raw foodist" (a label that had never fit me perfectly, anyway) and I welcomed more cooked vegan favorites, including more grains and legumes, back into my life. I found an effortless balance between the raw foods I so naturally gravitate toward, and the warm dishes that keep me grounded and add nourishment and heft to my diet. This is the diet that makes me thrive, and it's the diet that I continue to eat—and love—today.

At the start of this evolution with vegan and raw foods, a good friend of mine suggested that I start a food blog. "You're so passionate," she said. "Why not share that?"

She had a point: I was incredibly passionate, and I was also starting to accumulate an impressive collection of recipes. I liked the idea of sharing them, and of showing others that my diet—which might seem a little "out there" at first—was actually accessible, intuitive, and fun. I thought back to how intimidated I'd felt when I first began to explore vegan cooking (and later, raw food preparation). And I realized that I had a different perspective to share: the perspective of a young, busy, working person who hadn't grown up in the kitchen and wasn't a natural chef, yet who managed to create satisfying and tasty food in spite of it all. Food that just so happened to be all vegan and mostly raw.

This was the start of my blog, *Choosing Raw*. At first, it was small and intimate, read only by family and friends. As the weeks went by, though, the blog grew, and I realized that many other men and women could relate to parts of my story. I began receiving a steady stream of e-mails, many inquiries about my diet and how I ate. An idea that had been germinating for some time—the notion to begin an education in nutrition—became more compelling. I began pursuing a clinical nutrition degree from a naturopathic school at night. It didn't take me long to fly through the coursework, and very soon I was a practicing nutritionist, working remotely with clients around the world. It was an incredibly exciting moment for me: I had a chance to put my passion for nutrition into action, and, more important, I could help others to find the balance and joy that had eluded me for so long in the realm of food.

Choosing Raw

I'm often asked "why is the title of your blog *Choosing Raw* if you eat cooked food?" In other words, what does being "raw" mean to me?

The answer is that I'm not a raw foodist, not in the traditional sense of the word. "Raw foodists" are usually people who eat 100 percent (or close to 100 percent) raw food diets, and raw food diets consist only of foods that haven't been heated above a certain temperature (105°–115°F). Since I'm a great fan of stir-fries, roasted vegetables, and cooked grains, I certainly don't meet the criteria for "raw foodist." "High raw" is a term used to describe diets that are close to all raw, but not quite; depending on who you talk to, this might mean anywhere from 75 to 95 percent raw. That term describes me a little better, but it's still not quite right, since I sometimes eat less than 75 percent raw food—especially when I'm traveling or eating out.

In the end, the easiest way to describe my relationship to raw foods is to say that I'm a raw foods enthusiast. Raw foods have helped to make my diet more nutritious and creative, and they've influenced my culinary style tremendously. But I don't adhere to any particular percentage of raw vs. cooked, and I don't eat raw foods out of a sense of obligation. For me, the words "choosing raw" signify not a 100 percent raw foods lifestyle, but an overall approach to eating. Choosing raw means eating foods that are a little closer to the earth. It means minimal food preparation. It means dishes that are simple, nourishing, and whole. It often means raw food dishes, but it doesn't have to.

I want you to approach raw foods as a choice too. One way to begin your explanation of raw food is to remember that you're probably eating quite a few of them already, even if you're not thinking about them that way. Guacamole, gazpacho, salads, slaws: These are all raw, or mostly raw, foods. You can use these recipes to whet your appetite for raw food, and, if you like the way they make you feel, then you can continue to explore new ingredients and techniques. You can enjoy a raw recipe or a green smoothie without feeling pressure to commit to a 100 percent raw foods lifestyle. Being a raw foods enthusiast isn't an all-or-nothing prospect.

In this book, you'll find 125 recipes. All of them are vegan. Some of them are raw, and some of them are cooked. Some include a mixture of raw and cooked ingredients; it's okay to mix and match warm and cool foods without feeling as if you're breaking the rules. I'll start by sharing fifteen "essentials"—recipes I return to again, again, and again, along with a sampling of juices, snacks, and dressings that are staples in my kitchen as well. Then I'll share breakfasts, lunches, and dinners that I've divided into three levels. Level 1 presents vegan interpretations of such familiar classics as enchiladas, a breakfast scramble, and a hearty curry dish. Level 2 continues to feature vegan interpretations of dishes you may know and love already, such as risotto, but it also features some raw food recipes and techniques that will help you to freshen up your meals. Level 3 presents you with a wide array of creative yet accessible raw food dishes, including carrot and zucchini "pappardelle" and

Mediterranean cauliflower "rice." You don't have to move from level 1 to level 3—all of the recipes in this book are wholesome and healthy. But as you progress through the recipes, I hope you're inspired to step outside of your culinary comfort zone, to give raw food a chance, and to embrace the tremendous versatility of vegetables.

I've also formulated twenty-one flexible, easy-to-customize meal plans. The plans aren't prescriptive, and I don't intend for you to follow them to the letter. They're meant to give you an overall sense of how you might mix and match cooked and raw vegan food to create a lifestyle that is nutritionally balanced. Once you get the hang of things, I know you'll be able to branch out and start eating intuitively, perhaps adding some of your own recipes as you go along.

Before we get to the food, I'll walk you through the basics of healthy vegan nutrition. I'll explain exactly what raw foods are, why I enjoy them so much, and how they differ from regular vegan cuisine. I'll also address some of the most common myths and misconceptions surrounding vegan and raw food. I hope that you'll feel empowered and informed by the information I share.

Without further ado, let's start choosing raw.

Choosing Raw

PART I

The Why

THERE ARE HUNDREDS OF REASONS TO CONSIDER ADDING MORE
vegan and raw foods to your diet. I tend to think of them as falling into two
major categories: health and compassion. Health includes the ways in which
plant foods might benefit your body and help to protect you from chronic disease.
Compassion includes respect for our animal neighbors and an effort to tread
lightly on mother earth.

CHAPTER 1
Your Health

IN 2009, THE AMERICAN DIETETIC Association, now the American Academy of Nutrition Dietetics, released a new position on vegan and vegetarian diets. It stated that vegetarian diets are associated with lower risk of death from ischemic heart disease (the type of heart disease that's caused by hardening of the arteries). It went on to say that vegetarians and vegans have, on average, lower LDL, lower blood pressure, and lower rates of hypertension and type II diabetes than do nonvegetarians. Vegetarians have lower overall BMIs and lower overall cancer rates.[1]

This came as good news to plant-based eaters everywhere. For a long time, vegan diets had been regarded with doubt by some health practitioners, and certainly by the public at large. As recently as seven years ago, I was often told in passing that I couldn't get complete proteins as a vegan, or informed that I'd need to eat animal fats if I ever wanted to get pregnant, because fetal brains can't develop without them. As misleading as these claims are, they have a strong hold on popular imagination. Fortunately, the new ADA position, along with increasing research on the long-term effects of veganism, are helping to change our understanding of vegan nutrition. Nowadays, we know that it's possible to be a strong, healthy vegan for life, and that a plant-based diet may offer us protection against some of Western society's gravest diseases.

Cholesterol, Saturated Fat, and Heart Disease

No matter who you are or what you eat, your life has probably been touched by heart disease. It's the leading cause of death in the United States, claiming about 600,000 people every year (about one in four deaths, according to the CDC).[2] There are many factors involved in the development of heart disease, but risk factors include high blood pressure, high levels of LDL cholesterol, diabetes, and smoking. While it's possible to have a strong genetic predisposition to getting heart disease, lifestyle changes can make a big difference too.

You've probably heard that of the two types of cholesterol. LDL, or "bad," cholesterol, tends to build up on the inner walls of arteries, causing the "plaque" that can lead to a heart attack. HDL, or "good" cholesterol, on the other hand, is actually associated with a lower risk of heart attack. All cholesterol is not created equal, and in fact, very low cholesterol levels have been associated with depression and anxiety. The goal is not to make your cholesterol levels disappear, but, rather, to keep them within an advisable range and also to be sure that the ratio of total cholesterol to "good" (LDL) cholesterol is low. It's this ratio, more than any other measurement, that seems to be the best indicator of heart attack risk.

Vegans and vegetarians have, on average, lower levels of total cholesterol and LDL cholesterol than do nonvegans. And as far as that ratio of total cholesterol to LDL cholesterol goes, one examination of seventeen studies of Western populations between 1980 and 2003 showed that vegans had a better ratio than lacto-ovo vegetarians, pesco-vegetarians, and omnivores.[3] The risk of death from heart disease among vegans is also lower; one study showed it to be a whole 24 percent lower.[4] If heart disease runs in your family, adopting a whole foods, plant-centric diet is one of the most potent choices you can make to live a long, happy, and heart-healthy life.

Heart disease often comes hand in hand with type 2 diabetes, which is another epidemic in Western nations. Type 2 diabetes is particularly responsive to lifestyle changes—in particular, dietary changes—and, as it turns out, veganism has a protective effect here too. Studies comparing Seventh-Day Adventists, who consume largely vegan diets, to lacto-ovo-vegetarians and omnivores have indicated that vegans' risk of developing Type 2 diabetes may be about one-third of omnivores'.[5]

Macronutrients, Micronutrients, and Phytonutrients

What accounts for the remarkable benefits of a plant-based diet? Is it only the fact that plant-based eaters avoid excess animal protein and fat? Or do plant-based foods also have unique properties that can enhance our health? As it turns out, vegetables, fruits, legumes, and grains, which are the foundation of plant-based diets, have plenty of health-strengthening properties. Plant foods are often spoken of as being "nutrient dense"—which is just a way of saying that a particular food has a very high concentration of nutrients. These include macronutrients (protein, carbohydrates, and fat) and micronutrients (vitamins and minerals). Plant foods are particularly rich in micronutrients. Leafy greens provide us with vitamins A and K, as well as calcium, iron, and protein. Red bell peppers and grapefruit provide us with vitamin C. Sweet potatoes are brimming with vitamins A and C, as well as vitamin B6. Bananas are rich in potassium and magnesium, which help to keep our electrolytes balanced (and our body hydrated). Sunflower seeds and avocados are full of antioxidant vitamin E, which is a powerful anti-inflammatory agent. Quinoa—that magical grain seed so beloved in the vegan community—is rich in protein, magnesium, and folate. One would be hard-pressed to find fruits, vegetables, nuts, seeds, or whole grains that aren't rich in some essential vitamin or mineral.

Plants also boast phytonutrients, which have gotten quite a bit of attention in recent years for the role they may play in helping to reduce the risk of disease. Phytonutrients are the chemical compounds that give vibrant color to fruits and vegetables. On average, populations of people who consume a lot of phytonutrients tend to have lower rates of chronic illness than populations that don't. You've probably heard the name of a few notable phytonutrients before; lycopene, found in tomatoes, watermelon, and grapefruit, has been linked to a lower risk of prostate cancer. Lutein, found in green leafy vegetables, may help guard us against cataracts. Flavonoids, which include catechins and hesperidin, may help to guard against various kinds of cancers. Phytoestrogens in soy and flax are associated with a lowered risk of bone loss and a lower risk of endometrial cancer in women. Phytonutrients are *only* found in plant foods. The more plants you eat, the more phytonutrients you'll consume.

Among their many promising actions, phytonutrients can help to reduce bodily inflammation. While the word *inflammation* suggests illness, it's actually a natural part of your body's own defenses. When you get a cut and notice that the skin around it becomes red and swollen, this is inflammation at work. Blood flow to the injured area has been increased, and cells that help us to defeat pathogens are being shuttled in to promote wound healing. Inflammation in response to an injury or traumatic event is known as "acute inflammation." Problems arise when the normally healthy inflammatory response outstays its welcome, a condition called chronic inflammation. It can lead to disease, compromised immunity, and chronic pain. Chronic inflammation is particularly prominent in autoimmune diseases, such as rheumatoid arthritis, Hashimoto's thyroiditis, or Crohn's disease. But it plays a role in more commonplace complaints, such as asthma and seasonal allergies too, and it has even been implicated in cancer growth and coronary disease.[6]

Scientists are still struggling to understand the origins of excessive inflammation, as well as to figure out why it's more prominent in Western nations than Eastern ones. What we do know is that nutrition plays a significant role in mitigating inflammatory responses. The foods most likely to promote inflammation are refined sugar and grains, dairy, trans fats, animal fats, foods that are excessively high in omega-6 fatty acids (more about these on page 37), caffeine, and alcohol. Meanwhile, the foods that seem to cool inflammation's fires are fruits, vegetables, nuts, seeds, olive oil, whole soy foods, and green tea—foods that are conveniently abundant in a plant-based diet.

Systemic inflammation can wreak many

kinds of havoc in the body, and one of its possible side effects is the elevation of cortisol levels. Cortisol is a glucocorticoid, a hormone that increases the amount of glucose in our blood. Glucose gives us energy when we're under stress or in a crisis; it helps us to move, react, and think quick, so we want our bodies to be able to access it quickly. The problem is that many of us are so stressed—whether from work, our personal lives, or poor diet (known as nutritional stress)—that we have continually high levels of cortisol. Chronically elevated cortisol levels can lead to fatigue, weight gain (especially around the middle), infertility, digestive disorders, and depression. Cortisol leaves you feeling "tired but wired"—dragging your feet all day, but struggling to fall asleep at night because your mind is racing.

How do we lower cortisol? Yoga, meditation, chanting, abdominal breathing, and speed walking can all help. If you can't make time for these activities, rest assured that you can still take preventive action against elevated cortisol by avoiding foods that are associated with it. These are, not surprisingly, the same foods that trigger inflammation: refined carbohydrates, foods with imbalanced fatty acid profiles, animal fats, caffeine, and alcohol. Meanwhile (and not surprisingly) phytonutrient-rich diets—full of fruits, vegetables, nuts, seeds, and legumes—are associated with lower cortisol levels.

Good for the Gut

Of all of the healing properties that plant-based diets offer, I take particular excite-ment in their potential to help manage digestive illnesses. GI problems are by far the most common health challenge I come across as a nutritionist. In particular, I see a lot of IBS, or irritable bowel syndrome, which is the diagnosis I received as a teen. IBS is a complicated condition, and a constellation of factors are usually to blame, including bacterial imbalance, motility problems, and stress. The good news is that, while there doesn't seem to be a single dietary "cure" for IBS, vegan diets can be especially helpful. This is largely because they're high in fiber, and adequate fiber intake is crucial for managing the condition. Fiber is a dietary superstar: it's associated with a lower risk of type 2 Diabetes, obesity, and even cancer. Fiber helps to reduce plaque buildup in our arteries, sweeping through them like a broom. And of course, fiber is crucial for maintaining regularity and optimizing digestive health. The USDA recommendation for adult fiber intake is 25 grams per day for women and 38 for men, but the average American consumes only 15 grams daily. Why? Because so many foods that are common in the standard American diet, including soda, animal proteins, and refined carbohydrates, have little or no fiber at all. Transitioning to a plant-based diet—especially one that emphasizes raw food dishes—can help to flood your diet with fiber, ultimately keeping your system regular and healthy. (At first, fiber can cause a little bloating or discomfort, so start with a small increase and take it from there.)

An additional benefit of adding plant-based, fiber-rich foods to your diet is that they'll help you to maintain a healthy balance of bacteria in your gut. Our bodies are outnumbered ten to one by bacteria—a figure that may sound horrifying but is actually nothing more than a reflection of the natural symbiosis we've established with the microbes that surround us. We tend to think of bacteria as harmful, but the bacterial colonies that live on our skin and in our gut help to keep us healthy; they aid in digestion, detoxification, and bolstering our immunity. It's possible, though, for nasty bugs to crowd out the good ones, and, when this happens, GI disruption is a common symptom. To keep these bacteria in balance, it's important to eat foods that allow good bacteria to flourish and harmful bacteria to be minimized. Plant-rich diets, especially those that include the occasional helping of fermented veggies (such as kimchi, sauerkraut, or tempeh) can be helpful allies in maintaining the precious ecosystem of your digestive system.

Plant-Based Diet and Cancer

While the evidence for the advantages of a plant-based diet when it comes to gut health or protection against coronary disease is pretty well established, the relationship between plant-based diets and cancer is promising, if significantly more complex. Each type of cancer is different, so it's impossible to lump "cancer prevention" into a single category. And while it's tempting to believe that we can control our cancer risk altogether with lifestyle changes, cancers are deeply mysterious, and we don't yet understand how each one of them interacts with diet. What we do know is that certain kinds of cancers certainly do seem to respond

well to wholesome dietary choices and an active lifestyle. Higher fruit and vegetable consumption is associated with a decreased risk of breast cancer—especially estrogen receptor-negative breast cancer.[7] Red meat and processed meats are associated with a higher risk of colorectal cancer, while a Mediterranean diet—rich in legumes, vegetables, and polyunsaturated olive oil—may have a beneficial effect.[8] Further research is needed, but some preliminary data suggests that low fat, vegan diets and reduction of refined carbohydrates may help to prevent prostate cancer, and cruciferous vegetable intake is associated with lower prostate cancer risk as well.[9] In fact, more and more evidence seems to be pointing to phytochemicals as having a protective effect against cancers of all kinds.

A "Whole, Real Foods" Approach

All of these facts present a strong case for the benefits of vegan diets. But are *all* vegan diets healthy? Is there such a thing as an unhealthy vegan diet?

Sure. Or rather, there are vegan diets that are more wholesome or less wholesome (I hesitate to use the word *unhealthy*, which is too black and white for my liking). If you shape your diet around processed snack foods, sugary desserts, fried foods, and faux meats at the expense of fruits, vegetables, nuts, seeds, grains, and legumes, you may not experience all of the health benefits we've been talking about as readily. I like to encourage what's called a "whole foods" vegan diet: a diet that's centered around foods in their whole form. This includes whole grains, rather than refined flours; fresh fruits and vegetables, rather than canned; homemade meals, rather than frozen dinners; whole nuts and dried fruits, rather than protein bars with thirty-odd ingredients. Eating this way will be more nourishing for your body, and it will help to reduce your taste for sugar, fat, and salt, all of which tend to be abundant in processed foods (both vegan and nonvegan).

But of course, it's important to treat the "whole foods" philosophy realistically. It's all well and good to fantasize about a world in which we all create literally everything we eat from scratch (and grow it and farm it too!). But this isn't a realistic option for most of us. Life is hectic, and we all do the best we can. Plus, how do we define a "processed food?" Is store-bought almond milk a processed food? What about commercially made hummus? Fruit and nut snack bars? BPA-free canned beans? Tempeh? A healthy, organic frozen veggie burger? These foods all make frequent appearances in my diet, and they make it a lot easier for me to eat healthily when I'm busy. If we start to eschew literally everything that's undergone processing, we'll find ourselves with no snack foods when we're on the road, no options at airports, a scant list of choices at restaurants, and nothing to help us out in the kitchen when we're in a rush.

So, while I certainly advocate an "eat real food" approach, I don't think that some processed foods or vegan treats are going to kill you. In fact, I think that certain foods, such as vegan "cheese," veggie burgers, or frozen dinners, may help you to make a successful transition into plant-based eating,

which may bring long-term benefits into your life. (For more on transition foods, see Chapter 8, "Getting Started.") The goal is simply to eat whole, plant-based foods *most of* the time.

This is where I tend to find raw foods particularly helpful. When I got into raw food, I learned how to create salad dressings, nut milks, dips, spreads, and many other sorts of recipes from scratch. It shifted my emphasis from products to ingredients. Of course, there are ways to explore a whole foods ethos without getting into raw. But raw foods make it easy, colorful, and fun. Vegetables often serve as the centerpiece of raw food dishes (such as cauliflower "rice" or zucchini "pasta"), which means that "uncooking" (as some people like to call raw food preparation) is a useful lesson in crowding out the refined carbs and convenience foods we all tend to get overly reliant on, and replacing them with vegetables instead.

If you do spend any time exploring raw foods, you'll notice that they're often spoken of as the ultimate solution to each and every health woe. Raw websites promise you glowing skin and lustrous hair, boundless energy and graceful aging. These promises aren't unique to raw food circles: vegan diets on the whole are too often presented as health panaceas. While I'm as enthusiastic as anyone about the health potential of a plant-based diet, I find such claims problematic. It's wonderful that we can minimize the risk of so many kinds of chronic diseases through what we eat. But no matter how hard we try, we can't turn diet into a silver bullet prescription. And in spite of the fact that veganism can be an incredibly healthy diet, there is no conclusive evidence that it is the *only* healthy diet. Research supports the idea that a number of dietary approaches can be healthy and support longevity. But it casts a particularly favorable light on diets that are abundant in fruits, vegetables, nuts, seeds, legumes, grains, and healthy, polyunsaturated fats. Veganism is one of them. And I believe it is the diet that best allows us to protect our health while also preserving the lives of our animal neighbors.

CHAPTER 2
Beyond the Plate

EARLY IN MY VEGAN YEARS, I MADE almost a conscious point not to identify myself with veganism from an ethical standpoint. I'd leave the ethical stuff to other people, I thought, people who had calendars of baby animals on their bedroom walls, who fostered homeless kittens and took in stray dogs. I'd leave it to the hippies and the "angry vegans." Me? I wasn't touching ethics with a 10-foot pole. I'd stick to talking about the health benefits, the glowing skin, and the delicious recipes. Not the animals.

Now that animal rights are the defining feature of my relationship with veganism, I look back on that attitude with a mixture of amusement and embarrassment. I'm not sure why it took me so long to consider animals in my food choices. Part of it was the fact that I, like a lot of people, harbored a certain stereotype of "animal rights vegans"—angry, judgy—and didn't want to be associated with it. Part of it was fear of feel-

ing like an impostor. To jump into the ethical argument after so many years of being uninterested felt odd to me, like trying on a costume.

The final reason, and the most significant one, was that I simply was not accustomed to considering other living beings in my food choices. Eating had always been so fraught with stress and anxiety; these feelings didn't leave a lot of space for overall conscientiousness about the ethical, humane, and environmental dimensions of the food I ate. Interestingly enough, it was in developing more awareness as a consumer—particularly with regard to animal welfare—that I was able to develop a joyous, meaningful, and lasting relationship with food.

If you're reading this book primarily because you want to achieve lasting health, great. That's a wonderful reason to explore vegan food, and my goal is not to force a certain ethical perspective on you (or anyone).

But my veganism became richer when I started to consider how my choices as a consumer fit into a larger web, a system of food production that stretches far beyond me and my plate. It would now be impossible for me to talk about the lifestyle without describing this shift, and why it happened.

"It's Not All About Having a Perfect Bowel Movement"

A few years into my vegan journey, I visited the Woodstock Farm Animal Sanctuary, a place where abandoned and abused farm animals are able to live out their lives in peace and safety. I was volunteering at a fund-raising event, but I had some time to walk through the farm, observe the animals as they went about their lives, and appreciate their personalities. For the first time, the strangeness of keeping animals in captivity to produce food we don't need to eat hit home. It was unsettling.

Later that day, Woodstock FAS's director, Jenny Brown, gave a keynote speech as her guests dug into piping hot, fragrant plates of food. "At the end of the day," she said, "it's not all about having the perfect bowel movement. This is about the animals." I chuckled. Jenny might as well have been speaking to me directly. Of course, I felt no shame that I had explored veganism for healing. But in almost consciously ignoring animal issues, I'd been keeping my heart blocked off to a kind of awareness that would ultimately enrich my experience of being vegan. Nowadays I like to say that I went vegan for my health, but I stay vegan for animals.

Funnily enough, as soon as I became a little more open to animal rights—or simply a perspective that took animals into account—it started to feel incredibly common sense to me. You don't have to identify as an animal activist or even an animal lover to believe that animals should be spared pain, suffering, and captivity. Animals have consciousness, the ability to feel pain, and the capacity to form social bonds. Many animals also have a sense of self-awareness, as well as the ability to imagine a future. Anyone who has spent time around animals has witnessed these qualities in action. If you've ever had a companion animal (such as a dog or a cat), then you know that animals can suffer just as keenly as we do. You also know that they can rejoice, experience pleasure, and form deep, loyal, and abiding attachments. The pigs, cows, goats, turkeys, and other animals we keep on farms throughout this country are no less conscious than the pets we love so dearly in our homes. So why are we so able to accept that they suffer and die in conditions we'd consider absolutely appalling—and even immoral—for dogs, cats, or horses?

A traditional response to this question would be that we need animal foods to survive. But the fact is that we don't. Vegan diets have been shown to be completely safe, both short term and long term, so long as one has access to a B12 supplement (which we'll discuss soon). Given this fact, and because we can see plainly that farming animals for food causes them to suffer incredibly, isn't it our duty to respect them with our food choices?

Another way of thinking about this question is this: yes, we could eat meat. But given the world in which we live, should we?

Let's talk about that world. About 58 billion land animals die each year in factory farms and slaughterhouses. The USDA report on animal slaughter for 2012 states that 49.6 billion pounds of red meat were produced in 2012. This includes 33 million cows, 113.2 million hogs, and 2.18 million sheep.[1] And these numbers, mind you, are for the United States alone. This is a staggering amount of death for meat, a food that, eaten in excess, can increase one's likelihood of developing high blood pressure, heart disease, and type 2 diabetes. A food that we do not have to eat in order to be healthy.

The idea that animal farming is cruel is hard to accept if you grew up, as I did, with all sorts of idealized visions of what life on a farm is like. I spent my childhood summers in New Hampshire, where my father's family lived, drinking glasses of cold milk from the dairy farm down the road. I assumed that farm animals were cozy, well fed, and that they grew to a comfortable, advanced age before they somehow, magically, became food. The fantasy, sadly, is nothing like the reality. Here's a very small glimpse of what life on an average factory farm is like for a number of different farm animals.

Pigs

The average factory farm pig is born and promptly undergoes painful procedures—such as castration or the removal of its tail—without anesthesia. It proceeds to spend life biting at the cage behind which it lives, along with hundreds of others. Pigs that don't bite at their cages often bite off each others' tails;

depressed and helpless, most pigs allow this to happen. Pregnant pigs are kept in "gestation crates," with no more than a few millimeters in which to move before and after they give birth. Baby pigs that are sickly or weak are often clubbed to death or slammed into the ground.

Cows

Cows who are destined to be killed for beef spend their lives crowded together, up to their knees in their own excrement. Cows are ruminants, which means that their digestive system is meant to digest grass. And yet these cows are typically given a diet of soy and corn, which makes them sick. These cows typically live to the age of 24 or 36 months, at which point they're hung on a conveyor belt and then killed with a stun gun.

As grim as the lives of the average steer is, dairy cows are arguably worse off. These cows are continually impregnated so that they can produce milk. After they give birth, they're forcibly removed from their babies, who are then sold for veal or shipped to neighboring farms, where they will one day be slaughtered. Dairy cows are forced to produce so much milk that their udders frequently become infected and often degenerate early, at which point the cows are killed for leather or meat.

Chickens

Broiler chickens on factory farms are kept in sheds so crowded that the ammonia from their waste often burns the chickens' eyes.

They're given a diet that helps them to reach a mature weight in one third of their natural growing time. Rapid growth often leads to skeletal deformities, and many broiler chickens struggle to walk. At birth, their beak is seared off to prevent them from pecking at each other; this process, carried out with a hot blade or a laser, leaves the chickens in agony for weeks, and many starve to death afterward because they're unable to eat.

Egg-laying hens are packed into tiny cages, in which they can die of asphyxiation or dehydration. If they don't die and rot in their cages, they proceed to produce eggs at a rate so fast that their bones decline rapidly. "Spent hens," whose bones are breaking from so much egg production, are either transported to be killed, or gassed or composted on site. In one California farm, 30,000 live hens were fed into wood chippers. Egg laying hens die at staggering rates; in 2012, an estimated 8,576,194 chickens were killed for food in the United States.[2]

Baby male chicks, who are less valuable than female chicks because they can't produce eggs, are frequently ground up, or "masticated," after they are hatched.

What About "Certified Humane," Grass Fed, and Local Animal Foods?

Ten years ago, when I told people I didn't eat meat, the usual answer was, "Yeah, I wish I could do that, but I just can't give it up!" Today, what I usually hear is some version of, "Well, my meat is grass fed/local/certified humane, so it's okay."

Is it okay? Why don't we all just boycott

factory farms and eat local, organically farmed meats, dairy, and eggs instead?

Well, to start, such labels as "humane" or "grass fed" may not tell us the whole story. Yes, you can establish a nice rapport with a farmer at the farmers' market, but a number of individuals invariably end up caring for animals on a farm, and it's hard to know precisely what goes on to make the operation efficient. On many so-called humane egg laying farms, male chicks are still killed or sold as broiler chickens. Additionally, such terms as "free range" are essentially meaningless; many of the eggs labeled this way come from farms where animals are still cramped into tiny spaces. While it's nice to fantasize about dairy that's produced without cruelty, we often forget that dairy cows are almost always sold as beef when they stop producing milk. Even if you purchase dairy that is "local and organic," you still may be supporting slaughter with your dollar.

Beyond all this arguing about *how* animals die, we often lose sight of the fact that animals die. And if they don't, they spend their natural lives in captivity, often torn from their offspring. Some farms arrange for animals to have much higher quality of life and more humane deaths than others. This is, of course, better than what happens on a factory farm in the sense that less suffering is involved. But even small farms bring animals into the world and then kill them for unnecessary human consumption. I struggle to justify eating animal food when a simple B12 vitamin ensures that we can have rich, long, healthy lives without them.

Finally, eating animal foods—even those from more humanely oriented farms—serves to validate consumption of animals to the outside world. You may be willing to pay top dollar for grass fed, organic animal products, but that level of concern is not shared universally, and the demand for cheaper options persists. No matter how idyllic it is, the farm-to-table model, with the tiny, idealized farms it presents to our imaginations, may not be adaptable to a planet of over 7 billion people and growing. And so, for as long as we rely on animal products to sustain ourselves, there will be pressure to do it bigger and with more efficiency, which will mean more slaughter and more suffering. I'd personally rather do my part to show the world that life without any animal foods at all can be delicious, abundant, and peaceful.

The Environment

Animal suffering isn't the only non-health-oriented reason to eschew animal foods. Plant-based diets also have the potential to lessen a lot of the depletion of global resources and the environment that's so problematic today.

Most of us feel concern about global warming and the environment. We recycle. We use glass instead of plastic. We watch nature documentaries and donate money to organizations that protect endangered species. We ride bikes to work and organize carpools. But there's arguably one choice you can make that will benefit the environment far more than all of these actions taken together: switching to a plant-based diet. The food you eat is every bit as consequential to the environment as whether or not you choose to bike or drive to work, if not more so. In 2010, the UN commissioned a report on consumption and production, which included an assessment of land use and fossil fuel consumption. One of the study's conclusions was this: "Impacts from agriculture are expected to increase substantially due to population growth, increasing consumption of animal products. Unlike [with] fossil fuels, it is difficult to look for alternatives: people have to eat. A substantial reduction of impacts would only be possible with a substantial worldwide diet change, away from animal products."

It's estimated that agriculture is responsible for over 10 percent of US energy consumption, and about 17 percent of fossil fuel use.[3] Globally, it's responsible for 70 percent of freshwater consumption, 38 percent of total land use, and 14 percent of the world's greenhouse gas emissions. While plant agriculture represents a part of that figure, a very disproportionate amount of energy consumption is due to the meat, poultry, and dairy industries.[4] Why? Because raising animals, keeping them captive, and transporting them uses up land and carbon emissions. But so does growing and transporting all of the grains—soy and other crops—that are grown to feed the animals that are slaughtered. In other words, animal agriculture is doubly expensive in its consumption of resources.

We tend to think about energy consumption in terms of fossil fuels we burn, which then lead to CO2 emissions that destroy our ozone layer. But animal agriculture is also a culprit behind two other kinds of emissions: methane and nitrous oxide. Though they remain in the atmosphere for less time than carbon dioxide, they are in many ways more powerful greenhouse gases. Pound for pound, methane has a twenty times greater impact on climate change than carbon dioxide over a hundred-year period,[5] and nitrous oxide has a global warming potential that is up to 310 times greater than carbon dioxide's.

Seventy-four percent of nitrous oxide emissions come from agriculture, mainly from crop fertilizer. Rough estimates suggest that more of these emissions are from animal agriculture than plant.[6] If you're wondering where methane emissions come from, prepare yourself for the unsavory truth: They come from the stomach of ruminants, such as cows, and from animal waste. As cows digest corn, soy, grain, and grass (yes, even grass), they emit methane by belching and passing gas. That methane emissions from agriculture in 2003 totaled 182.8 million tons of CO2 equivalents says a lot about how many cows are held captive in factory farms. Methane and nitrous oxide are also emitted by the manure reservoirs and lagoons that result from mass-scale pork and beef production.

Critics of vegan diets often note that, if we were to phase out animal agriculture, we'd need to increase plant production, which would still consume fossil fuels. But even if we did, we wouldn't be growing any plant crops to feed to animals on factory farms. And we also wouldn't be creating enormous amounts of methane from animal waste, or using nitrous oxide to fertilize animal feed. That alone would remove a significant burden on our atmosphere.[7] And of course, it's worth thinking about the implications of feeding billions of pounds of grain and soy to animals, when about 870 million people—one in eight—are suffering from malnourishment. It has been estimated that 2.6 pounds of grain feed are used to produce every pound of beef. How much land and how many crops could be directed toward people, both in developed and developing countries, if they weren't bound up in animal agriculture?

It's also been estimated that, if you reduced the animal product intake in your diet to 20 percent (just 7.7 percent less than the national average of 27.7 percent), it would have the same environmental impact as switching from a typical sedan to a hybrid vehicle.[8] A few meatless dinners per week alone will reduce your environmental footprint dramatically. Such small changes, when made by many people, will have a tremendous difference when it comes to the environment.

PART II
The What

THIS SECTION WILL GUIDE YOU THROUGH THE BASICS OF ADDING more vegan and raw foods to your life. In chapter 3, we'll go over the fundamentals of vegan nutrition. In chapter 4, we'll talk about raw foods, and what makes them unique. In chapters 5 and 6, I'll answer some frequently asked questions and address common myths and misconceptions surrounding plant based diets.

CHAPTER 3
Vegan Nutrition

Plant-based eating can feel like a seismic shift at first, but the truth is that planning a healthy vegan diet isn't so different from planning any kind of healthy diet. You'll want to get a balance of complex carbohydrates, healthy fats, and protein. You'll need to be mindful of your calcium and iron intake, especially if you're a woman. You'll have to take a vitamin B12 supplement.

That's it. Nothing too crazy. And in fact, the only piece of advice in that list that differs from how you'd plan any kind of healthy diet is the bit about B12, which we'll get to. Vegan diets require a little bit of reading and research at the very start, but that's not because they're so much harder to manage than omnivore diets. It's only because they're new to most people.

Protein

Every vegan dreads the inevitable question: "Where do you get your protein?" As exasper-

ating as this moment can be, it's a natural inquiry. Most of us grew up associating "protein" with chicken, turkey, or meat. Where do plant foods fit into all of this?

Vegans get their protein from nuts and seeds, hemp, chia, grains, soy foods, and vegetables (which have a lot more protein than you think). Maybe you know this already, but, even if you do, you might still be wondering how much protein, exactly, you need. The AANP recommendation for protein—that's the dietetics gold standard—is that women get 0.8 grams of protein for every kilogram of body weight. That said, plant protein can be a little harder to assimilate than animal protein, which means that it's not a bad idea to go with 0.9 grams per kilogram body weight, or 0.4 grams per pound.[1] For a 145-pound woman, this would mean about 58 grams per day.

Will you wither away if you get less than this? Probably not, and, depending on your circumstances, you may feel fine getting a bit less than the 0.9 gram guideline. But a lot of people do feel more vibrant when they get ample protein, even if they weren't aware beforehand that they weren't getting enough. Keep in mind that protein adds up quickly. Suppose you start your day with a bowl of warm quinoa (or Quinoa Breakfast Pudding, page 175), a tablespoon of peanut butter, a tablespoon of flax meal, and a ½ cup of berries. You just ate 15 grams of protein—and you probably didn't have to think that hard about it.

It's always good to get protein from whole foods sources, but a high-quality plant-based protein powder may be helpful to you for a boost. I often use protein powder—usually hemp or brown rice—in my smoothies, and consider it a convenient and easy solution when I'm busy or traveling. A lot of protein powders are stuffed with artificial colors and sweeteners, so be discerning about what you choose; hemp, yellow pea, or rice protein is best. You can find a list of my favorite protein powder brands on page 74.

What About "Complete Proteins?"

Protein is made of amino acids. There are twenty-one amino acids in the human body. Of these, we can assemble twelve biologically. The remaining nine must be obtained from food. We call foods that contain all of the essential amino acids "complete proteins."

Animal proteins are naturally complete. For a while, it was thought that vegans and vegetarians had to make a special effort to combine different foods in order to get all nine amino acids at each meal. (One well-known example is the combination of beans with rice). It's not a bad idea to pair these foods together; getting variety within each meal is always wise from a nutrition standpoint. But recent studies have shown that vegans don't actually need to eat all of the amino acids with every meal in order to obtain adequate amounts of complete protein. The key is to eat varied meals overall. On top of that, certain vegan foods are already complete protein sources. They include quinoa, soy, hemp, amaranth, buckwheat, and chia seeds. Combine these nutritious foods with a steady rotation of beans, grains, greens, and you'll be well on your way to healthily meeting your protein needs.

Carbs

Poor carbs. They are the bugaboo of the nutrition world nowadays. They've been vilified by Atkins, spoken of with extreme suspicion in paleo camps, and now certain health writers would have us all believe that they and they alone are what makes Americans fat and causes our brains to decline.

The truth is, of course, more complex than this. Carbohydrates are our first line of energy, so it should come as no surprise that grains and legumes are the foundation of many global diets. Grains and legumes boast protein, iron, manganese, tryptophan, and countless other nutrients. They're packed with fiber, which helps to keep our digestive tract healthy. If you choose the right grains—whole grains, or grain products that are made with discernment—they'll provide you with sustained, slow-releasing energy.

In short, there's really nothing to fear about this food group. Which begs the question: why is everyone so carb-phobic?

The main issue is that the carbs we know today often bear little or no resemblance to the carbohydrates that have helped to sustain civilization since about 7,000 BC, when flax, wheat, and millet were first cultivated around the Euphrates River. In the 1950s, wheat was bred to be shorter and hardier in an effort to combat drought and global hunger. It worked, but it also meant that the gluten content of wheat was increased. At the same time, products once made with whole grains, including breads and cereals, were developed with refined flours instead (these are what remain after wheat germ has been stripped from the grain, and it's primarily starch, minus nearly all of the grain's nutrition). Refined grains are more likely to cause rapid spikes in blood sugar, and today, they're associated with diabetes, high triglycerides, high cholesterol, obesity, and heart disease.

You, the consumer, have the ability to seek out wholesome, nourishing whole grains instead of heavily refined ones. Saying that all grains are bad because some wheat products are excessively processed or sugary is like saying that a piece of fresh fruit is as questionable as a fruit roll-up. Carbohydrates will give you energy, nutrients, and they'll help you to feel grounded and full—an important consideration if your diet contains a lot of raw foods.

What About Gluten?

Gluten seems to be on everyone's mind these days. With diagnoses of celiac disease climbing, and wheat being named as the culprit behind inflammation, weight gain, acne, psoriasis, eczema, osteoporosis, digestive illness, and a slew of other health complaints, it's hard for us all not to wonder if we'd be better off avoiding the stuff as a matter of course.

Gluten is a protein that's found in wheat, barley, and a number of other grains. Some people cannot digest it at all, and, when they consume it, their body mounts an autoimmune response that destroys the small intestinal lining and can also impact fertility, bone health, and joints. This autoimmune response is also known as celiac disease, and strict avoidance of gluten is the only proper treatment. Some individuals don't test positive for celiac disease, but they still feel lethargic, achy, or bloated when they consume gluten, and find that removing it from their diet makes a profound difference. This is known as nonceliac gluten sensitivity, and it tends to encompass a spectrum of severity (unlike celiac disease, which is a more black-or-white diagnosis). Still other folks, including a lot of people with IBS or digestive travails, digest the sugar in wheat poorly, so they find that eliminating wheat can be helpful.

For every client of mine who has removed gluten and improved, I've also seen many who avoid it like the plague, only to confess that it hasn't really made a difference. At that point, gluten avoidance is more of a hassle than a health advantage, so it's worth approaching the choice to eliminate gluten carefully. Commercial muffins, cakes, and sugary cereals do the body no good, but that doesn't mean that all forms of gluten are equally insidious. Barley, farro (an ancient form of wheat), bulgur wheat, and sprouted-grain products can be nutrient dense and healthful.

If you're worried about gluten, chat with a knowledgeable health-care provider about your options. The only surefire way to diagnose celiac disease is with a biopsy of the small intestine, but a number of blood tests can screen for celiac disease quite sensitively, which is a good place to start. After that, you and your health-care provider can discuss how to proceed. It's more than possible to be a vegan who avoids gluten, especially because so many wholesome grains and grain flours on the market today are gluten free. But eating gluten will extend your range of options, so it's worth gathering some information before you make the choice to eliminate it altogether.

Fats

Like carbs, fat has been at the fore of many a nutrition discussion. Dietary fat plays an important role in our well-being. It adds flavor to food, increases satiety after a meal (which prevents overeating), gives us metabolic energy, and is important for the absorption of fat-soluble vitamins A, D, E, and K. While a few important studies have established that a very low-fat diet (10 percent or less of daily calories from fats) can reverse and prevent heart disease among people who were formerly eating mainstream diets, there is little evidence to show that such an approach is unconditionally necessary for good health. Meanwhile, many studies indicate that certain kinds of fats, including omega-3 fatty acids (which can be found in flaxseed and chia seed) and monounsaturated fats (such as olive oil and nuts) are associated with reduced inflammation, lower rates of heart disease, and reduced risk of type 2 diabetes.

Not all fats are created equal. Just as there are high-quality and low-quality carbs, there are high- and low-quality fats.

Polyunsaturated Fatty Acids (PUFAs)

Polyunsaturated fatty acids, or PUFAs, refer primarily to three types of fatty acids: omega-3, omega-6, and omega-9 fatty acids. These are known as "essential fatty acids" (EFAs) because they (like essential amino acids) can only be obtained through diet.

Omega-3 fatty acids are a hot topic these days. More and more, research suggests that omega-3s are beneficial to cardiovascular health.[2] They've also been shown to have anti-inflammatory effects, and they may even help to fight depression and anxiety. While fish oil supplements (one of the more reliable sources of omega-3s) aren't an option for vegans, there are a number of great, plant-based sources as well. The main ones are flaxseeds, chia seeds, and walnuts.

It gets a little more complicated, though. The foods I just mentioned contain alpha-linolenic acid, or ALA, which is just one type of omega-3 fatty acid. There are two others, EPA and DHA. The body can convert some amount of ALA into EPA and DHA, but not much. As the major dietary source of EPA and DHA is fish, vegans have been found to have relatively low DHA levels. This may be problematic, because DHA is one of the fatty acids that can help to prevent certain cancers, improve mood and psychiatric health, and aid in fetal brain development. [3]

The good news is that research has shown that certain species of marine algae can be used to produce supplementary DHA. Today, you can find DHA supplements in capsule form (the Deva brand is great) or in certain protein powders that have been enriched with algae. Though some vegans, especially those who consume quite a bit of walnuts and flax seed, may not need a EPA/DHA supplement, vegan health professionals are increasingly in agreement that taking 300 mg of DHA every day or every few days is probably wise, especially for pregnant women.

The other main type of essential fatty acids, omega-6 fatty acids (also known as linoleic acid, or LA), are plentiful in sesame seeds, sunflower seeds, pumpkin seeds, canola oil, and olive oil, as well as soybean, corn, and safflower oil. Omega-6 fatty acids have become far more abundant in American diets throughout the course of the twentieth century, thanks in part to the overconsumption of soybean oil in processed food products. [4] Some evidence suggests that omega-6 fatty acids and omega-3 fatty acids compete for the same metabolic pathways, and that eating too many omega-6 fatty acids will prevent the body from converting omega-3 fatty acids into EPA and DHA. [5] Because omega-6 fatty acids are easy to obtain in the modern diet (through processed foods) but omega-3s are a bit harder to obtain, our ratio of omega-6 to omega-3 consumption has changed dramatically; one estimate is that it has gone from a traditional ratio of about one or two to one to twenty or thirty to one. [6] An ideal ratio of may be between two to one and four to one. [7] As you get started with plant-based foods, it's wise to be mindful of this ratio. Walnuts, flax, and chia can help you to obtain more of those critical omega-3s.

Monounsaturated Fatty Acids (MUFAs)

Monounsaturated fatty acids can be found in various foods and oils, including olive oil, peanut oil, canola oil, avocados, macadamia nuts, cashews, and hemp seeds. Studies suggest that eating MUFAs can help to improve blood cholesterol and keep blood sugar even.

Saturated Fats

Overly high intake of saturated animal fat is also associated with heart disease risk and inflammation, so it's wise to consume it in moderation. Luckily, plant foods are generally low in saturated fats, and the ones they do contain may not be detrimental to health in the same way animal fat can be. The main fatty acid in coconut, called lauric acid, is nearly all saturated, but studies suggest that it isn't associated with the same harmful effects as saturated animal fats. [8] It may also be anti-inflammatory and antifungal.

Trans Fats

Trans fats are unsaturated fatty acids that have been industrially processed to be more stable. They increase "bad" cholesterol and may contribute to inflammation as well. Whenever you see the words *partially hydrogenated*, this means that you're looking at a product that contains trans fats. Steer clear.

What About Oil?

Oil tends to get vilified in certain vegan and raw circles, but there's no substantial evidence that moderate use of oils, coupled with a wholesome and plant-centric diet, is a health risk. Oils are a part of countless traditional diets, and countries with high consumption of olive oil tend to also have lower rates of heart disease. Of course, people in these countries also tend to eat less saturated fats than Americans do, along with lots of legumes, vegetables, and fruits. It's probably these habits, not the oil, that provide most protection; no one's saying that dipping a piece of bread in a bowl of olive oil is the trick to preventing heart disease! But if olive oil were as menacing as a Big Mac, it's unlikely that so many cultures that rely on it heavily would show epidemiological advantages. A number of studies have shown that diets rich in olive oil contribute to longer lasting weight loss than do low-fat diets.[9]

Oils aren't particularly nutrient dense, but certain oils, such as flax or hemp, offer us those crucial EFAs, whereas others, such as olive oil, contain polyphenols that fight inflammation and possibly even help to manage pain.[10] Because oils are so caloric, it's wise to use them with discretion. But unless you have a health condition that specifically demands it, there's no reason to avoid them. Fortunately, a small amount of oil goes a long way in cooking, so moderation is very manageable.

Calcium and Iron

Most new vegans I know spend a little too much time worrying about their protein intake and often spend too little time thinking about calcium, a crucial mineral. And along with the dread questions about protein, some well-meaning folks may ask vegans, "How do you get enough calcium?" Or (more likely) "how do you get enough calcium without dairy?"

It's simply not true that you need dairy to get adequate calcium. Dark leafy greens are a major calcium source. Legumes, nuts, seeds, blackstrap molasses, tofu, broccoli, and fortified foods (such as commercial almond, oat, hemp, or rice milk) are also great sources of calcium. Here's a handy list of vegan foods that are calcium rich:

Navy beans
Black beans
Great northern beans
Tofu (prepared with calcium sulfate)
Soybeans
Tempeh
Almond milk (fortified)
Almonds and almond butter
Sesame seeds
Tahini
Blackstrap molasses
Dried figs
Raisins
Collard greens
Broccoli
Kale

Adult women are advised to get about 1,000 milligrams of calcium daily. If you eat the above foods on a regular basis, it will be more than possible for you to meet your needs. Unfortunately, some research suggests that vegans tend to skimp on calcium, and that they have a higher risk of bone fracture as a result. This may be simple oversight: new vegans are inundated with advice on how to get adequate protein, but calcium may slip through the cracks. Floating around the vegan community are also some misleading ideas about calcium and its relationship to pH (I address these on page 53). But the good news is that vegans who consume as much calcium as nonvegans have the same risk of bone fracture.[11] So there's no need for any vegan to have compromised bone health; you simply need to be mindful of how much calcium you're getting.

One side note for raw foodies: fortified nut milks are one of the easiest ways for vegans to get calcium in their diet. If you make all of your nut milks from scratch, that's great, but, if you struggle to consume enough calcium-rich foods, you may want to consider using a mixture of homemade and commercially sold nut milk. I usually use organic, commercial, unsweetened almond, hemp, or soy milk in smoothies (or when I'm too busy to make nut milk at home), but I almost always use the homemade stuff in my raw muesli (page 155), or when I eat raw granola or fruit in the morning.

Absorption

Getting adequate calcium isn't quite as simple as eating calcium-rich foods. To absorb calcium, we need adequate amounts of vitamin D; 80–90 percent of the vitamin D we need comes from direct sunlight, but most of us wear sunscreen and work indoors. As a result, we rely on vitamin D in our diet too.

There are two forms of vitamin D: D2 (ergocalciferol) and D3 (cholecalciferol). Vitamin D3 is derived from animal sources, whereas D2 is usually made from yeast. While D3 stays active in the body longer than D2, they're both effective. It's not hard to find vegan D2 supplements, and a few vegan D3 supplements are now on the market as well. Whether or not you need to consider a vitamin D supplement is something you should chat about with your health-care provider; if your D levels are ever low or if you have a history of osteopenia or are at significant risk for it, then you may be a candidate. If so, you won't lack for vegan options.

Iron

Iron, like calcium, can be a little tricky to get a hold of as a vegan. In addition to this, the kind of iron found in plant foods (non-heme iron) isn't quite as easily absorbed by the body as is the heme iron found in animal foods. For this reason, vegans might want to get a little more iron than do nonvegans. Additionally, women need a little more iron than men because of blood loss through the menstrual cycle each month. The recommended daily iron intake is 18 milligrams daily for premenopausal women and 8 milligrams for men and postmenopausal women. Recommendations have been issued to vegetarians that are higher (1.8 times higher in one case), but if you maximize iron-rich foods in your diet and take care to avoid eating them with coffee or tea to enhance absorption, it's unlikely that such a discrepancy between plant-based and non-plant-based eaters is necessary.[12]

There are plenty of good, vegan iron

sources. Dark leafy greens—including spinach, chard, kale, bok choy, beet, and turnip greens—are rich in iron. Some of the other sources include:

Blackstrap molasses
Lentils
Soybeans
Quinoa
Tofu and tempeh
Black beans
Kidney beans
Black-eyed peas
Dried apricots
Raisins
Tahini/sesame seeds

Once again, whether or not you need to consider an iron supplement in addition to eating a variety of these iron rich foods is a conversation you should have with your health-care provider. Keep in mind too that our body absorbs iron better when we're also eating vitamin C. So it's a great idea to throw some citrus fruit or fennel into your bed of dark leafy greens!

Vitamin B12

Vitamin B12, also known as cobalamin, is the one vitamin that vegans have to supplement no matter what.

Vitamin B12 is made by bacteria. Cows and other ruminants both supply their own B12, thanks to the bacteria who live in their upper intestinal tract, and they often ingest it in the grass (and bits of soil) they eat, as do other land and marine animals. Consequently, fish, shellfish, meat, eggs, and yogurt all contain a lot of B12. Back in an era where we didn't clean our food so thoroughly, when our soil was less sanitized, and when most human beings spent their days outside tilling the land, we may have been able to get the B12 we need through freshly picked plant foods. But in our ultra sanitary culture, we simply don't expose ourselves to enough bacteria to get B12 without eating animal products.

Non-dairy milks, nutritional yeast, and some other vegan foods are fortified with B12, but that isn't always enough to ensure adequacy. Low B12 levels can lead to depression, anemia, weakness, and GI symptoms. Taking a B12 supplement—as little as 25 to 100 micrograms daily—is most likely enough to prevent a deficiency, though larger doses (1,000 micrograms daily) are commonly recommended. B12 supplements can be labeled as cobalamin, cyanocobalamin, or methylcobalamin, and any of them will do the trick if you take them regularly, but it's thought that methylcobalamin may be the most efficiently assimilated of these three.

Vegan critics love to insist that the fact that vegans have to take B12 is evidence that our diets are fundamentally "unnatural"—that is, they're not the diet that we evolved eating. I'm more interested in the diet that makes sense for us in the context of our present world than I am in eating exactly as we did in the distant past, but, even in the context of evolutionary history, the fact that vegans have to supplement B12 isn't a reflection of how natural our diets are. Vegans have to take B12 because we live in a world in which bacteria doesn't run amok, not because vegan diets are an affront to nature.

And as it turns out, vegans are not the only people who develop B12 deficiencies in the United States. As much as 15 percent of the population have suboptimal levels of B12. Older folks are particularly susceptible—so much so that all people over the age of fifty are advised to supplement.

No matter what sort of food you like to eat, if you choose a plant-based diet, then you'll need to be mindful of the nutrients just discussed. That said, raw food diets (or diets that are inspired by raw food recipes) are a little different, and it's worth saying a few words about what makes them unique.

CHAPTER 4
All About Raw Food

RAW FOODS ARE TECHNICALLY FOODS that have not been heated above 115°F, though some people go by 105°F, others, 118°F. The idea behind this is that all foods contain naturally occurring enzymes, which are denatured (made inactive) above 115°F. Our body produces digestive enzymes of its own, but raw foodists claim that, if we preserve the naturally occurring enzymes in our food, those enzymes will assist in digestion, sparing our body stress and effort.

In theory, this all sounds so . . . right. But the reality is more complex. Enzymes from food can assist in digestion, but their role is mostly preliminary. When you chew your food, enzymes (for instance, the bromelain in fresh pineapple) are released and can help break down food. This process continues from your mouth into the upper portion of the stomach, which has a pH of about 4.5 to 5.8. As food descends into the lower portion of your stomach, however, pH lev-

els drop to about 1.8—a harshly acidic environment—and enzymes become denatured, or rendered inactive. They're then broken down and digested just like any other protein you've eaten. They may play a helpful role in the early phase of digestion, which is why people with an impaired digestive system often benefit from taking digestive enzymes with their food. But since the vast majority of digestion and assimilation takes place in the small intestine, the action of food enzymes may be less critical than raw proponents suggest.[1]

In the absence of enzyme theory, it makes sense to ask why anyone would bother eating raw food. My answer is that the benefits of raw food go far beyond enzymes! Raw foods are hydrating, rich in fiber, and full of antioxidants. They're innovative, colorful, crispy, and fresh. There's a qualitative difference between raw and cooked food, which may be why many ancient traditions, including Ayurveda and Traditional Chinese Medicine, draw a distinction between the two and their impact on the body. For all of my skepticism about some of the miraculous claims associated with enzymes, I feel differently when I eat more raw food: more energetic, more inspired by my food. From a nutrition standpoint, there is truth to the idea that certain nutrients are depleted through the cooking process. B-complex vitamins are sensitive to heat, as are some antioxidants, including vitamin C. Cruciferous vegetables, such as kale,[2] lose antioxidant activity, and some beta-carotene content, when they're cooked. This isn't true for all nutrients, and it's certainly not the case that all cooked food is inferior to raw. In fact, cooking can release antinutrients, such as oxalates, which block absorption of iron and calcium. It can also help to break down plant cell walls, which increases the availability of some phytochemicals. (Cooking tomatoes, for example, decreases their vitamin C content, but it also activates lycopene, which is one of their cancer fighting compounds.) So there are tradeoffs when it comes to cooking vs. not cooking, which is why it's advisable to eat a diet that includes both raw and cooked foods.

The Difference Between Vegan and Raw Foods

Of course, most of us have a lot more experience cooking our vegetables (roasting, steaming, stir-frying) than we do eating them raw. Getting into raw food taught me to flex my creative muscles, and it showed me that a lot of vegetables I only ate cooked—including asparagus, beets, and spinach—could be absolutely delicious in their raw state. My culinary range expanded when I got into raw food, and I developed a greater appreciation of ingredients, a more sensitive approach to food preparation. There's something very powerful about consuming vegetables and herbs in their "naked" form; colors seem brighter, textures sharper, flavors more distinct. I emerged from my first few raw food experiments feeling as though I'd forged a more intimate connection with food, and that connection has lasted.

It's not always easy to discern how raw foods differ from regular vegan foods. Here's a quick list of the ingredients that comprise raw food diets:

- Raw and gently heated (<115°F) vegetables
- Sea vegetables (wakame, arame, hijiki, dulse, nori)
- Raw fruits
- Dried fruits
- Sprouted grains
- Sprouted legumes
- Nuts and seeds/nut and seed milks
- Condiments (apple cider vinegar, nama shoyu, miso, nutritional yeast, coconut aminos—not all of these are strictly raw, but they're fairly standard in raw cuisine, especially when used in moderation)

What isn't included are cooked vegetables, cooked grains, cooked legumes, or most commercial or processed foods. Sometimes this is a really good thing (for example, when it's helping us to avoid artificial sweeteners, really long ingredient lists, questionable food additives, and so on). Sometimes the distinction makes less sense: hummus, oatmeal, vegetable soup, and baked sweet potatoes are decidedly not raw, but all of these are perfectly healthful foods. I personally find sprouted grains and legumes harder to digest than cooked ones.

Balance Is the Key

The basic principles of vegan nutrition apply to raw vegan diets as well, but there are some particular challenges involved. Without tofu or tempeh, protein options are a little more limited. While some raw foodists do eat sprouted legumes and grains, these foods are generally more sparse in raw diets, which can further limit protein and calories. If you do choose to gravitate toward more raw foods, you'll need to take care to get a lot of hemp seeds, chia seeds, nuts, and green leafy vegetables to get adequate protein. It may be helpful for you to also use a high-quality, raw vegan protein powder, such as hemp, brown rice, or sprouted pea.

Another challenge of eating a raw food diet is that it's hard to get a lot of protein without also getting a lot of fat. When nuts become your primary protein source, you have to eat quite a few of them, and, in so doing, you can easily throw your macronutrient balance a little off kilter. No matter how well your body handles ample amounts of fat (and I speak as someone who thrives off nuts, seeds, avocados, and oil), there's still something to be said for everything in moderation.

Balancing raw food with cooked food can be the answer to this dilemma. Suppose you have a breakfast that's all raw and a little higher in delicious, healthy fat (such as my Cashew Banana Yogurt on page 203). For lunch, you might want to focus on something that's a little lower in fat and higher in protein, like a legume, grain, or soy-based meal (perhaps my Apricot Quinoa and Mint Salad on page 158, or my Easy Red Lentil, Sweet Potato, and Coconut Curry on page 167). If you serve a rich raw entrée for dinner (such as the Raw Lasagna on page 224, or Zucchini Pasta with Cashew Alfredo, page 107), you can serve it with some simple steamed greens and cooked lentils, sprinkled with lemon juice and my homemade Gomasio (page 129). This is not to suggest that you should feel squeamish about fat! But I do want you to understand how you can incorporate more of the richer raw recipes into your routine without feeling as though you've suddenly started to eat nuts for breakfast, lunch, and dinner. The meal plans on pages 85 to 89 will give you a very good sense of how to balance your plate with a combination of raw and cooked ingredients.

As with any healthy diet, folks who eat a lot of raw food need to be mindful of their calcium and iron intake. This is especially important because some raw leafy greens—prime calcium and iron sources—contain oxalic acid, which can block our body's absorption of calcium and iron. Light cooking decreases oxalic acid and therefore enhances calcium absorption, which is a good reason to consider lightly steaming some of your greens. If you prefer to eat your greens raw, seek out lower oxalate greens, such as broccoli, bok choy, dandelion greens, collard greens, kale, mustard greens, napa cabbage, turnip greens, and watercress. Raw foodists who make all of their own nut milks should also keep in mind that fortified, commercial nut milk is an easy source of calcium on a vegan diet, and, without it, it's more important still to be mindful of calcium intake. Sesame seeds and tahini, kale, broccoli, chia seeds, dried figs, and Brazil nuts are all good raw food sources of calcium.

The True Magic of Raw Cuisine

Once you have a sense of how to approach raw food healthfully, you can begin exploring its many wonderful culinary offerings. If you ask me, the real magic of a raw food diet is in creamy, unusual dressings, dips and sauces, as well as a couple of handy preparation methods (sushi rolls, collard green wraps, slicing vegetables to look like "pasta" threads). In fact, I tend to think about raw food not in terms of "recipes" (though I do have some tried-and-true recipes that I love) but rather in terms of "templates." There are a bunch of preparation methods that you can modify endlessly to create a surprisingly diverse array of meals. Here are the methods I rely on most when I'm making raw food at home:

Green smoothies
Salads
Slaws
Collard green wraps
Spiralized zucchini "pasta"
Raw sushi rolls
Blended raw soups
Zucchini or cucumber roll-ups (see page 219)
Chia pudding
Raw romaine leaf "tacos" (see page 191)

I'll walk you through all of these techniques in my recipe section. Once you've mastered the basic lineup, you'll be able to modify them in all sorts of different ways.

Naturally, raw food doesn't have to be quite this basic. In fact, some of the most impressive raw food—the kind you can order at raw food restaurants all over the country—is quite a bit more complex. A lot of it requires the use of a dehydrator, which can extend the preparation time for a raw recipe over several days. Because a food dehydrator is a significant investment (see page 75 for my recommendations if you're ready to take the plunge), and because I'm an impatient cook, most of my raw food recipes don't demand the use of a dehydrator. The ones that do are typically snacks: kale chips, dehydrated fruit or veggie chips, and raw granola. If you're inspired to make more "gourmet" raw food dishes, then there are a great many incredible resources out there. But for the most part, the food in this book will reflect the kind of simple dishes I make at home.

As you can see, I have a pretty relaxed approach to raw food. Unfortunately, there's a lot of dogma in the raw food world, which can make such an approach nearly impossible. Try not to get overly caught up in teeny tiny details (such as whether or not your almonds are really raw), or become overly rigid about trying to eat a certain amount of raw food each day. These sorts of fixations aren't necessary, especially since the evidence we have supports the idea that a raw/cooked balance is healthy. Instead, focus on having fun, on discovering new techniques, and on appreciating the ingenuity of raw food recipes.

CHAPTER 5

Frequently Asked Questions About Raw and Vegan Food

WE'VE ALREADY COVERED THE BA-sics of raw and vegan nutrition. Here are some of the most common questions I'm asked about this lifestyle.

Do I Need Many Fancy, Expensive Kitchen Tools to Explore Raw Food?

No. You can explore vegan and raw food with nothing more than a good set of knives, an inexpensive mandoline or vegetable slicer, and an open mind. Many of my favorite vegan and raw food dishes are salads, slaws, sandwiches or wraps, and simple cooked grains. None of them require any fancy appliances.

Of course, you'll widen your range of options if you're willing to invest in a couple of key appliances. I think that food processors, for example, are hugely helpful kitchen tools no matter what sort of diet you eat. They'll allow you to effortlessly chop and shred vegetables, puree nuts and beans (to make hummus, for example), and quickly chop up dried fruits and nuts for snack bars. Blenders can be had for a reasonable price, and they'll allow you to effortlessly make raw soups and smoothies.

Ultimately, you may become interested in a high-speed blender (such as a Vitamix) or a food dehydrator. These two gadgets can help you take raw food preparation in particular to a new level. But they're definitely not essential for exploration, and you'll still have tons of options without them.

I'm Very Active. Will Raw Foods Be Able to Support My Lifestyle?

While many athletes, yogis, and runners seem to thrive on a high raw diet, there's no reason to adhere to strict raw foodism while you train. By all means, load up on your favorite raw recipes, nutrient dense smoothies, and big salads. But you'll probably find that whole grains and legumes provide you with a lot of the energy your body needs to perform and recover too.

For guidance on athletic performance with vegan and raw food cuisine, I highly recommend *Thrive* and other titles by Brendan Brazier, a professional ironman triathlete.

I've Heard About Soaking and Sprouting Nuts and Seeds. What Is This, and Is It Hard to Do?

Nuts and seeds contain enzyme inhibitors, which can be difficult to digest. Soaking the nuts helps to neutralize these inhibitors, and it also initiates the sprouting process, which enhances the nuts' nutrition. Of course, soggy nuts are no fun to eat, so I really only recommend this if you're blending the nuts up into a nut pâté (see recipe on page 101), a pesto, or a dressing. For everyday snacking, it's fine to eat them without soaking.

What About Grains and Legumes? Do They Need to Be Soaked and Sprouted?

The good news about soaking and then sprouting grains and beans is that it enhances their nutrient density by removing certain antinutrients, which can block our absorption of the vital minerals in these nutritious foods. The bad news about eating soaked and sprouted grains or beans, rather than cooked ones, is that they don't taste all that great (not in my opinion, anyway!). And though some folks find sprouted grains and beans easier to digest, I actually find them to be much *harder* for my delicate GI system to handle.

My solution is to soak legumes and grains, but cook them afterward. That way I can maximize nutrition while also achieving an appealing texture and taste. If you want to try soaking, sprouting, and eating them raw, go for it. A simple Google search will lead you to many handy online tutorials.

What Do You Think About Fruitarian, or Mostly Fruit Diets?

Some raw foodists, who are often known as fruitarians, consume fruit only, whereas others follow a protocol called "80–10–10," in which one gets 80 percent of calories from carbohydrates, 10 percent from protein, and 10 percent from fats. While this way of eating seems to work for some, my feeling is that fruitarianism is a very restrictive way to live. It may not provide enough of the protein and complex carbohydrates that you need to stay fueled, nor the range and variety that seems to contribute to health and longevity. If you're considering this type of diet, be sure to chat with a health-care provider first.

How Much Fat Is Too Much on a Raw Food Diet?

Because strict raw foodists consume relatively few or no grains, legumes, and soy foods, a great deal of their overall energy tends to come from nuts, seeds, oils, and avocados. For this reason, it's not uncommon for raw foodists to get 35 to 50 percent of their caloric intake in the form of fats. This may work for you, and it may not. As you explore raw food, you can adjust the amount of fat you eat based upon what works for you.

For what it's worth, the USDA recommendation for adults (age nineteen or older) is for total fat intake to comprise 20 to 35 percent of their total calories. Less than 10 percent of calories should be from saturated fatty acids (though some health professionals have argued that this number is high). Of course, this isn't a rule: It's just a guideline, based upon what works for most people.

I've Stopped Getting My Period on a Raw Food Diet. Is This Normal?

There is nothing normal about not getting a period—unless you're pregnant or in menopause. It's not unusual to miss a month or two when you're under significant amounts of stress, but chronic amenorrhea is your body giving you a warning sign that's something's amiss, and it's definitely something to discuss with your doctor.

According to one study, a shocking 30 percent of women under the age of forty-five who were on raw food diets reported complete or partial amenorrhea. The higher raw their diets were, the more likely the amenorrhea.[1] It's likely that these women were simply not eating enough calories. They may also have been getting enough calories (from fats), but not enough variety overall. Studies like this are yet more evidence that you should consider adding raw foods to your diet without limiting yourself to them.

Do I Need to Incorporate Juicing into My Diet?

You can, but you definitely don't have to. Vegetable juice is a quick and delicious way to incorporate more greens into your routine! It makes a wonderful afternoon snack or prebreakfast drink. But since most plant-based eaters consume a ton of leafy greens already, you certainly don't have to invest in a juicer to reap the benefits of these powerful vegetables.

If you are curious about investing in a juicer, check out my recommendation on page 76, as well as my favorite juice recipes on page 112.

What's the Difference Between Blending and Juicing? Is One of Them Better for You?

There's a long-standing debate about whether blending or juicing is better for health. While the two methods are different and have different benefits, it's not necessary to choose between them.

When you juice fruits and vegetables, you remove the fiber. The advantage of this is that it makes it incredibly easy for you to digest and assimilate all of the wonderful micronutrients in the juice (vitamins, minerals, antioxidants). The downside is that fiber slows absorption of sugar into your bloodstream, so it's possible to get a little sugar spike from drinking juice, especially if it's on the sweeter side.

As with so many nutrition questions, this all comes down to personal preference and individual needs. Because juice is easy to digest and assimilate, it's a good option for people with a delicate digestive system. For folks who have sensitive blood sugar, blending may be a smarter option. Blended drinks, such as smoothies, are also more filling than juices, so they're much more suitable as a meal replacement.

What Do You Think About Juice Fasting?
While I'm a big fan of fresh fruit and vegetable juices, I'm not a fan of juice fasting. Unless you have a health condition that requires intermittent fasting, there's nothing you'll gain from fasting that you won't gain from eating healthfully. In the meantime, fasting can damage your metabolism, contribute to erratic eating patterns, and also start to reinforce disordered, restrictive thinking about food.

If you've been eating more than a usual amount of indulgences, and you want to give yourself a break, that's fine: Just focus on simple meals and lots of veggies for a couple of days. But depriving yourself of the food your body needs won't help you to find balance.

CHAPTER 6

Myths and Misconceptions

ANYONE WHO IS CURIOUS ABOUT NU-trition is sure to encounter a lot of "noise" out there, online and in books. It can be hard to separate the wheat from the chaff. Here are my responses to some of the most common myths and misconceptions about vegan and raw foods.

Raw Food Detoxes

It's commonly said that, as you begin to eat a vegan diet, you'll go through a "detoxifica-tion" process, during which your body will clean the years of dairy and meat out of your system. Symptoms attributed to this "detox" include headaches, fevers, skin eruptions, and bloating. Fear not: There's no evidence whatsoever for this claim. Of course you might have some hiccups as you make the transition to a plant-based diet: at first, the amount of fiber you're eating might lead to a little bloating or gas (this can be exacerbated by the fact that certain plant foods, such as beans or broccoli, contain sugars that are hard to break down). You may not be used to feeling lighter after meals, and that may lead you to feel hungry more often. If you haven't quite mastered how to eat adequate amounts of fat and protein with plant foods, you may feel a little sluggish, tired, or headachy.

The good news is that these problems will either normalize with time, or can be addressed with some simple dietary tweaks.

Vegan Diets Are Expensive and Difficult to Maintain

It's an unfortunate misconception that vegan diets are privileged and exceptionally expen-sive. In fact, veganism is what you make of it.

As with any way of eating, you can go vegan on the cheap, or you can approach it with more gourmet tastes. If you'd like to treat yourself to specialty ingredients, such as superfood powders or fancy raw chocolate, you certainly can. But the foundation of a vegan diet consists of affordable ingredients, such as whole grains, legumes, local produce, and nuts and seeds by bulk.

Sure, produce can be expensive, but it's no more expensive than high-quality fish, meat, or cheese. Plant-based proteins, including tofu, tempeh, lentils, beans, and quinoa, are far more cost efficient, per pound, than animal proteins are.

If you're exploring raw recipes and purchasing a lot of nuts and seeds, keep in mind that shopping in bulk bins at health food stores, or ordering in bulk online, can help to offset these costs substantially.

Being Vegan Is a Nice Idea, But It's Just Too Much of a Hassle in Restaurants

See page 81 for more on restaurant dining. It can be a little tough to eat vegan when you go out, but it's getting easier and easier. With a little creativity, confidence, and an open mind, you can find options on most menus.

Being Vegan Is Just Too Hard for the Average Person

It certainly doesn't have to be. Consider this:

You wake up. You make a bowl of rolled oats with some sliced banana and a scoop of peanut butter for breakfast. Or you blend up a cup of commercial almond milk, a frozen banana, some almond butter, and some spinach in a blender and drink it on your way to work.

At lunchtime, you walk from your office (or your campus) to the nearest salad joint and order a big salad with lots of veggies, some black beans, some raw nuts or seeds, and vinaigrette. Or maybe you get a cup of lentil soup and a side salad. Perhaps you've brought lunch instead: a wrap (whole grain or collard leaf) with some hummus (store-bought or homemade) and veggies.

As a snack, later in the day, you have a handful or two of trail mix and a piece of fruit.

For dinner, you defrost some leftover stew from your freezer and eat it with a salad you whip up at home. Maybe you make a HLT (hummus, lettuce, and tomato) sandwich on sprouted-grain bread. Or maybe you eat another nutrient-dense salad, full of fixings. Maybe you've got some zucchini hummus and quinoa lying around, so you mush them together and add some steamed greens. Maybe you make a stir-fry with tempeh and some organic, frozen mixed vegetables (ready in less than ten minutes). A little while after dinner, you eat some dark chocolate.

There you go: that was a day in the vegan life. As you can see, it wasn't painful, and it wasn't hard. In this day and age, vegan living is accessible and fun; you simply need to open your mind to a new set of options. For more meal plans, turn to page 85.

Vegans Are Always Weak, Delicate, and Sickly

One need only take a glance around the vegan community—blogs, cookbooks, athletic meetups, gyms, and potlucks—to see that the vegan community is full of individuals who are strong, fit, more than adequately nourished, and thriving. While it's true that, on average, vegans have lower BMIs than omnivores, the vegan community encompasses a wide variety of shapes and sizes.

Protein Is a Myth. Just Eat Plants, Man

The idea that we need to get enormous amounts of protein, all of it from animal sources, is a myth. And as things stand, we probably have more health problems due to excessive protein consumption in this country than we do health problems that result from a protein deficit. But protein's not an inconsequential concern, either, and as you transition to a plant-based diet you may find that you need to give a little extra thought to the amount of protein you eat. Try keeping loose track of your protein intake for a few days. If you're consistently below the recommended guidelines (covered on page 33), then go ahead and boost your intake.

If You Eat a Well-Rounded Diet, Then You Don't Need Any Supplements

It's ideal to get most of our nutrition from diet, and you shouldn't rely on supplements as a replacement for real food. Even if you're eating a well rounded diet, however, along with fortified foods, you still need to take a vitamin B12 supplement. Low B12 levels can lead to anemia, depression, and memory problems. It's a serious deficiency, and

there is no reason to put yourself at risk (see Chapter 3, page 40, for more on B12).

When it comes to other nutrients, such as omega-3 fatty acids, calcium, and magnesium, you'll need to evaluate things on a case-by-case basis. Some folks have absorption issues that make supplementation necessary. Women with histories of disordered eating or amenorrhea may want to take a calcium supplement to help protect against osteopenia (premature bone loss). No pill can stand in for the nutrition that food provides, but taking a strict antisupplement stance is short-sighted, and it may compel you to overlook important, individual needs.

Vegans Don't Need to Worry About Calcium Intake, Because They Eat a More Alkaline Diet

Perhaps you've heard that certain foods are acid forming once you digest them, and others are alkaline forming. To wrap your mind around the idea of pH, you'll need to travel back in time to high school chemistry, when you learned about the pH scale. This scale, which ranges from 0 to 14, measures how acidic or basic (alkaline) a substance is. Anything below 7 is considered acidic, and anything above 7 is basic, or alkaline. Nearly all of the enzymes that are necessary for biological function are optimally at a pH of 7.4. (Acidic digestive enzymes are an exception.) Any overall rise in bodily pH (alkalosis) or dip in pH (acidosis) is indicative of a major health crisis. Our bodies have a number of mechanisms in place to keep that pH range steady, because normal metabolic function and physical exertion can release acidic by-products.

Certain foods may also be acid-forming; these foods include meat, cheese, refined starches, coffee, alcohol, and some grains.

In the midnineties, a theory emerged that linked bone degeneration to acid-forming diets. There is some evidence that, when confronted with excess acid, our body may draw on mineral salts, including calcium, to neutralize the acid load,[1] leading to bone and muscle wasting. A number of researchers concluded that acidic diets therefore contribute to bone loss, and that vegan and vegetarian diets, which are lower in acid-forming meat and dairy, are better for bone health. The theory seemed to be validated by the fact that some studies of hip fracture showed that North Americans and Europeans (who eat more animal foods) were more at risk than Africans or Asians. Follow-up studies showed that people who consume more acid-forming diets had higher levels of calcium in their urine,[2] and that high-protein diets (which are presumably more acid-forming) were correlated with lower bone density.[3]

In recent years, however, evidence has suggested that these findings may not tell the whole story. Hip fracture rates aren't entirely conclusive (cultural factors, including balance, may impact the risk of fall), and a number of recent studies have failed to adequately establish a link between protein and bone loss.[4] In fact, some contemporary research suggests that protein may protect the bone matrix.[5] Because vegans do not have lower rates of bone fracture (in fact, the opposite is true), there is no reason to believe that they don't need the same amounts of dietary calcium as omnivores do.

Human Beings Were Meant to Be Vegan Because We Have a Long Digestive Tract

According to this theory, the fact that human beings have longer digestive tracts is a sign that we're natural herbivores; meat takes a long time to digest and "rots" in the gut, so carnivorous animals must have short digestive tracts, not long and windy ones. As much as I wish this were true—because let's face it, it's a fun talking point—it's not quite right. Meat can take a while to digest, because it's rich in fats, which slow down the digestion process. These fats also send signals of fullness to our brain, which is why meat can be so filling (and why people who have just switched over to a vegan diet often feel a pleasant sensation of "lightness" after they eat).

"Rot" is defined as "to undergo decomposition from the action of bacteria or fungi." Meat gets broken down by hydrocholoric acid in your stomach, along with everything else you eat, which ensures that bacteria and other pathogens are killed off. Meat may feel heavy to us, but nothing is rotting in there. On top of this, most evidence suggests that human beings evolved as omnivores (though this doesn't mean that we can't thrive as vegans in the modern world).

All Vegans Eat Is "Fake Meats" and Processed Foods. It's Better to Eat "Real Food," Paleo, or the Nourishing Traditions Diet

Saying that all vegans subsist on faux meat and fake food is like saying that all omnivores eat a SAD diet: it's an unfair generalization based on only a small sampling of eating habits. Some vegans enjoy faux meats, sure—along with processed snacks. But a huge number of vegans eat whole foods, minimally processed diets as well. If you want to eat processed food, you can do so no matter what sort of diet you choose; vegans are no more fond of it than is anyone else. In my whole time as a member of the vegan community, I've seen very few of the infamous "junk food vegans" that nonvegans are so fond of scapegoating.

If you want to eat a lot of processed food, you can do so no matter what sort of dietary orientation you follow. You can eat fast food hamburgers and cheese that comes out of an aerosol can, or you can eat faux chicken patties and soy cream cheese (for the record, soy cream cheese is a lot less scary than the stuff in the aerosol can). Vegans aren't any more inclined, by and large, to eat junk food than any other demographic.

Faux Meats Are Gross—And Hey, Aren't They Pretty Unhealthy Too?

Well, first let's define "faux meat." I've heard some people refer to tofu and tempeh this way, which isn't really fair. These are wholesome foods that have been cherished and prized in Asian cultures for hundreds of years (in their own right, not as a stand in for chicken or steak). Tofu is simply coagulated soy milk, which has been made from soaking, grinding, boiling, and straining dried or fresh soybeans. It's a pretty wholesome product, and nowadays it's easy to find tofu that is non-GMO, organic, and even sprouted. Tempeh is made from soy beans that have been fer-

mented, which helps to make their nutrients more bioavailable, then shaped into cakes. They're very far from Frankenfoods.

As for faux meats—vegan sausages, burgers, taco crumbles, and so on—it's important to remember that these products are intended to help spare animal lives and to provide folks who are inching toward a more plant-based diet with some familiar options. They serve a purpose that goes beyond the realm of nutrition alone. Besides, many of the current offerings are made from really high-quality plant ingredients. A new taco and burger mix, called Neat Meat, is made primarily from beans and nuts. Field Roast vegan sausage is made from seitan (a wheat product), potatoes, and spices. Wholesome veggie burgers, crafted from nuts, beans, whole grains, and even hemp seeds, are now abundant at health food stores. These products have it all: convenience, healthfulness, and a compassionate purpose.

You Can Eat as Much as You Want as Long as It's Raw, and You Won't Gain Weight

Weight loss discussions seem to be divided into two camps: those who believe that a calorie is a calorie is a calorie, and those who believe that it's what you eat, not how many calories you eat, that make you lose weight. Many conventional diet books tell us to track our calories meticulously, while raw foodists claim that you can eat whatever you want, so long as it's raw, and the pounds will melt off. Whom should we believe?

I think the truth lies in the middle of these two philosophies. If you eat a high-caloric food, such as a pumpkin seed pâté or a handful of nuts, that also has tremendous nutrient density, you'll be more nourished than you would if you were eating a handful of potato chips or Skittles. Healthy fats will keep you full, you won't have a blood sugar spike, and you consequently won't be tempted to overeat later on, which is not the case when you eat refined sugars or many processed foods.

That said, weight loss is still a matter of calories in and calories out; if you eat far more calories than you expend, you're going to gain weight. So even if you're filling up on nutritious raw fare, that doesn't mean you can consistently eat beyond what's healthy for your appetite without seeing some weight gain.

Vegan Diets Are Loaded with Omega-6 Fatty Acids and Not Enough Omega-3s, So They Cause Inflammation and Other Health Problems

We already touched on the omega-6 to omega-3 fatty acid ratio in Chapter 3. Vegan diets are sometimes critiqued for having a particularly imbalanced ratio. The claim is that vegans consume too many omega-6 fatty acids from canola oil, safflower oil, nuts, and seeds, and that they miss out on the omega-3 fatty acids in meat and fish. This critique has always baffled me, because there's nothing essential about canola oil in a vegan diet. Coconut oil and olive oil are fine for baking, while flax and hemp oils are ideal for salads and smoothies. As far as nuts and seeds go, you can balance the omega-6

fatty acids in sesame and sunflower seeds with plenty of omega-3s from flax, chia, and walnuts. It's really not hard to get a decent omega-6 to omega-3 ratio in your diet; it simply demands a little consciousness.

An Oil-Free Vegan Diet Is the Healthiest Diet

There's no robust evidence that moderate use of oils in an otherwise healthy, plant-centric diet is harmful to health. In fact, some oils may have healthful properties. Oil can also make a tremendous difference in cooking, and it's abundant in restaurant food. Trying to avoid it entirely can be the difference between a vegan diet that feels easy and a vegan diet that feels like it's full of restrictions.

If you're trying to lose weight, it's wise to be conscious of oils, since they're very caloric. But strict avoidance may be a lot more trouble than it's worth. For more on oil, see page 71.

It's Essential to Separate Proteins and Starches, Because They Require Different Digestive Environments and Will Cause Bloating If You Eat Them Together

Food combining—the idea that proteins and starches demand different stomach environments in order to digest efficiently and that we should separate these foods temporally when we eat them—is popular in certain raw food circles.

Food combining starts with a true premise: Different enzymes and different parts of the digestive tract are activated to digest proteins, starches, and fats. Starch digestion begins in our mouth (with salivary amylase, an enzyme that's responsible for the softening and sweetening of a bite of bread as you chew it) and is completed in the small intestine. Protein digestion begins in our stomach, where protease enzymes cleave protein molecules; these molecules are later absorbed in our small intestine. Fat digestion and absorption takes place mainly in the small intestine.

Food combining proponents go on to say that, because different areas of our digestive tract are activated to digest different food groups, we have to eat proteins, fats, and starches separately in order to avoid indigestion. This is where we move from fact to fiction. Sure, different enzymes work to digest different foods, but that doesn't mean we can't eat starches with proteins, or fruits with nuts. Let's say you eat a bite of the Quick Quinoa and Black Beans with Spicy Cilantro Vinaigrette (page 166). As you chew, salivary amylase will break down and soften the quinoa. A tiny amount of lingual lipase will act on the fat too, but not much. When the food reaches your stomach, it will start to be broken down by hydrochloric acid. As this happens, protease enzymes will start to work on the protein molecules from the black beans, cleaving them into smaller molecules that you can assimilate later on. Some of the fats from the oil in the dressing will be broken down too. All of these actions happen at once, as the food you ate gets churned into a giant ball called chyme.

When this mass reaches your small intestine, the sudden drop in pH will signal for more amylases to be released. The duodenum—the top of your small intestine—is somewhat alkaline, so it neutralizes the acidic chyme. At this point, carbohydrates are broken down and assimilated, along with fats. The proteins that you've already broken down get absorbed as the chyme moves through the small intestine too. By the time the digestive process passes the ileum, you've absorbed most of the nutrients you need. Indigestible fibers and sugars make their way to the large intestine, where they—along with bacteria, dead cells, and water—ultimately make their way to your toilet.

This is a delicate, perfectly orchestrated ballet. It's going on all the time, as you eat, sleep, and move. Sure, different molecules will be broken down and absorbed at different times, but you don't have to eat them one at a time; your body is perfectly capable of handling everything at once. In fact, there's good reason why you shouldn't separate your food; your meals are far more likely to have complete, well-rounded nutrition if you take care to eat fat, complex carbs, and protein with every meal. If it helps you to eat simply, then by all means, do. But don't feel that you need to subscribe to the often ornate rules of food combining in order to experience optimal digestion. Food combining theory is a gross underestimation of the strength and sophistication of your digestive system!

You Should Always Eat Fruit Alone and on an Empty Stomach

The central tenet of food combining is that fruits must be consumed alone and on an empty stomach. They're "lighter" than other foods, or so the logic goes, and if we eat them after heavier foods they won't be digested and will "ferment" in our stomach environment. Another popular theory is that fruit "spoils" when it is exposed to our stomach acid.

This premise is flawed on numerous fronts. Once again, fruit will be efficiently mixed up and digested with other food you've eaten; nothing will be forced to "wait" behind anything else. As for the fruit spoiling, it's impossible for anything to rot in the highly acidic stomach environment.

Fruit may feel "light" to us because it's so rich in water, but it's totally fine to eat it along with other foods. In fact, there may be some benefits to doing so. The vitamins in fruit can help our bodies to absorb other nutrients more efficiently: the vitamin C in an orange, for example, can help to make the iron in lentils and sautéed spinach more bioavailable. And if you eat fruit along with some protein and/or fat, the sugars will be absorbed more slowly into your bloodstream, which may be a good thing if you're sensitive to sugar.

Eating Spinach Raw Is Bad for You Because It Blocks the Absorption of Nutrients

Oxalic acid is a naturally occurring compound in leafy greens, such as spinach, kale, chard, parsley, collards, and beet greens, as well as in certain nuts, seeds, berry, and soy foods. Spinach is particularly high in oxalic acid—750 milligrams per 100-gram serving. Oxalic acid can be toxic, but it's not toxic in the amounts present in food.

When oxalic acid binds to certain minerals, such as calcium and iron, it forms salts called oxalates. These are typically passed in urine, but they can in some cases turn into kidney stones, especially for people who are predisposed to such stones in the first place. They don't pose a significant threat to most of us, but what is worth noting is that oxalates can block our absorption of calcium and iron. Spinach, beet greens, Swiss chard, okra, parsley, quinoa, soy foods, almonds, and cashews all have significant amounts of oxalates, so the amount of calcium or iron that is bioavailable from those foods may not be high.

Cooking may lower some of the oxalate content in foods, but by only 15 percent or so. It's a good rule of thumb to enjoy such foods as spinach and chard in both raw and cooked forms but also to eat a wide variety of leafy greens. Kale, collards, and mustard greens have lower oxalate content, so they're more reliable sources of calcium and iron than spinach or chard. That said, raw spinach certainly isn't "bad" for you—it simply may not deliver all of its full nutrient potential.

Soy Disrupts Hormones, Causes Breast Cancer, and Should Be Avoided

Antisoy sentiment has grown tremendously in recent years, thanks in part to the rhetoric of the paleo movement and advocates of "traditional" diets. This is unfortunate, because soy is one of the most nutrient dense foods in a plant-based diet. It's rich in calcium, complete protein, and iron. The phytoestrogens in soy are correlated with improved cholesterol levels, reduced risk of heart disease, and reduced inflammation. How did such a healthful food develop such a controversial reputation?

The source of most soy alarmism is the fact that soy contains phytonutrients called phytoestrogens. They behave similarly to estrogen in the body, but they're much weaker than estrogen itself. This fact has made many people leery of soy, and quick to suggest that it might increase breast cancer risk, but so far the evidence fails to validate that claim. In fact, it contradicts it. Phytoestrogens may attach themselves to estrogen receptors in the female body, blocking actual estrogen from promoting tumors. This may explain why numerous studies and meta analyses have found that soy has a protective effect against breast cancer development.[6] The protective effect is observed more strongly in Asian populations; in Western studies, soy seems to either have a modest protective effect, or no effect at all. This may be because soy is most beneficial for breast cancer development when it's consumed earlier in life.[7] For women who have had breast cancer in the past, current research suggests that soy has no effect on recurrence—even among women who have had estrogen positive cancers.[8] People who are at risk for breast cancer should of course avoid soy at their own discretion, but the research we have doesn't necessitate it.

Another major concern about soy is that it can impair thyroid function. Soy is a goitrogen, a food that can interfere with iodine uptake. Since iodine supports thyroid health, people who consume soy regularly may benefit from eating slightly more iodine (which is very available in seaweed, a plant-based staple).[9] However, studies have failed to show that soy causes hypothyroidism.[10]

Does it matter what type of soy you eat? Possibly. While health proponents tend to insist that fermented soy (tempeh and natto) is "safer" than tofu, neither food presents a health hazard, and they share many of the same benefits. However, soy does contain some antinutrients, called phytates, that can block our absorption of iron, zinc, manganese, and—to a lesser extent—calcium. It's unlikely that phytates pose a problem to people who eat balanced diets, and phytates have actually been shown to have some anti-inflammatory properties. But fermentation process will reduce the phytic acid in soy and make other nutrients more bioavailable, so tempeh is a good option for folks who are worried about zinc and calcium absorption.[11] That said, protein in soy becomes more available through processing, so tofu is a better protein source than edamame. For all of these reasons, it's wise to eat a combination of whole soy foods. Eating tofu, tempeh, or edamame along with vitamin C can aid in iron absorption too.

A final jab against soy foods is often the fact that soy is a common GMO crop. "90 percent of the soy grown in the US is genetically modified," you might be told. This is true, but it's also misleading. Most of the genetically modified soy grown in the United States is fed to animals on factory farms. It's actually much easier to find tofu and tempeh that are organic and non-GMO than it is to find tofu and tempeh that aren't. If you're eating GMO soy, it's most likely coming from either processed foods or meat, not tofu, tempeh, or edamame.

PART III

The How

THIS SECTION WILL HELP YOU EASE INTO VEGAN AND RAW foods. In chapter 7, I'll go over the essentials of grocery shopping, meal planning, stocking your pantry and fridge, and outfitting your kitchen with key appliances. In chapter 8, I'll chat about where you should begin your vegan and/or raw journey and give you tips on developing healthy, sustainable habits. Finally, in chapter 9, I'll guide you through twenty-one days of adaptable, plant-based meal plans.

CHAPTER 7
Setting Up

AWELL-STOCKED VEGAN KITCHEN IS A thing of plenty. In this chapter, we'll go over essential vegan pantry items, appliances you might find handy, and general tips for grocery shopping and meal planning.

Say What?

"Tamari," "tempeh," "aduki," "amaranth," and "nooch": as unusual as they may be now, these are all common ingredients in vegan and raw recipes. If you're new to plant-based eating, here's a short list of unusual ingredients that you'll probably discover along the way.

Açai

When açai, a fruit native to South America, hit the health food market nearly a decade ago, it was instantly catapulted to "superfood" status because of its supposedly co-

lossal antioxidant content. Recent studies, however, have shown that açai is not a better source of antioxidants than strawberries or grapes—in fact, it's a slightly *less* valuable source—and that a lot of the antioxidants are rendered inactive after digestion. This story illustrates the kind of mania that can often result when a shiny new ingredient gets a lot of buzz!

That said, there are still a lot of reasons to love açai. Açai berries have a gorgeous blue-black color and a deep, rich, almost chocolaty taste. Açai is usually sold in frozen, ready-to-blend packs, and it adds a lot of flavor to smoothies. My favorite way to prepare açai is in the açai bowl on page 209. It's a wonderful start to your day.

Agave Nectar

This is a sweet syrup made from the agave plant, which is native to Mexico and the

Southwestern United States. The nectar of the plant is extracted and commercially prepared to produce a sweetener that's mostly fructose. Agave nectar has a neutral flavor and is a suitable substitute for honey or sugar. There's been some controversy about agave's healthfulness lately, but I think that the fears are largely inflammatory. Agave nectar may not be a health food—after all, it's a concentrated sweetener—but it's fine to consume in moderation.

Almond Butter

Almond butter is like peanut butter, but it's made with raw or roasted almonds. It's delicious, protein rich, and has a slightly better fatty acid profile than peanut butter. I use it in pretty much everything (smoothies, on top of fresh fruit, spread on toast). It's readily available commercially and it's not hard to make your own, either.

Almond Flour

Almond flour is made from whole, blanched almonds. It's very fine, and it's wonderful in gluten-free baking. It can be hard to make baked goods work with almond flour exclusively, so I usually mix it with some type of whole-grain flour as well.

Amaranth

Amaranth is usually classified as a grain, but it's actually a pseudograin, or "grain seed." Cultivated in Asia and the Americas since ancient times, amaranth is rich in lysine, an essential amino acid, and it's suitable for those who avoid gluten. You can prepare it by "popping" it in a heated skillet, or you can cook it

as you would any other grain. It gets a little thick on its own, so I like to mix it with another, fluffier grain (such as quinoa or millet).

Apple Cider Vinegar

Apple cider vinegar (or ACV) is a type of vinegar made from (you guessed it) apple cider. You can purchase it in nearly any grocery store, but, if you can, it's worth purchasing unpasteurized apple cider vinegar, which contains a cloudy entity called "the mother" (really just a mass of cellulose and bacteria that develops from fermentation).

Apple cider vinegar is not only a delicious option for salad dressings but it's also a handy household cleaner. It's thought to be antifungal as well as antibacterial. No matter how you use it, it's a wise ingredient to keep in your home.

Avocado Oil

A type of oil that is pressed from avocados, avocado oil can be found in both refined and unrefined varieties. It has a high smoke point, which means that it's safe to cook with at high temperatures. This is especially true of refined avocado oil. It has a mild, nutty flavor. Great either for salads or for stir-fries, roasting, or grilling.

Barley

Barley is one of mankind's most ancient crops: it was first grown in western Asia, near the Nile River at around 7,000 BC. It is a plump, filling grain with plenty of chew. I like to eat it plain or as a breakfast cereal, but you can also toss it with vegetables and dressing to make a wonderful grain salad.

Blackstrap Molasses

Blackstrap molasses is the thick, dark syrup that remains after cane juice has been refined into sugar. It's a surprisingly nutrient dense ingredient, featuring significant amounts of iron and calcium. You can stir it into hot cereal, snack bars, puddings, or even into mashed sweet potatoes.

Bragg's Liquid Aminos

Bragg Liquid Aminos is a salty condiment (similar to soy sauce, tamari, or nama shoyu) that's derived from soybeans. It's high in a number of essential and nonessential amino acids.

Brown Rice Protein

A protein powder derived from brown rice that has been treated with enzymes that separate the starch from the protein. Brown rice protein is easily assimilated and works well in smoothies and baked goods. It has a slightly chalky taste, so it's nice to pair with sweeter fruits and bold flavors.

Brown Rice Syrup

A thick, golden syrup derived from cooked brown rice and barley sprouts. I think that brown rice syrup tastes a bit like caramel (which is a good thing!), and it works really nicely in snack bars and granola.

Buckwheat/Flour

Buckwheat, like amaranth, is what's known as a pseudograin. It's gluten free (don't let the name confuse you!), and it's rich in fiber and minerals. It's a staple food in certain parts of China, and some suggest that it's correlated with cardiovascular health and blood sugar control.

Buckwheat can be toasted and cooked (in this form, it's called kasha). I like to simply soak it overnight, rinse it well, and then either dehydrate or bake it (see my instructions for Buckwheaties, page 105). It's nutty, wholesome, and versatile, and it's a favorite ingredient in my raw granolas.

Finally, buckwheat flour is a great gluten-free flour to explore. It's hearty and nutty, and it adds an undeniably healthy—but not at all unpleasant—flavor to pancakes and baked goods.

Cacao/Cacao Nibs

Cacao is the raw version of cocoa. It tastes similar, but it's a little bolder, and you can use less of it to get a very dramatic, rich taste.

Cacao nibs are small, crunchy pieces of whole cacao beans. They're exceptionally high in antioxidants, and they have a subtle flavor: a little nutty, a little chocolaty, a little bitter. They add good flavor to smoothies and desserts, and they're lovely, crunchy toppings for puddings, cereals, and sliced banana.

Chia

Chia seeds (*Salvia hispanica*) grow into the chia plant, which is in the mint family. Chia is native to central and southern Mexico, and it was cultivated by the Aztecs over five centuries ago. Chia seeds plump up like tapioca when you add liquid to them, and they're exceptionally nutrient dense. They're high in protein, calcium, and omega-3 fatty acids.

The seeds can be used as pudding, or they can be ground up and used as a thickener in baking or smoothies.

Chickpea Flour

Chickpea flour is gluten free, rich in protein, and incredibly versatile. You can use it to make *socca* (a type of easy stove-top flatbread), in baking, to make falafel, or to make crepes. It's popular in Middle Eastern cooking in particular.

Coconut Nectar/Crystals/Flour

When coconut trees are tapped, they produce a syrup (much like maple syrup) that is sweet, low glycemic, and rich in amino acids. Coconut nectar has a caramel-like flavor, and it's very thick. It can be used in a one-to-one ratio to replace any sweetener.

Coconut crystals are derived from coconut nectar, and they share its properties. I think that coconut crystals taste like burnt sugar, and, as you'll see, I use them to flavor one decadent ice cream (page 245).

Coconut flour is a high-protein, high-fiber, and low-carbohydrate flour derived from defatted coconut. It works well in baked goods, especially when mixed with other types of flour, and it tastes, not surprisingly, like coconut. I enjoy coconut flour enough that I sometimes stir a tablespoon or two into my morning oats for added fiber and texture.

Dulse

Dulse is a type of edible seaweed, or sea vegetable, which is harvested in Canada and along coastal regions of the Atlantic. It's rich in iron and an excellent source of iodine. It is sold both in strips and as flakes (which you can sprinkle on food in place of salt). It happens to be my favorite type of sea vegetable, in part because of its irresistibly salty flavor. I add it to salads and soups whenever I'm craving something grounding and earthy.

Farro

Farro is a versatile, chewy grain. Like barley, it's one of the oldest cultivated grains on the planet. It also happens to be relatively high in protein and in iron (12 percent of the RDA of the latter per serving). I love to mix it with roasted vegetables or add it to soup. It can also be used to make a more wholesome version of risotto!

Flax

Flaxseed is a true superfood. First cultivated in ancient Babylon, flaxseeds have been associated with reduced risk of cancer, heart disease, stroke, and diabetes. They're inexpensive, versatile, and exceptionally rich in those precious and important omega-3 fatty acids. They're rich in fiber (soluble and insoluble), and they're also full of lignans, a type of antioxidant that has the same phytoestrogenic properties as soy.

Flax seeds won't be assimilated completely in their whole form, which means that, while they're fine to enjoy in crackers or raw breads, you'll benefit even more by eating ground flax meal. You can sprinkle it into smoothies, on oatmeal, or even on top of salads. Flax meal also makes a handy replacer for eggs in baked goods. Simply mix one ground tablespoon of meal with 3 tablespoons of water, and allow it to "gel" for 20 minutes before using it to replace one egg.

Goji Berries

Goji berries were one of the first highly publicized "superfoods." Popular in traditional Chinese medicine, these brilliantly colored, dried berries are rich in protein, vitamin A, vitamin C, iron, and antioxidants. You can enjoy them in any recipe that begs for the addition of something sweet and tart.

Hemp/Hemp Protein

Hemp seeds, as you may have guessed, come from the cannabis plant, but don't get too worried (or excited!): the plants used to harvest hemp seeds are bred for low THC content, and hemp products are processed so that THC content is literally negligible. Hemp seeds are extraordinarily nutrient dense. They're excellent sources of complete protein and have a balanced essential fatty acid profile.

Hemp protein, which is derived from hemp seeds, is probably my favorite type of protein powder. It's simple, easy to find without sweeteners or lots of added junk, and has a slightly nutty flavor.

Kelp

Kelp is another type of edible seaweed, or sea vegetable, that's notable for its mineral content. It is an excellent source of iodine, which is crucial for thyroid health.

Kelp is similar to Japanese kombu and can be purchased in a flake form. My favorite way to enjoy kelp, however, is in the form of kelp noodles. These incredible noodles are made from kelp, water, and sodium alginate (which is itself derived from brown seaweed). They're a little watery and crunchy, but, if you soak and dry them thoroughly before using them, you'll find that they're very versatile. They're a great stand in for pasta in raw food recipes, and they work well with a variety of sauces, from marinara to pesto to cashew Alfredo. Kelp noodles also happen to be an excellent source of calcium—15 percent of your daily value in one serving.

My favorite kelp noodles are made by the Sea Tangle Noodle Company. They can be purchased on Amazon, or online at http:// kelpnoodles.com.

Kombu

Kombu is a type of kelp seaweed. It is widely eaten in East Asia, where it's sometimes used to make stock. It's also pickled, dried, and even used to make a type of seaweed tea. It's thought that cooking beans with a strip or two of kombu will help to render them more digestible. I often add kombu to pots of beans at home, as well as to miso soup.

Lucuma

Lucuma is a fruit native to Peru. It contains B vitamins and is naturally sweet; to me, it tastes faintly of vanilla. It's also frequently compared to maple syrup. You can use it in smoothies or as an alternative sweetener.

Maca

Maca is a root vegetable native to the Andes of Peru. It's what's called an "adaptogen"—a name given to ingredients that are thought to help balance hormones and stress. It's also said to boost sexual desire and improve mood. I was skeptical about all of these claims until I saw a few studies that support maca's efficacy in stabilizing depression after menopause and increasing libido in men. Maybe there's something to all the hype!

Maca has a highly distinctive flavor, which people tend either to love or to hate. I'm not a big fan, but, when paired with the right ingredients, I can get into it. Check out my Mocha Maca Chia Pudding (page 200) or my Chocolate-Covered Superfood Clusters (page 235).

Millet (and Millet Flour)

If you've never cooked millet before, you're still probably familiar with it: it's the main ingredient in birdseed! But don't let that turn you off, because millet is wonderful. It is a small, round grain that's a major cop in Africa and southeast Asia. It's gluten free, easy to cook, slightly sweet, and rich in minerals. Millet can also be ground up into flour, and millet flour is actually one of my favorite options for gluten-free baking. It has a light texture and a subtly sweet taste. I find that it works best when used in combination with other gluten-free flours or with tapioca or potato starch.

Miso

Miso is a paste that is traditionally made from fermented soybeans and rice or barley malt. It is a staple in Japanese cooking but can add flavor to a wide variety of dressings, sauces, and soups. There are several kinds of miso, but mellow white miso, which—true to its name—is more subtle than red or brown miso, is my personal favorite.

Mulberries

Though they're not as commonplace as raisins, or as popularized as goji berries, dried mulberries are my personal favorite dried fruit. Mulberries are grown all over the world, from North America to Asia. White mulberries, which are native to east Asia, make unbelievably sweet, delicious dried fruit and can be found from various health food brands. They're so good that I rarely put them in recipes; I prefer to snack on them as they are, so that I can savor each bite.

Nama Shoyu

Nama shoyu is a lot like soy sauce, but it's preferred among raw foodies because it's unpasteurized and fermented, thus higher in enzymes than is regular soy sauce. Many brands are gluten free as well. I tend to use nama shoyu and tamari interchangeably.

Nori

Nori may be the most well known of edible seaweeds, because sheets of nori are what's used to wrap sushi rolls. I use raw (untoasted) nori sheets to make quick and easy wraps and snack rolls. Nori can also be found in a flake form, which makes it easy to sprinkle on salads and grains.

Nutritional Yeast

Nutritional yeast, lovingly known as "nooch" by those who use it often, is a secret weapon of vegan cooking. Nutritional yeast is made from *Saccharomyces cerevisiae*, a type of yeast that's grown on molasses and then washed, dried, and heated to deactivate the yeast properties. It doesn't have the properties of live yeast, and, no, it won't cause yeast infections or overgrowth. Nooch is rich in B-vitamins, including vitamin B12, folic acid, selenium, and zinc. It's almost always gluten free, but you should check labels to be sure it's certified if you can't consume gluten.

Nooch is famous for tasting "cheesy," so it's a staple in vegan cheese recipes, as a pasta topper, and it's wonderful on top of salads too. It also has what's described in Japanese as *umami*—a savory flavor that's often associated with certain animal proteins. For this reason, it's a great ingredient to use as you're transitioning. Though it may taste a little strange at first, most vegans ultimately fall head-over-heels in love with nooch. I myself order it in bulk and can happily eat it with a spoon.

Oat Flour

Oat flour is, as you might expect, flour made from finely milled oats. It's thick, wholesome, and more nutritious than other whole grain flours (it's high in fiber, and fairly high in protein as well). You can use it in quick breads, pancakes, muffins, or to bind vegetable burgers.

Quinoa/Flour/Flakes

A celebrated grain among health nuts everywhere, quinoa (pronounced "keen-wah") is famous for being a "complete protein" (that is, it contains all of the essential amino acids). It's also rich in manganese, magnesium, and folate. Quinoa is both nutritious and very light, so it's perfect for quick grain salads. It has a nutty taste, and it cooks up very quickly (15 to 20 minutes).

Quinoa flour is simply quinoa that has been finely ground. It adds nutty taste to baked goods and has a light texture, but it can be slightly bitter in large amounts, so I recommend mixing it with other gluten-free flours when you use it. Quinoa flakes are re-ally special; they're lighter than whole quinoa but have more texture than flour, and they cook up into a nutty, delicious breakfast porridge in about a minute. They can also be used as a binder in vegetable burgers, meatless meatballs, and more.

Sacha Inchi

Sacha Inchi is a plant native to the Peruvian Amazon rain forest. Its star-shaped fruit produces an edible seed that is exceptionally rich in omega-3 fatty acids, as well as vitamins A and E. Sacha inchi seeds can be roasted at low temperatures and eaten as snacks, or they can be used to produce a delicate oil, which, much like flax or hemp oil, is perfect for salads or smoothies.

Sunflower Seed Butter

Sunflower seeds are delicious in their own right, but they're also terrific when roasted and ground up into sunflower seed butter. Sunflower seed butter is usually a little salty and a little sweet. It's a nice departure from almond or peanut butter as usual and can generally be purchased at a good price.

Tahini

Tahini is a paste made from raw or roasted sesame seeds. It's one of the primary ingredients in traditional hummus, but, aside from this, it makes a perfect base for salad dressings. I also like to eat tahini on fresh banana slices, or even to use it in smoothies. You can purchase raw tahini, but it's very expensive, so for the sake of your budget, I recommend getting organic, roasted tahini instead (which also has more depth of flavor). Tahini is a good source of calcium.

Teff (flour)

Teff is indigenous to north Africa, where it has been a staple for years. It's a tiny grain but packs a lot of nutrition, including calcium, protein, and fiber. Teff flour is the traditional ingredient in injera, the spongy bread served in Ethiopian cuisine. Teff and teff flour are gluten free, and it's well worth exploring them if you're eliminating or minimizing gluten. Like many nonglutenous flours, teff flour is often best when combined with other flours and/or starches in baking.

Young Thai Coconut

Coconut is a familiar ingredient, but young Thai coconuts are more of a novelty. These coconuts are harvested while they're still green, so they don't have the characteristically brown, hairy coating of a regular coconut. They're full of sweet, fresh coconut water and gelatinous flesh. Young coconut meat is delicious: sweet, tender, mellow, and it blends up into incredible smoothies and sauces. You can also make your own coconut milk by blending the meat with water.

Thai coconuts can be pricey, and opening them can be tough, but they're well worth the effort once you discover their versatility and flavor. You can follow my instructions for opening a Thai coconut on page 224.

Vegan Kitchen VIPs

Here's a list of the ingredients that I find to be most essential in a plant-based kitchen. You'll probably find that some of them are more useful to you than others, based on your own eating style, likes/dislikes, and circumstances. As always, you can take what's helpful from this list, and leave behind what isn't.

Beans

Beans are a potent and powerful superfood, providing iron, calcium, protein, and numerous vitamins in one fell swoop. It's a good idea to have a few different types of beans on hand at all times. I happen to think that soaked and freshly cooked beans taste better (and are more digestible), but BPA-free, canned beans are a lifesaver when you're short on time. I like to have a mix of:

Chickpeas (garbanzos)
Great northern beans (cannellini)
Black beans
Navy beans
Kidney beans
Black-eyed peas
Lentils
Pinto beans
Kidney beans
Split peas (red, yellow, and green)

Grains

Healthy whole grains and psuedograins are one of the foundations of a vegan diet. Grains provide protein and carbohydrates—the building blocks of life—along with numerous micronutrients that vary from grain to grain. Human beings have relied upon whole grains since the dawn of agriculture, 10,000 to 7,000 BC, and they remain a foundation in diets around the world. If you're used to eating more conventional grains, such as rice or oats, this is a marvelous time to expand your palate.

An asterisk (*) denotes grains and grain products that are not gluten free. If you have celiac disease or gluten sensitivity, it's essential you keep them out of your pantry. If you avoid gluten for other reasons, then you should also avoid these foods. Stick with the grains and grain products not marked with an asterisk—those are naturally gluten free.

Whole Grains to Have on Hand
Quinoa
Millet
Brown rice
Farro*
Barley*
Amaranth
Buckwheat

What if whole grains aren't quite what you're craving? Here are some refined grain products that still get bonus points for being healthful (and tasty)!
Quinoa flakes
Steel-cut oats or rolled oats*
Quinoa pasta
Brown rice pasta
Sprouted-grain bread* (I like the Ezekiel or Alvarado St. Bakery brands)

If you're a baker, you can still harness the goodness of whole grains by purchasing unique, unconventional flours made from whole grains. Working with some of these flours will take some practice, but it will be well worth it when you can create baked goods that are as wholesome and nutritious as they are appealing.

Whole-Grain Flours to Have on Hand
Whole wheat pastry flour (this is a finely ground whole wheat flour, and it's less "gritty" tasting than regular whole wheat flour)* or a gluten-free all-purpose flour mix (I like Bob's Red Mill)
Oat flour*
Millet flour
Teff flour
Quinoa flour
Chickpea flour (not actually grain based, but very handy for savory baking)
Coconut flour (also not grain based, but it can add delicious texture to baked goods, as well as to hot cereal)
Buckwheat flour

All grains can go rancid after 3 months or so, especially when it's hot outside, so be sure to buy only as much as you can use in that time frame. Refrigerate flours when it's hot.

Oils
The right oils (olive, avocado, coconut, flax, hemp, and sacha inchi) in moderation are a source of healthy fat—and often a good anti-inflammatory agent. Here's a list of my go-to oils:
Coconut oil (organic, extra-virgin)
Toasted dark sesame oil (for flavoring; not to be used in large amounts)
Extra-virgin olive oil
Avocado oil (unrefined for salads, refined for high-heat cooking)
Flax oil
Hemp oil
Sacha inchi oil

One thing to keep in mind as you select oils is that certain oils can go rancid and even release toxins at high temperatures. Delicate oils, such as flax, hemp, or sacha inchi should be consumed cold, in salads or smoothies. Olive oil can stand up to moderate heat, but for really high-heat cooking, you're better off with either refined avocado oil or my personal favorite, coconut oil, which can withstand super high temperatures without losing its structure.

Vinegars/Broths/Condiments/Toppings

A good vinegar or condiment can make a meal. These are the ones that I use to flavor grains, salads, and other dishes.

Nama shoyu/Bragg's Liquid Aminos/Tamari/Coconut Aminos (These aren't all the same—shoyu is saltier than Bragg's—but they serve the same basic function, which is to add salt. Choose whichever is your favorite and suits your health needs. Gluten-free eaters can eat tamari that is certified gluten free, while those who are allergic to soy can consume coconut aminos.)

Marinara sauce (buy organic and lower sodium if possible)

Barbecue sauce (good for last minute marinades of tofu or tempeh, as well as grilled vegetables—try to find one that's organic and relatively low in sugar)

Ketchup (shop organic, and try to buy the brand with the least added sugar)

Apple cider vinegar

Rice vinegar

Balsamic vinegar

Low sodium vegetable broth or salt-free, organic vegetable bouillon cubes

Diced, canned tomatoes (I like the organic, fire-roasted tomatoes from Muir Glen)

Tomato paste

Nutritional Yeast

Herbs and Spices

Stock up on any of the herbs and spices you like the most. My favorites (and ones you'll find in the recipes here):

Curry powder

Cumin

Turmeric

Coriander

Smoked paprika

Cinnamon

Cloves

Nutmeg

Basil

Oregano or Italian herb blend

Salt-free herb-and-spice blend

Herbamare (a wonderful salt substitute that also contains an herb blend)

Sweeteners

People have different needs when it comes to sweeteners. If you're very sensitive to sugar, you may find that dates, which contain fiber that helps to prevent blood sugar spikes, are the best option for you. If you aren't sensitive to sweeteners, you can use whichever ones work best in the recipe you're making. Brown rice syrup and coconut syrup are very thick and sticky, while maple syrup and agave nectar are lighter.

If you can't consume sugar at all, then you can use stevia, a sweetener made from stevia leaf. It's sugar free and tastes very sweet, which makes it a popular sugar substitute in healthy eating circles. Research suggests, however, that it is in part the *taste* of sweetness, not only the presence of sugar itself, that raises blood sugar, so I'm generally wary of the value of artificial sweeteners, even plant-derived ones. Some folks find that stevia can cause bloating too. I tend to think it's better to use real sugar in moderation than rely on stevia too heavily.

With that, here's a list of the sweeteners I use most often:
Pitted dates
Agave nectar
Blackstrap molasses
Brown rice syrup
Coconut syrup
Maple syrup
Demerara sugar, evaporated cane juice, or coconut crystals
Stevia

Nuts, Seeds, and Nut Butters

Any of your favorite nuts and seeds should be household staples. This is especially true if you love raw food, since many raw recipes use nuts and seeds as a base. Here are my favorites. If you prefer roasted nut butters to raw ones, that's fine (roasted are usually cheaper and easier to find), but try to pick brands that are unsalted and unsweetened:
Almonds
Cashews
Pumpkin seeds
Pine nuts
Sunflower seeds
Sesame seeds
Walnuts
Chia seeds
Hemp seeds
Flax seeds
Almond butter
Sunflower seed butter
Peanut butter
Tahini

Note: Chia, flax, and hemp seeds must be kept in the fridge. It's not a bad idea to refrigerate other nuts as well, especially if you live in a hot environment and you're not going to use them right away. Try to choose organic when you can.

Dried Fruits

Dried fruits are the key to delicious raw desserts, and they're also great for homemade trail mix and snacking. Here are a few of the dried fruits I'm never without. When you're picking dried fruits, be sure to choose ones that are unsulfured and have no sugar added.
Dried, unsulfured apricots
Dried currants
Dried cherries
Pitted dates
Goji berries
Dried mulberries
Raisins

Plant Milks

As much as I love to make my own almond and hemp milks, I also tend to have a supply of store-bought plant milks around for when I need them in a pinch or simply don't have time to make a new batch. Commercial plant milks have an bonus, which is that they're fortified with calcium and B12. A cup of almond milk contains 35 to 45 percent of your daily recommended allowance of calcium—an easy way to squeeze in this essential nutrient! Here are my favorite plant milks.

You'll note that coconut milk is on the list. My preference is canned coconut milk, which is ideal for soups and stews. If you like, you can also pick up thinner coconut milk that comes in a carton (such as the So Delicious brand), but it won't add the same richness to food as the canned stuff.

Almond milk

Hemp milk

Full-fat coconut milk (in the can)

Light coconut milk (in the can)

Protein Powders and Superfoods

As I've mentioned, superfoods and protein powders are both optional parts of a plant-based diet. But they can be very fun to experiment with. Here is a list of the superfood ingredients that I tend to have at home:

Organic hemp protein (Navitas Naturals, Manitoba Harvest, and Nutiva are my favorite brands)

Organic brown rice protein (Sunwarrior and 22 Days Nutrition are my favorites)

Raw cacao powder (Navitas Naturals or Sunfood)

Cacao nibs

Maca powder (Navitas Naturals)

Lucuma powder (Navitas Naturals)

Your pantry doesn't need to contain all of these ingredients for you to have tremendous success with vegan and raw cooking. If you've got a couple of standard spices, some soy sauce, a good kitchen knife, and a lot of produce, you can make plant-based food. You can build your pantry slowly and gradually. It took me a while to amass the collection of appliances, herbs, spices, superfoods, grains, flours, nuts, and seeds that I have handy now. This didn't stop me from making a lot of really wonderful vegan and raw meals.

Appliances

A ton of plant-based recipes can be made with nothing more than a sharp set of knives, but, if you want to expand your repertoire to include homemade hummus, perfectly blended smoothies and soups, vegetable "pasta," and more, you can start to think about which appliances might be most useful to you. Here are my favorites, ranked in the order of how often I put them to use.

Food Processor

My Cuisinart 10-cup food processor is the appliance I use most often in my kitchen. I use it for soups, spreads, dips, hummus, nut pâtés, pestos, all fruit ice creams, homemade nut butter, and for grinding nuts and seeds. A lot of these things can be done with a high-powered blender too, but food processors are less expensive and in some ways more versatile. Whether you're transitioning to a plant-based diet or not, a food processor is a wise and worthy kitchen investment.

A 7- or 10-cup food processor costs between $50 and $150. A reasonably priced, refurbished machine can be had for less on eBay. Once you have it, you'll use it all the time, and a sturdy machine will last quite a while. Stay away from mini food processors; they're great for chopping opinions, garlic, and other vegetables, but they can't do the heavy lifting.

Blender

A blender will allow you to make fruit smoothies, pureed soups, puddings, and, depending on what sort of blender you have, much more. A basic blender (usually about $50 to $100) is perfectly suitable for smoothies and soups. High-speed blenders, which have far more power than regular blenders, are considerably more costly, but they open up a lot of fun possibilities—especially for raw food lovers. These machines can puree nuts into creamy sauces and soft nut cheeses, blend even the hardest vegetables (such as raw beets) into soup, and even turn whole grains into flour.

My high-speed blender of choice is the Vitamix 5200. It ranges in price from $449 to $650 but has a seven-year warranty and lasts for ages. If you're not ready for this kind of commitment, don't worry: a conventional blender is totally sufficient for most basic recipes.

Rice Cooker

Rice cookers are a game changer. They create perfectly fluffy rice, quinoa, millet, and other grains time and time again. If you, like me, tend to forget about grains when they're on the stove, you'll never have to worry about burning them again. Rice cookers can be purchased for as little as $25, and you can use them for lentils, oats, and steamed vegetables too.

Mandoline

Eating more vegetables means a lot more slicing, dicing, and chopping. This process is much easier if you have a mandoline on your side. It'll let you grate, chop, and slice vegetables into the shape you need. Mandolines are easy to use (but remember to use the protective hand guard, because the blades are sharp!) and you can find a good one online for under $30.

Spiralizer

Spiralizers are handy little devices that will slice zucchini, beets, turnips, or carrots into perfectly shaped "noodles." They're the trick to making perfect, vegetable-based pasta dishes. The model I like best is the Joyce Chen Saladacco slicer, which retails for about $25 online. You can also try the Paderno Spirooli slicer, which costs about the same amount. If you don't feel like purchasing a spiralizer, you can buy a julienne peeler (about $10), or you can simply use a regular vegetable peeler to create "ribbons" of vegetables.

Dehydrator

Dehydrators warm and dry food at low temperatures (around 115°F), so they're ideal for raw food lovers who want to be able to create breads, crackers, and other kinds of snacks without using an oven. I don't use my dehydrator nearly as often as I do my processor or my blender, but I do love using it for kale chips, zucchini chips, and raw granola (raw-nola). Although many of the items I dehydrate could work in an oven as well (raw granola, for example), dehydrators create unbeatably crispy textures. They can be a little intimidating at first, but they're actually very hands off: once you turn your dehydrator on, it does the work for you.

The best dehydrator on the market is the Excalibur. It comes in a five- or nine-tray model, both rectangularly shaped, so that you can easily create perfect, uniform sheets of raw breads or crackers. If an Excalibur is out of your reach (they retail at around $240), you can purchase a circular dehydrator, which costs only $40 to $60. These are fine for kale chips, dried fruit, and raw granolas.

Juicer

I use my juicer less than most other appliances, but I'm still grateful to be able to create fresh, homemade vegetable juice when I can. There are two types of juicers: centrifugal and single auger (there are also juicers called Norwalks that actually masticate and then press your juice, but these are prohibitively expensive for any average person). Centrifugal juicers have a fast, rotating blade that instantly shreds vegetables and fruits. The force of the blade's rotation ejects the pulp into a container that's included in the appliance, and the juice is released from a small spout. These juicers aren't ideal for delicate, leafy greens, and the juice won't stay fresh for more than an hour or two, but they're extremely economical and efficient. I've had a centrifugal juicer for five years (a Breville Juice Fountain Plus) and have loved it.

Single auger juicers have a slow, rotating auger that masticates produce and then squeezes out the juice. They're much better for leafy greens or wheatgrass, and the juice you make will stay fresh overnight in the fridge, so you can prepare morning juice the evening before you want to enjoy it. You can find horizontal or upright models; I recommend the Omega or the Hurom Slow Juicer. Both are excellent investments if you want to make juicing a major part of your lifestyle.

Grocery Shopping and Meal Planning

It takes a little time to get into a grocery groove when you're new to plant-based eating. It's easy to purchase too much produce and watch some of it go bad, or to purchase too little, and find that you've run out by midweek. Over time, you'll get the hang of it. To help you get started, here's a glimpse into my grocery system.

Each week, I pick up:

1. A short list of pantry items I'm running low on, plus

2. Staple ingredients (things I eat every single week, including kale, lettuces, avocados, sweet potatoes, tempeh, and zucchini) plus

3. Seasonal produce picks (items that I purchase occasionally or by season, including tomatoes, berries, peaches, asparagus, and more)

Common pantry items include plant milks, condiments, grains, nuts, seeds, nut butter, and dried legumes. My staple ingredients (you'll have your own list of favorites) include kale, lettuce, bananas, carrots, lemons, avocados, zucchini, broccoli, tempeh, and sweet potatoes. I also always peel and chop bananas to keep in my freezer for smoothies at a moment's notice. In the autumn, my seasonal favorites are apples, Brussels sprouts, cabbage, rutabaga, and parsnips; in the spring and summer I love fresh herbs, asparagus, heirloom tomatoes, berries, and basil.

Keeping Produce Fresh

I always tell new clients that the single-most important gift I'm going to give them isn't a recipe or a strategy or information about dining out. It's not a weight-loss technique, a lesson in the virtues of eating locally or seasonally, or an analysis of vegan nutrition. It's a storage tip, and it's life changing:

Store your produce in resealable plastic bags (or glass containers) with a damp paper towel. As they ripen, fruits and vegetables emit ethylene gas. Damp paper towels absorb some of this gas, which slows the ripening process and keeps produce crispier and fresher. If you're sick and tired of lettuce going soggy, this tip is well worth your time. Now, I don't mean that you should transfer a drippy, soaking paper towel to your containers or bags of produce. You're aiming for damp, and nothing more. Run the paper towel under water, then squeeze out extra moisture. Add it to your vegetables, and watch in amazement as they stay fresher longer. The towel will be fine as it is for up to 4 days; after that, you may wish to replace it with a fresh damp towel.

Making Time to Save Time

At least once every week, I carve out a little time for batch cooking and food prep. Batch cooking is the secret of busy home cooks everywhere: it means prepping big portions of grains, legumes, soups, and other dishes that can last through the week (and such things as grains and beans can stock your freezer for quick meals). I like to batch cook staples and dress them up or use them as needed. This includes:

1 large batch of quinoa
1 large batch of brown rice or barley
1 pot of beans
2 salad dressings (usually one nut/nut butter–based, one vinaigrette)
1 raw nut pâté
1 batch of raw crackers
1 large batch of hummus

Sometimes I substitute millet for quinoa, or a thick soup for plain beans, but you get the idea. I create basic recipes that I can mix and match together—grains that I can serve with a tahini dressing, a nut pâté that I can serve with raw crackers as a snack—as the week goes on.

The other important part of my prep process is washing, chopping, and storing veggies. As soon as I get home from a grocery haul, I stem, wash, and chop my kale, then transfer it to a plastic bag with a damp paper towel (see Keeping Produce Fresh at left). I do the same with broccoli florets and red pepper slices. Sometimes I use my food processor to grate carrots and cabbage, then store them for a couple of days. Everything else gets put away neatly. This is every bit as important as making salad dressings, grains, and beans—you can't throw together plant-based food without the plants!

If you're thinking, "that just sounds like

a lot of *work*," consider this: to make two salad dressings and a nut pâté takes about 30 or 45 minutes—about the same amount of time you might spend waiting for takeout to show up. While that happens, you can stick some quinoa in your rice cooker or let it simmer on the stove. Soaking beans and cooking rice don't take much effort—those things can happen while you're studying, doing work at home, shuffling laundry around, or watching TV. And using a dehydrator is particularly good for making snacks, because it demands no vigilance whatsoever. It's safe to leave the machine on as you go about your business.

Stock Your Freezer

One advantage of batch cooking is that you can freeze whatever you can't eat in a week and then have those portions at the ready when you're in a pinch. I rely on frozen quinoa, bean, and soup dishes from my freezer all the time. Freezing isn't great for a lot of raw food dishes, but raw dressings, marinara, and pesto all freeze very nicely.

CHAPTER 8

Getting Started

TRANSITIONING TO A VEGAN DIET doesn't have to be difficult. Here are six essential strategies that worked for me as I made the leap, and I hope they'll be helpful to you too.

1. Add First. Subtract Later

As you begin to transition over to plant-based foods, it's tempting to fixate on the stuff you *can't* eat. Rather than focusing on what veganism eliminates from your diet, focus on all the dishes you'll be adding. When I went vegan, I began experimenting with a lot of global cuisines I'd never tried, along with a slew of new herbs and spices and seasonings. When I went (semi) raw, I discovered many cool, innovative preparation methods that I'd never thought to try. My culinary talents grew, and my repertoire of food expanded.

For now, don't think about eliminating anything. Instead, think about adding a few meatless, vegan, or raw meals to your preexisting rotation each week. These meals will show you that vegan food is hardly a sacrifice. As the weeks go by you can continue to swap out more of your standard fare for these exciting new options.

2. When You're Ready to Subtract, Take It Step by Step

I've definitely come across folks who made the transition from omnivore to plant-based eater overnight. More often than not, though, a more gradual transition works best. Embrace a pace that works for you. I recommend eliminating one thing first—be it red meat, chicken, dairy, or eggs—and see where that step takes you. Trust yourself as you go along. It's great to challenge yourself, but, as with any significant change, setting realistic goals is important.

If you're already vegetarian, great! You're almost there. For you, the challenge is to find some easy and satisfying replacement for dairy and eggs. My Chickpea Tofu Tahini Scramble (page 152) can hold its own against any morning scramble, and, if you're a big fan of eggs, I welcome you to give it a try! Meanwhile, having Cashew Cheese (page 99) in your arsenal can be extremely helpful as you gradually transition away from regular cheese. Homemade almond milk (page 98) is also a wonderful culinary ally—it's so rich and delicious that you'll never miss the real stuff.

3. Keep It Simple

You may want to just jump in and make a show-stopping meal from a gourmet cookbook. But it's arguably more important that you learn how to master everyday fundamentals, as these are the recipes you'll rely on most heavily when you're coming home from a long day of work, struggling to put dinner on the table in 20 minutes or less, or packing lunch as you rush out the door.

Make a list of essential recipes that appeal to you (if you want some inspiration, the fifteen essentials on page 98 are a nice place to start). Get comfortable with them, and start to adapt them in different ways. This will give you a foundation in plant-based cooking, from which you can go on to explore more ornate dishes. You might also want to check out my tips for building a meal-size salad on page 139, since giant salads are easy to throw together according to what's in your fridge.

4. Embrace Transition Foods and Meals

Most of my recipes will help you to whip up food from scratch. But I'm certainly not opposed to using vegan substitutes in cooking.

Daiya (a melty, tasty vegan "cheese" made from tapioca starch), Earth Balance (a vegan butter substitute), commercial nut and soy milk, Field Roast sausage (which is so darn good that I've fooled omnivores with it at potlucks), and Sunshine Burgers (my favorite vegan burger, made with brown rice and sunflower seeds) were all staple foods for me as I made the switch. We're lucky to have so many great vegan products on the market these days, and it's fine to take advantage of them when you need to.

"Transition food," by the way, doesn't only have to mean something you buy at a store. It can also mean embracing vegan versions of dishes you already know, love, and take comfort in. If you love enchiladas, try my vegan enchiladas on page 163. If you love burgers, give my raw shroom burger a try (page 192). If you're a pasta fiend, check out any one of my zucchini pasta recipes (you can always skip the zucchini and use brown rice or quinoa pasta instead). One of the most enjoyable parts of exploring a new way of eating is that you'll try new foods and expand your diet, but it's also cool to "veganize" (or make a raw version of) recipes you already know and love. Sometimes, it's as easy as swapping cashew cream for dairy, or tempeh for bacon.

5. Find Community

Having support makes a big difference as you undertake any kind of lifestyle change. If you don't have friends or family members who share your interest in eating more vegan or raw food, that doesn't mean you have to set out on this journey alone. Join a vegan meet-up or find a potluck near you.

Check out Happy Cow (www.happycow.net) to find vegan-friendly restaurants in your area. Very often, the waitstaff or restaurant owner will be excited to tell you more about the local vegan or raw community. And use the Internet to your advantage: There are so many vegan and raw blogs out there, full of invaluable information and mouthwatering recipes. Many of the folks reading these blogs are just getting started too, and you may be able to encourage one another.

6. Eat Sustainably

A lot of online resources treat veganism as a kind of "detox" or slim-down plan, which means too little variety, too few hearty, satisfying foods, and too little emphasis on long-term health. Anyone can drink juice and eat salad for a couple of weeks, but, unless you take care to make your diet well rounded, you won't be able to sustain veganism long term.

Sustainability isn't often at the forefront of conversations about healthy living, but I think it should be. Many of us are easily seduced by dietary extremes, and their bold promises—weight loss, lightness, glow, whatever—but in the end, long-term health is associated with consistent, wholesome, varied, and realistic food choices.

For me, sustainability means making an effort to get a healthy balance of macronutrients—protein, carbs, and fat—at each meal. This isn't a rule, of course, but it's a good guiding principle, since each of these three groups will contribute energy and feelings of satiety. It also means eating regular meals at regular intervals, to avoid dips in blood sugar that can make you irritable, tired, and stressed out (cortisol levels tend to go up when we're hungry). It means avoiding calorie restricted diets that can lower your metabolism and ultimately lead to overconsumption. It means eating foods you crave: if you crave carbs, then seek out high-quality carbs (such as sweet potatoes and grains) and enjoy them. Strict avoidance of foods you really love will only create feelings of deprivation, and those feelings can prompt overeating later on. In all my years working in the nutrition world, it has been my observation that moderation—eating a little bit of everything, and indulging cravings sensibly so that they don't take on exaggerated lives of their own—is the best way to maintain balance.

CHAPTER 9

21 Days in the Life: The Meal Plans

ALL OF THE TIPS I'VE JUST MENTIONED will come together as you begin to construct a diet that's oriented around vegan and raw food. While most of us can explore a recipe or two, it can be tricky to get into the groove of eating a plant-based diet day in and day out. To help you navigate the process, I've put together twenty-one days of wholesome vegan food for you.

As you might imagine, these meal plans are not to be followed religiously. Intuition is a big part of adopting a sustainable diet, so I welcome you to adapt the plans as needed. You can always pick and choose recipes from Part 4, and assemble them as you like. It's also important to remember that the meal plans are theoretical in the sense that you may not have time to create as many recipes in close succession as they suggest. Chances are, you'll make a bunch of the recipes, but

spend the rest of the time eating leftovers and mixing them with simple salads or vegetable dishes. To make this easy for you, I've tried to incorporate leftovers into the meal plans whenever possible. If you're cooking for more than two people and don't tend to have leftovers, you can swap in whatever new recipes suit your fancy.

You'll find three meals and two snack options for each day. This is just a broad recommendation; if eating a greater number of small meals throughout the day, or three bigger meals instead of three meals and two snacks, fits your schedule better, that's fine. Each day, I offer up fresh juice as a midmorning snack option (as well as something a little more filling).

You can also *always* swap out any one of the breakfast, lunch, or dinner recipes and replace it with one you like more. And you can *always* trade a recipe for one of the following low-maintenance options.

Low-Maintenance Breakfasts

Raw banana breakfast wraps with a handful of Superfood Trail Mix

DIY Snack Bar with a banana

Basic Green Smoothie

Sprouted-grain toast with peanut or almond butter and sliced apple, banana, or pear

Quick oats or quinoa flakes, cooked to your liking, with a tablespoon of almond butter and fresh berries

Low-Maintenance Lunches

Meal-size salad of your choosing (see tips for building a meal-size salad on page 139)

Sprouted-grain wrap with mixed veggies and hummus or nut pâté of your choice

Collard wrap filled with veggies of choice, sliced tofu or tempeh, and your favorite dressing, dip, or spread

A store-bought, organic, vegan soup of choice (the Pacific brand makes some great options) warmed over the stove top. Stir in some chopped kale, spinach, or collards when it's warm, along with ½ cup of lentils or beans for a quick, easy, instant "stew."

A hearty snack plate: flax crackers, pita, sprouted-grain tortilla strips, or organic corn chips, along with a hummus or nut pâté, veggies, roasted chickpeas, and fruit for dessert

Low-Maintenance Dinners

Leftover grain of choice with frozen (and reheated), chopped veggies or spinach mixed in, a sprinkle of hemp seeds, and a dressing of choice

A small baked potato topped with coconut oil, cooked beans or grilled tofu, and steamed veggies of choice

Meal-size salad of your choosing

Sprouted-grain tortilla spread with cashew cheese or pesto, and topped with any veggies you like. Eat it just like that, or stick it in the oven for 15 to 20 minutes to soften the vegetables and warm it through. Serve with an easy side salad.

Raw vegetable "Napoleon": create layers of heirloom tomato, zucchini, cooked sweet potato, or cooked eggplant, and your favorite pesto or nut pâté/cashew cheese. Alternate layers until it's stacked high. Serve with steamed greens.

Batch cooking and having a well-stocked freezer (especially portions of frozen grains and legumes) will be tremendously helpful to you here. Having a few cups of frozen quinoa, for instance, would let you throw together either my quinoa and black bean salad (page 166) or my quinoa salad with apricots and mint (page 158) in a moment's notice. You could also mix frozen grains into leftovers, use them to add bulk to a salad, or heat them up with almond milk for a quick breakfast. Now's the time to put that rice cooker to use!

21 Days: Meal Plans

Day 1

Breakfast: Mango Coconut Chia Seed Pudding (page 172)

Midmorning snack: Fresh juices (page 112–114) or Reinvented Ants on a Log (page 124)

Lunch: Sweet Pea Hummus Tartines (page 156) served with a salad (any greens and veggies you like) and a dressing of choice

Afternoon snack: Superfood Trail Mix (page 120)

Dinner: Raw Carrot Falafel with Tangy Tahini Sauce (page 188), served over a generous salad (any greens and veggies you like) with ½ cup of cooked lentils.

Dessert: Simple Raw Vanilla Macaroons (page 237)

Day 2

Breakfast: Leftover Mango Coconut Chia Pudding with fresh berries (page 172)

Midmorning snack: Fresh juice *or* leftover Sweet Pea Hummus with vegetable crudités (page 152)

Lunch: Leftover Carrot Falafel (page 188), served with Hemp-Seed Tabouli (page 180) with yellow tomatoes and mint

Afternoon snack: An apple or banana

Dinner: Raw Pad Thai (page 191) sprinkled with 2 to 3 tablespoons of chopped peanuts, served with steamed vegetables and a cooked grain or legume of choice

Dessert: Leftover Macaroons

Day 3

Breakfast: Chickpea Tofu Tahini Scramble (page 152), served with steamed or fresh greens as desired and a dressing of choice

Midmorning snack: Fresh juice or fresh fruit as desired

Lunch: Leftover pad thai served with some cooked lentils or black beans

Afternoon snack: Blueberry, Mint, and Kale Smoothie (page 200)

Dinner: Un-Fried Vegetable Rice (page 227) served with steamed vegetables *or* a side salad (any greens and veggies you like) and a dressing of choice

Dessert: Leftover Macaroons

Day 4

Breakfast: Easy Berry Breakfast Pizza (page 153)

Midmorning snack: Fresh juice or seasonal fruit as desired

Lunch: Mango, avocado, and black bean salad over zucchini noodles (page 107), served with a side salad (any greens and veggies you like) and a dressing of choice

Afternoon snack: Superfood Trail Mix (page 120)

Dinner: Carrot and Millet Pilaf (page 165), served with leftover Tofu Tahini Scramble (page 152) or Mesquite Glazed Tempeh (page 165) and a small side salad (any greens and veggies you like) with a dressing of choice

Dessert: Dark chocolate *or* any raw dessert of choice

Day 5

Breakfast: Quinoa Breakfast Pudding (page 175)

Midmorning snack: Fresh juice or vegetable crudités with any dressing or nut pâté of your choosing

Lunch: Leftover Carrot and Millet Pilaf, served with steamed veggies or a side salad (any greens and veggies you like) with 2 tablespoons of hemp seeds and dressing of choice

Afternoon snack: Roasted chickpeas (any variation you like) (page 115)

Dinner: Portobello "Steak" and Rosemary Cauliflower Mashed Potatoes (page 196), steamed greens as desired or a side salad (any greens and veggies you like) and a dressing of choice

Dessert: Chocomole (page 110)

Day 6

Breakfast: Simple Avocado Toast (page 151)

Midmorning snack: Fresh juice or leftover roasted chickpeas

Lunch: Leftover Cauliflower Mashed Potatoes and portobello steak, served with a side salad (any greens and veggies you like) and a dressing of choice

Afternoon snack: Vegetable crudités with hummus of choice

Dinner: Acorn Squash, Frisée, and Brown Rice Salad with Toasted Hazelnuts, and Lemon Turmeric Vinaigrette (page 142)

Dessert: Leftover Chocomole

Day 7

Breakfast: Baked Sweet Potatoes with Vanilla Almond Butter and Goji Berries (page 175)

Midmorning snack: Fresh juice or seasonal fruit as desired

Lunch: Nori Rolls with Gingery Almond Pâté and Raw Veggies (page 182), served with a side salad (any greens and veggies you like) and a dressing of choice

Afternoon snack: Sweet and Savory Trail Mix (page 119)

Dinner: Leftover Acorn Squash, Frisée, and Brown Rice Salad (page 142) or Quick Quinoa and Black Bean Salad with Spicy Cilantro Vinaigrette (page 166)

Dessert: Chocolate-Covered Superfood Clusters (page 235)

Day 8

Breakfast: Mocha Maca Chia Pudding (page 200)

Midmorning snack: Fresh juice or Sweet and Savory Trail Mix (page 119)

Lunch: Sprouted-Grain Wraps with Kale-Slaw Filling (page 185)

Afternoon snack: Half of a leftover Sweet Potato with Vanilla Almond Butter from yesterday's breakfast

Dinner: Carrot and Zucchini Pappardelle with Pesto and Peas (page 229), leftover Kale-Slaw from lunch, cooked lentils or beans of choice

Dessert: Chocolate-Covered Superfood Clusters (page 235)

Day 9

Breakfast: Leftover Mocha Maca Chia Pudding (page 200) with fresh fruit

Midmorning snack: Fresh juice or Superfood Trail Mix

Lunch: Jicama Fiesta Rice Salad with Spicy Cilantro Vinaigrette (page 210); I add either cooked tofu or black beans

Afternoon snack: Cheesy or protein-packed Hummus Kale Chips (page 123)

Dinner: Zucchini noodles with leftover pesto (from the Pappardelle), a serving of cooked lentils or beans of choice, and leftover Kale-Slaw

Chocolate-Covered Superfood Clusters (page 235)

Day 10

Breakfast: Cashew Banana Yogurt with fresh berries (page 203)

Midmorning snack: Fresh juice or Zucchini Ranch Chips (page 119)

Lunch: Apricot, Quinoa, and Mint Salad (page 158), served over a bed of fresh greens

Afternoon snack: A couple of Nori and Pumpkin-Seed Cigars (page 116)

Dinner: Dinosaur Kale and White Bean Caesar Salad (page 141), or another meal-size salad of your choosing

Dessert: Coconutty for Chocolate Chip Cookies (page 230)

Day 11

Breakfast: Leftover Cashew Banana Yogurt with fresh berries

Midmorning snack: Fresh juice or leftover Zucchini Ranch Chips

Lunch: Collard wraps with Hemp Hummus, tempeh, and red peppers (page 130), served with a side salad (any greens and veggies you like) and a dressing of choice

Afternoon snack: A couple of Nori and Pumpkin-See Cigars (page 116)

Dinner: Leftover Apricot, Quinoa, and Mint Salad along with leftover Dinosaur Kalte and White Bean Caesar

Dessert: Coconutty for Chocolate Chip Cookies (page 230)

Day 12

Breakfast: Raw Vegan Bircher Muesli (page 155)

Midmorning snack: Fresh juice or seasonal fruit as desired

Lunch: Sweet Potato Salad with Miso Dressing (page 156), served with a side salad (any greens and veggies you like) and a dressing of choice

Afternoon snack: Leftover tempeh from yesterday's lunch wraps

Dinner: Raw or Cooked Ratatouille (page 222), a serving of quinoa, and a side salad (any greens and veggies you like) with a dressing of choice

Dessert: Coconutty for Chocolate Chip Cookies (page 230)

Day 13

Breakfast: Chocolate Açai Bowl (page 209)

Midmorning snack: Fresh juice or Sweet and Savory Trail Mix (page 119)

Lunch: Leftover Raw or Cooked Ratatouille, sprinkled with nutritional yeast and served over a big green salad with a dressing of choice

Afternoon snack: A couple of Hemp-Seed Power Balls (page 119)

Dinner: Pumpkin Quinoa Risotto with Pomegranate Seeds (page 195), served with steamed greens or a side salad (any greens and veggies you like) and a dressing of choice

Dessert: Dark chocolate or Simple Raw Vanilla Macaroons (page 237)

Day 14

Breakfast: Blueberry, Mint, and Kale Smoothie (page 200), leftover Raw-Nola from Chocolate Açai Bowl

Midmorning snack: Fresh juice *or* vegetable crudités with any dressing, dip, or hummus of choice

Lunch: Leftover Pumpkin Quinoa Risotto, served with a side salad (any greens and veggies you like) and a dressing of choice

Afternoon snack: Leftover Sweet and Savory Trail Mix

Dinner: Romaine, Cherry Tomato, and Arugula Salad with Chickpeas and Raw Parmesan (page 146), *or* any other meal-size salad of choice

Dessert: Cherry Vanilla Tahini Ice Cream (page 245)

Day 15

Breakfast: Raw Banana Breakfast Wraps (page 207)

Midmorning snack: Fresh juice *or* roasted chickpeas (any flavor you like) (page 115)

Lunch: Leftover Romaine, Cherry Tomato, and Arugula Salad with Chickpeas and Raw Parmesan *or* any meal-size salad of choice

Afternoon snack: Leftover hummus and vegetable crudités

Dinner: Easy Red Lentil, Sweet Potato, and Coconut Curry (page 167), topped with avocado or a few tablespoons of hemp seeds, served with steamed veggies or a side salad (any greens and veggies you like) and a dressing of choice

Dessert: Almost-Instant Chocolate-Covered Strawberries (page 236)

Day 16

Breakfast: No-Bake Sunflower Oat Bars, fresh fruit as desired (page 120)

Midmorning snack: Fresh juice *or* leftover roasted chickpeas

Lunch: Leftover red lentil curry, served with a side salad (any greens and veggies you like) and a dressing of choice

Afternoon snack: Cheesy or protein-packed Hummus Kale Chips (page 123)

Dinner: Basic Massaged Kale Salad (page 103) and Mesquite Glazed Tempeh (page 165), served with some cooked quinoa, if desired

Dessert: Almost-Instant Chocolate-Covered Strawberries (page 236)

Day 17

Breakfast: Plant Protein Shake (page 172)

Midmorning snack: Fresh juice *or* leftover kale chips

Lunch: Nori Rolls with Gingery Almond Pâté and Raw Veggies (page 182), served with a side salad (any greens and veggies you like) and a dressing of choice

Afternoon snack: Leftover roasted chickpeas

Dinner: Raw Cobb Salad (page 145) with leftover Mesquite Glazed Tempeh (page 165)

Dessert: Banana Soft Serve (page 111)

Day 18

Breakfast: Toasted Pumpkin Granola with Homemade Hemp Milk (page 148) and sliced apple or banana

Midmorning snack: Fresh juice *or* seasonal fruit as desired

Lunch: Leftover raw Cobb Salad (page 145) with leftover roasted chickpeas

Afternoon snack: Leftover Gingery Almond Pâté, vegetable crudités

Dinner: Raw mushroom burgers (page 192), served over a meal-size salad along with some quinoa or cooked lentils or beans

Dessert: Dark chocolate or any raw dessert of your choosing

Day 19

Breakfast: Leftover Toasted Pumpkin Granola with Homemade Hemp Milk (page 148) and sliced apple or banana

Midmorning snack: Fresh juice or leftover Gingery Almond Pâté with vegetable crudités

Lunch: Leftover raw mushroom burger with a meal-size salad

Afternoon snack: No-Bake Sunflower Oat Bars (page 120)

Dinner: Zucchini Pasta with Quinoa Meatless Balls (page 168), served with steamed vegetables *or* a side salad (any greens and veggies you like) with dressing of choice

Dessert: Chocolate-Covered Superfood Clusters (page 235)

Day 20

Breakfast: Almond Pulp Porridge (or regular oatmeal) with berries (page 209)

Midmorning snack: Fresh juice or Hummus Kale Chips (page 123)

Lunch: Easiest Vegan Pumpkin Soup (page 162) with Basic Massaged Kale Salad (page 103) or kale-slaw (page 185) and a few leftover Quinoa Meatless Balls

Afternoon snack: Leftover Toasted Pumpkin Granola

Dinner: Coconut Curry Kelp Noodles (page 223), Mesquite Glazed Tempeh (page 165), leftover kale salad from lunch

Dessert: Chocolate-Covered Superfood Clusters (page 235)

Day 21

Breakfast: Leftover Almond Pulp Porridge with fresh berries

Midmorning snack: Fresh juice *or* leftover Hummus Kale Chips (page 123)

Lunch: Collard wraps with Hemp Hummus (page 130), leftover Mesquite Glazed Tempeh (page 165), and red peppers, served with a side salad (any greens and veggies you like) and a dressing of choice

Afternoon snack: Leftover Easiest Vegan Pumpkin Soup

Dinner: Leftover Coconut Curry Kelp Noodles, served with steamed greens or a side salad (any greens and veggies you like) with a dressing of choice. Top the kelp noodles with roasted chickpeas or hemp seeds, if desired.

Dessert: Chocolate-Covered Superfood Clusters (page 235)

Specialized Meal Plans

Certain folks will have special needs or goals that call for particular kinds of meal planning. Below, I've tried to give you a sense of how you might modify a basic meal plan to fit a couple of special circumstances. First, a few meal plans for someone who's just getting started. These feature "tried-and-true" (level 1) recipes, and should feel familiar and accessible. Second, meal plans that place a particular focus on protein—great for those who are learning how to source adequate protein in a plant-based diet. And finally, meal plans for folks whose aim is to go high(er) raw while remaining well nourished and balanced.

Starter Meal Plans

1.

Breakfast: Simple Avocado Toast (page 151)
Midmorning snack: Seasonal fresh fruit
Lunch: Easiest Vegan Pumpkin Soup (page 162), Basic Massaged Kale Salad (page 103)
Afternoon snack: Hemp Hummus (page 130) with vegetable crudités of choice
Dinner: Sweet Potato Black Bean Enchiladas (page 163) or Quick Quinoa and Black Bean Salad with Spicy Cilantro Vinaigrette (page 166), served with a side salad (any greens and veggies you like) and a dressing of choice
Dessert: Chocomole (page 110) or Coconutty for Chocolate Chip Cookies (page 130)

2.

Breakfast: Millet and Almond Zucchini Muffins with fresh fruit of choice (page 148)
Midmorning snack: Reinvented Ants on a Log (page 124)
Lunch: Leftover enchiladas with side salad (any vegetables, greens, and dressing you like) *or* Kale Salad with Sweet Potato, Almonds, and Creamy Maple Chipotle Dressing (page 141)
Afternoon Snack: Fresh juice or leftover Hemp Hummus and vegetable crudités of choice
Dinner: Easy Red Lentil, Sweet Potato, and Coconut Curry (page 167) or leftover Quick Quinoa Salad with Black Beans and Spicy Cilantro Vinaigrette, served with a side salad (any greens and veggies you like) and a dressing of choice
Dessert: Banana Soft Serve (page 111)

Higher Protein Meal Plans

1.

Breakfast: Chickpea Tofu Tahini Scramble (page 152)

Midmorning snack: Sweet and Savory Trail Mix (page 119)

Lunch: Sprouted-Grain Wraps with Kale-Slaw Filling (page 185); Easy Red Lentil, Sweet Potato, and Coconut Curry (page 167)

Afternoon snack: Plant Protein Shake (page 172)

Dinner: Pumpkin Quinoa Risotto (page 195) served with steamed greens or a side salad (any greens and veggies you like) and a dressing of choice

Dessert: Any dessert of choice, or dark chocolate

2.

Breakfast: Plant Protein Shake (page 172)

Midmorning snack: Hummus of choice with vegetable crudités

Lunch: Leftover Chickpea Tofu Tahini Scramble *or* Curried Chickpea and Carrot Salad (page 162) with a side salad of choice, such as my Basic Massaged Kale Salad (page 103) or Kale-Slaw (page 185)

Afternoon snack: 3 or 4 Hemp-Seed Power Balls (page 119)

Dinner: Carrot Millet Pilaf with Mesquite Glazed Tempeh (page 165) and leftover Kale-Slaw or Basic Massaged Kale topped with a couple of tablespoons of hemp seeds

Dessert: Any dessert of choice, or dark chocolate

High(er) Raw Meal Plans

1.

Breakfast: Basic Chia Pudding (page 108) with fresh berries

Midmorning snack: Cheezy (page 123) or Hummus Kale Chips (page 123)

Lunch: Raw Cobb Salad (page 145)

Afternoon snack: Plant Protein Shake (page 172)

Dinner: Heat-Free Lentil and Walnut Tacos (page 191), Basic Massaged Kale Salad (page 103)

Dessert: Any raw dessert of choice

2.

Breakfast: Almond Pulp Porridge (page 209)

Midmorning snack: Classic Zucchini Hummus (page 130) with vegetable crudités *or* sprouted-grain tortilla

Lunch: Creamy Basil and Ginger Noodles (page 210) with ½ cup of cooked or sprouted lentils, leftover Basic Massaged Kale Salad (page 103)

Afternoon snack: 2 Nori and Pumpkin-Seed Cigars (page 116)

Dinner: Coconut Curry Kelp Noodles (page 223) or Raw Lasagna (page 224) with side salad (any greens, veggies, and dressing you like)

Dessert: 3 to 4 Hemp-Seed Power Balls (page 119), or any raw dessert of choice

PART IV

The Food

NOW, FOR THE BEST PART: THE FOOD! IN THE FOLLOWING PAGES, you will find 125 of my favorite vegan and raw food recipes. I begin with fifteen "essentials." These dishes have earned a time-honored status in my kitchen. They range from almond milk to raw zucchini "pasta" to a basic green smoothie. They showcase techniques that I think are essential to anyone who is exploring vegan cooking with an emphasis on raw food.

Next, I'll share five juices, ten snacks, twenty dressings, dips, and sauces, and "meal-size salads"—salads that are nutrient dense and hearty enough to serve as a complete meal. Snacks will help you to stay fueled on the go, while the dips and sauces will allow you to dress up vegetables, grains, and salads.

Finally, we'll launch into our three levels of vegan and raw breakfasts, lunches, and dinners. As you'll see, the levels take you from a foundation of cooked vegan recipes to more raw food dishes. You don't have to start with level one and make your way toward levels two and three: I'm simply presenting food in a sequence that moves from what's probably more familiar to what's slightly more exotic, to help you to feel more comfortable putting raw vegetables at the front and center of your diet. Feel free to take any recipes from any level and mix and match them as you please.

Banana Soft Serve, page 111

The Recipes

B EFORE I SAY ANYTHING ELSE ABOUT these recipes, let me say this: you are welcome—nay, encouraged—to make these recipes your own. While I can't promise you that major modifications might not be a problem, I can guarantee you that small changes, in accordance with your taste, will only enhance the recipes. Go ahead and omit herbs or spices you don't like, and replace them with ones you do. If you hate one of the vegetables, feel free to use another one that you enjoy more. If the dressing option for a salad isn't your thing, use another from the "dips, dressings, sauces, and spreads" section. Modifying a recipe is always a small gamble, but it's how you'll begin to know and trust your own tastes.

Substitutions

Part of making a recipe your own is knowing how to substitute ingredients you might not have for ones you do. Substitutions aren't only a matter of taste or convenience: They may also be necessary for readers with various food allergies. My recipes tend to be forgiving, but not every single substitution is a guaranteed success, so here's a list of appropriate swaps:

Almonds: Replace with hazelnuts, pecans, walnuts, or cashews

Cashews: Replace with macadamia nuts or pine nuts

Walnuts: Replace with pecans, cashews, or almonds

Pecans: Replace with walnuts or almonds

Pumpkin seeds: Replace with sunflower seeds

Sunflower seeds: Replace with pumpkin seeds

Sesame seeds: Replace with hemp seeds

If you're allergic to all tree nuts: Try using legumes or hummus in place of nuts and nut pâtés. Some people with tree nut allergies can still consume seeds, so pumpkin, sesame, and sunflower seeds will be very helpful.

If you're allergic to bananas: Try replacing bananas in these recipes with frozen mango, which is also very sweet and creamy.

If you're allergic to soy: In most of the following recipes, soy can be omitted and replaced with another plant-based protein source (such as beans, hummus, nuts, or seeds).

If you're allergic to gluten: With very few exceptions, the recipes in this book are gluten free, though people with gluten allergies should definitely be sure to purchase individual products that are certified GF and safe from cross-contamination. The only recipes that definitely have gluten are the Avocado Toast and Sweet Pea Hummus Tartines, in which you can easily substitute certified gluten-free bread.

If you don't eat beans: You can try using nuts or nut pâté in place of legumes or hummus. In general, people who don't digest beans well can replace them with tofu or tempeh for protein. Nuts and seeds will also provide protein, and some folks who don't digest most legumes well may still be able to tolerate these.

Essential Techniques

Soak your beans before cooking:

Making beans from scratch is a great habit to get into: it's cheaper than buying canned beans, it leaves you with zero risk of toxins from cans getting into your food, and home-cooked beans are simply so much tastier (especially in hummus) than canned. If you do boil beans from scratch, soaking them beforehand may make a difference in terms of digestibility because it releases the tricky sugars that cause discomfort.

You can either do a "quick soak" or a "long soak."

For a "quick soak," rinse and pick over your beans, cover them with water (one part beans to three parts water) and boil them for 5 minutes. Let them sit for an hour after, and then cook through.

For a long soak, pick over and clean beans, cover them in water (one part beans to three parts water) and then let them soak for 8 hours, or overnight. Drain and change the water before cooking through. For most beans, this will mean about an hour of simmering.

Blending:

While blending is definitely one of the easiest techniques, there are still some essential tricks of the trade to master.

If you're using a high-speed blender, it's important to use the tamp attachment to facilitate the blending process. This is especially true if you're making something thick, such as hummus or nut pâté. If you use a regular blender, stop a few times while you're blending to mix your ingredients with a spoon, and then continue blending. Note that, in a high-speed blender, you'll need to be working with a certain amount of volume to get things blending and use the tamper—tiny batches of nut cheese or hummus, for example, won't blend smoothly. If you're considering cutting a recipe in half, you may want to simply make the whole batch and share your leftovers.

Always start your blender on the lowest setting, then gradually increase the blender speed until you reach its highest setting.

Successful Smoothies:

Whether you're using a conventional or high-speed blender, always add your liquid first—it will get things blending. Next, add your frozen fruit, then protein powders, cacao, spices, or other flavorings. Add ice last, so that it doesn't overblend and cause the smoothie to get too watery. Fresh fruits get blended in last, along with ice.

Working with a Food Processor (hummus, nut pâté, and nut cheese):

This can be a little tricky at first, but as long as you get used to stopping the processor frequently to scrape the bowl down, you'll be on your way to creamy and consistent hummus, nut pâtés, and nut cheeses. Some tips:

When blending nuts or legumes, start with a small amount of liquid to get things moving. After about 30 seconds, stop the power, scrape the bowl down, turn the motor back on, and then drizzle in the remainder of your liquid, until you have a good consistency.

Be patient. With banana soft serve, nut pâté, and hummus alike, the food processor takes a little bit of time to whip things up perfectly. The longer you're willing to wait, the more even your results will be!

I usually soak nuts or seeds before using them in the processor, but if you don't have time, you can still get great results. Simply add dry nuts or seeds to the processor first, grind them up finely, and then start adding your liquid.

Prepping vegetables:

When preparing vegetables to sauté, try to chop them into evenly sized pieces.

When adding vegetables into the blender (for a raw soup, for example), a rough chop is fine, but try to be consistent about how large the pieces are. Add liquid to the blender first.

When slicing vegetables thinly, always place the vegetable onto a flat surface.

To mince herbs, stack leaves as best you can onto a flat surface, then use a very sharp knife to cut them. For many herbs (chives, basil leaves, cilantro), it's sometimes easier simply to snip them with a knife.

Making Raw Zucchini Pasta:

While it's easiest to use a spiralizer for raw zucchini pasta (a low-cost and worthy investment), there are plenty of other ways to prepare it. You can use a julienne peeler, which creates long, thin strips of any vegetable you like. You can also lay your zucchini down on a flat surface and run a regular vegetable peeler along it lengthwise, peeling off thin ribbons as you go. You can even use a box grater to grate the zucchini, and treat it as mini noodles! Don't let not having a spiralizer stop you from enjoying the pleasures of raw pasta.

Making Raw "Rice":

Simply pulse coarsely chopped vegetables in the food processor until they're the consistency of long grain rice. The vegetables I use most often for this are parsnip, cauliflower, jicama, and carrot. The first three have the most authentic rice appearance, but they're all delicious options. Work in small batches (about 2 cups of veggies at a time) to get a consistent texture.

15 Essentials

THESE ARE FIFTEEN OF THE DISHES THAT I CAN'T LIVE WITHOUT. THEY ALSO HAPPEN to be some of the best-loved recipes from my blog. Many of these are so simple that they resemble techniques more than recipes, which is fine, because it means you can adapt them easily to suit your tastes.

CLASSIC ALMOND MILK

ALMOND MILK HAS A RICH, CREAMY texture and taste; a little vanilla and sea salt elevate it to perfection. If you've never tried homemade almond milk before, you're in for a treat.

It's easier to make almond milk in a high-speed blender, but so long as you strain it, any kind of blender will work. If you're using a regular blender, it's especially important to soak your almonds for eight hours or more beforehand. To strain the almond milk, you can use cheesecloth, a nut milk bag (available at health food stores or online) or even a paint bag from a hardware store!

MAKES 3 CUPS MILK

1 cup almonds
4 pitted dates
¼ teaspoon sea salt
1 teaspoon vanilla extract, or 1 vanilla
   bean, cut lengthwise down the center,
   seeds scraped out with a spoon

1. Soak the almonds overnight, or for at least 8 hours. Drain and rinse them.

2. Place the almonds, the dates, the sea salt, the vanilla, and 4 cups of filtered water in a blender. Blend for at least one full minute on high speed, until the mixture looks totally uniform and creamy.

3. When it looks well blended, stop the blender. Over the mouth of a large container—a 2-quart mason jar, a large jug, or a pitcher—drape cheesecloth, folded over once to make a double layer. Secure it in place with a rubber band, so that it's fixed over the mouth of the container. I often quickly transfer my unstrained almond milk to another container, and then use the blender itself as my container in which to strain it.

4. Pour the almond milk through the cheesecloth. You may need to do this in small increments, because it takes a little while to strain. As you wait for it to strain, you can gently remove some of the almond "pulp" that is building up in the cheesecloth and set it aside.

5. When all of the almond milk has been poured through the cheesecloth, let it sit for a while to strain completely. Scoop up the pay and reserve for use later (for example, Almond Pulp Milk Porridge [page 209]). Store the almond milk in a clean container in the fridge. It will last for 2 to 3 days.

BASIC GREEN SMOOTHIE

GREEN SMOOTHIES MAY BE EVERY-one's favorite raw food intro recipe. They are a quick, accessible way to incorporate more greens into your diet, and the flavor combinations are endless. Here's a simple, easy-to-customize recipe that won't let you down no matter how many times you make it.

MAKES 2 SERVINGS

2 bananas, peeled, cut into rough pieces, and then frozen
1 cup frozen blueberries
1½ cups almond milk
2 tablespoons almond or peanut butter
Pinch ground cinnamon (if desired)
2 cups spinach, well rinsed

Blend all the ingredients in a blender until smooth. Serve.

CASHEW CHEESE

CASHEW CHEESE AND CASHEW CREAM are secret weapons of vegan cooking. More than any other ingredient, they add the richness that we associate with dairy to vegan dishes. Cashews are incredibly soft, mild tasting nuts, so they blend up to perfection.

This basic cashew cheese should have a texture not unlike cream cheese or spreadable goat cheese. You can, however, add more water (up to a cup) to turn it into a thick cashew cream instead, which will have the texture of heavy whipping cream. You can add more or less water to suit your needs. The recipe is generous; once you start using cashew cheese in salads, on top of soups, or in wraps, you'll likely find that it runs out fast. But feel free to cut the recipe in half if you don't need the full yield.

MAKES 1 ½ CUPS CHEESE

2 cups raw cashews, soaked overnight and drained of soak water
½ teaspoon sea salt
4 tablespoons nutritional yeast
2 tablespoons freshly squeezed lemon juice
1 clove garlic, minced (optional)
Freshly ground black pepper

1. Place the cashews, salt, nutritional yeast, lemon, and garlic in a food processor fitted with the "S" blade. Pulse until the cashews are broken up well.

2. Run the motor and drizzle in ⅓ cup of water. Keep blending until the mixture is very smooth and creamy. You may need to stop a few times to scrape the bowl down—be patient! The key to perfect cashew cheese is to scrape the bowl down a lot, and also to blend for a very, very long time. Your ideal cashew cheese should be thick, but easy to spread. Add a little extra water if needed.

3. Check the cashew cheese for seasoning. Add black pepper to taste. Cashew cheese will keep in an airtight container for up to 5 days in the fridge.

Homemade Hemp Milk, page 101

HOMEMADE HEMP MILK

MAKES 4 CUPS MILK

1 cup shelled hemp seeds
4 pitted Medjool dates
1 pinch sea salt
1 vanilla bean, cut lengthwise down the
    center, seeds scraped out with a spoon

Blend all the ingredients, along with 3½ cups of water, in a high-speed blender until smooth. Shake before serving. Hemp milk will keep, sealed in the fridge, for 1 or 3 days.

NUT OR SEED PÂTÉ

IT MAY SOUND PECULIAR TO HEAR A vegan talking about "pâté" at all, but nut and seed pâtés are staple Ingredients in my diet. Pâté is, of course, just a figure of speech. It's made of nuts or seeds that have been soaked, softened, and blended up with seasonings and water. It has thick, spreadable texture, and it's incredibly versatile— use it in collard wraps, with vegetables for dipping, or wrapped up into nori sheets.

MAKES 2 CUPS PÂTÉ

1½ cups seeds (pumpkin, sesame, or
    sunflower) or nuts (almonds, cashews,
    macadamia, walnuts, pistachios, and
    Brazil nuts all work)
1 tablespoon tamari, nama shoyu, or
    Bragg's Liquid Aminos
1 tablespoon apple cider vinegar or freshly
    squeezed lemon juice
1 clove garlic, minced (optional)
OPTIONAL: A few tablespoons of any herbs, spices, or add-ins you like. Rosemary, dill, basil, cumin, paprika, sun dried tomatoes, olives, and roasted red peppers all make wonderful additions.

1. Cover the nuts or seeds with enough water to submerge them by a few inches, and soak them overnight, or for 6 hours or more. In the morning (or when you're ready) discard the soak water and rinse them a little in a colander or metal strainer.

2. Add the nuts or seeds, the tamari, the vinegar, and the garlic, if using, to the bowl of a food processor fitted with the "S" blade. Run the motor for a minute or two, until the mixture is coming together (the consistency will be coarse and wet).

3. With the motor still running, drizzle in ½ cup of water in a thin stream (if it starts to get at all watery, you can use a little less water—how much you need will depend on how much liquid your nuts/seeds absorbed). Continue blending until the mixture is thick but smooth and spreadable. Season to taste with black pepper.

Nut pâtés keep in the fridge for at least 3 to 4 days, and sometimes up to 5.

GREEN SOUP (BLENDED SALAD)

THINK OF GREEN SOUP AS THE SAVORY alternative to all of those delicious green smoothies you'll be experimenting with in your raw adventures. Though not quite as sweet as green smoothies, of course, green soups are equally nutritious, and they're a wonderful vehicle for your freshest produce. The following is a basic recipe, but you can certainly make it your own by adding different vegetables (zucchini in place of cucumber, for example) and seasonings.

MAKES 1 LITER SOUP (ABOUT 3 OR 4 SERVINGS)

1 pound cucumber, cut into sections
1 small Haas avocado, pitted and flesh
   scooped out
1 cup coconut water or filtered water
½ cup chopped parsley or cilantro
   (dill also works)
Juice of 1 lemon (about 1½ tablespoons)
½ teaspoon sea salt
2 large stalks celery, cut into quarters
1 cup spinach (optional)
TOPPINGS: Diced tomato, zucchini, cucumber, mango, avocado, fresh herbs, or any other vegetables or fruits of choice. Drizzling a few tablespoons of cashew cream into the soup is also a wonderful addition.

Blend all the ingredients in a blender until creamy and smooth. Add more water as necessary. Sprinkle with your toppings of choice, and serve.

HERBED FLAX CRACKERS

FLAX CRACKERS ARE COMMERCIALLY available nowadays, but why buy them when it's incredibly easy to make your own? Note that the flax seeds need to soak for 3 hours, for a thick, spreadable texture that makes for a super crispy, savory snack.

Flax crackers can either be dehydrated or baked in the oven. If you have a dehydrator, you may find that it results in a crispier and more preferable texture. But both methods will work.

MAKES ABOUT 30 CRACKERS

½ cup dark flaxseeds
½ cup golden flaxseeds (alternatively, you
   can use all golden flaxseeds)
¼ cup ground flax meal
1½ tablespoons Bragg's Liquid Aminos or
   tamari or nama shoyu
2 tablespoons apple cider vinegar
1 tablespoon chopped fresh rosemary, or
   2 teaspoons dried
2 teaspoons minced fresh thyme, or 1
   teaspoon dried

1. If you're using an oven, preheat it to 350°F.

2. Mix all the ingredients in a large mixing bowl. Add 1½ cups of water. Allow the ingredients to sit for 3 hours, at which point they should thicken up completely.

3. To dehydrate: spread the mixture onto a Telfex-lined dehydrator sheet. Use a pizza dough roller to score into cracker-size squares. Dehydrate at 115°F for 8 hours or

Green Soup (Blended Salad), page 102

so. Place another Teflex-lined sheet on top of it and then flip it over. Dehydrate the other side for 2 more hours, break into crackers, and serve.

To bake: line a baking sheet with parchment. Spread the cracker mixture over it thinly (less than ¼ inch) with a spatula and score lightly with a pizza roller. Bake for 25 minutes at 350°F. If the crackers are not yet browning, return them to the oven and continue baking until they're golden brown. Remove, and allow to cool completely before breaking the crackers apart and enjoying.

Stored in an airtight container in the fridge, flax crackers will keep for up to 2 weeks.

BASIC MASSAGED KALE SALAD

TO ME, THE PHRASE *MASSAGED KALE* IS so ordinary and commonplace that it doesn't strike me as the slightest bit odd. But if you're wondering what it means to

Basic Massaged Kale Salad, page 103

"massage" a cruciferous vegetable, it simply means cutting the kale up into small pieces, and then using your hands to forcefully rub your dressing of choice into the greens. If you don't have a dressing on hand, you can just rub some avocado and lemon into the kale—this is very delicious too!

MAKES 4 SMALL OR 2 GENEROUS SERVINGS

5 cups tightly packed kale, washed
1 cup finely shredded red cabbage
1 cup shredded carrot
2 tablespoons freshly squeezed lemon juice
2 teaspoons hemp oil
¼ teaspoon sea salt
1 teaspoon pure maple syrup
1 small avocado, chopped into 1-inch chunks

1. Place the kale, cabbage, and carrot in a large mixing bowl. Mix well.

2. Add all the remaining ingredients to the bowl. "Massage" the kale with your hands well, until the kale is wilted and creamy and the avocado is all smooshed in.

Leftover kale salad will keep overnight in the fridge.

5-MINUTE GUACAMOLE

THIS GUACAMOLE IS EASY TO MAKE, AS the title suggests, and it's both savory and sweet (since the tomatoes and pepper add a lot of sweetness to the dish). This guacamole is great with vegetables, mushed into salad, in wraps and burritos, and by the spoonful. There's no wrong way to enjoy something this simple and delicious.

MAKES 2 TO 4 SERVINGS

2 large Haas avocados, peeled, pitted, and cubed
Juice of 2 limes
½ cup packed chopped fresh cilantro
1 teaspoon pure maple syrup or agave nectar
½ chop chopped red onion (optional)
½ cup seeded and finely diced red bell pepper
1 cup quartered cherry tomatoes
Sea salt and freshly ground black pepper

1. Mash the avocado, lime juice, cilantro, and maple syrup together with a fork, until it's creamy but still has some texture.

2. Add the onion, pepper, and tomatoes. Season with salt and pepper to taste, and serve.

You can sprinkle some lemon juice on top of the guacamole and store it overnight—this will help to preserve color, and it will keep for a second day.

BUCKWHEATIES

BUCKWHEAT IS FULL OF FIBER, MINERals, and it's relatively high protein. My favorite way to enjoy buckwheat is to simply soak it for a day or two, then rinse it thoroughly and either dehydrate it (for a raw version) or toast it in the oven. I then add it to

Zucchini Pasta with Red or White Sauce, page 107

fresh fruit and eat it as a cereal, or I use it in one of my many delicious raw granola (raw-nola) recipes (such as my Cacao Granola and Banana Coconut Raw-Nolas on pages 202 and 205). Because it's reminiscent of cereal, many raw foodies call dehydrated buck-wheat "Buckwheaties."

2 cups raw buckwheat groats

1. Place the buckwheat in a bowl and submerge it in enough water to cover it by several inches. Let it soak overnight. Rinse it thoroughly through a sieve (it will be very slimy).

2. If you're baking the buckwheat, preheat your oven to 325°F.

3. If you have a dehydrator, dehydrate the buckwheat for 6 to 8 hours at 115°F, until it's totally dry. Set aside for use. If you don't have a dehydrator, you can lay the buckwheat onto a baking sheet lined with parchment paper or foil and bake at 325°F for 35 to 40 minutes (or when the buckwheat is turning golden), stopping halfway through to move the groats around on the baking sheet a little. Allow the groats to cool completely before serving.

Dried buckwheat will keep for several weeks in an airtight container.

ZUCCHINI PASTA WITH RED OR WHITE SAUCE

ZUCCHINI PASTA IS A RAW FOOD staple. It's easy, it's fun to eat, and totally versatile. I've included here my "red sauce" (raw marinara) and my "white sauce" (a cashew-based Alfredo). Pesto is also a lovely topper, or other kind of pasta sauce, you like. If you're in a pinch, you can use your favorite canned, organic, commercially pre-pared marinara sauce.

If you don't have a spiralizer (see page 75), you can use a vegetable peeler to slice the zucchini into long, thin "ribbons" instead.

MAKES 4 SERVINGS

**4 medium zucchini or summer squash
Raw Marinara Sauce (page 135) or Raw
  Cashew Alfredo (page 134)**

1. Use a spiralizer to cut the four zucchini into long, thin ribbons, or use a julienne peeler to achieve the same effect. You can also use a regular vegetable peeler to slice the zucchini into long, thin ribbons.

2. To assemble your zucchini pasta, divide the zucchini noodles among four bowls. Prepare your sauce of choice, and top each bowl with a heaping ¼ cup of sauce. If you like, you can add shredded carrots, chopped cherry tomatoes, sun-dried tomatoes, mushrooms, or any other vegetables to your "pasta" bowl.

DIY SNACK BARS

THIS IS A HOMEMADE SPIN ON THE dried fruit and nut bars you might be familiar with. I'm all for purchasing a snack bar when you're in a pinch, but it's nearly as easy to make them at home—and, if you do it regularly, a whole lot cheaper and healthier. These raw bars can be easily customized however you'd like to with add-ins (see my suggestions for some ideas!).

MAKES 12 SNACK BARS

1¾ cups almonds, cashews, walnuts,
    Brazil, or macadamia nuts
Pinch sea salt
2 cups pitted dates
OPTIONAL ADD-INS: ¼ cup cacao nibs,
2 tablespoons lemon or orange zest,
1 teaspoon cinnamon, ¼ cup goji
berries or mulberries, 1 teaspoon maca,
2 tablespoons raw cacao powder

1. Line an 8 by 12–inch or 9–inch square baking dish with plastic wrap or foil.

2. Place the nuts and a pinch of salt into a food processor fitted with the "S" blade and process until they are ground up (about 1 minute).

3. Add the dates and process until the mixture is uniform and the nuts and fruit are broken-down. Add any add-ins you are using, and pulse to combine. When you can squeeze some of the mixture in your hand and have it hold together, it's ready.

4. Empty the dough into the lined pan and press it down with your fingers so that it's uniformly thick and even. Refrigerate for about 30 minutes or more.

5. Cut into ten to twelve bar shapes. Wrap individually in plastic wrap or waxed paper. Store in an airtight container for up to 2 weeks, enjoying as desired. The bars will also freeze well.

BASIC CHIA PUDDING

WHEN YOU SOAK CHIA SEEDS, THEY plump up to look like tapioca pudding, with a similar texture. I absolutely love them this way, and chia pudding is probably my favorite raw food breakfast of all time. It also makes for a great snack. Here's my basic recipe; check out my Mango Coconut Chia Pudding (page 172) and Mocha Maca Chia Pudding (page 200) as well.

One of the best things about making chia pudding is that you can mix it together in the evening, let it sit overnight, and grab it to go in the morning!

MAKES 2 SERVINGS

6 tablespoons chia seeds
2 cups homemade or store-bought
    almond milk
Seeds of 1 vanilla bean or 1 teaspoon
    vanilla extract
2 tablespoons pure maple syrup or agave
    nectar

1. Stir all the ingredients together in a medium-size mixing bowl. Allow the

Basic Chia Pudding, page 108

Chocomole, page 110

mixture to sit for a minute, then stir again. Continue to stir once every 8 to 10 minutes for 30 minutes.

2. Let the mixture sit for a few hours. Serve with fresh berries, if desired.

Chia pudding will keep for up to 4 days in the fridge.

CHOCOMOLE

CHOCOLATE PUDDING WITH AVOCADO, you say? Believe it. As strange as it sounds, avocado actually makes a wonderful, neutral, creamy base for this delicious raw riff on chocolate pudding. Once you experience this easy and beloved raw food dessert, you'll be hooked! Amp the flavor by adding a teaspoon of ground cinnamon and a touch of chili powder.

MAKES 2 GENEROUS SERVINGS

1 large, ripe Haas avocado, peeled and
   pitted
¼ cup pure maple syrup
1 teaspoon vanilla extract or one vanilla
   bean, sliced lengthwise and seeds
   scooped out with a spoon
¼ cup raw cacao powder
Pinch sea salt

1. Place all the ingredients in a food processor fitted with the "S" blade or a high-
speed blender. Add ¼ cup of water and begin
blending.

2. Add more water as needed, until the
mixture is totally smooth and has the texture of thick chocolate pudding.

Leftovers will keep in the fridge for 2 days.

BANANA SOFT SERVE

WHEN I FIRST BEGAN MY BLOG, I
posted this technique—an old trick
in the raw food world—along with the title
"this post will change your life." It certainly
changed mine when I first discovered it;
I couldn't believe that anything so simple
could also be so hopelessly delicious. Frozen bananas processed make a texture that
is divinely ice cream–like. You can make this
in either a food processor or a high-speed
blender. Once you get the hang of it, feel
free to chop in dried fruit, nuts, chocolate
chips, nut butter, or anything else you love!
MAKES 2 SERVINGS

2 large or 3 small bananas, peeled, cut
   into large chunks, and frozen
OPTIONAL ADD-INS: cacao nibs, vegan
dark chocolate chips, raisins, chopped
dates, peanut butter, chopped nuts or
seeds, fresh strawberries, crystallized
ginger, etc.

1. Place the banana chunks into a food
processor fitted with the S" blade and turn
machine on. Let the motor run for a couple
of minutes—seriously, a full minute or two!
At first, the bananas will just make a ton of
noise and bounce around in the processor.

2. After a few minutes, they'll begin to
magically take on a super-creamy texture.
As soon as they do, you can stop the processor and add your add-ins, if you care for any.
Give the machine a few pulses to incorporate
the add-ins fully. Scoop up the mixture and
serve just like ice cream.

Banana soft serve is best served immediately. However, if you have some left over,
you can transfer it to a freezer-safe container and freeze it. To serve again, transfer the frozen portion to your food processor and process it again, so that it takes on
the creamy texture once more before you
serve it.

5 Juices

JUICES ARE A QUICK LINE OF ENERGY AND A WAKE-UP CALL TO THE SENSES. THEY'RE delicious, incredibly nutrient dense, fun to make, and easy to customize. I tend to enjoy juices midmorning (*after* my morning coffee!), but I also sometimes enjoy them as an afternoon snack. I've offered juice as a midmorning snack option in my meal plans, but you can do whatever works for you.

COOK'S NOTE: Juices are easiest to prepare in a juicer (see page 76 for my recommendations). If you don't have a juicer, however, you can make most juices by blending your ingredients in a Vitamix or a regular blender and then straining them through cheesecloth or a nut milk bag. This will remove the fiber, just as a juicer will, and allow you to enjoy the sweet and nutritious liquid that remains. (Note that, unless you're working with a high-speed blender, it'll be hard to blend up harder vegetables, such as carrots and beets, so stick with cucumbers, apples, greens, and other easy-to-blend veggies and fruits.)

GREEN LEMONADE

LIKE MANY CLASSIC GREEN JUICE COMbinations, this recipe combines apple, ginger, lemon, and a ton of green goodness.

Green lemonade is a wonderful way to start your day. I often enjoy it as a snack between meals, as a preworkout treat, or I sip it with my dinner if I'm craving extra greens.
MAKES 1 SERVING

1 green apple
1 (1-inch) knob fresh ginger
5 large stalks celery
1 cucumber
1 large handful fresh parsley
5 leaves kale
1 lemon, halved, peel cut off and
    discarded

Run all the ingredients through your juicer, and serve, or follow the note above about making juices in a blender.

CUCUMBER COOLER

HERE'S A CRISP, REFRESHING SUMmertime drink that's mildly sweet and also very hydrating. Coconut water adds a good dose of electrolytes, so I've often been known to sip this after a hot yoga class!
MAKES 1 SERVING

1 cucumber
1 large pear or 1 cup cubed pineapple
1 large handful (about ½ cup) fresh mint,
    plus a sprig, for serving
½ lime
½ cup coconut water

Green Lemonade, page 112

Run the cucumber, pear, mint, and lime through your juicer or follow the note about making juice in a blender, above. Mix the juice with the coconut water, and serve with a sprig of mint.

THE VEGGIE BOWL

THIS JUICE IS NOT FOR THE FAINT OF heart; it's brimming with veggies, and lots of them, along with a good dose of spicy ginger. But if you love vegetables, you're sure to love it too. This is a great winter juice, since it's more warming than a lot of other green juices.

MAKES 1 SERVING

3 large carrots
1 beet
4 large stalks celery
1 large handful of spinach, fresh parsley, or other dark green
1 small cucumber
1 (1-inch) knob fresh ginger

Run all the ingredients through your juicer, and serve, or follow the note about making juices in a blender (page 112).

SPRING GREENS

THIS JUICE ISN'T VERY SWEET, WHICH makes it ideal for folks who are being mindful of sugar. It's also super refreshing, and the addition of fresh dill—an unusual herb in juices—always makes me think of springtime.

MAKES 1 SERVING

1 medium zucchini
1 medium cucumber
2 stalks celery
4 leaves Swiss chard
1 handful watercress
2 lemons
½ cup fresh dill

Run all the ingredients through your juicer and serve, or follow the note about making juice in a blender (page 112).

JUNGLE GREENS

THIS JUICE IS SWEET, SOUR, AND SASSY. Cilantro adds a summery kick, while pineapple and chard give you plenty of vitamins A and K. If you're not a cilantro lover, feel free to substitute parsley.

MAKES 1 SERVING

1½ cups cubed pineapple
1 cup broccoli florets
3 large stalks Swiss chard or kale
1 large handful (about ½ cup) fresh cilantro
1 cucumber
2 stalks celery

Run all the ingredients through your juicer and serve, or follow the note about making juice in a blender (page 112).

10 Snacks

NACKING IS IMPORTANT NO MATTER WHAT SORT OF DIET YOU EAT, BUT VEGAN AND raw foods offer a ton of easy and delicious snack options. Having a dehydrator makes some of these (such as kale or zucchini chips) easier, but you certainly won't need one to make "reinvented" ants on a log, DIY Snack Bars, or salty, delicious roasted chickpeas.

EASY ROASTED CHICKPEAS

ROASTED CHICKPEAS HAVE ALL OF the crunch and saltiness you might associate with chips and other savory snacks, but they're packed with heart healthy fiber and protein.

As you'll see, this is another "template" recipe that you can customize to your heart's content. Use what you have to give these a kick of acid and salt, and feel free to experiment with some of the flavor options below.

MAKES 2 CUPS CHICKPEAS

2 cups cooked chickpeas
1 tablespoon olive or coconut oil
1 tablespoon tamari, nama shoyu, or
   Bragg's liquid aminos
1 tablespoon freshly squeezed lemon
   juice, balsamic vinegar, or apple cider
   vinegar

1. Preheat your oven to 375°F.
2. Mix the chickpeas, oil, tamari, and lemon. Place them on a parchment or foil-lined baking sheet and bake for about 35 minutes, stirring them around halfway through (if you like them super crunchy, you can bake them for up to 45 minutes). When they're quite nicely toasted, remove them from the oven.

You can store your roasted chickpeas in an airtight container in the fridge for up to a week.

FLAVOR OPTIONS

Cinnamon and Sugar
Before cooking for the same amount of time and at the same temperature as the original recipe, toss the chickpeas in a tablespoon of coconut oil, 3 tablespoons of coconut sugar or demerara sugar, and 1 teaspoon of ground cinnamon.

Spicy Southwestern
Before cooking for the same amount of time and at the same temperature as the original recipe, toss the chickpeas in a tablespoon of olive oil, a teaspoon of ground cumin, ½ teaspoon of ground coriander, a teaspoon of chili powder, ½ teaspoon of paprika, a pinch of cayenne pepper, and sea salt to taste.

Lemon Herb

Before cooking for the same amount of time and at the same temperature as the original recipe, toss the chickpeas in a tablespoon of olive oil, a tablespoon of chopped fresh rosemary (or a teaspoon of dried rosemary), a teaspoon of fresh thyme (or ½ teaspoon dried), a teaspoon of fresh oregano (or ½ teaspoon dried), sea salt to taste, and a clove of garlic, minced. Squeeze two lemons over the beans and mix well before roasting.

Curry Kick

Before cooking for the same amount of time and at the same temperature as the original recipe, toss the chickpeas in a tablespoon of coconut oil, a teaspoon of fresh curry powder, a pinch of cayenne, a tablespoon of tamari, and a teaspoon of pure maple syrup or agave nectar.

NORI AND PUMPKIN-SEED CIGARS

THESE TASTY AND UNUSUAL RAW snacks are inspired by Bonobo's, a restaurant that was a fixture of the New York City raw scene for a number of years before it (sadly) closed its doors a few years ago. You can choose either to serve the cigars fresh, or to dehydrate them for a slightly longer life. They're rich in minerals and healthy fat, and they're a great option when you're in the mood to snack on something savory.

MAKES 12 CIGARS

1¼ cup pumpkin seeds, soaked for at least 2 hours and drained
2 tablespoons freshly squeezed lemon juice
2 tablespoons tahini
1½ tablespoons low-sodium tamari, low-sodium nama shoyu, coconut aminos, or Bragg's liquid aminos
1 clove small garlic, minced (optional)
Freshly ground black pepper
2 scallions, green and white parts, chopped
6 sheets nori (toasted or untoasted is fine)

1. Place the pumpkin seeds, lemon, tahini, tamari, garlic, pepper, and scallions in a food processor fitted with the "S" blade. Pulse a few times to combine. With the motor running, drizzle in ½ cup of water, or just enough for the pâté to take on the texture of hummus (thick, but easily spreadable).

2. Cut a sheet of nori in half, vertically, down the center. Spread each half with 2 generous tablespoons of pâté.

3. Using a knife or an inverted spatula, spread the pâté in a thin, even layer over the nori sheet.

4. Roll the nori sheet up from right to left. Let it sit for a few moments. Slice the roll into bite-size pieces or leave as it is.

OPTIONAL: You can dehydrate the nori roll for 8 hours to get a dry, dehydrated snack that is great for travel and will keep for up to 2 weeks when stored in the fridge. Otherwise, the rolls will keep for 2 or 3 days in the fridge.

Easy Roasted Chickpeas, page 115

Hemp-Seed Power Balls, Sweet and Savory Trail Mix, and Zucchini Ranch Chips, page 119

SWEET AND SAVORY TRAIL MIX

THIS IS A PERFECT TRAIL MIX WHEN you want something a little more filling and substantial than the usual fruit + nut combination. Roasted chickpeas give the mix extra fiber, protein, and iron, and they add a wonderful savory touch.

MAKES 4 CUPS TRAIL MIX

1 batch roasted chickpeas (page 115)
1 cup almonds
1 cup raisins

Mix all the ingredients together. Store in an airtight container in the fridge for up to 10 days.

HEMP-SEED POWER BALLS

THESE BALLS HAVE ALL THE TASTE OF snack bars, but they're smaller, so you can pop one or two when you're in the mood for a mini snack. They've also got a nice protein boost in the form of hemp protein and seeds.

MAKES 16 BALLS

1 cup almonds
¼ teaspoon sea salt
3 tablespoons hemp protein
1 cup tightly packed, Medjool dates
½ cup shelled hemp seeds

1. Place the almonds, the sea salt, and the protein powder in a food processor fitted with the "S" blade. Process until the ingredients are loosely ground.

2. Add the Medjool dates. Keep processing until the ingredients are smooth and evenly incorporated.

3. Form the mixture into balls 1½ inches in diameter. Roll them in the shelled hemp seeds. Refrigerate for an hour prior to eating.

Stored in an airtight container in the fridge, these will keep for 2 weeks.

ZUCCHINI RANCH CHIPS

LIKE KALE CHIPS, THESE ZUCCHINI ranch chips are an easy and tasty way to get green vegetables in your diet. The recipe calls for Herbamare, which is a very delicious, organic seasoning blend. If you don't have it, sea salt on its own will do fine.

MAKES 1½ TO 1¾ CUPS ZUCCHINI CHIPS

3 medium or large zucchini, unpeeled, sliced thinly (about ¼ inch thick) on a mandoline or with a paring knife
1 tablespoon freshly squeezed lemon juice
1 tablespoon olive oil
½ teaspoon Herbamare or sea salt
1 teaspoon crushed garlic (about 1 small clove) or ½ teaspoon garlic powder
2 tablespoons finely chopped fresh dill or 2 teaspoons dried

1. If you're preparing chips in an oven, preheat your oven to 450°F.

2. Mix all the ingredients together with your hands in a large mixing bowl.

3. To prepare the chips in the dehydrator: Dehydrate at 115°F for 6 to 8 hours, or until they're considerably shrunken and dry, but not yet crispy. Flip the chips over, and continue to dehydrate for another 4 hours, or until they're crispy.

To prepare the chips in the oven: Bake at 450°F for about 25 minutes, or until lightly browned.

Store chips in an airtight container in the fridge for up to a week.

NO-BAKE SUNFLOWER OAT BARS

NOTHING MAKES ME HAPPIER THAN A wholesome, filling snack bar that doesn't require me to turn on my oven! These are great for when you're getting tired of the same old date and nut bars. I personally love the taste of sunflower seed butter in these bars, but peanut, almond, or cashew will work very well too (and peanut butter will give it a quintessential childhood "comfort food" taste).

MAKES 10 TO 12 BARS

2½ cups rolled oats (use certified gluten-free oats if needed)
1 cup sunflower seeds (raw or toasted)
½ cup raisins
½ cup cacao nibs
⅔ cup sunflower seed, cashew, peanut, or almond butter
6 tablespoons agave nectar or brown rice syrup

1. Line a small (7 by 11 inches, or 9-inch square) baking dish with foil or plastic wrap.

Mix oats, sunflower seeds, raisins, and cacao nibs in a large bowl.

2. Whisk together the nut butter and ½ cup of sweetener. Pour over the oat mixture, and mix well, until everything is sticky and combined. If the mixture is too dry, you can add more sweetener as needed.

3. Press the mixture into the lined baking dish. Cover with another layer of foil or plastic wrap, press well into the baking dish, and refrigerate for 4 hours. Cut into bar shapes, wrap, and keep refrigerated until ready to use. They ought to keep for 2 weeks.

SUPERFOOD TRAIL MIX

TRAIL MIX IS A FAVORITE ON-THE-GO snack. This version contains some slightly unusual ingredients, including cacao nibs, goji berries, and mulberries—all potent sources of antioxidants.

MAKES 5 CUPS TRAIL MIX

1 cup raw cashews
1 cup raw pistachios
½ cup pumpkin seeds
½ cup cacao nibs
1 cup goji berries
1 cup dried mulberries

No-Bake Sunflower Oat Bars, page 120, and DIY Raw Snack Bars, page 108

Classic Cheesy Kale Chips, page 123

Mix all the ingredients together in a large mixing bowl. Store in an airtight container for several weeks, enjoying as desired.

CLASSIC CHEESY KALE CHIPS

KALE CHIPS ARE PROBABLY THE MOST well-known raw food snack. If you've never tasted these salty, savory, "cheesy" chips, then you're in for a major treat, and, if you have tasted them, this is your chance to create them at home.

I've tried making these in the oven many times over, without any real success; they don't quite get the crispy quality that is so essential for them to work. You can make these in either a rectangular or a low-cost, circular dehydrator. Either way, you'll be delighted as soon as you bite into your first chip. For a higher protein option, check out the Hummus Kale Chips on the right.

MAKES 4 SERVINGS

1 cup raw cashews, soaked for at least 2 hours (or overnight), drained, and rinsed off
Juice of 1 lemon
1 small red bell pepper, seeded and chopped into rough pieces
1 tablespoon mellow white miso
¼ teaspoon salt
⅓ cup nutritional yeast
1 bunch curly kale, washed, dried, and torn into bite-size pieces (about 12 ounces, or 6 cups after prep)

1. Combine all the ingredients, except the kale, in a high-speed blender and add 2 tablespoons of water. Blend until smooth, using your tamper attachment to facilitate. Add another tablespoon or two of water if the mixture is much too thick. You can also use a food processor for this step, stopping to scrape it down frequently as you blend.

2. Place the kale pieces in a large mixing bowl and drench them in the sauce. Use your hands to mix the kale and the sauce evenly and thoroughly. It will seem like a lot of sauce, but you'll be glad for it when you have super cheezy and flavorful kale chips!

3. Place the kale onto two Teflex-lined dehydrator sheets, and dehydrate at 115°F for about 4 hours.

4. Flip the kale chips gently to expose the less dry parts, and keep dehydrating until they're totally crispy, about 4 more hours.

Store the kale chips in an airtight container in the fridge for up to 2 weeks.

HUMMUS KALE CHIPS

THESE KALE CHIPS ARE A LITTLE lower in fat and a little higher in protein than the cheesy kale chips. The addition of chickpeas adds a nutritional boost, and garlic, lemon, and tahini bring to life the flavor of fresh hummus.

MAKES 4 SERVINGS

1 cup cooked chickpeas

½ cup tahini

3 tablespoons freshly squeezed lemon juice

1 clove raw garlic, minced

1 teaspoon sea salt

1 bunch curly kale, washed, dried, and torn into bite-size pieces (about 12 ounces, or 6 cups, after prep)

1. Combine the beans, tahini, lemon juice, garlic, sea salt, and ¼ cup of water in a high-speed blender or food processor. Blend until smooth, using your tamper attachment to facilitate blending, or stopping often to scrape the bowl down. Add another tablespoon or two of water if the mixture is much too thick.

2. Place the kale pieces in a large mixing bowl and drench them in the sauce. Use your hands to mix the kale and the sauce evenly and thoroughly.

3. Place the kale onto two Teflex-lined dehydrator sheets, and dehydrate at 115°F for about 4 hours.

4. Flip the kale chips gently to expose the less dry parts, and keep dehydrating until they're totally crispy, about 4 more hours.

Store the kale chips in an airtight container in the fridge for up to 2 weeks.

REINVENTED ANTS ON A LOG

THIS IS A SLIGHTLY OFFBEAT SPIN ON A classic snack—and more sophisticated for adult palates. I use almond butter, which is a little more subtle than peanut butter, as a base, and, in place of raisins, I use goji berries, which are richer in both protein and antioxidants. You can get very creative with the dried fruit you use here. Dried pineapple, mango, mulberries, blueberries, or strawberries would all be delicious.

MAKES 2 SERVINGS

4 stalks celery, washed and dried

4 tablespoons almond or cashew butter

4 tablespoons goji berries

Trim the celery. Spread 1 tablespoon of nut butter in the groove of each stalk. Line up about a tablespoon of goji berries along the nut butter. Serve.

Reinvented Ants on a Log, page 124

20 Dips, Dressings, Sauces, and Spreads

READERS OF MY BLOG OFTEN TELL ME THAT THEY ASSOCIATE ME WITH SALAD DRESS-ing, and I can't imagine a better compliment. Dressings, dips, and sauces will get you excited about vegetables, both raw and cooked. They can make or break a salad, liven up a boring bowl of grains, or add life to zucchini noodles or raw "rice."

APPLE CIDER VINAIGRETTE

I EAT MANY DIFFERENT TYPES OF VINAI-grettes, made with all sorts of oils and vinegars and citrus fruits for acid. This vinaigrette, though, is a great basic to have on hand. A mixture of olive oil, raw apple cider vinegar—which is rich in enzymes, antibacterial, and may aid in fighting fungal infections—and some sweetness from maple syrup, it's universally appealing and works on a variety of different salads.

MAKES ¾ CUP DRESSING

½ cup olive oil
¼ cup apple cider vinegar
¼ to ½ teaspoon sea salt
1 tablespoon Dijon mustard
2 tablespoons pure maple syrup

Whisk all the ingredients together until smooth. You can use a blender or food processor to mix as well.

Store in an airtight container in the fridge. The dressing will keep for several weeks.

LEMON TURMERIC VINAIGRETTE

TURMERIC IS NOTABLE FOR ITS ANTI-inflammatory properties, so I try to eat a lot of it when I've been particularly active or when I'm under stress. It's not always easy to find uses for this wonderful, brilliantly colored herb, so I'm always looking for new ideas. This dressing is a perfect vehicle for turmeric and has a slightly sweet-and-sour taste.

MAKES 1 ¼ CUPS VINAIGRETTE

⅓ cup hemp, flax, or olive oil
½ fresh Haas avocado peeled and pitted
¼ cup freshly squeezed orange juice
2 tablespoons freshly squeezed lemon juice
1 teaspoon ground turmeric
½ teaspoon ground ginger, or 1 teaspoon grated fresh
1½ tablespoons agave nectar or pure maple syrup
¼ teaspoon sea salt, or to taste

Blend all the ingredients together in a blender or food processor.

Store in an airtight container in the fridge. The dressing will keep for a week.

GREEN HERB DRESSING

THIS IS A VERY LOOSE ADAPTATION OF the very famous Green Goddess dressing by Annie's Organic, which is beloved among hippies, healthy eaters, and foodies everywhere. My version features three different herbs—basil, parsley, and dill. You can use whichever herbs you have on hand (tarragon, chives, and thyme would also be lovely), but do be sure that they're fresh. Dried herbs don't work the same way in this recipe.

MAKES 1 ¼ CUPS DRESSING

1 cup packed fresh parsley
¼ cup fresh dill
½ cup packed fresh basil
¼ cup tahini
½ teaspoon Herbamare (a very delicious and healthy seasoned salt and herb mix) or sea salt
3 tablespoons freshly squeezed lemon juice
¼ cup olive oil
1 green onion, green part only, chopped

Blend all the ingredients, along with ½ cup of water, in a blender until smooth.

Store in an airtight container in the fridge. Dressing will keep for 5 days.

SPICY CILANTRO VINAIGRETTE

THIS TART, TANGY, AND VERSATILE vinaigrette is light and bright enough for green salads (or as an accompaniment for my Jicama Fiesta Rice (on page 210), but it also makes a fantastic marinade for vegetable kebabs or grilled tofu.

MAKES 1 SCANT CUP DRESSING

½ cup extra-virgin olive oil
4 tablespoons freshly squeezed lime juice
1 tablespoon agave nectar
½ teaspoon salt
½ teaspoon cumin (optional)
¼ teaspoon cayenne (more as desired)
½ cup tightly packed fresh cilantro

Blend all the ingredients together in a blender, food processor, or magic bullet.

Store in an airtight container in the fridge. The dressing will keep for a week.

ALMOND BUTTER AND SUN-DRIED TOMATO DRESSING

THERE'S SOMETHING MAGICAL ABOUT the marriage of almond butter and tomato, no matter how improbable it sounds! You can make this dressing as thick or as thin as you like. I use 1 scant cup of water for a thinner salad dressing, and just over ½ cup to make a sauce, which I then use on zucchini noodles, to dip veggies in, or in raw wraps.

For something in between—a rich, creamy salad dressing—use ¾ cup as instructed. Be sure to make this dressing when tomatoes are in season; canned tomatoes won't have as much sweetness or flavor.

MAKES 1¾ CUPS DRESSING (DEPENDING ON THE SIZE OF YOUR TOMATO)

1 medium beefsteak or Jersey tomato, quartered
½ cup raw almond butter
6 sun-dried tomatoes, soaked for 10 minutes, water discarded
1 tablespoon tamari, Bragg's Liquid Aminos, or nama shoyu
1 pitted date

Blend all the ingredients with ¾ cup of water in a blender until smooth.

Store in an airtight container in the fridge. The dressing will keep for 4 days.

CREAMY MAPLE CHIPOTLE DRESSING

SAVORY SUN-DRIED TOMATOES, creamy cashews, and smoked paprika: When combined with sweet maple syrup, they create a spicy, sweet, and altogether scrumptious salad dressing. Use this on any salad you like, but it's particularly good with my Raw Cobb (page 145) or my kale salad with sweet potatoes and almonds (page 141).

MAKES 1½ CUPS DRESSING

1 cup cashews, soaked in water for at least 2 hours and drained
¼ cup oil-packed sun-dried tomatoes,
½ teaspoon smoked paprika
1 teaspoon chipotle powder or 2 chipotle peppers in adobo
1 tablespoon pure maple syrup
2 tablespoons apple cider vinegar

Blend the ingredients and ¾ cup of water in a high-speed blender until smooth.

Store in an airtight container in the fridge. The dressing will keep for a week.

GINGER MISO DRESSING

THIS SALTY, SWEET, AND DELICIOUS dressing features the timeless combination of miso and ginger, along with the creamy addition of tahini. I like to serve it over zucchini noodles, with steamed broccoli, or over a big salad of romaine, red bell peppers, steamed snow peas, and raw shiitake mushrooms. It's also a great topper for warm brown rice.

MAKES 1½ CUPS DRESSING

¼ cup miso (I prefer mellow white miso, but red miso and chickpea miso are also fine)
¼ cup pure maple syrup or agave nectar
½ cup tahini

2 tablespoons low-sodium tamari, low-sodium nama shoyu, Bragg's Liquid Aminos, or Coconut Aminos
2 tablespoons fresh, grated fresh ginger, or 1 teaspoon powdered ginger

Blend all the ingredients, along with ¾ cup of water, in a high-speed blender until smooth. Add more water if the mixture is too thick.

Store in an airtight container in the fridge. The dressing will keep for up to 10 days.

CARROT MISO DRESSING

THIS RICH DRESSING FOR SALADS, FOR dipping raw vegetables, or for slaws is lower in fat than some of my other dressings, and full of fresh, spicy flavor from the ginger.

MAKES 3 CUPS DRESSING

3 to 4 large carrots, chopped
3 tablespoons mellow white miso
1 tablespoon tamari or nama shoyu
1 tablespoon freshly squeezed lemon juice
3 large, pitted Medjool dates
1 (1-inch) knob fresh ginger, peeled
1 tablespoon toasted sesame oil

Blend all the ingredients in a high-speed blender along with 1 cup of water. You'll have to start on low and work the speed up; your machine will sound a little angry, but, once it gets blending, it'll simmer down! Add more water as needed. Dressing will keep in an airtight container for up to 6 days.

MULTISEED GOMASIO

GOMASIO IS A TRADITIONAL JAPANESE condiment made with sesame seeds, dried seaweed, and salt. It is fabulous sprinkled over a bowl of warm grains (especially rice or millet), but you can also use it to top salads, slaws, and roasted root vegetables.

I love sesame seeds, but, for an added boost of protein and zinc, I like to add hemp seeds and pumpkin seeds to my gomasio as well.

MAKES ¾ CUP GOMASIO

¼ cup hemp seeds
¼ cup pumpkin seeds
¼ cup sesame seeds
1 tablespoon kelp or dulse granules
½ teaspoon sea salt

Add all the ingredients to a food processor fitted with the "S" blade. Process until the seeds are ground up well (you can either leave a little texture, or make it powdery—it's up to you!).

Store in a glass jar in the fridge for up to 2 weeks.

CLASSIC ZUCCHINI HUMMUS

ISA CHANDRA MOSKOWITZ, A VEGAN CU-linary superstar and longtime activist, has said that hummus is a vegan food group. I agree wholeheartedly. I'm often asked whether or not hummus is raw, and the answer is technically "no," not if you prepare it traditionally. (Cooked chickpeas are, of course, cooked!) You can make a raw hummus using sprouted chickpeas, but I wouldn't recommend it; they tend to be incredibly bitter.

Instead, try this incredible hummus recipe, which uses zucchini as a base. It's a little thinner than some of my other hummus recipes, but it's mellow, fresh, and a suitable option for folks who have a hard time digesting beans.

MAKES 2 SCANT CUPS (ABOUT 8 SERVINGS)

4 cups (12 ounces) chopped zucchini
½ cup tahini
½ teaspoon sea salt
Freshly ground black pepper
2 tablespoons freshly squeezed lemon juice
½ teaspoon ground cumin (optional)

1. Blend all the ingredients until smooth in a high-speed blender or food processor (if using a food processor, you may need to stop a few times, scrape the bowl, and continue blending).
2. Check the hummus for seasoning. Season to taste, and serve.

Stored in an airtight container in the fridge, zucchini hummus will keep for up to 4 days.

HEMP HUMMUS

THIS RECIPE, WHICH I'VE ADAPTED from my blog, is probably my all-time favorite hummus. Hemp seeds add healthy fat and a hefty dose of protein to a classic set of hummus flavors. Feel free to add some garlic if you like, but I like to keep this one light and bright without it.

This is a dense, hearty hummus, so I enjoy serving it with light, crispy vegetables, including jicama, cucumber rounds, celery, and romaine lettuce leaves.

MAKES 6 SERVINGS

¼ cup hemp seeds
½ teaspoon sea salt
½ teaspoon ground cumin
2 cups cooked chickpeas
2 to 3 tablespoons freshly squeezed lemon juice
1 tablespoon olive oil

1. Grind the hemp seeds, sea salt, and cumin in a food processor until finely ground.
2. Add the chickpeas and lemon juice, and pulse a few times to combine.
3. Run the motor of the food processor, and, while it's running, drizzle in ¼ cup of water in a thin stream. Keep processing, stopping on occasion to scrape down the bowl, until the mixture is very smooth. Drizzle in the olive oil, allow the mixture

to process for one more moment, and then transfer to a serving bowl. Serve with a sprinkle of additional hemp seeds, if desired.

Stored in an airtight container in the fridge, this hummus will keep nicely for up to 4 days.

CURRIED SWEET POTATO HUMMUS

SWEET POTATO AND CURRY GIVE THIS hummus an exotic flavor, a wonderful, spicy fragrance, and—thanks to the curry powder—some anti-inflammatory properties too. I like to serve this hummus with slices of endive, radicchio, kale, and other, slightly bitter vegetables for a nice contrast with the sweetness of the potatoes, but you can also serve it with apple slices when you're in the mood for a sweet snack.

MAKES 6 SERVINGS

2 cups skinned, cubed sweet potato
  (1-inch cubes)
2 cups cooked chickpeas
3 tablespoons almond butter
½ to 1 teaspoon toasted sesame oil
2 teaspoons curry powder
1 tablespoon apple cider vinegar
1 tablespoon tamari or nama shoyu

1. First, cook your sweet potatoes. You can either fill a medium-size pot halfway with water, add the sweet potatoes, and then boil them until they're fork tender (about 15 to 20 minutes) or you can place them in a strainer or sieve and position it over the pot before covering it with a lid. The potatoes will take about 20 minutes to steam through. If you have a rice cooker that is also a vegetable steamer, you can steam the potatoes according to the manufacturer's instructions.

2. Place the sweet potatoes in your food processor and pulse until they're roughly mashed. Add the chickpeas, almond butter, sesame oil, curry powder, apple cider vinegar, and tamari. Pulse a few times to combine them. Scrape the sides of the processor down with a spatula.

3. With the motor running, pour ½ cup of water into the processor in a thin stream. Keep processing until the hummus is creamy. You can add a little more water as needed. You may need to scrape the bowl down a few more times.

4. Check for seasoning, and adjust to taste. Serve.

Stored in an airtight container in the fridge, this hummus will keep nicely for up to 4 days.

RED LENTIL AND WALNUT HUMMUS

THIS IS REALLY MORE A DIP THAN A hummus. While it's more time-consuming than any of my other hummus recipes, it has a depth of flavor, thanks to garlic and paprika, that's quite special. If you're short on time, you can skip toasting the walnuts (step 2), but toasting them will contribute a lot more flavor to the dish!

The hummus is great with vegetable

Classic Zucchini Hummus (page 130), Hemp Hummus (page 130), Curried Sweet Potato Hummus (page 131)

crudités (I especially like celery, button mushrooms, and broccoli), but it also works perfectly with sprouted-grain toast points or flax crackers.

MAKES 2 CUPS HUMMUS

1 cup dried red lentils
¾ cup walnuts
1 to 2 garlic cloves, finely chopped
¼ cup tahini
2 tablespoons freshly squeezed lemon
    juice, or to taste
1 teaspoon paprika (or ½ teaspoon
    smoked paprika for a "smoky" flavor)
1½ teaspoons sea salt
¼ teaspoon freshly ground black pepper

1. Bring 2 cups of water to a boil in a small saucepan. Add the lentils and reduce the heat to low. Simmer the lentils until almost all of the liquid has been absorbed and the lentils are tender, about 15 minutes. Drain the lentils through a fine-mesh strainer and let them cool to room temperature, about 20 minutes.

2. While the lentils cook, toast the walnuts. Heat a small saucepan or skillet over medium heat and add the nuts. Toast them, moving the pan around constantly, until they're just golden brown and fragrant (2 to 3 minutes). They'll continue to cook when you remove them from the heat, so be sure not to toast them too long. Remove them from the heat and set aside.

3. Place the lentils, walnuts, garlic, tahini, lemon, paprika, salt, and pepper in a food processor fitted with the "S" blade. Process until the mixture is very smooth, drizzling in a few tablespoons of water as needed to achieve a perfect consistency. Stop a few times to scrape the bowl down. Serve with a sprinkle of paprika if desired.

Stored in an airtight container in the fridge, this hummus will keep nicely for up to 4 days.

RAW CASHEW ALFREDO

YOU'LL BE AMAZED THAT THERE'S NOT a drop of cream in this velvety sauce. Cashew Alfredo is great on zucchini pasta, of course, but it's also delightful drizzled onto soup, with chili, or to thicken up other sauces.

MAKES 1½ CUPS SAUCE

1 cup cashews, soaked overnight and
    drained of water
2 tablespoons freshly squeezed lemon
    juice
1 teaspoon agave nectar
1 teaspoon mellow white miso
1 clove garlic, minced (optional)
Sea salt
¼ cup nutritional yeast

Place all the ingredients in a blender. Add ½ cup of water and blend until smooth. Add more water as needed until the sauce has the consistency of regular Alfredo sauce. Store in the fridge for up to 5 days, and enjoy over pasta, stirred into soups, or as a topping for roast vegetables.

HEMP PARMESAN

MOST RAW PARMESAN RECIPES DE-mand the use of a dehydrator. I developed this recipe as a quick, easy, and almost instant alternative. You can use the hemp Parmesan as a topping for salad or pasta dishes, or you can sprinkle it on top of steamed vegetables. It's delicious, and it's also very nutrient dense: hemp provides healthy fatty acids, while nutritional yeast provides B vitamins. Both ingredients are protein rich, so this is also a nice way to give any meal a little protein boost.

MAKES 1 SCANT CUP PARMESAN

½ cup hemp seeds
½ cup nutritional yeast
Sea salt and freshly ground black pepper

Place all the ingredients into a food processor and process until evenly mixed. Store in a glass jar in the fridge for up to 2 weeks.

RAW MARINARA SAUCE

THIS BASIC RAW MARINARA DEMANDS nothing more than the use of your blender, but it tastes as if it's been simmering on a stove top. What gives the recipe such depth is the addition of sun-dried tomatoes. I make a lot of the marinara at once, then freeze it in small batches so that I can use it on a moment's notice.

MAKES 2 CUPS SAUCE

2 cups chopped Jersey or Roma tomatoes
1 cup chopped sun-dried tomatoes, hydrated in water and then drained
¼ teaspoon sea salt
1 tablespoon apple cider vinegar
1 tablespoon pure maple syrup
2 tablespoons fresh oregano, or 1 teaspoon dried
¼ cup chopped fresh basil, or 2 teaspoons dried

Blend all the ingredients with 1 tablespoon of water in a high-speed blender or food processor until totally smooth. Store in the fridge for up to 5 days, or freeze.

BASIC VEGAN PESTO

IF YOU THINK PESTO WITHOUT PARME-san is destined to be lackluster, think again. This pesto is every bit as delicious as the traditional stuff, thanks to the flavor of nutritional yeast!

Pestos are a perfect way to dress up vegetables, grains, and pasta dishes, of course. You can use a wide array of greens as a base (including kale, sage, parsley, cilantro, and arugula) and almost any nuts or seeds you like (including hemp seeds, walnuts, pumpkin seeds, pine nuts, and macadamia nuts). The kale and pistachio recipe that follows is a good example. You can make double batches of pesto and freeze as needed; I sometimes like to freeze pesto in ice cube trays, pop a single cube out, and mix it directly into warm brown rice or quinoa pasta.

MAKES 1 GENEROUS CUP PESTO

2 cups tightly packed fresh basil
½ cup walnuts, raw or toasted
1 clove garlic, roughly chopped
½ cup extra-virgin olive oil
Sea salt and freshly ground black pepper
1 tablespoon freshly squeezed lemon juice
3 tablespoons nutritional yeast

1. Place the basil, walnuts, and garlic in a food processor fitted with the "S" blade. Pulse to combine, until the mixture is coarsely ground.

2. Turn the motor on and drizzle the olive oil in a thin stream. Add the sea salt, pepper, lemon, and nutritional yeast, and pulse a few more times to combine. This will keep for 5 days in the fridge or can be frozen as needed.

KALE AND PISTACHIO PESTO

A SAVORY, NUTRITIOUS PESTO KALE gives this recipe a little bit of bitterness and bite, so I think it's perfect served over sweet roasted root vegetables.

MAKES 1 HEAPING CUP PESTO

½ cup pistachios
¾ teaspoon sea salt
1 clove garlic, chopped
1 cup tightly packed fresh basil
2 cups loosely chopped kale
⅓ cup olive oil
1 tablespoon freshly squeezed lemon juice
3 tablespoons nutritional yeast

1. Grind the pistachios and sea salt together in a food processor fitted with the "S" blade until coarsely ground. Add the garlic, basil, and kale. Pulse a few more times to break down.

2. Turn on the motor and drizzle in the olive oil slowly. When the olive oil has been incorporated, pulse in the lemon juice and nutritional yeast. Store in a jar or other airtight container in the fridge for 5 days. You can freeze any pesto you don't have a chance to use.

SIMPLE RAW VEGAN AVOCADO MAYONNAISE

A VOCADO CREATES THE RICH, FATTY texture of mayonnaise perfectly, and lemon and mustard give it a traditional flavor. This spread is a treat in wraps, sandwiches, or even as a thick dressing for chopped salads.

MAKES ½ TO ¾ CUPS MAYONNAISE

1 small or medium Haas avocado, cut in
 half and pitted
1 tablespoon freshly squeezed lemon juice
2 teaspoons Dijon mustard (optional)
⅛ to ¼ teaspoon sea salt
2 tablespoons olive oil

1. Place the avocado, lemon, mustard, if using, and salt in a food processor or high-speed blender and process until it's blended well. Stop a few times to scrape the bowl down if need be.

5-Minute Guacamole, page 105

2. With the motor running, drizzle in your olive oil. Continue blending until the mixture has taken on a creamy, light texture.

Store in an airtight container in the fridge. Will keep for 2 days.

RAW CORN SALSA

MOST OF US KNOW HOW DELICIOUS grilled or boiled sweet corn is but are less familiar with the wonderful taste of raw corn. I like raw corn so much that I often eat it sliced straight off the cob, but this raw corn salsa is a slightly more dressed up and flavorful way to enjoy it.

MAKES 3 CUPS SALSA

1 ripe avocado, peeled, pitted, and diced into ½-inch pieces
1 ripe, seeded red tomato, diced into ½-inch pieces
2 cups shucked fresh corn
2 green onions, green parts only, chopped
½ teaspoon red chili flakes
⅓ cup chopped fresh cilantro or parsley
Sea salt and freshly ground black pepper
2 to 3 tablespoons freshly squeezed lime juice
2 tablespoons extra virgin olive oil

Mix all the ingredients in a mixing bowl and season to taste. Serve with any dish that calls for salsa. Store in the fridge for up to 3 days.

5 Meal-Size Salads (and Meal-Size Salad How-To)

ONE OF THE MOST POPULAR POSTS ON MY BLOG IS CALLED "HOW TO BUILD A MEAL-Size Salad." The idea for the post came to me when client after client complained that salads weren't keeping them full enough at lunchtime. When I probed a little, it became clear that their salads weren't doing the trick because they were far too skimpy: nothing more than greens, a couple of veggies, and a vinaigrette. There's nothing wrong with that kind of combination for a side dish, but greens and dressing do not a meal make.

Meal-size salads include all of those handy macronutrient groups we keep talking about: protein, fat, and carbs. To compose a meal-size salad, you simply need to throw together foods that are rich in these different nutrients. Here are some options:

Proteins	Complex carbs	Fats
Tofu or tempeh	Legumes	Avocado
Hemp seeds	Whole grains	High-quality oils
Quinoa	Potato (sweet or white)	Nuts and seeds
Nutritional yeast	Root vegetables	Nut or seed butters
Peanuts		
Legumes		

Add at least two of these to each salad, and you'll never again complain about how salads don't fill you up. If you want a few options, here are some of my favorites.

Dinosaur Kale and White Bean Caesar Salad, page 141

DINOSAUR KALE AND WHITE BEAN CAESAR SALAD

CREAMY AND SAVORY, THIS SPIN ON Caesar salad uses kale as the base, of course, instead of plain 'ole romaine, and features sun-dried tomatoes, which add smoky and salty flavors to the dish. Navy beans give the dish heft and a great deal of nutrition too, so you can count on this salad to fill you up!

MAKES 4 TO 6 SERVINGS

Salad Ingredients

14 ounces of dinosaur kale, stems removed, cut into thin strips
⅔ cup sun-dried tomatoes, rehydrated in hot water and sliced into narrow strips (oil soaked tomatoes are also fine, if that is what you prefer)
1½ cups cooked cannellini beans

Dressing Ingredients

½ cup raw cashews, soaked overnight and drained
¼ cup hemp seeds (substitute more cashews if you don't have hemp)
¼ cup nutritional yeast
¼ teaspoon salt
3 tablespoons freshly squeezed lemon juice
Freshly ground black pepper
2 pitted Medjool dates
1 teaspoon kelp granules (optional, but good for re-creating the anchovy taste)
1 cup chopped celery

1. Blend all the dressing ingredients, as well as ¾ cup of water, together in a blender (a high-speed blender will work best, but, if you have a regular one, that's okay).

2. Pour dressing over the kale and "massage" it with your hands, until the kale has gotten a bit soft and wilted in texture. You can start with ½ cup of the dressing and add more, until the kale is dressed to your liking. Reserve extra dressing for veggie dipping or future salads.

3. Add the tomatoes and beans, and give the salad another quick toss with your hands, so that everything is coated in dressing. Serve.

KALE SALAD WITH SWEET POTATO, ALMONDS, AND CREAMY MAPLE CHIPOTLE DRESSING

THIS SALAD TURNS KALE INTO COMfort food, thanks to the addition of comforting sweet potatoes and a gently spiced, sweet, and creamy dressing. This is a perfect salad to make in the autumn, when both kale and sweet potatoes are in season.

If you prefer avocado to almonds, feel free to use a small, chopped Haas avocado in place of the almonds here. I like to keep the skins on my sweet potatoes, but, if you prefer to peel them before chopping, feel free!

MAKES 4 SERVINGS

2 medium sweet potatoes, cut into 1-inch cubes (about 3 cups)
2 tablespoons coconut or olive oil
Sea salt and freshly ground black pepper
1 Batch Creamy Maple Chipotle Dressing (page 128)
1 large bunch kale, stemmed, washed, dried, and cut into bite-size pieces (about 12 ounces after preparation)
1 cup red bell pepper, seeded and diced
⅓ cup sliced or slivered almonds

1. Preheat the oven to 400°F. Toss the sweet potatoes with the oil in a large mixing bowl. Transfer the potatoes to a foil or parchment–lined baking sheet and season to taste with sea salt and black pepper. Roast until potatoes are browning and tender (about 20 to 25 minutes). Allow the potatoes to cool for 15 minutes, or until you're ready to make the salad. This step can be done a day in advance.

2. In a large mixing bowl, massage ½ cup of the dressing into the raw kale until it starts to soften. Continue to add dressing as needed until the kale is well coated. Add the pepper, almonds, and sweet potato, and toss everything to combine. Serve.

ACORN SQUASH, FRISÉE, AND BROWN RICE SALAD WITH TOASTED HAZELNUTS

THIS IS THE ULTIMATE WINTER SALAD. Though fresh frisée serves as a base, it's brown rice, toasted hazelnuts, and savory winter squash that give this salad its flavor, texture, and heft. The salad makes great leftovers, and it's also a beautiful dish to plate. It's one of the salads I most enjoy serving to friends.

MAKES 4 SERVINGS

1 acorn squash (2 pounds)
2 tablespoons coconut or olive oil
Sea salt and freshly ground black pepper
½ cup hazelnuts
1 batch Lemon Turmeric Vinaigrette (page 126)
4 heaping cups frisée
1½ cups cooked brown rice

1. Preheat the oven to 400°F. Cut the acorn squash in half, remove the seeds, and cut crosswise into slices ½ inch thick. Toss the slices in coconut oil, sea salt, and pepper. Place the slices on a parchment-lined baking sheet and bake for 30 or 35 minutes, or until the slices are golden brown. Allow them to cool for 15 minutes.

2. While the squash is cooking, place the hazelnuts in a shallow baking dish or pie pan and add them to the oven for 4 or 5 minutes, or until they're just becoming fragrant. Rub

Acorn Squash, Frisée, and Brown Rice Salad with Toasted Hazelnuts, page 142

Raw Cobb Salad, page 145

off the skins and set them aside. Prepare the vinaigrette.

3. Mix the hazelnuts, frisée, and brown rice in a mixing bowl, along with ¼ cup of vinaigrette. Divide the mixture among four plates and then top each with one quarter of the cooled squash slices. Enjoy.

RAW COBB SALAD

EGGPLANT BACON IS ONE OF MY FAvorite vegan culinary inventions. It's easy to prepare, versatile, and, while it certainly won't fool a committed bacon lover, it's as bold and salty as any plant-based eater could hope for. Plus, it's rich in fiber, potassium, and numerous minerals—a healthier alternative to the "real stuff."

This Cobb salad seems simple enough, but the flavors are surprisingly complex. It's hearty, full of healthy fat to keep you satisfied, and it looks really pretty too.

MAKES 4 SERVINGS

Salad Ingredients
6 cups chopped romaine lettuce,
2 cups chopped Jersey or heirloom tomatoes (½-inch dice)
1 large Haas avocado, cut into 1-inch chunks
1 cup Cashew Cheese (page 99)
1 cup diced Eggplant Bacon (recipe follows)
2 tablespoons chopped fresh chives

Eggplant Bacon Ingredients
4 tablespoons low-sodium tamari, low-sodium nama shoyu, or coconut aminos
2½ tablespoons apple cider vinegar
1 tablespoon pure maple syrup
½ teaspoon smoked paprika
1 tablespoon olive oil
1 medium eggplant, cut in half and sliced lengthwise into long strips ¼ inch thick

1. To make the eggplant bacon, mix the tamari, vinegar, maple syrup, paprika, and olive oil together. Pour the marinade into a shallow baking dish. Add the eggplant strips and allow them to marinate for at least 2 hours, or overnight.

2. Place the eggplant strips onto a Teflex-lined dehydrator sheet. Dehydrate for 6 hours. Flip the strips over and dehydrate for another 2 hours, or until crispy.

Alternatively, you can place the strips onto a parchment-lined or greased baking sheet and bake them at 400°F for 15 to 20 minutes, or until golden, flipping halfway through. They won't be super crispy, as with the dehydrator version, but they'll still taste fantastic.

3. To assemble the salad, mix all the ingredients together, or divide them evenly into fourths, and arrange them in strips on your serving plates. Dress with either Apple Cider Vinaigrette (page 126), or Creamy Maple Chipotle Dressing (page 128).

Romaine, Cherry Tomato, and Arugula Salad with Chickpeas and Raw Parmesan, page 146

ROMAINE, CHERRY TOMATO, AND ARUGULA SALAD WITH CHICKPEAS AND RAW PARMESAN

THIS SALAD IS A PERFECT WAY TO CELebrate summer produce. Spicy arugula is a perfect contrast for sweet, juicy cherry tomatoes and chopped romaine. If you don't have chickpeas on hand, you can substitute lentils, black beans, or any other legume of your choosing.

MAKES 4 SERVINGS

3 heaping cups chopped romaine lettuce,
3 heaping cups arugula
2 cups halved cherry tomatoes
2 cups chickpeas
1 batch Apple Cider Vinaigrette (page 126), or Lemon Turmeric Vinaigrette (page 126)
½ cup Hemp Parmesan (page 130)

1. Mix all the ingredients except for the Hemp Parm together in a large salad bowl. Top with dressing to taste (about ⅓ or ½ cup, more as needed).

2. Divide the salad into four bowls or plates and sprinkle each with 2 tablespoons of Hemp Parm. Serve.

LEVEL 1
Tried and True

L EVEL 1 RECIPES ARE INTENDED TO GUIDE YOU INTO THE WORLD OF VEGAN AND RAW food. A lot of these recipes may be new to you, but they'll still evoke the flavors and textures of foods that are familiar. Among these recipes, you'll find a tofu "scramble" (like scrambled eggs, but better!), toasted pumpkin granola, a curried chickpea salad (which stacks up pretty nicely to curried chicken salad, if you ask me), and scrumptious vegan enchiladas. You won't miss the meat with food this satisfying and flavorful.

Breakfast

TOASTED PUMPKIN GRANOLA WITH HOMEMADE HEMP MILK

I LOVE PUMPKIN IN ANYTHING AND EVerything, but I especially love it in this delightful granola. I often create raw granolas (or raw-nolas—see page 202 for one of my favorites), but sometimes I crave the toasted flavor of a traditional recipe. When I do, this is my go-to.

MAKES 6 CUPS GRANOLA

4 cups rolled oats
¾ cup pumpkin seeds
½ cup raisins
3 tablespoons chia seeds
1 teaspoon ground cinnamon
¼ teaspoon grated nutmeg
¼ teaspoon ground cloves
2 tablespoons flax meal
½ cup pumpkin puree
2 tablespoons melted coconut oil
¼ cup almond butter
⅓ cup pure maple syrup

1. Mix the oats, seeds, raisins, chia, cinnamon, nutmeg, cloves, and flax in a large mixing bowl. Whisk together the pumpkin, coconut oil, almond butter, and maple syrup. Pour the wet ingredients over the dry and combine thoroughly.

2. Preheat the oven to 325°F. Spread the mixture onto two parchment or foil-lined baking sheets. Bake the granola for 20 minutes or so. Remove the granola from the oven and stir gently with a spoon. Bake for another 15 minutes, or until nicely toasted. Let cool completely, and serve with Homemade Hemp Milk, page 101.

MILLET AND ALMOND ZUCCHINI MUFFINS

I'VE NEVER BEEN MUCH OF A BAKER, but there's no better way to entice people into veganism than with a tray of warm, freshly baked goods. The zucchini in this recipe provides moistness, but you won't taste it at all. It's a great recipe to serve to kids (or grown-ups) who are struggling to warm up to vegetables.

Whole wheat pastry flour and spelt flour work well in most vegan baking endeavors, but, since many of my readers don't eat gluten, I try to create gluten-free goodies when I can. It's taken me a long, long time to come up with a muffin recipe that's vegan and gluten free but not loaded up with starches or gums. Gluten-free baking can be a little tricky without eggs, but, in this recipe, flax meal does the work, and the almond and millet flours create a perfect "crumb."

MAKES 6 MUFFINS

Toasted Pumpkin Granola with Homemade Hemp Milk, page 148

1 cup blanched almond flour
¾ cup + 2 tablespoons millet flour
1 teaspoon baking soda
¼ teaspoon sea salt
1 teaspoon ground cinnamon
½ cup almond milk
1 teaspoon apple cider vinegar
1 small banana
¼ cup pure maple syrup
2 tablespoons flax meal
2 tablespoons coconut oil
1 cup grated zucchini

1. Preheat your oven to 350°F. Line or grease a six-cup muffin tin.

2. Whisk the flours, baking soda, sea salt, and cinnamon together in a large mixing bowl.

3. In a blender, blend the almond milk and apple cider vinegar until frothy. Add the banana, maple syrup, flax, and oil, and blend until smooth.

4. Add the wet ingredients to the dry ones, and mix until incorporated. Add the zucchini, and mix again.

5. Spoon mixture into the six prepared muffin cups. Bake for 30 to 35 minutes, or until the muffins are golden and a toothpick inserted into the center emerges clean.

These muffins are best when eaten immediately but can be stored in an airtight container for up to 2 days. Freeze any muffins you don't intend to eat quickly—they freeze very well!

Superfood Trail Mix, page 120

Simple Avocado Toast, page 151

SIMPLE AVOCADO TOAST

ONE OF MY ALL-TIME FAVORITE BREAK-fasts. If you've never tried creamy, delectable avocado "smooshed" onto crispy sprouted-grain bread, now is the time to change that. I find avocado to be a better toast topping than butter or cream cheese ever was, and it's so much richer in antioxidants and healthy, unsaturated fats.

You can dress up avocado toast however you like. Tomato, radishes with sea salt, sprouts, arugula, and sweet potato chunks are all favorite additions of mine.

MAKES 2 SERVINGS

4 slices sprouted-grain bread
   (such as Ezekiel or Alvarado St.
   Bakery bread)
1 large, ripe Haas avocado
Sea salt and cracked black pepper
1 tablespoon freshly squeezed lemon or
   lime juice (optional)

1. Toast four slices of bread until crispy.

2. Cut the avocado in half and remove the pit. Then cut into quarters. Scoop out the flesh and layer one quarter onto each slice of toast. Use a fork to smoosh the avocado into the bread.

3. Sprinkle each slice with sea salt and black pepper to taste. Drizzle a little lemon or lime juice on top, if desired.

CHICKPEA TOFU TAHINI SCRAMBLE

SCRAMBLE WILL TAKE ON A WHOLE new meaning when you try this egg-free breakfast dish. With a little nutritional yeast, spices, and a good block of extra firm tofu, you can create a high-protein, nourishing meal that's worthy of any fine brunch—vegan or otherwise!

This tofu scramble gets extra protein and healthy fat from the addition of chickpeas and tahini.

MAKES 4 SERVINGS

1 tablespoon coconut oil
1 cup diced onion
1 red bell pepper, seeded and chopped
1½ cups, chopped into small pieces, broccoli
1 block (about 16 ounces) extra-firm tofu
1 cup chickpeas
1 tablespoon low-sodium tamari
3 tablespoons tahini
1 tablespoon Dijon mustard
2 tablespoons nutritional yeast

1. Heat the coconut oil over medium or high heat in a large skillet. Sauté the onion and pepper in the coconut oil until they're

Chickpea Tofu Tahini Scramble, page 152

Easy Berry Breakfast Pizza, page 153

just getting soft (about 4 minutes). Add the broccoli and sauté for another 4 to 5 minutes.

2. Using your hands, break up the tofu into pieces. They should be bite-size, but not enormous—try to imagine that you ultimately want this to look like scrambled eggs. Add the tofu to the skillet along with the chickpeas, and heat through.

3. Whisk together the tamari, tahini, and mustard. Add them to the skillet and stir to combine everything. Finally, add the nutritional yeast and give it all a quick stir. Serve warm.

EASY BERRY BREAKFAST PIZZA

THIS BREAKFAST IS FESTIVE AND pretty but easy to prepare (hint: there's no actual pizza crust preparation involved!), and it features one of my favorite marriages: avocado and berries. The avocado spread makes a delightful pudding in its own right.
MAKES 2 INDIVIDUAL PIZZAS

Raw Vegan Bircher Muesli, page 155

Avocado Spread/Pudding Ingredients

1 large Haas avocado, pits removed and flesh scooped out

2 pitted dates or 1½ tablespoons pure maple syrup

1 vanilla bean, seeds scraped out

Pinch of sea salt

½ cup almond milk (plus more as needed)

"Pizza" Ingredients

4 Ezekiel sprouted-grain tortillas (brown rice tortillas are a good option if you don't eat gluten or wheat)

2 cups fruit of choice (I particularly like berries, banana slices, pomegranate seeds, mango, or kiwi)

½ cup finely chopped and loosely packed fresh mint

1. Place all of the pudding/spread ingredients in a high-speed blender or a food processor and blend until you reach a smooth, creamy consistency. If you're using a food processor, you may want to opt for agave nectar or maple syrup instead of dates, since they'll blend up more easily.

2. Spread the avocado mixture evenly over the two tortillas. Arrange the fruit over each tortilla, then sprinkle half the mint over each. Serve.

RAW VEGAN BIRCHER MUESLI

SWISS PHYSICIAN MAXIMILIAN OSKAR Bircher-Benner is thought by some to be the father of the raw foods movement.

At his sanitarium in Zurich, Bircher-Benner encouraged his patients to eat less meat and bread and more raw fruits and vegetables, and it was he who invented muesli, a now famous morning cereal made of dry rolled oats, dried fruit, and nuts.

This Bircher muesli is made without the traditional addition of yogurt or dairy; instead, I use homemade almond milk for richness (hemp milk will work too). It's also packed with super fruits such as goji berries and mulberries, as well as chia seeds, which provide antioxidants and omega-3 fatty acids. This dish is perfectly appropriate for hot summer temperatures, but it's filling enough to hold its own in the depths of winter too.

MAKES 4 SERVINGS

2 cups rolled oats

⅔ cup slivered almonds

1 large Fuji or Honeycrisp apple (or apple of choice), grated with a mandoline or box grater (about 1 cup)

⅓ cup goji berries

⅓ cup dried mulberries

4 tablespoons chia seeds

3 cups homemade or store-bought almond milk (homemade will be richer)

Place all the ingredients in a large bowl and soak overnight. In the morning, you can add a little extra almond milk, if needed, before serving.

Lunch

SWEET PEA HUMMUS TARTINES WITH SUNFLOWER SPROUTS

THIS ELEGANT LUNCHTIME "TARTINE" is ideal for spring. It features sweet pea hummus, which has a lighter texture and lemony flavor. If you can't find sunflower sprouts, you can top the tartine with any kind of sprout you like, or a simple sprinkling of raw greens, such as arugula or frisée.

You can use sprouted-grain bread, millet bread, or any commercially sold bread that suits you in this recipe.

MAKES 4 SERVINGS

2 cups cooked chickpeas
1½ cups fresh or frozen green peas, lightly steamed
¼ cup olive oil
2 to 3 tablespoons freshly squeezed lemon juice (to taste)
½ teaspoon sea salt
1 clove garlic, minced
2 tablespoons chopped fresh herbs (parsley, dill, or whatever you like)
8 slices wholesome bread of choice, toasted
2 cups sunflower sprouts or alfalfa or broccoli sprouts

1. Place all the ingredients except for the herbs, bread, and sprouts in a food processor or high-speed blender. Blend until creamy and smooth. Add some water if the mixture is too thick. At the end, pulse in fresh herbs, if using.

2. Spread ¼ cup of the hummus over each slice of bread. Top with ¼ cup of sprouts, and serve.

Stored in an airtight container in the fridge, the hummus will keep for up to 4 days.

SWEET POTATO SALAD WITH MISO DRESSING AND CHIVES

THIS SALAD IS SWEET, SALTY, AND filling. It's a perfect wintertime lunch component, and the chives give it perfectly subtle seasoning.

I hate peeling and chopping potatoes, so I prefer to roast them for this recipe, then scoop out the flesh. If you would rather peel them, cut them into ¾-inch chunks, and boil or steam them. That's fine too!

MAKES 4 SERVINGS

4 medium sweet potatoes (about 10 ounces each)
2 tablespoons mellow white miso

2 tablespoons olive oil

2 tablespoons hot water

1 tablespoon pure maple syrup or agave nectar

1 tablespoon brown rice vinegar

1 teaspoon freshly squeezed lemon juice

1 teaspoon toasted sesame oil

½ teaspoon ginger powder (if you use a high-speed blender to make this dressing, you can use ½ tablespoon grated fresh ginger instead)

½ ounce (12 grams) fresh chives

1. Preheat the oven to 400°F. Roast the potatoes until each is tender when pierced with a fork. Remove them from the oven and let cool. Cut the potatoes in half and scoop the flesh out. Cut into ¾-inch chunks (these will be rough, because the potato is soft) and set aside.

2. Whisk together the miso, oil, water, maple syrup, vinegar, lemon, sesame oil, and ginger, or use a blender or food processor to combine them well.

3. Toss the potatoes, chives, and dressing together (you may not need to use all of the dressing) and serve.

The salad will taste even better after the flavors marry for a day or two and can be kept for up to 4 days in the fridge.

Sweet Pea Hummus Tartines with Sunflower Sprouts, page 156

Sweet Potato Salad with Miso Dressing and Chives, page 156

APRICOT QUINOA AND MINT SALAD

FRESH MINT AND DRIED APRICOTS ARE a wonderful combination, and pine nuts add a perfect amount of crunch. If you like, you can use fresh apricots instead, or you can use toasted pine nuts for a little extra flavor. While the taste of mint adds unique freshness to this recipe, you can use basil, chives, dill, or any seasonal herbs that you have handy instead.

MAKES 4 SERVINGS

1 cup dry quinoa
2 cups low sodium vegetable broth
or water
½ cup chopped fresh mint
⅔ cup dried, sliced into thin pieces,
unsulfured apricots
½ cup pine nuts
½ cup Apple Cider Vinaigrette (page 126)
Sea salt and freshly ground black pepper

1. Transfer the quinoa to a metal sieve and rinse it under cold water. Transfer to a medium-size pot and add the broth. Bring the liquid to a boil, reduce the heat to a simmer, and place a lid on the pot, leaving it slightly askew so that steam can escape as the quinoa cooks. Continue simmering until all liquid is absorbed and the quinoa is plump (20 to 25 minutes). Fluff with a fork and let sit until the quinoa has cooled (this can be done a day or two in advance).

2. When the quinoa is cool, transfer it to a large mixing bowl and add the mint, apricots, and pine nuts. Add about ½ cup of the Apple Cider Vinaigrette to the bowl, and mix well. Season to taste with salt and pepper, add more vinaigrette if needed, and serve.

ASPARAGUS QUINOA SUSHI ROLLS

QUINOA IS A FUN, FLAVORFUL, AND gluten-free alternative to traditional brown rice in sushi rolls. It can be a little hard to work with because it's less sticky than regular sushi rice, but a little practice will give you the hang of it. Part of what makes the quinoa in this recipe so tasty is the addition of mirin, a sweet rice wine that is often used in Japanese cooking. Mirin is very pricey, so, if you don't wish to use it, adding a little sweetener here will do the trick.

MAKES 4 ROLLS

Apricot Quinoa and Mint Salad, page 158

Step 1: Asparagus Quinoa Sushi Rolls

Step 2: Asparagus Quinoa Sushi Rolls

Step 3: Asparagus Quinoa Sushi Rolls

3 cups cooked quinoa

2 tablespoons brown rice vinegar

1 teaspoon sesame oil

1½ tablespoons tamari, nama shoyu,
Bragg's Liquid Aminos, or coconut
aminos

1 tablespoon mirin (optional; if you don't
have mirin, add 1 teaspoon sweetener
of choice, such as agave nectar, pure
maple syrup, or coconut sugar)

4 nori wrappers

4 large stalks asparagus, lightly steamed

1 small avocado, sliced into ½-inch-thick
slices

1. Mix the quinoa, rice vinegar, sesame oil, tamari, and mirin (or sweetener) together in a mixing bowl.

2. Lay a sheet of nori, shiny side down, on a flat, dry surface in front of you. The shorter end of the sheet should be facing you. Spread ¾ cup of quinoa over the sheet, starting at the bottom. Allow ⅓ of the wrapper to remain bare (the third that is farthest away from you, at the top).

3. Lay an asparagus spear horizontally across the quinoa, about 2 inches from the bottom of the sheet. Top it with a few slices of avocado. Starting from the bottom, gently roll the nori up, applying pressure as you go. When you get to the top, moisten the top edge of the nori roll; this will help the roll stick together.

4. Use a very sharp knife to slice the roll into pieces (about five). Repeat with the three remaining nori sheets. Serve with tamari for dipping, or any dressing you like.

You can prepare the quinoa as instructed, and store it for up to 3 days in the fridge, rolling the sushi as desired.

CURRIED CHICKPEA AND CARROT SALAD

THIS SALAD IS REMINISCENT OF CUR-ried chicken salad (which I used to love), but the fiber makes it even more satisfying. If you've tried a similar dish with mayonnaise, you'll be surprised at how well tahini works as an alternate.

I like to serve this salad with greens and veggies, and sometimes a cup of soup as well. It also works as a dinner entrée, with some quinoa and steamed veggies.

MAKES 4 SERVINGS

Salad Ingredients
3 cups cooked chickpeas
1½ cups grated carrots
½ cup currants or raisins

Dressing Ingredients
3 tablespoons tahini
1 tablespoon freshly squeezed lemon
   juice
1 tablespoon apple cider vinegar
2 tablespoons water
1 tablespoon tamari, nama shoyu,
   Bragg's Liquid Aminos, or coconut
   aminos
2 teaspoons pure maple syrup
1 teaspoon curry powder

1. Combine the salad ingredients in a large mixing bowl.

2. Whisk all the dressing ingredients together.

3. Dress the salad ingredients with the dressing. Serve.

The chickpea salad will keep for up to 3 days in the fridge.

EASIEST VEGAN PUMPKIN SOUP

THE TITLE PRETTY MUCH SAYS IT ALL. Using fresh puree of pumpkin will certainly enhance this soup, but, to make it true to its name, go ahead and used canned, organic pumpkin instead.

MAKES 2 SERVINGS

1 can (15 oz.) organic pumpkin puree,
   or 1½ cups fresh pureed pumpkin,
   butternut squash, or sweet potato
1¼ cups organic vegetable broth
¼ cup cashews, soaked for 2 hours and
   drained, or ¼ cup silken tofu, 3 tablespoons cashew butter, or 3 tablespoons
   tahini
1 tablespoon pure maple syrup
1 teaspoon pumpkin pie spice
1 clove garlic, minced (optional)
¼ teaspoon sea salt (or to taste—will
   depend on the saltiness of your vegetable broth)
Freshly ground black pepper

Blend all the ingredients in a blender until smooth. Heat gently over a stove, and serve.

The soup will keep for up to 4 days in the fridge, and it can easily be frozen.

Dinner

SWEET POTATO BLACK BEAN ENCHILADAS

THIS RECIPE IS A LOT OF WORK, BUT the labor will be well worth it when you bite into these incredibly flavorful enchiladas. They may be the most beloved cooked recipe on my blog, and I've made them for countless dinner parties, potlucks, and get-togethers.

If you're in a pinch, simply use an organic, canned tomato sauce and whisk in a teaspoon of chili powder or cumin, rather than preparing the sauce as directed. With this sweet, fragrant sweet potato and black bean filling, you can't possibly go wrong.

MAKES 4 SERVINGS

Sauce Ingredients

1 tablespoon olive oil
1 cup diced onion
2 cloves garlic, minced
½ tablespoon chili powder
1 teaspoon ground cumin
1 teaspoon fresh oregano, or ½ teaspoon dried
1 (14-ounce) can diced tomatoes (I like Muir Glen fire roasted)
1 teaspoon pure maple syrup
Sea salt

Enchilada Ingredients

3 large sweet potatoes
1 cup yellow onion
Coconut oil
2 cups (or 1 [15-ounce] can) cooked black beans
1 tablespoon almond butter
1 tablespoon freshly squeezed lime juice
½ to 1 teaspoon salt (to taste)
1 teaspoon cumin
1½ teaspoons chili powder
Freshly ground black pepper
8 to 10 corn or whole-grain tortillas
¼ cup minced fresh curly parsley (optional)

1. Preheat the oven to 375°F.

To make the enchilada sauce, heat the olive oil in a medium-size skillet or pot. Sauté the onion for 3 minutes. Add the garlic and continue cooking for another 5 minutes, or until the onion is translucent.

2. Add the chili powder, cumin, oregano, tomatoes, maple syrup, and ⅓ cup of water. Add sea salt to taste. Cook for another minute or two, until all the ingredients are warmed through.

3. Transfer the sauce to a blender or food processor, and blend until smooth. Add water to adjust the consistency as you wish. Set the sauce aside until you're ready to use it.

4. Pierce the sweet potatoes with a fork, place them on a foil-lined baking sheet, and

Sweet Potato Black Bean Enchiladas, page 163

bake until tender (35 to 45 minutes). When the potatoes are cool enough to be handled, scoop the flesh, mash it a little with a fork, and set it aside. You can discard the skins or use them as desired.

5. Sauté the onion in the coconut oil until translucent. Add the sweet potatoes, black beans, almond butter, lime juice, salt, cumin, chili powder, and black pepper, and mix well with a wooden spoon. You can use a potato masher to get it all well combined! You want the final mixture to look like a very chunky mash.

6. Preheat the oven to 350°F.

7. Assemble your enchiladas by rolling about ¼ to ⅓ cup of the filling into each of your tortillas, and laying them side by side in a small rectangular baking dish. Cover them with all of the enchilada sauce (they're supposed to be smothered).

8. Bake for about 25 minutes, until the sauce has darkened and enchiladas are hot (if you make the filling ahead and refrigerate it, you'll maybe need a few more minutes than this). Serve, sprinkled with parsley if desired.

The enchiladas can easily be frozen and will keep for up to 4 days in the fridge.

CARROT AND MILLET PILAF WITH MESQUITE GLAZED TEMPEH

TEMPEH, LIKE TOFU, IS TREMENDOUSLY high in protein, has been associated with reduced cholesterol, and has a high calcium content. Unlike tofu, it's fermented, which helps to make some of the nutrients, such as zinc and calcium, more bioavailable. It's also rich in vitamin B5, vitamin B6, and it boasts nearly a quarter of your daily recommended iron intake.

I use tempeh in stir-fries or on top of salads all the time. My favorite way to serve tempeh, though, is to marinate it with mesquite, and then bake or grill it. Mesquite is a legume native to northern Mexico. It's smoky, sweet, and incredibly flavorful. You can find mesquite online or in specialty shops. If you can't get your hands on it, though, the recipe will still be delicious without it.

MAKES 4 SERVINGS

Tempeh Ingredients

2 tablespoons tamari, nama shoyu, Bragg's Liquid Aminos, or coconut aminos
1½ tablespoons apple cider vinegar
1½ tablespoons pure maple syrup
2 teaspoons mesquite powder
1 teaspoon chili powder
½ teaspoon toasted sesame oil
8 ounces tempeh, sliced into ½-inch-thick slices

1. Whisk together all the ingredients, except the tempeh, in a mixing bowl. Lay the tempeh slices in a shallow, small dish (I use a 7 by 11–inch baking pan) and pour the marinade over them. Allow them to marinate for a few hours (or while you're at work, if you like).

2. Preheat your oven to 350°F. Transfer the tempeh to the oven and bake for 25 to 30 minutes, or until the tempeh is browning. Set the tempeh aside.

Pilaf Ingredients

1 tablespoon coconut oil
1 clove garlic, minced
1 cup chopped yellow onion
1 cup chopped carrot
1½ teaspoons mild curry powder
¼ teaspoon sea salt
1 teaspoon turmeric
Pinch cayenne
1 cup millet
1 cup carrot juice (fresh or commercial)
1⅓ cups vegetable broth

1. Heat the coconut oil in a large pot or medium-size Dutch oven. Add the garlic and onion and sauté over medium heat for 4 to 5 minutes, or until the onion is translucent. Add the carrot and sauté for another 5 minutes.

2. Add the curry, sea salt, turmeric, and cayenne to the pot and combine with the vegetables. Add the millet and cook it for a minute or so, before adding the carrot juice and vegetable broth.

3. Bring mixture to a boil and lower the heat to a simmer. Place the lid of the pot or oven on, ajar, and simmer for 30 minutes, or until all the liquid has been absorbed. Check on it at 25 minutes, and, if it looks close to ready, remove it from the heat. Once the millet is ready, fluff it with a fork and allow it to sit for 5 minutes before serving.

4. Divide the pilaf onto four plates. Top it with a quarter of the tempeh, and serve with a fresh salad.

Tempeh will keep for up to 4 days in the fridge. Millet pilaf will keep for up to 3 days, and leftovers can be frozen.

QUICK QUINOA AND BLACK BEAN SALAD WITH SPICY CILANTRO VINAIGRETTE

THIS SALAD IS A PERFECT SOLUTION when you're short on time but hoping to impress with bold, tangy flavors. As soon as the quinoa is cooked, you can throw the dish together in minutes (and it's a perfect reason to keep some batch cooked quinoa on hand). It's one of the most popular entrées on my blog. Feel free to replace the vinaigrette with any vinaigrette of your choosing, but the spicy cilantro gives it a really nice kick.

MAKES 4 SERVINGS

1 cup dried quinoa, rinsed
Dash salt
1 cup seeded and neatly diced cucumber
1 cup seeded and neatly diced red bell
　pepper
1½ cups cooked black beans, or
　1 (15-ounce) can
10 to 15 fresh basil leaves, chopped into
　thin strips, plus more for garnish
1 batch Spicy Cilantro Vinaigrette
　(page 127)

1. Cook the quinoa in salted water until tender and fluffy (use a rice cooker or follow the package instructions). Remove from the heat, let cool, and place in a bowl.

2. Add the chopped vegetables, black beans, and basil to the cooked quinoa.

3. Dress the salad with ⅔ cup of the Spicy Cilantro Vinaigrette. (Add more or less of the

Carrot and Millet Pilaf with Mesquite Glazed Tempeh, page 165

dressing as desired.) Garnish with basil and serve.

The salad will keep for up to 3 days and tastes particularly nice after the flavors have mingled overnight.

EASY RED LENTIL, SWEET POTATO, AND COCONUT CURRY

HEARTY, FILLING, AND NUTRITIOUS, this curry can be prepped beforehand and warmed when you're ready to eat, but it's actually quick enough that you can make it at the last minute too. As soon as the vegetables are chopped, the hard work is done. Red lentils have many of the same nutrients as beans (iron, protein), but their rapid cooking time makes them a convenient alternative.

MAKES 4 SERVINGS

1½ tablespoons coconut oil
1 cup diced onion
1 cup dried red lentils
1 medium sweet potato, cut into 1-inch cubes
1 large carrot, split lengthwise and chopped
½ teaspoon ground turmeric
1 tablespoon mild curry powder
1 teaspoon ginger powder
½ teaspoon sea salt

Freshly ground black pepper
3½ cups vegetable broth or water
½ cup coconut milk

1. Heat the oil in a large pot over medium heat. Sauté onion until it's turning a little golden. Add the lentils, potato, carrot, and spices/seasonings, and stir to combine everything.

2. Add the water or broth and bring to a boil. Reduce the heat to a simmer and cook for 25 minutes, or until the lentils and sweet potato are tender. Stir in the ½ cup of coconut milk. Serve.

Curry will keep for up to 4 days in the fridge. Leftovers can be frozen.

ROOT "RAWVIOLI" WITH NUT CHEESE AND PESTO

RAWVIOLI IS A CLASSIC RAW FOOD dish. It's usually made with beets, but turnip slices and jicama slices work very well too. Feel free to dress the rawvioli up with marinara sauce instead of pesto, or dress with cashew cream. If none of those options suit your fancy, a simple sprinkle of herbs is fine too!

MAKES 4 SERVINGS

Rawvioli Ingredients
2 large beets, scrubbed, peeled, and
   rinsed

Nut Cheese Ingredients
1 batch Cashew Cheese (page 99)
1 tablespoon fresh oregano, or 2
   teaspoons dried

Pesto Ingredients
1 batch Kale and Pistachio Pesto (page
   136).

1. Cut the beets in half through the center, horizontally (so you're separating the top half from the bottom, not the right side from the left side). Use a mandoline to slice them into very thin (almost paper thin) slices. You'll want between thirty-two and forty slices altogether (four or five rawvioli per person).

2. Prepare the Cashew Cheese. At the end, stir in the oregano.

3. Prepare the Kale and Pistachio Pesto.

4. Place four or five beet slices on a serving place. Place a heaping tablespoon of cashew cheese on top of each slice. Place another beet slice on top of the cheese, and press down slightly to flatten the rawvioli. Top with a dollop of pesto. Repeat on the three remaining plates, and serve.

ZUCCHINI PASTA WITH QUINOA MEATLESS BALLS

THIS RECIPE TAKES TIME AND EFFORT, but they will be well worth it if you're looking to create the taste of traditional Italian comfort food with a whole foods, semiraw spin! The quinoa balls are delicious,

Root "Rawvioli" with Nut Cheese and Pesto, page 168

and you can throw them into salads or snack on them if you have leftovers. As with nearly any recipe in which I call for my raw marinara, you can use your favorite organic, store-bought marinara instead. In that case, all you'll need to do is spiralize your noodles and prepare the meatless balls.

MAKES 4 SERVINGS

Pasta Ingredients

4 small zucchini, spiralized or cut with a julienne peeler

Marinara Ingredients

Organic, store-bought marinara sauce of choice or 1 batch Raw Marinara Sauce (page 135)

Quinoa Meatless Balls Ingredients

MAKES 24 TO 30 MEATBALLS

1 tablespoon olive oil
¾ cup onion, diced
1 clove garlic, minced
1 cup chopped button or baby bella mushrooms
½ cup chopped, sun-dried tomatoes, soaked in warm water for 10 minutes or more, then drained
2 cups cooked quinoa
2 tablespoons chopped fresh oregano (or 1 teaspoon, dried)
½ cup cooked cannellini or navy beans
Sea salt and freshly ground black pepper

Zucchini Pasta with Quinoa Meatless Balls, page 168

1. Heat the olive oil in a large sauté pan over medium heat. Add the onion and garlic. Cook until the onion and garlic are translucent (5 minutes). Add the mushrooms and continue cooking until the mushrooms are tender, another 4 to 5 minutes or so.

2. Add the sun-dried tomatoes, quinoa, oregano, and beans to the pan. Stir until everything is warm and evenly mixed, about 2 minutes.

3. Transfer all the ingredients to a food processor. Pulse to combine, and then process until the ingredients are mostly uniform, about a minute.

4. Roll the ingredients into 1-inch balls.

Let them sit for 30 minutes. While you wait, preheat the oven to 400°F and line a large baking sheet with parchment. Place the balls on the baking sheet and bake for 20 to 25 minutes, or until they're lightly browned.

To assemble:

Divide the zucchini among four serving bowls. Top with ⅓ to ½ cup of marinara sauce, and a quarter of the meatballs.

Marinara sauce will keep for up to 5 days in the fridge and can be frozen. The quinoa meatballs can be frozen and will keep in the fridge for up to 4 days.

LEVEL 2
Something New

L EVEL TWO RECIPES ARE DESIGNED TO TAKE YOU OUTSIDE YOUR COMFORT ZONE—BUT not too much. Here you'll find more raw food recipes, including a dressed up chia pudding, raw wraps made from collard leaves, and nori rolls stuffed with a savory raw nut "pâté." I'll also show you familiar dishes that have been dressed up with unconventional ingredients, like quinoa "risotto." I hope these dishes will help you to think outside the box a little, and whet your appetite for raw food.

Breakfast

PLANT PROTEIN SHAKE

THE NEXT TIME SOMEONE GIVES YOU A hard time about protein and vegan diets, you can tell them that this easy vegan smoothie has as much protein as two eggs. It also has healthy, omega-3 fatty acids, phyto-nutrients, magnesium, potassium, natural sugars to sustain your morning energy, and it tastes delicious. Hemp protein is probably my favorite variety of vegan protein powder; the taste takes a little getting used to, but I've come to really love it—and the many health benefits it provides.

MAKES 2 SERVINGS

2 large frozen bananas
2 tablespoons hemp seeds
4 tablespoons hemp protein
1½ cups almond or hemp milk
Seeds from ½ vanilla bean, or 1 teaspoon
    vanilla extract
OPTIONAL: 1 to 2 heaping cups baby
spinach
OPTIONAL: 1 pitted date (if you prefer
your smoothie to be sweeter)

Blend all the ingredients together in a blender and serve. Add more almond or hemp milk as needed.

MANGO COCONUT CHIA PUDDING

THIS BREAKFAST WILL BRIGHTEN YOUR morning with its tropical flavors. Sweet, juicy mango meets creamy coconut chia pudding and a hint of vanilla. You can either mix in the mango or layer it on the bottom, as shown, but it will be easier to store if you keep the components separate. The pudding should last about 3 days in the fridge.

Since coconut milk is very rich, I mix it with almond milk to avoid overpowering the pudding. Commercial almond milk works well here, since it's not quite as creamy as the coconut.

MAKES 4 SMALL OR 2 LARGE SERVINGS

½ cup coconut milk
1 cup almond milk
2 tablespoons pure maple syrup
1 teaspoon vanilla extract or the seeds of
    1 vanilla bean
⅓ cup chia seeds
1½ cups diced fresh mango
¼ cup unsweetened shredded coconut

1. Whisk or blend together the coconut and almond milk, maple syrup, and vanilla.
2. Combine the liquid with the chia seeds. Stir until combined. Let the mixture sit for 5

Mango Coconut Chia Pudding, page 172

Baked Sweet Potatoes with Vanilla Almond Butter and Goji Berries, page 175

minutes, then stir again. After another few minutes, give it one final stir before allowing it to sit for an hour or more. (If you're letting it sit for more than an hour, refrigerate the pudding.)

3. Spoon a quarter of the mango into the bottom of four serving bowls or glasses. Top with a quarter of the chia pudding. Top with one tablespoon of shredded coconut. Serve.

The chia pudding will keep in the fridge for 3 days.

BAKED SWEET POTATOES WITH VANILLA ALMOND BUTTER AND GOJI BERRIES

SWEET POTATOES MAY SEEM LIKE AN odd choice for breakfast. Nevertheless, they're not only warm, grounding, and satisfying but also rich in beta-carotene, fiber, and minerals. For folks who are tired of oatmeal or other hot breakfast cereals, they'll fulfill your carb craving and add variety to your routine.

You can serve baked sweet potatoes with coconut oil and a sprinkle of granola, if you like, or even top them with black beans for a savory breakfast option. This recipe, though, is my favorite serving idea: almond butter, vanilla, and a sprinkle of nutrient-rich goji berries.

MAKES 2 SERVINGS

2 medium sweet potatoes, unpeeled
¼ cup almond butter
1 teaspoon vanilla extract
½ teaspoon ground cinnamon
1 tablespoon pure maple syrup
2 to 3 tablespoons almond milk
¼ cup goji berries

1. Preheat the oven to 375°F. Wash the sweet potatoes, then prick them with a fork. Lay them on a baking sheet and bake until they're totally tender, about 45 minutes.

2. While the potatoes are baking, mix the almond butter, vanilla, cinnamon, maple syrup, and almond milk together using a fork or a small whisk.

3. Split the potatoes open. Drizzle half of the almond butter mixture over each. Top with half of the goji berries, and serve.

The almond butter can be doubled and stored for up to 2 weeks.

QUINOA BREAKFAST PUDDING

MOST OF US ARE USED TO THINKING about quinoa in the context of savory recipes. As it turns out, this super-grain is every bit as delicious in the morning. Try replacing your standard bowl of oats with a warm bowl of quinoa. You can serve the quinoa plain and top it with some almond butter and banana, or, if you'd like to get a little fancy, give this simple, yet decadent breakfast pudding a try. Coconut milk makes the pudding incredibly delicious and satisfying. Be sure to get full fat coconut milk; the "lite" stuff just isn't the same!

MAKES 4 SERVINGS

1 cup dry quinoa
1¼ cup full-fat coconut milk
1 vanilla bean, split lengthwise, seeds
  scraped out
Pinch sea salt
2 tablespoons pure maple syrup
2 cups berries (optional)

1. Transfer the quinoa to a sieve and run it under cold water to rinse it off. Drain the quinoa well.

2. Transfer the quinoa to a medium-size pot. Add 1 cup of the coconut milk, along with 1 cup of water. Add the vanilla bean, sea salt, and maple syrup and give it all a stir.

3. Bring the mixture to a boil, and reduce the heat to a simmer. Place the lid of the pot on, slightly ajar, so that some steam can escape. Simmer the quinoa until all of the liquid is absorbed and the quinoa is tender, about 15 or 20 minutes. Stir in the remaining ¼ cup of coconut milk.

4. Divide the pudding into four serving bowls. Top with fresh berries, if desired. Serve.

Leftover pudding will keep for a night or two in the fridge and can easily be reheated.

PEACHY KEEN SMOOTHIE

THIS SIMPLE SMOOTHIE IS A WONDERful way to enjoy ripe, juicy peaches in the summer (when you get tired of putting them into my Raw Peach Cobbler, page 233). If you have a high-speed blender, go ahead and use whole almonds in the recipe. If you don't, I recommend using almond butter instead (and using almond milk, rather than coconut water). The addition of cinnamon and ginger makes this smoothie taste like dessert.

MAKES 2 TO 3 SERVINGS

3 cups sliced peaches, fresh or frozen
2 tablespoons flax meal
¼ cup almonds (or 3 tablespoons almond
  butter if you don't have a high-speed
  blender)
1 cup coconut water or almond milk
1 teaspoon ground cinnamon
½ teaspoon ginger powder (or 2 teaspoons
  grated fresh ginger)

Blend all the ingredients until very smooth.

Quinoa Breakfast Pudding, page 175

Avocado Black Bean Breakfast Scramble, page 179

AVOCADO BLACK BEAN BREAKFAST SCRAMBLE

THIS HASHLIKE SCRAMBLE IS BOTH filling and fresh—a perfect example of how harmoniously raw and cooked ingredients can work together! It's also rich in protein from beans and nutritional yeast and packed with fiber, which means that it's a nutritious start to your day.

MAKES 4 SERVINGS

2 large avocados (about 12 ounces),
    peeled and, pitted, and diced into
    ¾-inch chunks
1½ tablespoons freshly squeezed lime
    juice
¼ teaspoon sea salt
Freshly ground black pepper
2½ tablespoons nutritional yeast
1 red bell pepper, seeded and chopped
1 large carrot, grated (about ½ cup)
⅓ cup diced red onion
½ cup minced fresh parsley
1 cup cooked black beans
8 lettuce or cabbage leaves
4 slices sprouted-grain bread (optional)

1. Place the avocados in a large mixing bowl and, using a fork, mash them lightly with the lime juice, sea salt, pepper, and nutritional yeast.

2. Add the pepper, carrot, onion, parsley, and beans. Mix well, until the avocado resembles a "scramble" and the veggies are distributed evenly.

3. Scoop into lettuce or cabbage leaves and serve (about two per person). You can also eat this piled high on sprouted-grain toast.

To keep leftovers fresh, sprinkle them with lemon juice before storing in an airtight container in the fridge. Kept this way, the hash should last for 2 days.

Lunch

RAW GAZPACHO

GAZPACHO IS ONE OF THOSE RECIPES we all know and love and eat all the time but rarely think to classify as "vegan" or "raw." This recipe has traditional flavors, but I've left out the bread crumbs. Once you toss all of the ingredients into your blender, all you need to do is press a button to get a delicious, nutritious soup.

With this gazpacho, and all raw soups, I like to add a little topping for texture and variety. I suggest the corn salsa on page 138 as an accompaniment, but, if you don't have time, you could just add some avocado chunks to the soup and start to dig in. A dollop of cashew cream is also delightful!

MAKES 4 SERVINGS

4 large vine tomatoes, quartered
¼ cup sun-dried tomatoes, soaked for at least an hour and rinsed off
1 red bell pepper, seeded and cut into chunks
1 cucumber, peeled and cut into chunks
½ white or yellow onion, roughly chopped
1 clove garlic, minced
1½ teaspoons pure maple syrup
2 tablespoons freshly squeezed lime or lemon juice
¼ teaspoon sea salt
Freshly ground black pepper
3 tablespoons extra-virgin olive oil

1. Blend all the ingredients except for the olive oil in a blender, adding ¼ cup of water or more as needed.

2. With the blender running, drizzle in the olive oil until the soup is creamy and smooth.

3. Divide the gazpacho into four serving bowls. Top with any mixed vegetables you like (cucumber, peppers, tomato, avocado) or a salsa of choice (such as my Raw Corn Salsa, page 138).

The gazpacho is best served fresh, but it will keep overnight if you don't polish it all off at once.

HEMP-SEED TABOULI WITH YELLOW TOMATOES AND MINT

HEMP-SEED TABOULI IS ANOTHER classic raw food recipe. While I'm all for making tabouli the traditional way—with bulgur wheat, or even an unusual grain, such as quinoa or millet—tabouli takes on a whole new life when it's created with nutrient dense, protein rich hemp seeds. In this recipe, I like to use bright green mint as well as parsley, and I love to use yellow tomatoes for a pop of unexpected color. Of course, red tomatoes will work fine if you don't have yellow ones, and you can use all parsley if mint isn't on hand.

MAKES 4 SERVINGS

Raw Gazpacho, page 180

1 cup fresh parsley

½ cup fresh mint

¼ teaspoon sea salt

4 medium yellow vine or Jersey tomatoes, chopped

1 cup shelled hemp seeds

2 tablespoons hemp oil

2 tablespoons freshly squeezed lemon juice

1. In a food processor fitted with the "S" blade, process the parsley, mint, and sea salt until minced.

2. Transfer the herbs and salt to a large mixing bowl. Add the tomatoes, hemp seeds, hemp oil, and lemon juice. Mix well, and serve.

Stored in an airtight container in the fridge, the tabouli will keep for 2 days.

NORI ROLLS WITH GINGERY ALMOND PÂTÉ AND RAW VEGGIES

ONCE YOU'VE MASTERED THE QUINOA sushi rolls on page 159, you'll be ready to dip your toes into the waters of raw sushi. There are many ways to make raw sushi rolls: you can fill them with raw "rice" made of parsnips or cauliflower, or you can mash up avocado as a filling and then pile them with veggies. I think the easiest raw sushi method, at least at first, is to spread a layer of nut pâté onto a nori sheet and then add veggies of your choosing, before you roll it all up to perfection.

MAKES 4 SERVINGS

Gingery Carrot Almond Pâté Ingredients

MAKES 1 ¼ CUPS PÂTÉ

1 ¼ cup almonds, soaked overnight and drained

½ teaspoon sea salt

2 pitted dates

1 tablespoon minced or grated ginger, or ½ teaspoon ginger powder

⅔ cup shredded carrot

½ teaspoon ground turmeric

Nori Roll Ingredients

4 raw or toasted nori sheets

1 bell pepper, cut into matchsticks

1 medium cucumber, cut into matchsticks

1 cup spiralized jicama or zucchini

1. To make the pâté, place almonds, sea salt, dates, ginger, carrot, and turmeric in your food processor. Pulse to combine. Turn on the motor and drizzle in ¼ cup of water. Keep processing until the mixture has the texture of a rich pâté—dense, but spreadable. Add extra water as needed (you'll probably need about ⅓ cup).

2. Lay a sheet of nori, shiny side down, on a flat, dry surface in front of you. The shorter end of the sheet should be facing you. Spread ⅓ cup of pâté over the sheet, leaving ⅓ of the sheet blank (this should be the third that is farthest away from you). Place ½ cup of the vegetables in a straight, horizontal line across the pâté, about 2 inches from the bottom of the sheet.

3. Working from the bottom end of the nori sheet (the end closest to you, with the

filling on it), roll the sheet upward. Moisten the top edge with water and be sure to hold it down for a moment or two when you've rolled the whole sheet up. Repeat with three more sheets and let the rolls soften for a few moments. Using a clean, sharp knife, cut each roll into five or so pieces. Serve with some tamari, if desired.

The nori rolls will keep overnight in the fridge. Otherwise, the gingery carrot almond paste will keep for up to 5 days, and you can make new rolls as needed!

COLLARD WRAPS WITH HEMP HUMMUS, TEMPEH, AND RED PEPPERS

THIS IS AN EASY, ACCESSIBLE WAY TO get into collard wraps. The marriage of mesquite tempeh and tomato is reminiscent of a BLT. I love this lunch because, if you prep the components early in the week, it's easy to assemble, and also because it's incredibly high in protein.
MAKES 4 SERVINGS

4 medium collard leaves
1 batch Hemp Hummus (page 130)
1 large Jersey or heirloom tomato, cut into thick slices
1 batch Mesquite Glazed Tempeh (page 165)

1. Prepare the collard leaf according to instructions on page 184.
2. Spread about ⅓ cup of hemp hummus along the center of the collard leaf. Layer a quarter of the tomato over the hummus, and top with a quarter of the hummus.
3. Roll the collard wrap up according to my tutorial (page 184). Slice the wrap in half, and serve.
  Collard wraps can be kept overnight in the fridge.

SPROUTED-GRAIN WRAPS WITH KALE-SLAW FILLING

THE KALE-SLAW IN THIS RECIPE IS wonderfully versatile and tasty. If you'd rather serve it on its own or as a side dish, that's fine—no need to stuff it into a wrap! But I think it makes a great wrap filling, especially when it's topped by some creamy avocado.
MAKES 4 SERVINGS

6 cups stemmed, washed, dried, and finely chopped raw kale
1 red bell pepper, seeded and diced
1 cup shredded carrot
½ cup Apple Cider Vinaigrette (page 126)
⅓ cup golden raisins (regular is fine too)
¼ cup raw sunflower seeds
¼ cup sliced almonds
4 Ezekiel sprouted-grain tortillas (or brown rice tortillas)

1. Mix the kale, pepper, and carrots in a large mixing bowl. Add ½ cup of the Apple Cider Vinaigrette (you can use more or less, to taste) and "massage" the kale well with your hands, until it's well coated and softened.
2. Add the raisins, seeds, and almonds. Toss the salad well to combine.
3. Stuff each tortilla with a heaping cup of kale salad. Wrap up the tortilla as you would a burrito. Repeat with the remaining wraps. Serve each with a bit of extra remaining kale-slaw.

Carrot, Avocado, and Turmeric Soup, page 187

CARROT, AVOCADO, AND TURMERIC SOUP

CARROT AND AVOCADO WAS MY FIRST ever raw soup. Nothing could be easier: Carrot juice and avocado blend up easily, so you can use a food processor, any blender, or a magic bullet. The soup is a little spicy and a little sweet, and pumpkin seeds give it the perfect hint of crunch.

MAKES 2 SERVINGS

2 ½ cups fresh carrot juice (bottled is okay if you can't get your hands on fresh)
1 medium or large Haas avocado peeled and pitted
½ teaspoon powdered ginger powder (or 1 teaspoon fresh, grated)
½ tablespoon tamari
½ teaspoon ground turmeric
1 tablespoon freshly squeezed lime juice
¼ cup pumpkin seeds

1. Blend all the ingredients except for the pumpkin seeds in a blender or food processor until rich and creamy.

2. Heat a skillet over medium heat and add the pumpkin seeds and a sprinkle of salt to the skillet. Toast the pumpkin seeds until they're just turning golden. Quickly transfer them to a cool plate.

For a raw version, you can soak the pumpkin seeds overnight and drain them. Dust them with a pinch of salt and dehydrate them at 115°F for 6 to 8 hours, or until totally dry.

3. Divide the soup into two bowls and top with the pumpkin seeds.

Dinner

RAW CARROT FALAFEL

FALAFEL IS ONE OF MY FAVORITE foods, but I often find that it's too greasy when prepared conventionally. These falafel, which I first created when I had a ton of pulp left over from making carrot juice, impart all the wonderful flavor of regular falafel, minus the deep frying.

Once you make the falafel, you can use them in pita, pile them into romaine leaves, put them on your salads, or snack on them as they are. And this is one of those recipes where there's little difference between the dehydrator version and the baked version, so no need to fear if you don't have a dehydrator at home!

MAKES 4 SERVINGS

1 cup sesame seeds
½ teaspoon sea salt
1½ cups carrot pulp from juicing or
    1½ cups finely grated carrot, squeezed
    firmly between paper towels to remove
    excess moisture
2 cloves garlic, minced
1 tablespoon freshly squeezed lemon juice
¼ teaspoon ground cumin (optional)
2 tablespoons flax meal
¼ cup fresh curly parsley

1. Grind the sesame seeds and sea salt in a food processor until finely ground.

2. Add the carrot pulp, garlic, lemon, cumin, if using, and flax, along with ⅓ cup of water. Process until the mixture is smooth.

3. Add the parsley to the processor and pulse to combine.

4. Shape the mixture into twelve small patties. Dehydrate at 115°F for 6 hours, flipping once through.

Alternatively, preheat the oven to 350°F. Bake the falafel for 15 minutes. Flip and cook for another 10 minutes, or until golden brown on both sides. Top with tangy tahini sauce, and serve.

Stored in an airtight container in the fridge, both dehydrated and baked falafel will keep for up to 4 days. They can also be frozen.

TANGY TAHINI SAUCE

MAKES 1 SCANT CUP SAUCE

½ cup water
¼ cup tahini
¼ teaspoon sea salt
3 tablespoons freshly squeezed lemon
    juice
1 clove garlic, minced
1 teaspoon agave nectar or pure maple
    syrup

Raw Carrot Falafel, page 188, and Hemp Seed Tabouli with Yellow Tomatoes and Mint, page 180

Heat-Free Lentil and Walnut Tacos, page 191

Combine all the ingredients in a blender or food processor. Blend and serve.

Tahini dressing will keep for a week in the fridge and can also be served over salads, with raw veggies, and warm grains.

HEAT-FREE LENTIL AND WALNUT TACOS

TO ME, THIS DISH EMBODIES FLEXI-ble, high raw cuisine at its finest. Using romaine leaves as a "taco" and walnut as part of the taco "meat" are standard raw foodie tricks, but the addition of cooked lentils adds extra protein, iron, and healthy complex carbs. This is a stress-free meal, easy to whip up at a moment's notice if you have some lentils in the freezer, and you can top it however you like!

MAKES 4 SERVINGS

Taco Filling Ingredients

1½ cups raw walnuts
½ teaspoon sea salt (or to taste)
10 sun-dried tomatoes, soaked in warm water for 10 minutes and drained
½ teaspoon chili powder
¼ teaspoon ground cumin
¼ teaspoon ground coriander
1 cup cooked brown or green lentils

Serving Ingredients

8 large romaine leaves (cabbage, radicchio, and butter lettuce leaves also work well)
1 cup salsa of choice
1 avocado, pitted and sliced

1. Place the walnuts and sea salt in a food processor and pulse to break the nuts down until crumbly.

2. Add the tomatoes, spices, and lentils to the processor. Pulse until the mixture is well incorporated. Check for seasoning, and add additional salt, cumin, or chili as needed. Add a few tablespoons of water, if needed, to bind the mixture together.

3. Divide the filling into the romaine leaves. Top each with 2 tablespoons of salsa and a few avocado slices. Serve.

RAW PAD THAI

KELP NOODLES ARE MADE FROM KELP, a type of seaweed that's rich in calcium, iron, and especially rich in iodine. The noodles are made with the use of sodium alginate, a type of salt, and they're typically made without the use of heat, which is why they're very popular with raw foodists. They're a little bit crunchy, very light, and they make for a wonderful alternative to conventional wheat pasta. Iodine is necessary in the diet, but it's possible to overconsume it, so I don't recommend eating kelp noodles more than once or twice a week.

As you'll see, I like to serve kelp noodles in a variety of ways, but this pad Thai recipe is one of my favorites. The sauce is deeply enriched by the use of tamarind paste, a specialty ingredient made from tamarind fruit that can be found at any Asian market, or through online retailers.

MAKES 4 SERVINGS

Pad Thai "Noodle" Ingredients

1 package (12 ounces) kelp noodles
1 cup carrot, julienned or peeled into slips
    with a vegetable peeler
1 cup julienned or spiralized zucchini
1 cup shredded red cabbage
½ cup chopped cilantro

Pad Thai Sauce Ingredients
(makes 1 cup)

6 tablespoons almond butter
1 tablespoon tamarind paste
1 teaspoon toasted sesame oil
1 tablespoon tamari
1 tablespoon pure maple syrup
½ teaspoon powdered ginger (or 1
    tablespoon grated, fresh ginger)
½ cup water

1. Soak the kelp noodles in warm water for 10 to 15 minutes. Shake them dry, then pat them very dry with a paper towel or kitchen towel. Use a pair of scissors to snip them into smaller pieces.

2. Blend all the sauce ingredients, along with one ½ cup of water, in a blender until smooth.

3. Mix the noodles thoroughly with the vegetables and cilantro. Add ½ cup of sauce and mix in. Add more sauce if needed, until the noodles are thoroughly coated with sauce. Serve, garnished with cilantro.

The pad Thai sauce will last for a week in the fridge. The noodle dish will keep for 2 days in the fridge.

RAW SPINACH AND MUSHROOM BURGERS

I ABSOLUTELY LOVE CREATING RAW "burgers"—it's proof that any recipe, even one associated fundamentally with meat-eating, can be playfully created in raw vegan form. These burgers are packed with antioxidant-rich vegetables, including both spinach and mushrooms. You can either bake or dehydrate the burgers, and the leftovers are excellent.

MAKES 4 BURGERS

2 tablespoons low sodium tamari, low
    sodium nama shoyu, or coconut aminos
1 teaspoon smoked paprika
1 tablespoon pure maple syrup or agave
    nectar
1½ tablespoons apple cider vinegar
3 large portobello mushroom caps,
    cleaned and chopped
1¼ cups dried pumpkin seeds
½ cup chopped carrot (or carrot pulp left
    over from juicing)
½ cup chopped celery (or celery pulp left
    over from juicing)
1 cup baby spinach
1 teaspoon rosemary or thyme

1. Mix the tamari, paprika, maple syrup, and apple cider vinegar in a bowl. Add the mushrooms and mix them well into this marinade. Let them sit for about 2 hours.

2. In a food processor fitted with the "S" blade, grind the pumpkin seeds until smooth.

Raw Pad Thai, page 191

3. Remove the mushrooms from the marinade (reserving leftover marinade as you do) and add them to the processor. Process until the mixture has very little texture, but isn't as smooth or uniform as a nut pâté. If it's overly thick, add a few tablespoons of leftover marinade.

4. Add the carrot, celery, spinach, and thyme, and pulse to incorporate it all, still leaving some texture in the mixture.

5. Shape the mixture into four patties and dehydrate at 115°F for 3 hours. Flip the burgers and continue dehydrating for another 3 or 4 hours, or until they're still a little pliant, but firm on the outside.

Alternatively, you can bake these at 325°F for 30 to 35 minutes, flipping once. Serve.

Spinach burgers, whether raw or baked, will keep in an airtight container in the fridge for up to 4 days. They can also be frozen.

Pumpkin Quinoa Risotto with Pomegranate Seeds, page 195

PUMPKIN QUINOA RISOTTO WITH POMEGRANATE SEEDS

EVERYONE LOVES CONVENTIONAL RIsotto, but there's no denying that it can get a little heavy—not to mention time-consuming! Quinoa risotto cooks much more quickly than a traditional risotto dish, and it boasts more complete protein and minerals. I especially love quinoa risotto when it's paired with creamy pumpkin and a surprising bite of pomegranate seeds.

As always, this recipe is customizable. Pureed butternut squash, acorn squash, or sweet potato will be fine in place of the pumpkin, and, if you don't have the pomegranate seeds, you can omit them entirely or try a sprinkle of goji berries for the same tanginess and sweetness.

MAKES 4 SERVINGS

1 tablespoon olive or coconut oil
1½ cups chopped onion
1 cup quinoa, rinsed in a sieve
2⅔ cups low sodium vegetable broth
1½ cups pumpkin or butternut squash puree
3 tablespoons nutritional yeast
1 tablespoon freshly squeezed lemon juice
¼ teaspoon sea salt (add more to taste)
½ cup pomegranate seeds

1. Heat the olive oil over medium-high heat in a large pot. Add the onion and sauté, stirring frequently, for 5 to 8 minutes, or until the onion is translucent and browning.

2. Add the quinoa and stir it in with the onion for a few minutes, to lightly toast the grain. Add 2 cups of the broth and bring to a boil. Reduce to a simmer and cook, covered, but with the lid of the pot slightly ajar.

3. When the quinoa has absorbed almost all of the liquid (15 to 18 minutes), stir in 1 cup of the pumpkin with an additional ⅓ cup of vegetable broth. Stir until the mixture has absorbed the liquid, about 3 minutes. Add the remaining ½ cup of pumpkin and ⅓ cup of broth, along with the nutritional yeast, lemon, and salt. Keep cooking until the quinoa is no longer liquidy but has the creamy texture of a risotto, about 5 minutes. Stir in the pomegranate seeds at the very end, or use them as a garnish when you plate each dish. Serve.

Leftover risotto will thicken up in the fridge, but you can reheat it with a splash of almond milk or vegetable broth. This dish will keep for 3 days. If you plan on having leftovers, you may want to sprinkle the pomegranate seeds on top of the risotto when you serve, rather than mixing them in, so that their color holds up. Leftover risotto can be frozen as well.

PORTOBELLO "STEAK" AND ROSEMARY CAULIFLOWER MASHED POTATOES

MY BEST FRIEND'S HUSBAND, WHO is by no means a raw vegan, requests these cauliflower "mashed potatoes" nearly every time I visit them. I don't blame him—who knew that nuts, cauliflower, and seasoning could create something so delicious? The portobello "steaks" in this recipe are incredibly easy to prepare (just let them marinate), so while the meal feels like a "fancier" raw dish, it's actually very accessible.

Serving the mashed potatoes with the steak will enhance their flavor. If you serve them on their own, you may wish to add a little nutritional yeast.

MAKES 4 SERVINGS

⅓ cup olive oil
¼ cup balsamic vinegar
¼ cup pure maple syrup
3 tablespoons tamari or nama shoyu
Pinch freshly ground black pepper
4 portobello mushroom caps, stems removed and gills scraped out (you can do this with a small spoon; simply scrape the inside of the mushroom until the dark gills come out easily)

1. Mix all the ingredients except for the mushrooms in a small casserole pan.

2. Submerge the four mushroom caps in the marinade. One hour will be enough for

Portobello "Steak" and Rosemary Cauliflower Mashed Potatoes, page 196

them to be ready, but it's even better to cover them and let them marinate overnight in the fridge. When ready to serve, pat off any excess marinade and serve with rosemary cauliflower mashed potatoes (recipe follows).

ROSEMARY CAULIFLOWER MASHED POTATOES

MAKES 4 SERVINGS

¾ cup pine nuts or cashews
½ teaspoon sea salt
1 pound (one average-size head) cauliflower, chopped
2 tablespoons nutritional yeast
1½ tablespoons freshly squeezed lemon
   juice
⅓ cup water
2 tablespoons chopped fresh rosemary

1. Place the pine nuts and sea salt in your food processor and process until finely ground.

2. Add half of the cauliflower and pulse until it's broken down into small pieces. Add the rest, along with the nutritional yeast, and pulse a few more times to break it down as well.

3. Turn the motor of the processor on and drizzle in the lemon and the water. You may need to stop several times to scrape the bowl down. Continue blending until the mixture is fluffy, light, and totally smooth.

4. Add the rosemary to the food processor and pulse to incorporate it. Serve the mashed potatoes with the mushrooms and a drizzle of extra marinade.

Store the mushrooms and cauliflower mashed potatoes in airtight containers in the fridge. Both will keep for 2 days.

LEVEL 3
Brave New World

EVEL THREE RECIPES WILL TAKE YOU DEEPER INTO RAW FOOD TECHNIQUES AND recipes. Here you'll find an exotic, chocolaty "açai bowl," a mocha maca chia pudding, jicama "rice," coconut curry kelp noodles, and even a raw ratatouille! As you explore this level, you'll meet ingredients that may be new to you (such as açai and maca), as well as unexpected flavor pairings, like basil and almond butter.

One of the best things about exploring raw foods is that you come across novel textures and flavors, and learn to be more innovative with the vegetables you already know and love. The idea of turning zucchini and carrots into "pappardelle" might sound odd at first, but, when you try it, you'll see how the idea of a pasta bowl can be given a fresh face. I hope these recipes will steer you in fun new directions, and inspire you to use fresh vegetables in creative ways.

Breakfast

MOCHA MACA CHIA PUDDING

MACA HAS A SWEET, NUTTY, AND slightly malty flavor. It tends to pair very well with sweet foods, and I enjoy it in chocolate, in puddings, and in smoothies.

In this dish, maca meets a touch of espresso and chocolate, which keeps the flavor very subtle. Because maca is gently stimulating, this dish is a fantastic morning wake-up call. If you think that the combination of maca plus espresso is too strong for you, feel free to use decaf espresso powder.

MAKES 2 SERVINGS

2 cups homemade almond milk
1 tablespoon pure maple syrup or agave nectar
4 tablespoons raw cacao (or unsweetened cocoa) powder
2 teaspoons maca
1 tablespoon instant espresso
6 tablespoons chia seeds

1. Blend the almond milk, maple syrup, cacao powder, maca, and espresso in a blender until smooth.

2. Pour the mixture over the chia seeds in a medium mixing bowl and stir. Allow the pudding to sit for a minute, then stir again. Continue to stir once every 8 to 10 minutes for 30 minutes.

3. Let the pudding sit, refrigerated, for a few hours. Serve with fresh berries.

Stored in an airtight container, the pudding will keep for up to 4 days.

BLUEBERRY, MINT, AND KALE SMOOTHIE

THIS IS A GREENER GREEN SMOOTHIE than my basic green smoothie. You'll taste the kale here, along with the refreshing mint.

This smoothie features avocado, which adds tremendous creaminess, as well as a wonderful, fluffy texture!

MAKES 4 CUPS SMOOTHIE

1 banana
2 cups frozen blueberries
½ Haas avocado (about 1½ ounces)
1 tablespoon flax meal
2 cups almond milk
2½ cups tightly packed kale
¼ cup tightly packed fresh mint
1 pitted date (2 if you prefer a bit more sweetness)

Blend all the ingredients in a high-speed blender until smooth. Serve.

Plant Protein Shake, page 172, and Blueberry, Mint, and Kale Smoothie, page 200

Chocolate Raw-Nola, page 202

CHOCOLATE RAW-NOLA

THIS RAW-NOLA IS SUPER CRISPY, IT'S not overly sweet, and it's full of chocolate. What more could a person ask for?
MAKES 2 ½ CUPS (4 TO 6 SERVINGS)

6 pitted Medjool dates
1 cup water
1 teaspoon vanilla
¼ cup cacao powder
Dash sea salt
1 ¼ cup Buckwheaties (page 105)
⅓ cup cacao nibs
¼ cup hemp seeds

2 tablespoons flax meal (for the oven version only)

1. Blend the dates, water, vanilla, cacao powder, and sea salt in a blender until smooth. If you don't have a high-speed blender, you may want to soak and drain the dates beforehand.

2. Mix the buckwheaties, cacao nibs, and the hemp seeds together. If you're baking the granola, add the 2 tablespoons of flax meal. Stir in ½ to ⅔ cup of the chocolate sauce—just enough to coat the groats, seeds, and nibs very generously, but not enough to drown them.

3. Transfer the granola to a dehydrator sheet lined with Teflex and dehydrate for 6 to

8 hours, stopping halfway through to gently mix up the granola and break it into pieces (unless you dehydrate it overnight, in which case you can just let it do its thing).

If you don't have a dehydrator, transfer the granola to a parchment-lined baking sheet. Set the oven to 350°F and toast for 20 minutes. Remove the granola from the oven and allow it to air dry until completely cool. Stored in a sealed container, it will keep for up to 2 weeks. It will remain extra crispy if stored in the fridge.

CASHEW BANANA YOGURT

GREEK YOGURT IS ONE OF THE LAST nonvegan foods I stopped eating, and it was one of my favorites. I've seen all sorts of super complex recipes for fermented, homemade yogurts, but this simple recipe is my go-to.

This yogurt calls for a probiotic powder. You don't have to go out and purchase one to make it. If you take any kind of probiotic

Cashew Banana Yogurt, page 203

Banana Almond Coconut Raw-Nola, page 205

supplement, you can simply empty two to three capsules into the recipe and enjoy. If you don't want to, or don't have a probiotic powder at all, that's fine. Just go ahead and enjoy the taste of this sweet, tangy treat.

MAKES 4 SMALL OR 2 LARGE SERVINGS

1 cup cashews, soaked for 2 hours or more, then drained
2 large bananas
1½ tablespoons freshly squeezed lemon juice
⅔ cup coconut water (½ cup if you're using a food processor)
1 pinch sea salt
½ teaspoon probiotic powder (optional; you can simply open up a few probiotic capsules for this!)

Blend all the ingredients in a high-speed blender until smooth.

Alternatively, place all the ingredients, except the coconut water, in a food processor and pulse a few times to combine. Turn the motor on and drizzle in the coconut water in a thin stream. Keep processing until the mixture is very smooth.

Stored in an airtight container in the fridge, the yogurt will keep for 2 days.

BANANA ALMOND COCONUT RAW-NOLA

THIS RAW-NOLA IS SWEET, FRAGRANT, and bursting with the taste of delicious coconut.

MAKES 4 TO 6 SERVINGS

¼ cup almond butter
⅓ cup agave nectar
2 tablespoons melted coconut oil
1 small banana
1 tablespoon flax meal
1½ cups dehydrated buckwheat groats
1 cup sliced or slivered almonds
1 cup dried shredded coconut

1. Blend the almond butter, agave nectar, coconut oil, banana, and flax meal in a blender until smooth.

2. Mix the buckwheat, almonds, and coconut in a large bowl. Pour the sauce over the mixture and mix thoroughly with your hands.

3. Spread the raw-nola on a Teflex or parchment–lined dehydrator tray. Dehydrate at 115°F overnight (8 hours). Move the granola around a bit to break it up, and dehydrate for another 6 hours. Serve.

If you don't have a dehydrator, transfer the granola to a parchment-lined baking sheet. Set the oven to 350°F and toast until it's lightly browned, 20 to 25 minutes. Remove the granola from the oven and allow it to air dry until completely cool.

Stored in a sealed container, the raw-nola will keep for up to 2 weeks. It will remain extra crispy if stored in the fridge.

Step 1: Raw Banana Breakfast Wraps

Step 2: Raw Banana Breakfast Wraps

Step 3: Raw Banana Breakfast Wraps

RAW BANANA BREAKFAST WRAPS

THIS IS THE RAW FOODIE'S EQUIVA-
lent of a drive-in breakfast. It's one
of my favorite options when I'm truly in a
rush—just wrap your bananas, add some nut
butter, drizzle your sweetener, and go!

The pairing of greens with banana can
seem odd at first, but remember: if you've
ever had a green smoothie, then you've enjoyed this combination before. I do recommend using a more mild tasting green for the
wraps. Romaine, butter lettuce, and Boston
lettuce are all perfect.

MAKES 2 TO 4 SERVINGS

4 large Boston, butter, or romaine lettuce
  leaves
6 tablespoons peanut or almond butter
4 large bananas
4 teaspoons pure maple syrup or agave
  nectar

1. Lay a lettuce or chard leaf on a flat, dry
surface. Spread it with about a tablespoon
and a half of nut butter.

2. Place the banana in the center of the
leaf. Drizzle it with sweetener. Roll up the
leaf around the banana, and secure it with
a toothpick, if desired (I usually eat the roll
before I have a chance to!). Repeat with the
remaining leaves, and enjoy.

Almond Pulp Porridge, page 209

ALMOND PULP PORRIDGE

WHEN I FIRST MADE THIS RECIPE, I was hoping I could find a way to make the pulp that's left over from making almond milk (see page 98 for the recipe) salvageable. I didn't have high expectations, so you can imagine my surprise when this "porridge" turned out to be satisfying and flavorful! Feel free to add in any spices or mix-ins you like.

MAKES 4 SERVINGS

Pulp left over from 1 batch of my home-made almond milk (2 scant cups)
2 pitted dates
Seeds from ½ vanilla bean or 1 teaspoon vanilla extract
Pinch salt
2 tablespoons almond milk
1 teaspoon ground cinnamon or pumpkin pie spice
1 medium apple, cored and diced
⅓ cup raisins (substitute cacao nibs if you don't care for raisins)

1. In a food processor fitted with the "S" blade, process the pulp, dates, vanilla, salt, almond milk, and cinnamon until smooth.

2. Transfer the mixture to a bowl. Stir in the apple and raisins. Divide among the bowls, top with a little more almond milk and raisins (if desired) and serve.

The porridge is best served fresh but will keep overnight in the fridge as well.

CHOCOLATE AÇAI BOWL

CACAO BRINGS OUT ALL THE WONDERful, rich, chocolaty notes in açai berry, and this breakfast recipe, which is half smoothie, half granola bowl, celebrates the two ingredients in all of their harmony. I use any raw-nola I happen to have at home as a topper; I've included two of my favorite options here. One will complement chocolate flavor, while the other helps to highlight the tropical notes in this recipe!

SERVES 2

1 frozen açai pulp packet (the Sambazon brand is very good)
2 large frozen bananas
6 Brazil nuts
1¼ cups coconut water
3 tablespoons cacao powder
¾ cup raw-nola of choice

In a high-speed blender or food processor, blend all the ingredients, except the raw-nola, until smooth. Top each with half of the raw-nola, and serve.

Lunch

CREAMY BASIL AND GINGER NOODLES

THESE NOODLES HAPPENED ALMOST by accident. I was making an almond butter and ginger dressing, and I just so happened to have summer basil teeming in my fridge. I wondered if these ingredients might all taste good together, and, lo and behold, they did. Ginger and basil is now a favorite flavor combination of mine, and it's never more simple than it is in this delicious raw "noodle" dish.

MAKES 4 SERVINGS

Noodle Ingredients

1 package (between 12 and 16 ounces) kelp noodles
1 cup halved cherry tomatoes
¼ cup thinly sliced fresh basil

Sauce Ingredients

⅓ cup almond or cashew butter
½ cup water
¼ cup fresh basil
¼ teaspoon sea salt
½ teaspoon powdered ginger (or 2 teaspoons fresh, grated)

1. Soak the kelp noodles in warm water for 10 to 15 minutes. Shake them dry, then pat them very dry with a paper towel or kitchen towel. Use a pair of scissors to snip them into smaller pieces.

2. Blend all the sauce ingredients together in a blender until smooth. Pour the sauce over the noodles and use your hands to mix them well. Add the tomatoes and mix well. Serve, topped with the fresh basil.

Leftover noodles will keep overnight in the fridge. The nut butter and basil sauce will keep for up to 5 days in an airtight container in the fridge.

JICAMA FIESTA RICE SALAD

RAW "RICE" CAN BE MADE BY PULSING one of your favorite, firm vegetables up in a food processor. Cauliflower, parsnip, and jicama are my favorite vegetables to use, but you can get creative and chop up beets or carrots too.

This raw "rice" features jicama, a highly underutilized vegetable. Jicama, also known as Mexican yam, has a crunchy, watery texture. It's rich in vitamin C, iron, and potassium. I like to slice jicama into matchsticks and sprinkle it with lime juice for a refreshing snack, dip it into guacamole, and, most of all, put it to use in this colorful dish.

MAKES 4 SERVINGS

Creamy Basil and Ginger Noodles, page 210

2 medium or large jicama, peeled and roughly chopped (about 6 cups)
1 cup seeded and diced bell pepper
1 cup diced cucumber
1 Haas avocado, cubed
½ cup tightly packed fresh cilantro
⅔ cup Spicy Cilantro Vinaigrette (page 127)

1. Place half of the jicama into a food processor fitted with the "S" blade and pulse until it starts to look like rice (you may need to stop once or twice to mix up the jicama so that it chops evenly). Transfer it to a bowl. Place the remaining jicama in the processor and repeat the process.

2. Use a piece of cheesecloth, a thin kitchen towel, or a nut milk bag to squeeze any excess moisture out of the jicama. It will release quite a lot of liquid, so squeeze hard!

3. Transfer the jicama to a mixing bowl and add the pepper, cucumber, avocado, and cilantro. Dress with the cilantro vinaigrette, and serve.

Leftover salad will keep, stored in an airtight container in the fridge, for 2 days.

Jicama Fiesta Rice Salad, page 210

Raw Corn Chowder, page 213

RAW CORN CHOWDER

LIKE ALL RAW SOUPS, THIS CHOWDER is super low stress—simply blend, top, and enjoy. Corn, cashews, and almond milk give you all the richness you'd expect from a chowder, while a little smoked paprika and garlic add zest to the dish. I like to top mine with tomatoes and avocado, per the instructions, but you can choose any other vegetables to chop in.

If you like, you can also blend only 3 cups of corn to make the soup, and stir in the remaining cup to give it texture. I enjoy it both ways—totally blended, and a little chunky.

MAKES 4 SERVINGS

4 cups raw corn kernels (if you don't have raw, or corn isn't in season, you can also use frozen and thawed kernels)
⅓ cup cashews, soaked in water for 2 hours or more, then drained
½ cup almond milk

1 red bell pepper, seeded and roughly
    chopped
½ teaspoons smoked paprika
½ teaspoon sea salt
1 teaspoon minced garlic
1 cup heirloom or vine tomatoes, chopped
    into ½-inch pieces
1 cup Haas avocado (about 1 large fruit),
    chopped into ½-inch pieces

1. Blend all the ingredients except for the avocados and tomatoes with 1 cup of water, in a blender until very smooth.

2. Transfer the chowder to four serving bowls. Top each bowl with ¼ cup of chopped tomatoes and ¼ cup of chopped avocado.

Stored in an airtight container in the fridge, the soup will keep for up to 2 days.

DILLY RAW VEGAN SUNFLOWER "TUNA SALAD"

CONVENTIONAL, CANNED TUNA CONtains mercury, is frequently subject to recalls due to contamination or leaky seals, is lousy for the environment, and is, of course, incredibly cruel to tunas. Why bother when you can make this delicious, nourishing raw food version instead?

Dilly Raw Vegan Sunflower "Tuna Salad," page 214

Sunflower seeds are rich in vitamin E, an antioxidant, as well as phytosterols that may help to lower cholesterol. Paired with all the fixings of traditional tuna salad—pickle, onion, dill, lemon, and seaweed to evoke the ocean—they make this dish come alive. You can serve the tuna salad over greens for a raw meal, or you can go the traditional route, and pile it on top of some toast.

MAKES 4 SERVINGS

1¼ cups sunflower seeds, soaked for at least 2 hours
1 large dill pickle, chopped (about ½ cup)
½ cup chopped white onion
¼ cup tightly packed, minced fresh dill

3 tablespoons pickle juice
2 tablespoons freshly squeezed lemon juice
1 tablespoon dulse or kelp flakes
2 tablespoons finely chopped fresh dill

1. Place the sunflower seeds in a food processor fitted with the "S" blade and pulse until they're well combined but not totally smooth.

2. Add the remaining ingredients and pulse again, until everything is broken down and uniform.

The salad will keep in an airtight container for up to 4 days.

ZUCCHINI PASTA WITH MANGO, AVOCADO, AND BLACK BEAN SALSA

MANGO AND AVOCADO SALAD IS A summertime classic. In this recipe, I take that recipe one step further by adding black beans and cilantro. I then pile it on top of spiralized zucchini for a quick, easy, and refreshing meal.

MAKES 4 SERVINGS

2 ripe Haas avocados, halved, pitted, and
    cut into ¾-inch cubes
3 tablespoons freshly squeezed lime juice
2 ripe Ataulfo mangoes, peeled, pitted,
    and cut into ½-inch cubes
¼ cup chopped fresh cilantro, plus more
    as garnish
½ teaspoon sea salt
Freshly ground black pepper
1 teaspoon agave nectar or pure maple
    syrup
2 tablespoons extra-virgin olive oil
1½ cups cooked black beans, or 1
    (14-ounce] can
4 medium zucchini, spiralized

1. Toss all the ingredients except for the zucchini in a mixing bowl. Combine well.

2. Divide the zucchini onto four plates. Top each with a quarter of the mango mixture. Sprinkle with extra cilantro, and serve.

To store, keep the zucchini pasta and the mango mixture separate. Both will keep, stored in an airtight container in the fridge, for 2 days.

Zucchini Pasta with Mango, Avocado, and Black Bean Salsa, page 216

ZUCCHINI ROLL-UPS

ZUCCHINI ROLL-UPS ARE SO PRETTY that the first time I saw them, I assumed they must be incredibly hard to make. Actually, they're incredibly easy to make, once you get the hang of it. I'll walk you through all the steps here. In no time, you'll be on your way to creating a variety of beautiful zucchini roll-ups, filled with your favorite seasonal toppings.

One cautionary note: the roll-ups tend to get a little watery as you let them sit, so it's best to eat them right away once they're prepared. If you want to prep them in advance, simply get the filling and the strips ready beforehand, then wrap and roll when you're ready to eat.

SERVES 4

3 large zucchini, shaved lengthwise into long, very thin strips (about 48 strips total)

1 batch hummus, nut pâté, or cashew cheese of choice (I like to use my gingery almond paste, cashew cheese, or curried sweet potato hummus)

1 large cucumber, cut into matchsticks (about 1½ cups)

2 cups alfalfa or broccoli sprouts

1 cup fresh herbs (basil, dill, cilantro, parsley, etc.)

Toothpicks (optional)

1. To make a roll, lay about six zucchini strips lengthways and very close together, overlapping significantly. Spread 2 tablespoons of topping (hummus, nut pâté, cashew cheese) horizontally across the bottom of the layered zucchini strips.

2. Place some cucumber matchsticks horizontally across the topping. Add a small handful of sprouts and a sprinkle of fresh herbs.

3. Roll the whole thing up, from the bottom to the top. Secure with a toothpick, if desired. Repeat until you've used up all of the zucchini. You should have eight rolls in total, two per serving.

Extra rolls will keep in the fridge overnight.

Dinner

MEDITERRANEAN CAULIFLOWER RICE WITH SMOKY RED PEPPER SAUCE

I'M HALF GREEK, AND THIS DISH EVOKES many of the Mediterranean flavors I grew up with: cumin, dill, and buttery pine nuts. It's reminiscent of the orzo bowls that were abundant in my grandmother's home, but, in place of pasta or grains, it features refreshing cauliflower "rice." The smoky red pepper sauce, by the way, is a winner in its own right. You can use it for salads, on veggie kebabs, or over quinoa. I especially like to drizzle it over grilled tofu.

MAKES 4 SERVINGS

Rice Ingredients

1½ pounds (4 scant cups) cauliflower florets
½ cup pine nuts
¼ teaspoon sea salt
Freshly ground black pepper
½ teaspoon ground cumin
¼ cup chopped fresh dill (plus more for garnish)
¼ cup dried currants

Smoky Red Pepper Sauce Ingredients

1 large red bell pepper, cut into pieces
½ cup tahini
½ cup water
½ teaspoon sea salt
½ teaspoon smoked paprika
1 tablespoon apple cider vinegar
1 pitted date

1. Place half of the cauliflower, pine nuts, sea salt, pepper, and cumin in the bowl of a food processor fitted with an "S" blade. Pulse until the cauliflower is broken into small pieces. Add the remaining cauliflower and the dill and pulse until all of the cauliflower is the size of medium grain rice.

2. Remove the cauliflower from the food processor; mix the currants into the cauliflower mixture.

3. Blend the pepper, tahini, water, salt, paprika, vinegar, and date in a blender until smooth. Divide the rice into four portions and spoon 3 to 4 tablespoons of the sauce over the rice. Garnish with dill, and serve.

Rice leftovers will keep, stored in an airtight container in the fridge, for 2 days. If stored separately, the red pepper sauce will keep for up to 5 days.

Mediterranean Cauliflower Rice with Smoky Red Pepper Sauce, page 220

RAW OR COOKED RATATOUILLE

THOUGH THE WORD "RATATOUILLE" may conjure up images of casserole dishes, roasting fragrantly in the oven, this raw spin on the French classic is surprisingly delicious. I love it without any heating at all, but I offer up a dehydrator option for gentle heating, and an oven option if you're craving a more traditional presentation. Raw jicama or cauliflower rice make wonderful accompaniments, as does a bed of warm quinoa.

I recommend making this dish when tomatoes and zucchini are at the peak of their season—it will make the dish so much fresher and more flavorful. I like to use oil-packed sun-dried tomatoes, but the dried ones will be fine too, so long as you soak them in warm water for 20 minutes prior to using. Pine nuts add a delightful crunch, but, if you're craving a heartier meal, you can stir in cooked or sprouted lentils or chickpeas.

MAKES 4 SERVINGS

2 zucchini, halved lengthwise and cut into
 ¼-inch slices
1 large carrot, peeled and sliced thinly
 into coins
1 bell pepper, seeded and diced
1 large heirloom tomato, seeded and diced

Raw or Cooked Ratatouille, page 222

¼ cup minced fresh parsley

2 teaspoons minced fresh thyme or
1 teaspoon dried

2 teaspoons minced fresh oregano or
1 teaspoon dried

1 tablespoon freshly squeezed lemon
juice

2 tablespoons olive oil

½ cup, sliced into thin strips, sun-dried
tomatoes

1 clove garlic, minced

½ teaspoon sea salt

Freshly ground black pepper

1 cup pine nuts, cooked or sprouted
lentils, or chickpeas

1. Combine all the ingredients except for the pine nuts in a large mixing bowl. Adjust the seasonings to taste (you can add more herbs if you like, or more lemon for a more tart taste).

2. Let all the ingredients marinate for a few hours, so that the flavors can marry. If you're serving it cool, simply stir in the pine nuts or legumes and plate. If you're heating it, use one of the options below, and stir in the pine nuts or legumes right before serving.

OVEN OPTION: Preheat the oven to 400°F. Place the vegetables in a small casserole dish and cook for 15 minutes. Give the vegetables a stir, and cook for another 10 minutes, or until they're soft throughout.

DEHYDRATOR OPTION: Set your dehydrator to 140°F. Spread the vegetables onto two Teflex-lined dehydrator sheets, and dehydrate for an hour before serving them warm.

If you keep the dish raw, it will last overnight in the fridge. If you cook or dehydrate it, it will last for up to 3 days.

COCONUT CURRY KELP NOODLES

O PENING YOUNG THAI COCONUTS CAN be a hassle, and I admit that I don't use coconut enough for this reason. Every time I purchase one, though, I'm reminded of how delicious and versatile young coconut meat is. In this recipe, crispy kelp noodles are smothered with a sauce made of young coconut meat and seasoned with ginger and curry. It's exotic, bold, and altogether delicious. Instructions for opening a young coconut are listed below, but, if you don't feel like it, fear not: I offer an option with coconut milk instead!

MAKES 4 SERVINGS

Noodle Ingredients

1 package (12-ounce) kelp noodles, rinsed,
drained, and patted dry

1 cup green peas, lightly steamed or
blanched (frozen and defrosted is
fine too)

1 cup thinly sliced shitake mushrooms

1 cup grated carrot

⅓ cup thinly sliced fresh basil

Sauce Ingredients

Meat of 1 young Thai coconut (1 cup)

½ cup coconut water

2 pitted dates

2 tablespoons nama shoyu or tamari

1 teaspoon ginger powder or 1 tablespoon
grated fresh

2 teaspoons curry powder

1 teaspoon sesame oil

1 tablespoon apple cider vinegar

1. Soak the kelp noodles in warm water for 10 to 15 minutes. Shake them dry, then pat them very dry with a paper towel or kitchen towel. Use a pair of scissors to snip them into smaller pieces.

2. Blend all the sauce ingredients together in a high-speed blender until smooth.

3. Mix all the noodle ingredients together in a mixing bowl. Add the sauce and use your hands to combine all the ingredients thoroughly. Serve, garnished with basil.

COOK'S NOTE: If you don't have young Thai coconut, that's fine. Omit the coconut meat and water, and replace them with ¾ cup of full-fat coconut milk.

Stored in an airtight container, the sauce will keep for 3 days in the fridge. Dressed noodles will keep for 2 days.

How to open a young Thai coconut

You'll need a flat, clean surface and either a cleaver or a really large kitchen knife with a "heel."

1. Trim away some of the exterior flesh of the coconut by working your knife around the point. The idea is to make the top a little bit flatter.

2. Put your noncleaver hand behind your back and keep it there! This is an important precaution. Next, gently tap the surface of the coconut. You'll be able to hear where it's a bit hollow sounding. You want to aim your knife blows in this area. You'll be making four cuts in a square shape around the top point of the coconut. Administer your first blow, and then take three more to connect the square.

3. Take a large kitchen knife and cut through any spots that the cleaver missed so the square comes loose.

4. Peel away the top. The coconut will be full of pure, delicious, hydrating coconut water. You'll want to save this, so pour it into a container. Then scrape out the meat with a spoon. The meat will keep for about 4 days in the fridge, and it can also be frozen. The water will keep for 3 days in the fridge.

RAW LASAGNA

ONE OF THE GREATEST RAW RESTAU-rants in the world is New York City's Pure Food and Wine. There, owner Sarma Melngailis and her team of incredible chefs turn out dishes that never cease to astound me with their creativity and elegance. The restaurant's signature dish is an heirloom tomato and basil lasagna with nut cheese and pesto. It's superb, and, while I'll never quite re-create it at home, I've certainly tried many times over.

This lasagna is my favorite homemade, raw spin on the traditional Italian dish. It's not nearly as beautiful or as complex as Sarma's, but it's pretty darn tasty. There is plenty of prep work involved—this is not an easy raw dinner—but once you've made all of the various spreads (pesto, nut cheese) it's pretty easy to assemble.

MAKES 8 SERVINGS

Lasagna Ingredients

2 to 3 large zucchini, cut in half and then lengthwise into strips (⅛ inch thick) on a mandoline

2 large heirloom tomatoes, sliced into ¼-inch-thick rounds

Pesto Ingredients
1 batch Basic Vegan Pesto (page 135)

Cashew Cheese Ingredients
1 batch Cashew Cheese (page 99)

Marinara Ingredients
1 batch Raw Marinara Sauce (page 135)

1. Place one layer of zucchini along the bottom of a 9 by 13–inch rectangular casserole dish. Slightly overlap the edges of the zucchini pieces. Spread ½ cup of the cashew cheese over the zucchini slices, then top that with ⅓ cup of the raw marinara.

2. Lay one layer of tomato rounds over the marinara. Spread ½ cup of pesto over the tomatoes.

3. Repeat these layers once more. After the tomato layer, add one final layer of zucchini slices. Cut into eight pieces, and serve.

The lasagna will keep for up to 3 days, covered, in the fridge. Note that some liquid will collect from the veggies as it sits, so you should occasionally pour the liquid out of the dish to keep it fresh.

Raw Lasagna, page 224

Un-Fried Vegetable Rice with Scallions and Ginger, page 227

UN-FRIED VEGETABLE RICE WITH SCALLIONS AND GINGER

THERE'S CLEARLY NOTHING "FRIED" about this fried rice, but that doesn't mean it's not bursting with flavor. Scallions, ginger, and mirin (Japanese rice wine) endow this raw "rice" bowl with incredible taste. If you're craving something warm, you can use one of the two heating options listed at the end of the recipe. And if you'd prefer to use cauliflower or parsnip rice instead, go for it.

Mirin is an expensive ingredient. A little goes a long way, but, if you'd prefer not to use it, that's fine. Add a teaspoon of maple syrup to the dish instead, and add the full 2 teaspoons of vinegar.

MAKES 4 SERVINGS

1 large (or two smaller) jicama, peeled and turned into "rice" (per the instructions for my Jicama Fiesta Rice, page 210, be sure to squeeze off excess moisture before using)
1 cup broccoli, chopped into small pieces (you can use a food processor, or you can even grate the broccoli on the large setting of a box grater)
1 cup raw shitake mushrooms, stems removed and sliced into thin strips
½ cup snow peas, sliced into small pieces
2 scallions, green parts only, diced
1 tablespoon olive oil
1 teaspoon sesame oil
1 tablespoon mirin (optional)
1 teaspoon grated fresh ginger
1 to 2 teaspoons rice vinegar or apple cider vinegar
1 tablespoon tamari, nama shoyu, coconut aminos, or Bragg's Liquid Aminos
2 tablespoons chopped Thai or regular basil (optional)

1. Mix the jicama rice, broccoli, mushrooms, snow peas, and scallions in a large mixing bowl.

2. Whisk together the olive oil, sesame oil, mirin, ginger, vinegar, and tamari. Pour this marinade over the vegetable mixture.

3. Use your hands to mix all the ingredients together. Add in the basil if desired, and serve as is, or use one of the heated options, below.

STOVE-TOP OPTION: Heat a large frying pan or wok over low heat. Add the "rice" and heat it gently, stirring often, until it's as warm as you like it. Mix in the basil, if desired, and serve.

DEHYDRATOR OPTION: Spread the rice evenly onto two Teflex-lined dehydrator sheets and dehydrate at 140°F for 1 hour. Mix in the basil, if desired, and serve.

Leftover rice will keep, stored in an airtight container in the fridge, for 2 days. If it gets a little watery, you can use a colander to squeeze out any extra liquid before serving.

Carrot and Zucchini Pappardelle with Pesto and Peas, page 229

CARROT AND ZUCCHINI PAPPARDELLE WITH PESTO AND PEAS

THIS DISH IS LIGHT, FLAVORFUL, AND beautiful to look at. Instead of the usual zucchini "noodles," I use a vegetable peeler to create wide, thin strips of zucchini that resemble "papardelle" pasta. Pesto and steamed peas are the perfect way to dress it all up. This is a light, summery entrée, so feel free to serve it with something substantial, such as grilled tofu or a hearty salad.

MAKES 4 SERVINGS

4 large carrots, peeled
2 small or medium zucchini, trimmed
1 cup peas, blanched or steamed
1 batch Kale and Pistachio Pesto
 (page 136)

1. First, prepare your carrot noodles. Place one of your carrots on a flat surface. Run a wide mouthed vegetable peeler along the length of the carrot to create a long, thin strip. Continue doing this until you're down to the last of the carrot—you can save this bit for snacks. Repeat with remaining carrots. Slice the noodles in half if they're very thick.

2. Next, make your zucchini noodles. You can use a mandoline or V-slicer to do this by putting the mandoline on its thinnest setting and running the zucchini along the mandoline lengthwise. You'll get long, thin strips of zucchini. Stack them together and cut them in half. If one edge of your "noodle" is full of seeds, you can slice off a strip of the seeded area, and discard it.

You can also use a vegetable peeler to make the zucchini noodles, just as you did the carrot noodles. Lay the zucchini flat on a table, trim off the ends, and then use a vegetable peeler to shave off one long, lengthwise piece. Keep working from end to end, creating long, flat noodles. Again, cut them in half and trim off any seedy parts.

3. Mix the carrot and zucchini noodles in a large mixing bowl. Add ⅓ cup of the pesto and massage it into the noodles. Add more pesto as needed, until the noodles are well coated. Mix in the peas and serve.

Leftover noodles will keep in the fridge for 2 days.

13 Desserts for Everyone

DESSERT RECIPES MAY BE THE MOST CELEBRATED PART OF RAW FOOD CUISINE, AND with good reason: they deliver decadence and taste along with healthy fats, antioxidants, and natural, unrefined sugars. I often think that raw desserts taste better than the original recipe they've reinterpreted. And the fact that you don't have to turn on your oven is a great bonus!

COCONUTTY FOR CHOCOLATE CHIP COOKIES

THESE COOKIES TASTE EVERY BIT AS sweet and indulgent as a cookie should, but they're surprisingly nutritious. Walnuts contribute healthy omega-3 fatty acids, while coconut lends its anti-inflammatory properties and cacao nibs give the cookies a little antioxidant boost. Whether for the benefits or the taste, I enjoy these cookies both as midday snacks and as dessert.

MAKES 16 TO 18 COOKIES

2 cups walnuts
1¼ cups tightly packed, pitted Medjool
    dates
1½ cups unsweetened dried coconut
1 teaspoon coconut oil
3 tablespoons pure maple syrup or agave
    nectar
1 teaspoon ground cinnamon
⅛ teaspoon sea salt
⅓ cup cacao nibs

1. Place the walnuts, dates, coconut, and coconut oil in a food processor fitted with the "S" blade. Process for just under a minute, or until the mixture is starting to stick together.

2. Add the agave nectar and cinnamon. Process quickly (about 10 seconds) to combine.

3. Pulse in the cacao nibs. Roll into 1-inch balls and press down into flat, round cookies. Store in the fridge until ready to use.

Stored in an airtight container in the fridge, they'll keep for at least 2 weeks.

FIG BARS

IT'S AMAZING TO ME THAT A DESSERT this good can be free of refined flour or refined sugar. These fig bars have all of the chewiness and sweetness of traditional Fig Newton cookies, but they're made with wholesome almonds, oats, and real dried figs.

MAKES 9 BARS

Coconutty for Chocolate Chip Cookies, page 230

Fig Bars, page 230

Filling Ingredients

3 cups water
2 cups dried figs
1 teaspoon vanilla extract

Base Ingredients

½ cup almonds
1½ cups rolled oats
⅛ teaspoon sea salt
6 pitted Medjool dates
2 tablespoons pure maple syrup
1 tablespoon melted coconut oil

Topping Ingredients

¾ cup sliced almonds

1. Bring the water to a boil, and pour it over the figs. Let the figs soak for at least 1 hour (or for as long as 6).

2. Grind the almonds in a food processor fitted with the "S" blade until they're relatively smooth. Add the oats and continue grinding until both are quite finely ground. Pulse in the sea salt.

3. Add the Medjool dates to the food processor, along with the maple syrup and coconut oil. Process until the mixture is evenly incorporated. Press into an 8–inch square baking dish.

4. Drain the figs, reserving the water they soaked in, and transfer them to a clean food processor. Process them with the vanilla. Add the soak water as needed, until you have the consistency of a fig jam.

5. Spread the fig mixture over the oat/almond mixture. The fig layer should be ¼ inch thick, or a little thicker. Reserve extra fig mixture to use in place of jam on your favorite toast.

6. Top the fig layer with almonds. Refrigerate the bars for a few hours, until they set. Cut into nine squares, and enjoy.

Store the fig bars in an airtight container in the fridge. They will keep for up to 2 weeks this way.

RAW PEACH COBBLER

SUMMER IS THE BEST SEASON FOR RAW desserts. After all, what better way is there to show off a bounty of berries or stone fruits than in a decadent raw treat?

In this raw spin on summery fruit cobbler, juicy peaches are married with a pecan crumble topping and kissed with a hint of cinnamon and nutmeg. The recipe is easy to make and even easier to devour.

MAKES 6 TO 8 SERVINGS

Topping Ingredients

1 cup pecans
1⅓ cups pitted Medjool dates
⅛ teaspoon sea salt

Filling Ingredients

2 tablespoons pure maple syrup
1 teaspoon ground cinnamon
¼ teaspoon grated nutmeg
2 teaspoons freshly squeezed lemon juice
4 cups skinned, pitted, and sliced peaches

1. Whisk together the maple syrup, cinnamon, nutmeg, and lemon juice. Drizzle onto the fresh fruit, and allow it to marinate for an hour or so.

Raw Peach Cobbler, page 233

2. In a food processor fitted with the S" blade, grind the pecans until they've become a coarse meal. Add the dates and sea salt, and process until the mixture is still crumbly but sticks together easily.

3. Turn the peaches out into an 8-inch square cake pan, a pie dish, or a small, rectangular casserole dish. Sprinkle the topping over the peaches.

Leftover cobbler will keep in an airtight container in the fridge for up to 3 days.

CHOCOLATE-COVERED SUPERFOOD CLUSTERS

MAKING CHOCOLATE FROM SCRATCH sounds like a major undertaking, but it's actually incredibly easy! Once you get the hang of it, you'll be tempted to customize homemade chocolate in hundreds of different ways. In this recipe, I add a hint of maca to my standard raw chocolate mixture, which is then mixed with almonds and goji berries. The result is a delicious, anti-oxidant packed treat that's equally good as a snack or a dessert.

To make chocolate from scratch, you can use either melted coconut oil or coconut butter. For this recipe, butter works best, because the chocolate will keep its shape when it cools. Coconut butter is expensive, but a little goes a long way, and it's so fun to use in recipes that it's an ingredient well worth investing in.

MAKES 14 TO 18 CLUSTERS

6 tablespoons raw cacao powder
⅓ cup melted coconut butter
¼ cup coconut syrup or agave nectar
1 teaspoon maca powder
Pinch of sea salt
⅔ cup whole, raw almonds
½ cup goji berries

1. Use a whisk to mix the cacao, melted coconut butter, coconut syrup or agave nectar, maca, and sea salt together until it's totally smooth.

2. Add the almonds and goji berries and mix well. Line two baking sheets with parchment, and use a tablespoon to drop the mixture, heaping tablespoon by heaping tablespoon, onto the parchment. Leave about 1½ inches of space between the clusters, as they'll spread out. You should have about twenty clusters.

3. Transfer the sheets to the fridge immediately. Chill for 30 minutes or longer.

Store the clusters in the fridge. They will keep for up to 3 weeks.

RAW KEY LIME PIE

WHILE I WAS GROWING UP, KEY LIME pie was one of my favorite desserts. When I went vegan, I just assumed that it would become a fond memory, until I tried my first raw Key lime pie and was astonished at how incredibly creamy and delicious it was. This recipe uses both cashews and avocado to create a perfect filling texture and flavor.

MAKES ONE 9-INCH PIE

Crust Ingredients

2 cups cashews
½ cup shredded, unsweetened coconut
1 cup pitted dates
⅛ teaspoon sea salt

Filling Ingredients

1 large Haas avocado, pitted and peeled
1½ cups raw cashews, soaked in water for
    at least 2 hours and drained
½ cup melted coconut oil
¼ cup freshly squeezed lime juice
½ cup pure maple syrup or agave nectar
1 teaspoon vanilla extract
Pinch sea salt
1 tablespoon lime zest (optional)

1. To make the crust, add the cashews, coconut, pitted dates, and sea salt to your food processor, fitted with the "S" blade. Process until the ingredients are mixed and broken down well, and they stick together when you collect a small handful and squeeze.

2. Press the crust ingredients evenly into the bottom of on oiled, 9-inch springform pan.

3. Blend the filling ingredients together in a high-speed blender or food processor until silky smooth. Spread the filling over the crust and use a spatula or inverted knife to make the top very smooth.

4. Chill the pie in the freezer for an hour, then transfer it to the fridge and let it set for another 3 hours, or overnight. Cut into slices and serve.

Alternatively, you can make four tartlets in place of one pie. (See instructions for No-Bake Tartlets on page 243 for basic tips).

Cover and store the pie in the fridge for up to 3 days, or in the freezer for up to 10. If you freeze the pie, defrost the slices in the fridge for several hours before serving.

ALMOST INSTANT CHOCOLATE-COVERED STRAWBERRIES

APERFECT SHORTCUT FOR RAW CHOColate making is to skip melting the coconut butter and simply use melted coconut oil and cacao powder instead. The chocolate is delicate (it'll melt in warm temperatures), but it's a perfect coating for any dessert you don't mind keeping cool. My favorite way to use it is as a coating for plump, juicy summer strawberries.

MAKES 12 LARGE STRAWBERRIES

¼ cup melted coconut oil
2 tablespoons coconut syrup or agave nectar
¼ cup raw cacao powder
Pinch sea salt
12 large strawberries

1. Whisk together the oil, coconut syrup, and vanilla. Add them to the cacao and salt, and whisk together until smooth.

2. Dip the strawberries in the mixture until well coated, and lay on a foil or parchment–lined baking sheet.

3. Refrigerate for at least 30 minutes before serving.

The strawberries will keep in the fridge for up to 4 days.

SIMPLE RAW VANILLA MACAROONS

MACAROONS WERE ONE OF THE first raw treats I made, and they have remained a favorite ever since. These macaroons are full of vanilla and coconut flavor, all elevated with a touch of sea salt. If you don't have a dehydrator, that's fine. The macaroons will firm up well in the fridge. Be patient, though, because they'll be a little soft while you're shaping them.

MAKES 16 TO 20 MACAROONS

¾ cup raw cashews
¼ teaspoon sea salt
2 cups unsweetened shredded coconut
1 vanilla bean, cut lengthwise, seeds scraped out with a spoon (substitute 2 teaspoons vanilla extract)
1 tablespoon coconut butter
¼ cup agave nectar
1 teaspoon coconut oil

1. Grind the cashews and salt in a food processor until fairly finely ground (about a minute and a half).

2. Add all of the remaining ingredients and process until they are mixed very well.

Raw Key Lime Pie, page 235

3. Use a tablespoon measure to shape the mixture into bite-size macaroons. Place them on a Teflex-lined dehydrator sheet (or, if you don't have a dehydrator, a parchment-lined baking sheet).

4. If you have a dehydrator, dehydrate the macaroons at 115°F for 6 to 8 hours, or until they've firmed up considerably. If you don't, that's fine—you can shape them and then transfer them to the fridge for a few hours, at which point they'll be nice and firm.

Stored in an airtight container in the fridge, they'll keep for at least 2 weeks.

BLUEBERRY CHEESECAKE

I F YOU THINK AUTHENTIC CHEESECAKE flavor is impossible without the cheese, think again. Raw cheesecake happens to be one of the most authentic tasting raw desserts, thanks to the magical combination of cashews and coconut oil.

The cheesecake is easier to prepare in a high-speed blender than a food processor, but the processor can work if that's what you have. Just be sure to soak your cashews overnight! If you don't have cashews, macadamia nuts are a perfect substitute.

MAKES 1 9-INCH ROUND CAKE, OR 8 TO 10 SERVINGS

Crust Ingredients
1½ cups almonds
Pinch sea salt
2 cups pitted Medjool dates

Filling Ingredients
3 cups cashews, soaked in water overnight and drained
¼ teaspoon sea salt
⅔ cup melted coconut oil
Seeds of 1 vanilla bean, or 2 teaspoons vanilla extract
¼ cup freshly squeezed lemon juice
½ cup agave nectar

Topping Ingredients
2 cups blueberries
2 teaspoons freshly squeezed lemon juice
2 tablespoons agave nectar or pure maple syrup

1. Place the almonds and sea salt in a food processor and grind roughly. Add the dates and process until the mixture is well processed and sticks together when you squeeze a bit in the palm of your hand. Press the mixture evenly into the bottom of a 9-inch springform pan.

2. Use a high-speed blender or food processor (high-speed blender is preferable, but a food processor will work as well) to process all the filling ingredients thoroughly, until they are silky smooth. If you're working with a processor, you may need to stop often to scrape it down. Pour the mixture over the layer of crust and use an inverted knife to smooth it over. Place the cheesecake in the freezer for an hour, then transfer it to the fridge and let it set overnight.

3. When the cheesecake has set, blend 1 cup of blueberries, the lemon, and the agave nectar in a blender until smooth. Transfer to a small bowl and stir in the remaining whole blueberries. Pour the mixture over the

Blueberry Cheesecake, page 238

cheesecake (or you can spoon it over individual slices). Serve.

Cover and store the cheesecake in the fridge for up to 3 days, or in the freezer for up to 10. If you freeze the cake, defrost the slices in the fridge for several hours before serving.

RAW VEGAN BLUEBERRY GINGER ICE CREAM

THIS ICE CREAM TASTES ENTIRELY TOO delicious to be dairy free and made without an ice cream maker! Ginger and blueberries are a surprisingly harmonious combination, and the color of the finished ice cream is phenomenal. Garnish with fresh mint or a few extra blueberries before wowing your friends.

MAKES 4 SERVINGS

½ cup cashews, soaked for 2 hours or more and drained
4 frozen bananas
2 heaping cups frozen blueberries
1½ tablespoons fresh, grated ginger (or 1 teaspoon ginger powder if you're using a food processor)
1 tablespoon freshly squeezed lemon juice
4 tablespoons almond or hemp milk (may not be needed for the food processor version)

IF YOU'RE USING A HIGH-SPEED BLENDER: Blend all the ingredients together in a high-speed blender. Use the tamper attachment to facilitate blending. Add a little more almond milk, if necessary, to facilitate blending.

IF YOU'RE USING A FOOD PROCESSOR: Place the cashews in a food processor and process until they're broken down. Add the bananas and let the motor run until they've turned into soft serve (instructions on page 111). When you have soft serve consistency, add the blueberries, powdered ginger, and lemon, and blend until totally smooth. Add the almond milk only if you need a thinner consistency; you may not. Serve.

Leftover ice cream can be transferred to a sealed storage container and frozen for up to a week, then reprocessed in the food processor just prior to serving.

CARROT CAKE CUPCAKES WITH CREAM CHEESE FROSTING

THEY SAY THAT NECESSITY IS THE mother of invention. I created this dessert when I had a surplus of carrot pulp leftover from juicing. I can't imagine a better way to use up a seemingly undesirable ingredient! These raw "cupcakes" are delightfully tasty, and they're full of healthful Ingredients, including walnuts, raisins, and carrots, of course. And if you don't have any carrot pulp, using shredded carrots is also fine. Whether you use the pulp or the carrots themselves, be sure to squeeze them thoroughly to remove excess moisture before you blend them to create the cupcake base.

MAKES 6 CUPCAKES

Cupcake Ingredients

1 cup walnuts (not soaked)
1 cup dates
2 cups carrot pulp or grated raw carrots,
   squeezed thoroughly with paper towels
   or cheesecloth to remove excess
   moisture
1 teaspoon ground cinnamon
½ teaspoon ginger powder
Pinch grated nutmeg
⅛ teaspoon sea salt
¾ cup raisins

Frosting Ingredients

1 cup cashews, soaked overnight and
   drained
¼ cup agave nectar or pure maple syrup
Dash sea salt
1 teaspoon freshly squeezed lemon juice
2 tablespoons coconut oil

1. Process the walnuts and dates in a food processor fitted with the "S" blade until they're crumbly.

Raw Vegan Blueberry Ginger Ice Cream, page 240

2. Add the carrot pulp or grated carrots, cinnamon, ginger, nutmeg, and sea salt. Process until the mixture is uniform and sticking together.

3. Add the raisins and pulse to combine.

4. For the frosting, place the cashews, agave nectar, sea salt, lemon juice, and coconut oil in a high-speed blender or food processor. Process until the mixture is broken down. Drizzle in ¼ cup of water, and then continue adding water until the mixture has the texture of a buttercream frosting (¼ cup of water may be plenty!). Continue blending until totally smooth.

5. Pack the carrot cake dough into six muffin tins or ramekins and refrigerate for about

No-Bake Tartlets with Raw Vegan Chocolate Ganache Filling, page 243

an hour. Remove them from the fridge, and frost with the frosting mixture. Serve.

If you're not going to eat the cupcakes all at once, you can store the cakes and the frosting separately. The frosting will keep for a week in the fridge, and the cakes can be frozen for up to 3 weeks or kept in the fridge for up to 4.

NO-BAKE TARTLETS WITH RAW VEGAN CHOCOLATE GANACHE FILLING

THESE TARTLETS LOOK SO ELEGANT and enticing that anyone will think you spent a long time making them. While they're a little more complex than some of my other desserts, they're actually quite easy to prepare, and they are the very definition of rich, decadent chocolate goodness.

Try making the crust a day or two in advance of the filling to streamline the process.

MAKES 6 TARTLETS

Crust Ingredients

1½ cups raw walnuts
1½ cups pitted dates
¼ teaspoon sea salt, plus an extra pinch for the filling
3 tablespoons cacao powder (or cocoa powder)

Filling Ingredients

⅓ cup pure maple syrup
1 cup cashews, soaked overnight or for at least 4 hours and drained
¼ cup cacao (or cocoa) powder
⅓ cup coconut oil
1 teaspoon vanilla extract
Fresh raspberries or other fruit (optional)

1. To make the crust, grind the walnuts, dates, salt, and cacao powder together in a food processor until everything is well combined and sticking together.

2. Press the crust into six 4-inch tartlet shells, making sure to keep the thickness even and to get the sides nice and high. Refrigerate for 1 hour or more (up to a day or 2).

3. In a high-speed blender, blend the cashews, maple syrup, cacao powder, oil, vanilla, ¼ cup of water, and a pinch of sea salt. Let it blend for as long as necessary to make it completely, silky smooth.

4. Pour the filling into the tartlet shells and use a small knife to spread it evenly. Place the shells in the freezer for an hour, and then transfer to the fridge for at least 3 hours before serving, to let the ganache set. Top with fresh raspberries, if desired!

Stored in the fridge, with a layer of plastic wrap draped gently over them, the tartlets will keep for 5 days. They can also be frozen for up to 10 days and allowed to defrost in the fridge for several hours before serving.

Burnt-Sugar Coconut Ice Cream, page 245

BURNT-SUGAR COCONUT ICE CREAM

THIS IS THE SORT OF RECIPE THAT might give anyone the confidence to explore veganism. It's rich, decadent, and extraordinarily simple. Even die-hard ice cream lovers will go crazy for it. Quite a feat with only four ingredients!

MAKES 3 TO 4 CUPS ICE CREAM

2 cans full-fat coconut milk, chilled in the fridge overnight
¾ cup coconut crystals or cane juice or organic sugar
Seeds of 1 vanilla bean, scraped, or 1 teaspoon vanilla extract
Pinch sea salt

1. Blend or whisk the ingredients together quickly (if you blend them for too long, they'll start to warm up, which will make freezing the ice cream harder).

2. Transfer the ingredients to an ice cream maker and freeze according to the manufacturer's instructions. Chill in the freezer for an additional hour, scoop, and serve.

Ice cream can be stored for up to a week in a sealed container in the freezer, then rechurned before serving.

CHERRY VANILLA TAHINI ICE CREAM

ANOTHER EASY RAW BLENDER "ICE cream." Though bananas and tahini may sound like a highly unusual combination, they're delicious together, and the addition of cherries and vanilla makes it all sing.

MAKES 4 SERVINGS

3 large bananas, peeled, cut into pieces, and frozen
¼ cup tahini
Seeds of 1 vanilla bean or 1 teaspoon vanilla extract
1 cup frozen cherries
2 tablespoons raw or toasted sesame seeds

1. Place the bananas, tahini, and vanilla in the bowl of a food processor or high-speed blender. Process or blend until the bananas have turned into soft serve.

2. Add the cherries and pulse until they're broken up into pieces and incorporated into the ice cream.

3. Divide the ice cream into four bowls and top with 1½ teaspoons of sesame seeds each.

Leftover ice cream can be transferred to a sealed storage container and frozen for up to a week, then reprocessed in the food processor just prior to serving.

Metric Conversions

The recipes in this book have not been tested with metric measurements, so some variations might occur. Remember that the weight of dry ingredients varies according to the volume or density factor: 1 cup of flour weighs far less than 1 cup of sugar, and 1 tablespoon doesn't necessarily hold 3 teaspoons.

GENERAL FORMULA FOR METRIC CONVERSION	
Ounces to grams	multiply ounces by 28.35
Grams to ounces	multiply grams by 0.035
Pounds to grams	multiply pounds by 453.5
Pounds to kilograms	multiply pounds by 0.45
Cups to liters	multiply cups by 0.24
Fahrenheit to Celsius	subtract 32 from Fahrenheit temperature, multiply by 5, divide by 9
Celsius to Fahrenheit	multiply Celsius temperature by 9, divide by 5, add 32

VOLUME (LIQUID) MEASUREMENTS		
1 teaspoon	= ⅙ fluid ounce	= 5 milliliters
1 tablespoon	= ½ fluid ounce	= 15 milliliters
2 tablespoons	= 1 fluid ounce	= 30 milliliters
¼ cup	= 2 fluid ounces	= 60 milliliters
⅓ cup	= 2⅔ fluid ounces	= 79 milliliters
½ cup	= 4 fluid ounces	= 118 milliliters
1 cup or ½ pint	= 8 fluid ounces	= 250 milliliters
2 cups or 1 pint	= 16 fluid ounces	= 500 milliliters
4 cups or 1 quart	= 32 fluid ounces	= 1,000 milliliters
1 gallon	= 4 liters	

WEIGHT (MASS) MEASUREMENTS		
1 ounce	= 30 grams	
2 ounces	= 55 grams	
3 ounces	= 85 grams	
4 ounces	= ¼ pound	= 125 grams
8 ounces	= ½ pound	= 240 grams
12 ounces	= ¾ pound	= 375 grams
16 ounces	= 1 pound	= 454 grams

OVEN TEMPERATURE EQUIVALENTS, FAHRENHEIT (F) AND CELSIUS (C)		
100°F	=	38°C
200°F	=	95°C
250°F	=	120°C
300°F	=	150°C
350°F	=	180°C
400°F	=	205°C
450°F	=	230° C

VOLUME (DRY) MEASUREMENTS	
¼ teaspoon	= 1 milliliter
½ teaspoon	= 2 milliliters
¾ teaspoon	= 4 milliliters
1 teaspoon	= 5 milliliters
1 tablespoon	= 15 milliliters
¼ cup	= 59 milliliters
⅓ cup	= 79 milliliters
½ cup	= 118 milliliters
⅔ cup	= 158 milliliters
¾ cup	= 177 milliliters
1 cup	= 225 milliliters
4 cups or 1 quart	= 1 liter
½ gallon	= 2 liters
1 gallon	= 4 liters

LINEAR MEASUREMENTS	
½ inch	= 1½ cm
1 inch	= 2½ cm
6 inches	= 15 cm
8 inches	= 20 cm
10 inches	= 25 cm
12 inches	= 30 cm
20 inches	= 50 cm

Recipe List by Meal

Milks, Juices, Smoothies
Classic Almond Milk
Homemade Hemp Milk
Green Lemonade
The Veggie Bowl
Cucumber Cooler
Jungle Greens
Spring Greens
Basic Green Smoothie
Plant Protein Shake
Peachy Keen Smoothie
Blueberry, Mint, and Kale Smoothie

Breakfast
Buckwheaties
Toasted Pumpkin Granola with Homemade
    Hemp Milk
Raw Vegan Bircher Muesli
Chocolate Açai Bowl
Chocolate Raw-Nola
Banana Almond Coconut Raw-Nola
Mocha Maca Chia Pudding
Cashew Banana Yogurt

Almond Pulp Porridge
Mango Coconut Chia Pudding
Quinoa Breakfast Pudding
Raw Banana Breakfast Wraps
Simple Avocado Toast
Easy Berry Breakfast Pizza
Millet and Almond Zucchini Muffins
Baked Sweet Potatoes with Vanilla Almond
    Butter and Goji Berries
Chickpea Tofu Tahini Scramble
Avocado Black Bean Breakfast Scramble

Snacks
Herbed Flax Crackers
DIY Snack Bars
Reinvented Ants on a Log
Superfood Trail Mix
Sweet and Savory Trail Mix
Easy Roasted Chickpeas (and Variations)
Hemp-Seed Power Balls
No-Bake Sunflower Oat Bars
Classic Cheesy Kale Chips
Hummus Kale Chips

Zucchini Ranch Chips
Nori and Pumpkin-Seed Cigars

Lunch

Sweet Pea Hummus Tartines with
   Sunflower Sprouts
Sweet Potato Salad with Miso Dressing and
   Chives
Curried Chickpea and Carrot Salad
Dilly Raw Vegan Sunflower "Tuna Salad"
Apricot Quinoa and Mint Salad
Jicama Fiesta Rice Salad
Hemp-Seed Tabouli with Yellow Tomatoes
   and Mint
Easiest Vegan Pumpkin Soup
Green Soup (Blended Salad)
Raw Gazpacho
Raw Corn Chowder
Carrot, Avocado, and Turmeric Soup
Asparagus Quinoa Sushi Rolls
Nori Rolls with Gingery Almond Pâté and
   Raw Veggies
Collard Wraps with Hemp Hummus,
   Tempeh, and Red Peppers
Sprouted-Grain Wraps with Kale-Slaw
   Filling
Zucchini Roll-Ups
Zucchini Pasta with Mango, Avocado, and
   Black Bean Salsa
Creamy Basil and Ginger Noodles

Dressings, Sauces, Dips, and Spreads

Apple Cider Vinaigrette
Lemon Turmeric Vinaigrette
Spicy Cilantro Vinaigrette
Carrot Miso Dressing
Green Herb Dressing
Almond Butter and Sun-Dried Tomato
   Dressing

Ginger Miso Dressing
Creamy Maple Chipotle Dressing
Multiseed Gomasio
Hemp Parmesan
Raw Marinara Sauce
Raw Cashew Alfredo
Raw Corn Salsa
Basic Vegan Pesto
Kale and Pistachio Pesto
Classic Zucchini Hummus
Curried Sweet Potato Hummus
Red Lentil and Walnut Hummus
Hemp Hummus
Simple Raw Vegan Avocado Mayonnaise
Cashew Cheese
Nut or Seed Pâté
5-Minute Guacamole

Salads

Basic Massaged Kale Salad
Dinosaur Kale and White Bean Caesar Salad
Acorn Squash, Frisée, and Brown Rice
   Salad with Toasted Hazelnuts
Romaine, Cherry Tomato, and Arugula
   Salad with Chickpeas and Raw Parmesan
Raw Cobb Salad
Kale Salad with Sweet Potato, Almonds,
   and Creamy Maple Chipotle Dressing

Dinner

Quick Quinoa and Black Bean Salad with
   Spicy Cilantro Vinaigrette
Sweet Potato Black Bean Enchiladas
Raw Carrot Falafel with Tangy Tahini Sauce
Heat-Free Lentil and Walnut Tacos
Raw Spinach and Mushroom Burgers
Carrot and Millet Pilaf with Mesquite
   Glazed Tempeh

Pumpkin Quinoa Risotto with Pomegranate
Seeds
Easy Red Lentil, Sweet Potato, and Coconut
Curry
Coconut Curry Kelp Noodles
Raw Pad Thai
Raw or Cooked Ratatouille
Root "Rawvioli" with Nut Cheese and Pesto
Zucchini Pasta with Red or White Sauce
Zucchini Pasta with Quinoa Meatless Balls
Un-Fried Vegetable Rice with Scallions and
Ginger
Mediterranean Cauliflower Rice with Smoky
Red Pepper Sauce
Raw Lasagna
Carrot and Zucchini Pappardelle with Pesto
and Peas
Portobello "Steak" and Rosemary
Cauliflower Mashed Potatoes

Desserts

Fig Bars
Simple Raw Vanilla Macaroons
Coconutty for Chocolate Chip Cookies
No-Bake Tartlets with Raw Vegan Ganache
Filling
Raw Peach Cobbler
Raw Key Lime Pie
Blueberry Cheesecake
Carrot Cake Cupcakes with Cream Cheese
Frosting
Chocolate-Covered Superfood Clusters
Almost-Instant Chocolate-Covered
Strawberries
Basic Chia Pudding
Chocomole
Banana Soft Serve
Raw Vegan Blueberry Ginger Ice Cream
Cherry Vanilla Tahini Ice Cream
Burnt-Sugar Coconut Ice Cream

Resources

Vegan Nutrition Information

Becoming Raw, Brenda Davis, Vesanto Melina, and Ryan Berry

Becoming Vegan, Brenda Davis and Vesanto Melina

Vegan for Life, Virginia Messina and Jack Norris

Vegan for Her, Virginia Messina with JL Fields

The Plant Powered Diet, Sharon Palmer, RD

Health and Wellness

Crazy Sexy Diet, Kris Carr

Gutbliss, Robynne Chutkan, MD

Superimmunity, Joel Fuhrman, MD

Ultrametabolism, Mark Hyman, MD

Anti-Cancer, David Servan-Schreiber, MD

Compassionate Living

Beg, Rory Freedman

Veganist, Kathy Freston

Main Street Vegan, Victoria Moran

Why We Love Dogs, Eat Pigs, and Wear Cows: An Introduction to Carnism, Melanie Joy, PhD

Eating Animals, Jonathan Safran Foer

Vegan and Raw Food Cookbooks

Thrive Foods, Brendan Brazier

Let Them Eat Vegan! Dreena Burton

Eat, Drink & Be Vegan, Dreena Burton

Crazy Sexy Kitchen, Kris Carr

Raw Food for Everyone, Alissa Cohen

Practically Raw, Amber Shea Crawley

The Vegan Table, Colleen Patrick Goudreau

Everyday Raw, Matthew Kenney

How It All Vegan, Sarah Kramer

Raw Food, Real World, Sarma Melngailis

Veganomicon, Isa Chandra Moskowitz

Vegan with a Vengeance, Isa Chandra Moskowitz

Candle 79 Cookbook, Joy Pierson, Angel Ramos, and Jorge Pineda

Ani's Raw Food Kitchen, Ani Phyo

Quick Fix Vegan, Robin Robertson

Going Raw, Judita Wignall

Informative Websites

The Vegetarian Resource Group (www.vrg.org)
The Vegan Society (http://www.vegansociety
.com)
Vegan Health (http://www.veganhealth.org)
Vegan Outreach (http://www.veganoutreach
.org)
Try Veg (http://www.tryveg.com/cfi/toc/)

Vegan Dining and Travel

Happycow (www.happycow.net)
Veg Dining (http://www.vegdining.com/
Home.cfm)

Food Companies I Love

Protein Powder and Performance Products

22 Days Nutrition (http://www.22days
nutrition.com/)
Plant Fusion (http://plantfusion.net/)
Sun Warrior (http://sunwarrior.com/)
Vega (http://myvega.com)

Superfoods

Manitoba Harvest (http://manitobaharvest
.com/)
Navitas Naturals (http://navitasnaturals.com/)
Nutiva (http://nutiva.com/)
Sun Foods (http://www.sunfood.com/)

Snacks and Goodies

Brad's Raw Chips (http://www.bradsrawchips
.com/)
Go Raw (http://www.goraw.com/)
Livin' Spoonful (http://livinspoonful.com/)

Lydia's Organic (http://www.lydiasorganics
.com/welcome.html)
Pure Bar (http://thepurebar.com/)

Online Grocery Storefronts

Blue Mountain Organics (http://www.blue
mountainorganics.com/store/index.htm)
One Lucky Duck (http://www.oneluckyduck
.com)
Nuts.com (http://www.nuts.com)
The Raw Food World (http://www.theraw
foodworld.com)
Vitacost (http://www.vitacost.com)

Personal Care

Vegan makeup, shampoo, body lotions, facial care, and nail polish are all available. The best way to figure out which brands don't test on animals or use animal products is to do some online research. PETA (http://peta.org/living/) keeps an extensive and frequently updated list. Cruelty Free Face (http://crueltyfreeface
.com) is also a great resource. When you read labels, avoid anything with lanolin, beeswax, oleic acid, allantoin, squalene, gelatin, glycerin (often animal-derived), keratin, milk protein, mink oil, or musk oil.

Clothing/Shoes

There are many hip and compassionate labels on the market these days:

Outerwear

The North Face, Land's End, and LL Bean all make parkas with Thermaloft in place of down. Check out the websites, or call the company to get details. For high-fashion vegan coats, Vaute Couture makes beautiful, fashionable garments that are also ridiculously soft!

Clothing

The best place to start looking for vegan apparel is Etsy; not only will you find vegan options, but many of them will be budget friendly as well. Modcloth (http://modcloth.com), Lulus (Lulu's (http://lulus.com) and Piperlime (http://piperlime.com) always have vegan options. For all vegan shopping, check out Alternative Outfitters (http://alternativeoutfitters.com).

Footwear

Vegan footwear has exploded, and there's something for everyone. Classy shoe lines abound; some of my favorites are Olsen Haus (http://olsenhaus.com), Beyond Skin (http://beyondskin.co.uk), Neuaura (http://neuaurashoes.com), and Novacas (http://www.novacas.com). A wide selection of vegan shoes can be found at MooShoes, which has a flagship location on New York's Lower East Side but also has an online store (http://mooshoes.com). The online retailer Zappos also offers vegan alternatives.

References

Chapter 1

1. W. J. Craig and A. R. Mangels, "Position of the American Dietetic Association: Vegetarian Diets," *Journal of the American Dietetic Association* 109 (2009): 1266–1268.

2. K. D. Kochanek, J. Xu, S. L. Murphy, A. M. Minino, and H. Kung, "Deaths: Final Data for 2009," National Vital Statistics Reports 60 (2011).

3. Virginia Messina and Jack Norris, *Vegan for Life* (Cambridge, MA: Da Capo, 2011), 173.

4. T. J. Key, G. E. Fraser, M. Thorogood, P. N. Appleby, V. Beral, G. Reeves, M. L. Burr, et al., "Mortality in Vegetarians and Nonvegetarians: Detailed Findings from a Collaborative Analysis of 5 Prospective Studies," *American Journal of Clinical Nutrition* 70 (1999): 516S–524S.

5. D. A. Snowdon and R. L. Phillips, "Does a Vegetarian Diet Reduce the Occurrence of Diabetes?" *American Journal of Public Health* 75 (1985): 507–512; S. Tonstad, T. Butler, R. Yan, and G. E. Fraser, "Type of Vegetarian Diet, Body Weight, and Prevalence of Type 2 Diabetes," *Diabetes Care* 32 (2009): 791–796.

6. D. B. Lowe and W. H. Storkus, "Chronic Inflammation and Immunologic-Based Constraints in Malignant Disease," *Immunotherapy* 3 (2011): 1265–1274.

7. S. Jung, D. Spiegelman, L. Baglietto, L. Bernstein, D. A. Boggs, P. A. van den Brandt, J. E. Buring, et al., "Fruit and Vegetable Intake and Risk of Breast Cancer by Hormone Receptor Status," *Journal of the National Cancer Institute* 105, no. 3 (February 2013): 219–236.

8. C. Bamia, "Mediterranean Diet and Colorectal Cancer Risk: Results from a European Cohort," *European Journal of Epidemiology* 28 (2013): 317–328.

9. J. Freedland and W. J. Aronson, "Dietary Intervention Strategies to Modulate Prostate Cancer Risk and Prognosis," *Current Opinion in Urology* 19 (2009): 263–267; G. W. Watson, L. M. Beaver, D. E. Williams, R. H. Dashwood, and E. Ho, "Phytochemicals from Cruciferous Vegetables, Epigenetics, and Prostate Cancer Prevention," *American Association of Pharmaceutical Scientists Journal* 15, no. 4 (2013): 951–961.

Chapter 2

1. USDA, National Agricultural Statistics Service, Livestock Slaughter 2012 Summary, April 2013.

2. USDA, National Agricultural Statistics Service, Livestock Slaughter 2012 Summary, February 2013.

3. L. Horrigan, R. S. Lawrence, and P. Walker, "How Sustainable Agriculture Can Address the Environmental and Human Health Harms of Industrial Agriculture," *Environmental Health Perspectives* 110 (2002): 445–456.

4. E. G. Hertwich, E. van der Voet, A. Tukker, M. Huijbregts, P. Kazmierczyk, M. Lenzen, J. McNeely, and Y. Moriguchi, "Assessing the Environmental Impacts of Consumption and Production: Priority Products and Materials" (Nairobi, Kenya: United Nations Environment Programme, 2010), 12.

5. US Environmental Protection Agency, "Methane and Nitrous Oxide Emissions from Natural Sources" (Washington, DC: Environmental Protection Agency, 2010).

6. E. Gidon and P. A. Martin, "Diet, Energy, and Global Warming," *Earth Interactions*, 10, no. 9 (2006): 1–17, 9.

7. Ibid.

8. Ibid., 12.

Chapter 3

1. Messina and Norris, *Vegan for Life*, 1

2. S. Lorente-Cebrián, A. G. Costa, S. Navas-Carretero, M. Zabala, J. A. Martínez, and M. J. Moreno-Aliaga "Role of Omega-3 Fatty Acids in Obesity, Metabolic Syndrome, and Cardiovascular Diseases: A Review of the Evidence," *Journal of Physiology and Biochemistry* 69 (2013): 633–651; E. J. Chan and L. Cho, "What Can We Expect from Omega-3 Fatty Acids?" *Cleveland Clinic Journal of Medicine* 76 (2009): 245–251.

3. J. M. Bourre, "Dietary Omega-3 Fatty Acids for Women," *Biomedicine and Pharmacotherapy* 61 (2007): 105–112.

4. T. L. Blasbalg, J. R. Hibbeln, and R. R. Rawlings, "Changes in Consumption of Omega-3 and Omega-6 Fatty Acids in the United States During the 20th Century," *American Journal of Clinical Nutrition* 93 (2011): 950–962.

5. Sharon Palmer, *The Plant-Powered Diet: The Lifelong Eating Plan for Achieving Optimal Health, Beginning Today* (New York: Experiment, 2012), 168–169.

6. A. P. Simopoulos, "Essential Fatty Acids in Health and Chronic Disease," *American Journal of Clinical Nutrition* 70 (1999): 560S–569S.

7. Elson M. Haas and Buck Levin, *Staying Healthy with Nutrition: The Complete Guide to Diet and Nutritional Medicine* (Berkeley, CA: Celestial Arts, 2006), 68.

8. P. T. Voon, T. K. Ng, V. K. Lee, and K. Nesaretnam, "Diets High in Palmitic Acid (16:0), Lauric and Myristic Acids (12:0 + 14:0), or Oleic Acid (18:1) Do Not Alter Postprandial or Fasting Plasma Homocysteine and Inflammatory Markers in Healthy Malaysian Adults," *American Journal of Clinical Nutrition* 94 (2011): 1451–1457; A. B. Feranil, P. L. Duazo, C. W. Kuzawa, and L. S. Adair, "Coconut Oil Is Associated with a Beneficial Lipid Profile in Pre-Menopausal Women in the Philippines," *Asia Pacific Journal of Clinical Nutrition* 20 (2011): 190–195.

9. M. M. Flynn and S. E. Reinert, "Comparing an Olive Oil–Enriched Diet to a Standard

Lower-Fat Diet for Weight Loss in Breast Cancer Survivors: A Pilot Study," *Journal of Women's Health* 19 (2010): 1155–1161.

10. D. E. Cintra, E. R. Ropelle, J. C. Moraes, J. R. Pauli, J. Morari, C. T. Souza, R. Grimaldi, et al., "Unsaturated Fatty Acids Revert Diet-Induced Hypothalamic Inflammation in Obesity," *PLoS One* 7 (2012): e30571; A. Camargo, J. Ruano, J. M. Fernandez, L. D. Parnell, A. Jimenez, M. Santos-Gonzalez, C. Marin, et al., "Gene Expression Changes in Mononuclear Cells in Patients with Metabolic Syndrome After Acute Intake of Phenol-Rich Virgin Olive Oil," *BMC Genomics* 11 (2010): 253.

11. P. Appleby, A. Roddam, N. Allen, T. Key, "Comparative fracture risk in vegetarians and nonvegetarians in EPIC-Oxford," *European Journal of Clinical Nutrition* 61 (2007):1400–6. Epub February 2007.

12. Messina and Norris, *Vegan for Life*, 62–65.

Chapter 4

1. Davis, 218–220.

2. E. Sikora and I. Bodziarczyk, "Composition and Antioxidant Activity of Kale (Brassica oleracea L. var. acephala) Raw and Cooked," *Scientiarum Polonorum Technologia Alimentaria* 11 (2012): 239–248.

Chapter 5

1. C. Koebnick, C. Strassner, I. Hoffman, and C. Leitzmann, "Consequences of a Long-Term Raw Food Diet on Body Weight and Menstruation: Results of a Questionnaire Survey," *Annals of Nutrition and Metabolism* 43 (1999): 69–79.

Chapter 6

1. J. Dwyer, E. Foulkes, M. Evans, and L. Ausman, "Acid/Alkaline Ash Diets: Time for Assessment and Change," *Journal of the American Dietetic Association* 85 (1985): 841–845.

2. T. Remer and F. Manz, "Potential Renal Acid Load of Foods and Its Influence on Urine pH," *Journal of the American Dietetic Association* 95 (1995): 791–797; H. Macdonald, S. A. New, W. D. Fraser, M. K. Campbell, and D. Reid, "Low Dietary Potassium Intakes and High Dietary Estimates of Net Endogenous Acid Production Are Associated with Low Bone Mineral Density in Premenopausal Women and Increased Markers of Bone Resorption in Postmenopausal Women," *American Journal of Clinical Nutrition* 81 (2005): 923–933.

3. B. A. Ince, E. J. Anderson, and R. M. Neer, "Lowering Dietary Protein to U.S. Recommended Dietary Allowance Levels Reduces Urinary Calcium Excretion and Bone Resorption in Young Women," *Journal of Clinical Endocrinology and Metabolism* 89 (2004): 3801–3807; S. A. Schuette, M. B. Zemel, and H. M. Linkswiler, "Studies on the Mechanism of Protein-Induced Hypercalciuria in Older Men and Women," *Journal of Nutrition* 110 (1980): 305–315; F. Manz, T. Remer, E. Decher-Spliethoff, M. Hohler, M. Kersting, C. Kunz, and B. Lausen, "Effects of a High Protein Intake on Renal Acid Excretion in Bodybuilders," *Z Ernahrungswiss* 34 (1995): 10–15.

4. J. Calvez, N. Poupin, C. Chesneau, C. Lassale, and D. Tome, "Protein Intake, Calcium Balance and Health Consequences," *European Journal of Clinical Nutrition* 66 (2012): 281–295.

5. A. L. Darling, D. J. Millward, D. J. Torgerson, C. E. Hewitt, and S. A. Lanham-New,

"Dietary Protein and Bone Health: A Systematic Review and Meta-Analysis," *American Journal of Clinical Nutrition* 90 (2009): 1674–1692.

6. X. O. Shu, Y. Zheng, H. Cai, K. Gu, Z. Chen, W. Zheng, and W. Lu, "Soy Food Intake and Breast Cancer Survival," *Journal of the American Medical Association* 302 (2009): 2437–2443; L. M. Butler, A. H. Wu, R. Wang, W. P. Koh, J. M. Yuan, and M. C. Yu, "A Vegetable-Fruit-Soy Dietary Pattern Protects Against Breast Cancer Among Postmenopausal Singapore Chinese Women," *American Journal of Clinical Nutrition* 91 (2010): 1013–1019; A. H. Wu, W. P. Koh, R. Wang, H. P. Lee, and M. C. Yu, "Soy Intake and Breast Cancer Risk in Singapore Chinese Health Study," *British Journal of Cancer* 99 (2008): 196–200.

7. L. A. Korde, A. H. Wu, T. Fears, A. M. Nomura, D. W. West, L. N. Kolonel, M. C. Pike, et al., "Childhood Soy Intake and Breast Cancer Risk in Asian American Women," *Cancer Epidemiology, Biomarkers and Prevention* 18 (2009): 1–10; X. O. Shu, F. Jin, Q. Dai, W. Wen, J. D. Potter, L. H. Kushi, Z. Ruan, et al., "Soyfood Intake During Adolescence and Subsequent Risk of Breast Cancer Among Chinese Women," *Cancer Epidemiology, Biomarkers and Prevention* 10 (2001): 483–488.

8. B. J. Caan, L. Natarajan, B. A. Parker, E. B. Gold, C. A. Thomson, V. A. Newman, C. L. Rock, et al., "Soy Food Consumption and Breast Cancer Prognosis," *Cancer Epidemiology, Biomarkers and Prevention* 20 (2011): 854–858.

9. M. Messina and G. Redmond, "Effects of Soy Protein and Soybean Isoflavones on Thyroid Function in Healthy Adults and Hypothyroid Patients: A Review of the Relevant Literature," *Thyroid* 16 (2006): 249–258.

10. Davis, 107.

11. Davis, 44.

Acknowledgments

MY FIRST EXPRESSION OF GRATITUDE goes to my mother, Rallou Hamshaw, for loving me, supporting me, and embracing me as I am. I love you, Mom.

This book would not exist without the vision and confidence of my agent, Chris Parris-Lamb. Chris, thank you for taking my writing seriously, for encouraging me to do the same, and for championing this project from start to finish. I'm so thankful for our friendship.

Kris Carr, I can't tell you how deeply I appreciate your confidence in me. Thank you for your beautiful words, for reminding me why I do what I do, and for setting such an elegant example of what it means to change the face of health and wellness. Corinne Bowen, thank you for all of your help with this book.

Renée Sedliar, thank you for being the best editor I could have imagined: intelligent, efficient, witty, and deeply attuned to my voice and my message. This book is so much better because of you. Thanks, too, to everyone at Da Capo Lifelong: Cisca Schreefel, thank you for handling the production process nimbly;

Lisa Diercks, thank you for your beautiful interior design; Alexander Camlin, thank you for making the cover come to life; and Jenna Gilligan, thanks for your expert help with publicity and promotion.

Hannah Kaminsky, you are phenomenal. Thank you for making this book come alive, for keeping me sane through the recipe testing process, and for being a true friend. I literally could not have done it without you. Jeff Skeirik, thank you for my fabulous author photo, and for being such a light in the raw foods community.

I am eternally grateful to my amazing group of recipe testers: Elizabeth Amrien, Sarah Brown, Beth Horwitz Fox, Courtney Pool, Andrea Manka, Amy Skretta, Melanie St. Ours, Hannah Terry-Whyte, Heather Waxman, Melissa Davison, and Janet Mulawney. Thank you for your hard work, and for tolerating my scattered brain with grace. Valerie Mirko, thank you for putting nearly as much work into recipe testing as I did, and for being an exceptional neighbor and friend.

A big, loving thank-you to all of the George-town post-bacc students whom I was lucky for being an exceptional neighbor and friend.

A big, loving thank-you to all of the Georgetown post-bacc students whom I was lucky enough to call my peers in the last three years. I don't know what I would have done without you. Special thanks to my brothers-in-arms, Luke Nankee and David Coon. You are going to be phenomenal doctors, and I'm proud to have passed through the fire by your side. Reed Macy, thank you for being an unwavering friend and confidante. I look forward to watching you save the world.

Blanche Christerson, thank you for all of your love, support, and good counsel.

Chloe Polemis Berthelsen, thank you for being the best sister I could hope for, for always giving me space in which to grow and change, and for your extraordinary, unwavering belief in me. I love you so much.

Nelly Ward, thank you for your wise perspective, your sound advice, and your tireless wit. How lucky I am to have grown up with you. Rose Lichter-Marck, thank you for encouraging me to be courageous and authentic, and for inspiring me with your example. Christina Wilson, thank you for being my soul sister and kindred free spirit. If I could insert an emoji here, I would.

Jordan Heimer, thank you for getting it, always. Jim Rutman, thank you for your compassion, kindness, and support. Sam Douglas, thank you for your thoughtfulness, good humor, and your unfailing wisdom.

Steven, I'll be forever grateful for your curiosity about my taste in literary magazines. Thank you for your companionship, your encouragement, and for finding hundreds of different ways to make me smile.

My veganism is continually enriched by the example set by my peers and friends in the activist and food blogging communities. JL Fields, I am so glad we decided to spend an afternoon together at the pool three years ago. I adore you. Jasmin Singer and Mariann Sullivan, thank you for encouraging me to be more confident as an activist, for your tireless work on behalf of animals, and for your remarkable friendship. Cassie Karopkin, it's because of you that I let animals into my heart. Thank you for recognizing my capacity for compassion. Heidi Kristoffer, thank you for your wise listening ear, and for helping me to embrace an uncertain future. *Om Ganesha.* Brendan Brazier, thank you for agreeing to lunch with a random blogger years ago, and for the many dinners and walks and conversations that have followed. Never balance.

Sarma Melngailis, I have you to thank for first showing me how exciting and beautiful raw food could be. Thank you, thank you. Huge thanks, too, to Mark, Joy, Bart, and Benet and the wonderful Candle Cafe community in New York.

Angela Liddon, Ashley McLaughlin, Anne Mauney, Dreena Burton, Ricki Heller, Heather Nauta, Christy Morgan, Allyson Kramer, Lisa Pitman, Nicole Axworthy, Kristy Turner, Meghan Telpner, Brittany Mullins, Jaime Karpovich, Sayward Rebhal, Jackie Sobon, Michelle and Lori Corso, Gina Harney, Evan Thomas, Abby Heugel, Janessa Philomon-Kerp, Casey Stevens, Janae Wise, Allesandra Seiter, Ela Harrison Gordon, Alicia Sokol, Elenore Bendel-Zahn, Cadry Nelson, Amanda McGuire, Emma Potts: It is an honor to inhabit the blogosphere along with you all. So much love. Melissa Davison, I owe you my entire blogging career. Thanks for encouraging me to put my passion for raw food and veganism into words.

Kathy Patalsky, thank you for inspiring me with your gorgeous blog, your incredible business acumen, your sly sense of humor, and your generous heart. I love our friendship.

In the last two years I was lucky enough to find a professional mentor, colleague, and dear friend, all in the person of Robynne Chutkan. Robynne, you inspire me in more ways than you'll ever realize. I look forward to a lifetime of kale, yoga, spirited conversation, and a shared confidence that we can find new ways to help people.

Finally, my deepest gratitude goes to the men and women who have read *Choosing Raw* over the years. Thank you for allowing me to share the food I love so much with you, for trusting me with your thoughts, words, and stories, and for engaging with my work so intelligently and critically. Thank you for allowing me to grow and evolve. You have inspired me to be more thoughtful, more conscious, and more compassionate, and I am eternally grateful. I hope you'll enjoy the book.

Index

C

Cabbage
- Avocado Black Bean Breakfast Scramble, *178*, 179
- Basic Massaged Kale Salad, 103–105, *104*
- Heat-Free Lentil and Walnut Tacos, *190*, 191
- Raw Pad Thai, 191–192, *193*

Cacao nibs
- Almond Pulp Porridge, *208*, 209
- Chocolate Raw-Nola, *202*, 202–203
- Coconutty for Chocolate Chip Cookies, 230, *231*
- DIY Snack Bars, 108, *121*
- No-Bake Sunflower Oat Bars, 120, *121*
- Superfood Trail Mix, 120–123, *150*

Cacao powder
- Almost Instant Chocolate-Covered Strawberries, 236
- Chocolate Açai Bowl, 209
- Chocolate-Covered Superfood Clusters, 235
- Chocolate Raw-Nola, *202*, 202–203
- Chocomole, 109, *109*
- Mocha Maca Chia Pudding, *109*, 200
- No-Bake Tartlets with Raw Vegan Ganache Filling, *242*, 243

Caesar Salad, Dinosaur Kale and White Bean, *140*, 141
Calcium, 38–39, 45–46, 53–54, 58
Cancer, 19, 58–59
Carbohydrates, 34–35, 56–57

Carrots
- Avocado Black Bean Breakfast Scramble, *178*, 179
- Basic Massaged Kale Salad, 103–105, *104*
- Carrot, Avocado, and Turmeric Soup, *186*, 187
- Carrot and Millet Pilaf with Mesquite Glazed Tempeh, 165–166, *167*
- Carrot and Zucchini Pappardelle with Pesto and Peas, *228*, 229
- Carrot Cake Cupcakes with Cream Cheese Frosting, 240–243
- Carrot Miso Dressing, 129
- Coconut Curry Kelp Noodles, 223–224
- Curried Chickpea and Carrot Salad, 163
- Easy Red Lentil Sweet Potato and Coconut Curry, 167–168
- Nori Rolls with Gingery Almond Pâté and Raw Veggies, 182–183, *183*
- Raw Carrot Falafel, 188, *189*
- Raw or Cooked Ratatouille, *222*, 222–223
- Raw Pad Thai, 191–192, *193*
- Raw Spinach and Mushroom Burgers, 192–193
- Sprouted-Grain Wraps with Kale-Slaw Filling, 185
- The Veggie Bowl, 114

Cashew butter
- Creamy Basil and Ginger Noodles, 210, *211*
- Easiest Vegan Pumpkin Soup, 162
- No-Bake Sunflower Oat Bars, 120, *121*
- Reinvented Ants on a Log, 124, *125*

Cashews
- Blueberry Cheesecake, 238–240, *239*
- Cashew Banana Yogurt, *203*, 203–205
- Cashew Cheese (or cashew cream), 99
- Classic Cheesy Kale Chips, *122*, 123
- Cream Cheese Frosting, 240–243
- Creamy Maple Chipotle Dressing, 128
- Dinosaur Kale and White Bean Caesar Salad, *140*, 141
- DIY Snack Bars, 108, *121*
- Easiest Vegan Pumpkin Soup, 162
- No-Bake Tartlets with Raw Vegan Ganache Filling, *242*, 243
- Nut or Seed Pâté, 101
- Raw Cashew Alfredo, 134
- Raw Corn Chowder, *213*, 213–214
- Raw Key Lime Pie, 235–236, *237*
- Raw Vegan Blueberry Ginger Ice Cream, 240, *241*
- Rosemary Cauliflower Mashed Potatoes, *196*, 198
- Simple Raw Vanilla Macaroons, *232*, 237–238
- substitutions, 95
- Superfood Trail Mix, 120–123, *150*

Cauliflower Mashed Potatoes, Rosemary, *196*, 198

A SEAT BY THE HEARTH

OTHER BOOKS BY AMY CLIPSTON

THE AMISH HOMESTEAD SERIES

A Place at Our Table

Room on the Porch Swing

THE AMISH HEIRLOOM SERIES

The Forgotten Recipe

The Courtship Basket

The Cherished Quilt

The Beloved Hope Chest

THE HEARTS OF THE LANCASTER GRAND HOTEL SERIES

A Hopeful Heart

A Mother's Secret

A Dream of Home

A Simple Prayer

THE KAUFFMAN AMISH BAKERY SERIES

A Gift of Grace

A Promise of Hope

A Place of Peace

A Life of Joy

A Season of Love

NOVELLA COLLECTIONS

Amish Sweethearts

NOVELLAS

A Plain and Simple Christmas

Naomi's Gift included in *An Amish Christmas Gift*

A Spoonful of Love included in *An Amish Kitchen*

Love Birds included in *An Amish Market*

Love and Buggy Rides included in *An Amish Harvest*

Summer Storms included in *An Amish Summer*

The Christmas Cat included in *An Amish Christmas Love*

Home Sweet Home included in *An Amish Winter*

A Son for Always included in *An Amish Spring*

A Legacy of Love included in *An Amish Heirloom*

No Place Like Home included in *An Amish Homecoming*

NONFICTION

A Gift of Love

PRAISE FOR AMY CLIPSTON

"This heartbreaking series continues to take a fearlessly honest look at grief, as hopelessness threatens to steal what happiness Allen has treasured within his marriage and recent fatherhood. Clipston takes these feelings seriously without sugarcoating any aspect of the mourning process, allowing her characters to make their painful but ultimately joyous journey back to love and faith. Readers who have made this tough and ongoing pilgrimage themselves will appreciate the author's realistic portrayal of coming to terms with loss in order to continue living with hope and happiness."
—*RT BOOK REVIEWS*, 4 STARS, ON *ROOM ON THE PORCH SWING*

"A story of grief as well as new beginnings, this is a lovely Amish tale and the start of a great new series."
—*PARKERSBURG NEWS AND SENTINEL* ON *A PLACE AT OUR TABLE*

"Themes of family, forgiveness, love, and strength are woven throughout the story . . . a great choice for all readers of Amish fiction."
—*CBA MARKET MAGAZINE* ON *A PLACE AT OUR TABLE*

"This debut title in a new series offers an emotionally charged and engaging read headed by sympathetically drawn and believable protagonists. The meaty issues of trust and faith make this a solid book group choice."
—*LIBRARY JOURNAL* ON *A PLACE AT OUR TABLE*

"These sweet, tender novellas from one of the genre's best make the perfect sampler for new readers curious about Amish romances."
—*LIBRARY JOURNAL* ON *AMISH SWEETHEARTS*

"Clipston is as reliable as her character, giving Emily a difficult and intense romance worthy of Emily's ability to shine the light of Christ into the hearts of those she loves."
—*RT BOOK REVIEWS*, 4½ STARS, TOP PICK! ON *THE CHERISHED QUILT*

"Clipston's heartfelt writing and engaging characters make her a fan favorite. Her latest Amish tale combines a spiritual message of accepting God's blessings as they are given with a sweet romance."
—*LIBRARY JOURNAL* ON *THE CHERISHED QUILT*

"In the first book in her Amish Heirloom series, Clipston takes readers on a roller-coaster ride through grief, guilt, and anxiety."
—*BOOKLIST* ON *THE FORGOTTEN RECIPE*

"Clipston delivers another enchanting series starter with a tasty premise, family secrets, and sweet-as-pie romance, offering assurance that true love can happen more than once and second chances are worth fighting for."
—*RT Book Reviews*, 4½ STARS, TOP PICK! ON *The Forgotten Recipe*

"Clipston is well versed in Amish culture and does a good job creating the world of Lancaster County, Penn. . . . Amish fiction fans will enjoy this story— and want a taste of Veronica's raspberry pie!"
—*Publishers Weekly* ON *The Forgotten Recipe*

"[Clipston] does an excellent job of wrapping up her story while setting the stage for the sequel."
—*CBA Retailers + Resources* ON *The Forgotten Recipe*

"Clipston brings this engaging series to an end with two emotional family reunions, a prodigal son parable, a sweet but hard-won romance, and a happy ending for characters readers have grown to love. Once again, she gives us all we could possibly want from a talented storyteller."
—*RT Book Reviews*, 4½ STARS, TOP PICK! ON *A Simple Prayer*

". . . will leave readers craving more."
—*RT Book Reviews*, 4½ STARS, TOP PICK! ON *A Mother's Secret*

"Clipston's series starter has a compelling drama involving faith, family, and romance . . . [an] absorbing series."
—*RT Book Reviews*, 4½ STARS, TOP PICK! ON *A Hopeful Heart*

"Authentic characters, delectable recipes, and faith abound in Clipston's second Kauffman Amish Bakery story."
—*RT Book Reviews*, 4 STARS ON *A Promise of Hope*

". . . an entertaining story of Amish life, loss, love and family."
—*RT Book Reviews*, 4 STARS ON *A Place of Peace*

"This fifth and final installment in the Kauffman Amish Bakery series is sure to please fans who have waited for Katie's story."
—*Library Journal* ON *A Season of Love*

"[The Kauffman Amish Bakery] series' wide popularity is sure to attract readers to this novella, and they won't be disappointed by the excellent writing and the story's wholesome goodness."
—*Library Journal* ON *A Plain and Simple Christmas*

A SEAT BY THE HEARTH

An Amish Homestead Novel

AMY CLIPSTON

 ZONDERVAN®

For editor Jean Bloom with love and appreciation.
Thank you for using your amazing talent to polish my books and
keep my characters and timelines straight. You're a blessing!

GLOSSARY

ach: oh
aenti: aunt
appeditlich: delicious
Ausbund: Amish hymnal
bedauerlich: sad
boppli: baby
bopplin: babies
brot: bread
bruder: brother
bruderskind: niece/nephew
bruderskinner: nieces/nephews
bu: boy
buwe: boys
daadi: granddad
daadihaus: a small house built onto or near the main house for grandparents to live in
daed: father
danki: thank you
dat: dad
Dietsch: Pennsylvania Dutch, the Amish language (a German dialect)
dochder: daughter
dochdern: daughters
Dummle!: Hurry!

Englisher: a non-Amish person
faul: lazy
faulenzer: lazy person
fraa: wife
freind: friend
freinden: friends
froh: happy
gegisch: silly
gern gschehne: you're welcome
grossdaadi: grandfather
grossdochder: granddaughter
grossdochdern: granddaughters
grossmammi: grandmother
gross-sohn: grandson
Gude mariye: Good morning
gut: good
Gut nacht: Good night
haus: house
Ich liebe dich: I love you
kaffi: coffee
kapp: prayer covering or cap
kichli: cookie
kichlin: cookies
kind: child
kinner: children
krank: sick
kuche: cake
kumm: come
liewe: love, a term of endearment
maed: young women, girls
maedel: young woman
mamm: mom

mammi: grandma

mei: my

Meiding: shunning

mutter: mother

naerfich: nervous

narrisch: crazy

onkel: uncle

Ordnung: the oral tradition of practices required and forbidden in the Amish faith

schee: pretty

schmaert: smart

schtupp: family room

schweschder: sister

schweschdere: sisters

sohn: son

Was iss letz?: What's wrong?

Willkumm: Welcome

Wie geht's: How do you do? or Good day!

wunderbaar: wonderful

ya: yes

zwillingbopplin: twins

AMISH HOMESTEAD
SERIES FAMILY TREES

Edna m. Yonnie Allgyer
|
Priscilla

Marilyn m. Willie Dienner
|
Simeon (deceased)
Kayla m. James "Jamie" Riehl
Nathan

**Eva m. Simeon (deceased)
Dienner**
|
Simeon Jr. ("Junior")

Nellie m. Walter Esh
|
Judah
Naaman

Laura m. Allen Lambert
|
Mollie Faith (mother—Savilla—
deceased)

Irma Mae m. Milton Lapp
|
Savilla

Florence m. Vernon Riehl
|
James ("Jamie") Riehl (mother—
Dorothy—deceased)
Walter Esh (father—Alphus
Esh—deceased)
Mark Riehl (Laura's twin)
(mother—Dorothy—deceased)
Laura (Mark's twin) m. Allen
Lambert (mother—Dorothy—
deceased)
Roy Esh (father—Alphus Esh—
deceased)
Sarah Jane Esh (father—Alphus
Esh—deceased)
Cindy Riehl (mother—
Dorothy—deceased)

Kayla m. James "Jamie" Riehl
|
Calvin

Elsie m. Noah Zook
|
Christian
Lily Rose

NOTE TO THE READER

While this novel is set against the real backdrop of Lancaster County, Pennsylvania, the characters are fictional. There is no intended resemblance between the characters in this book and any real members of the Amish or Mennonite communities. As with any work of fiction, I've taken license in some areas of research as a means of creating the necessary circumstances for my characters. My research was thorough; however, it would be impossible to be completely accurate in details and description, since every community differs. Therefore, any inaccuracies in the Amish and Mennonite lifestyles portrayed in this book are completely due to fictional license.

ONE

Priscilla Allgyer's hands trembled as her taxi sped down the two-lane road. When the Allgyer's Belgian and Dutch Harness Horses sign came into view, her stomach seemed to twist.

She turned to her son, who'd nodded off in the booster seat beside her.

"Ethan." She nudged him. "Ethan, wake up. We're here."

"Already?" His honey-brown eyes fluttered open as he yawned. "But I just fell asleep." He peered out the window as the Prius steered up the winding rock driveway.

When they reached the top, she could see her father's line of red barns and stables. She'd been away for eight years, but all the buildings looked as pristine as if they'd just been painted. Perhaps they had. The white split-rail fence lining the enormous, lush, rolling green pasture where his beautiful horses frolicked looked the same. The large, two-story whitewashed house where she was born and raised seemed just as immaculate. Every building, every blade of grass on her father's horse farm was as impeccable as she remembered.

If only her childhood had been as perfect.

"This is where you grew up, Mom?"

1

"Yes." Her chest constricted as the taxi bumped over the rocks. She cleared her throat and tried to shake off the apprehension coiling through her. When she left all those years ago, she promised she'd never return.

But here she was with nothing but a few dollars to her name and a child she'd had out of wedlock.

"It's nice." Ethan pointed to the row of barns after unbuckling himself. "It's a horse farm?"

She nodded. Ethan lowered his window, and the humid July air mixed with the familiar aroma of moist earth and horses permeated the taxi and overpowered her senses.

"I can touch the horses?"

She shrugged. "I imagine so." *If my father even allows us to stay.*

She shoved that thought away. Aside from a few nights in a motel and then a homeless shelter, her parents were her only hope. Priscilla would do anything to give her son a safe home.

When she noticed movement in the corner of her vision, she turned toward her father's largest barn. The door had swung open, and a man stood with his back to the driveway. He looked taller than Robert Yoder, the farmhand who had worked for her father since she was a teenager. His shoulders seemed broader too.

The taxi came to a halt in front of the house, and Priscilla's attention was drawn to her childhood home. Her palms began to sweat as she studied the wraparound porch. Her father's harsh voice and biting criticisms echoed in her mind, and when she closed her eyes and rubbed her temples against a coming headache, she could still see his disappointed face.

This was a mistake. Her father would never forgive her. Maybe they should have stayed in Baltimore with Trent. Her left hand moved to her right bicep, hidden by the three-quarter sleeve of her purple shirt. The situation there might have improved if she'd tried harder to keep Trent happy.

But it wasn't safe to keep Ethan in that environment! It was her duty to protect her son.

"Miss?" The taxi driver turned to face her. "I think we're here."

Priscilla had just opened her mouth to respond when a tap near Ethan's open window startled her. She spun toward it and was surprised to find Mark Riehl peering in.

"Can I help—" He stopped, recognition sparkling in his bright-blue eyes. "Priscilla?"

"Mark. Hi." She tried to force a smile, but it felt more like a grimace.

"Your *dat* didn't mention you were coming home today." He glanced toward the house and then back at her.

"I didn't tell either of my parents I was coming." Her throat suddenly felt bone-dry.

"Oh." He smiled. "They're going to be surprised."

That was an understatement. "Yes, they sure are."

Mark turned his attention to Ethan and smiled. "Hi. I'm Mark." He extended his arm through the open window, and Ethan shook his hand.

"Hi. I'm Ethan. I'm six and a half. We're here to visit my grandparents."

"It's nice to meet you." Mark grinned as his eyes flickered back to Priscilla.

She swallowed a groan. Why did Mark Riehl, one of her schoolmates and an acquaintance from her youth group, have to be at her father's farm when she arrived? Coming home was difficult enough. Facing a peer from her past made it even more painful. News of her arrival would rage through the community like wildfire, and she was certain that judgment would follow.

"Miss?" The driver faced her again. "Are you going to get out of the car? Or do you want me to take you somewhere else?"

Priscilla hesitated as anxiety gushed through her. If she told the driver to take her to the nearest motel, she and Ethan could try this again tomorrow. But Mark had already seen her and—

"Let's go, Mom!" Ethan's insistence broke through her thoughts.

Mark stepped back from the door as Ethan wrenched it open, climbed out of the taxi, and started for the front porch. Mark bent down and leaned inside. "Do you have any luggage?"

"Yes, I do." She pointed toward the trunk. "We have two big suitcases."

"I'll get them for you." Mark tapped the roof to signal the driver to open the trunk, pushed the door closed, and then disappeared around the back of the car.

Priscilla paid the fare and thanked the driver before getting out. The stifling heat slammed into her like a brick wall as she turned to where Mark had both suitcases already sitting on the driveway.

"Ethan," Mark called as he closed the trunk, "why don't you come pull one of these suitcases to the bottom of those steps for me?"

"Okay!" Ethan jogged back down the porch steps and grabbed the handle of one of the suitcases before bumping it along the rock path.

Priscilla fingered the strap of her purse as the yellow taxi steered back down the driveway. She should have asked the driver to take them to a motel. Her mother might welcome her, but her father would most likely slam the door in her face.

"Priscilla?"

She looked up and found Mark studying her. He seemed taller than she remembered. While he'd always been taller than she was, as were most of her peers, he looked as if he towered over her five-foot-two stature by at least eight inches. Not only were his shoulders broader than she recalled, but his striking blue eyes seemed even more intelligent. He was more handsome than she remembered, too, with his light-brown hair, strong jaw, and electric smile.

He had an easy demeanor as well, and she bit back a frown. Mark Riehl had always been aware of just how attractive he was, and he enjoyed the attention of all the young women who followed him around, waiting for him to choose one of them to be his girlfriend.

Mark's twin sister, Laura, had been one of her best friends, but Mark had never seemed to notice Priscilla. No one did. She'd always felt as if she faded into the background with all the young men in their youth group. They noticed Laura and the other, prettier young women instead.

A smile turned up the corners of Mark's lips. "Are you ready to go into the *haus*?" He nodded toward the front porch. "Your *dat* walked inside a few minutes ago. I think your *mamm* is making supper."

"Mom!" Ethan's voice held a thread of whining as he called from the porch steps. "I'm hungry, and I need to use the bathroom."

"I'm coming." She started up the path with Mark at her side, and an awkward silence fell between them.

"What's that house for?" Ethan pointed toward the small cottage behind her parents' large farmhouse.

"That's called the *daadihaus*."

Ethan snickered. "The *what* house?"

"It's where my grandparents lived when I was little." Her heart felt heavy at the memory of her father's mother, who was widowed when Priscilla was still just a toddler. If only *Mammi* were still alive. She would've welcomed her and her son home. "My father's farmhand, Robert Yoder, lives there."

"He doesn't live there anymore." Mark lifted the suitcase he'd been pulling and carried it up the porch steps. "He quit a little over a year ago and moved to Ohio with his new *fraa*."

"What's a *fraw*?" Ethan scrunched his nose.

"*Fraa* means wife." Priscilla turned back to Mark. "Robert moved to Ohio?"

"*Ya*." He set down the suitcase. "He met a woman who was here visiting relatives, and they fell in love. They married, and he moved to Ohio, where she was from." He went back down the steps for the second suitcase.

"Who's working for my father, then?"

"I am." When Mark reached the porch again, he opened the screen door and set each suitcase inside the family room. Then he held the door open for her and Ethan.

Questions swirled through her mind. Why would Mark work for her father when his own father owned a dairy farm? Wouldn't he be expected to help run the family business?

As she followed Ethan into the house, memories mixed with the smell of fried chicken wafted over her. She scanned the family room. It was just as she remembered. The two brown sofas her parents purchased before she was born still sat in the middle of the room, flanked by their favorite tan wing chairs. The two propane lamps and the matching oak end tables and coffee table were the same too.

The doorway at the far side of the room led to a hallway that led to her parents' bedroom and a bathroom. The staircase to the four upstairs bedrooms and another bathroom sat to her left. The stairs seemed to beckon her to venture to the second floor to see if her old room was still decorated the way it was when she'd snuck out of the house that night, leaving a note promising to never return.

Ethan took her hand in his and tugged. "Where are my grandparents?"

"Your grandmother is probably through there." Priscilla pointed to the doorway to her right.

Taking a deep breath, she steered Ethan into the large kitchen. Her mother stood at the stove, her back to the doorway, turning over pieces of chicken with a pair of metal tongs.

"Yonnie, I told you I would call you when supper was ready." She lowered the flame and half turned around. When her eyes focused on Priscilla and Ethan, she gasped and whirled. The tongs dropped to the floor with a clatter. "Priscilla?"

"Hi, *Mamm*." Tears stung Priscilla's eyes.

Mamm's mouth worked, but no words escaped.

"Hi." Ethan skipped over to her. "I'm Ethan, your grandson." He looked back at Priscilla over his shoulder. "How do you say grandson in Dutch?"

"*Gross-sohn*," Priscilla responded, her voice thick with raging emotion.

Mamm made a strangled noise and pulled Ethan into her arms. "My prayers have been answered!"

Priscilla wiped her eyes as guilt, hot and biting, nearly overcame her.

Mark leaned against the doorframe and folded his arms over his chest. "You haven't taught him Dutch." It was a statement, not a question.

"No." She shook her head. "His father didn't like me to speak it."

"Huh." Mark rubbed his clean-shaven chin.

"Priscilla." *Mamm* closed the distance between them and pulled her into a crushing hug, forcing the air from Priscilla's lungs. Then she stepped back and touched Priscilla's face. "You look tired."

"It's been a long day." Priscilla looked up at her mother, taking in her affectionate, dark-brown eyes and pretty face. Lines reflected the eight years that had passed.

"I can't believe you're here." A sheen of tears glistened in her eyes as she caressed the thick ponytail that cascaded past Priscilla's shoulders to the middle of her back. "Why didn't you call or write so I could prepare? I would have had your favorite meal ready for you."

"This wasn't planned. I mean, I had been hoping to come visit, but I . . . Well, I wasn't sure when I was going to be able to . . ." Her hand fluttered to her right bicep again.

There was so much she wanted to share with her mother, but she couldn't hurt her that way. Besides, they had an audience. Not only was Ethan there, but Mark Riehl, a man she'd never trust with her deepest secrets, was still watching them.

"I wanted to surprise you." Priscilla tried to smile, but her mother's eyes were assessing her. *Mamm* could probably sense she wasn't telling the truth.

"Are you back for *gut*?" *Mamm* touched Priscilla's cheek again.

"Possibly. Would that be okay?" Priscilla could hear the humiliating thread of supplication in her voice. She cleared her throat and glanced at Ethan, who had taken a seat at the long kitchen table where Priscilla had eaten all her meals while growing up.

"Of course it will be okay." *Mamm* nodded with emphasis. "This is still your home."

Will Dat *agree with that?* Priscilla felt her lips press together with apprehension.

"Would you like me to carry the suitcases upstairs for you?" Mark asked.

Priscilla spun toward the doorway. Mark shifted his weight on his feet as if he were eager to leave.

"No, I think I can handle them, but thanks for offering."

Mark lifted an eyebrow. "They're pretty heavy. I don't mind carrying them up for you before I go." He gestured toward the suitcases. "Just let me know where you want them."

"It's fine. Really," Priscilla said, insisting.

Mark nodded. "All right. It was nice seeing you. I'll head home now." He nodded at her mother. "I'll see you tomorrow, Edna. *Gut nacht.*" He turned to go.

"No, wait," *Mamm* called after him. "Stay for supper."

Priscilla studied her mother. Why would her mother invite Mark to stay? Did she think his presence might keep her father from lashing out?

"*Danki,* but I need to get home." He jammed his thumb toward the front door. "*Mei schweschder* and her family are coming over for supper tonight."

"Laura?" Priscilla asked, her heart swelling with affection for her best friend. How she'd missed both Laura and their mutual best friend, Savilla Lapp, over the years. Leaving them behind had been almost as difficult as leaving her mother.

"*Ya.*" Mark smiled. "She'll be *froh* to hear you're back."

"Oh. Tell her I said hello." Would Laura accept her back into the community after learning she'd had a child out of wedlock?

"I will."

A door clicked shut somewhere in the house, and then Mark looked toward the far end of the family room. "Hi, Yonnie. I was just getting ready to leave."

"Where did these suitcases come from? Is someone here visiting? Why didn't I know about this?"

Priscilla trembled at the sound of *Dat*'s voice. The moment had arrived. Her father might tell her and Ethan to leave. She held her breath and sent a silent prayer to God.

Please let him take pity on Ethan and me. I need to stay until I can earn enough money to rent a safe place for us. Please help me be the mother Ethan deserves.

"Yonnie!" *Mamm* called. "You have to see who's here! It's a miracle."

"Ethan." Priscilla held out her hand. "Come here and meet your grandfather."

Ethan crossed the kitchen to stand next to her, a smile spreading across his face. Surely her father wouldn't break her son's heart.

Dat appeared in the kitchen doorway, and although his dark-brown hair was now threaded with gray, he was the same tall, wide, overbearing man she remembered.

"Priscilla?" He seemed surprised, but then the look in his dark eyes turned fierce. "What are you wearing?" His eyes moved up and down her attire.

Her cheeks heated as she brushed her sweaty palms over her worn jeans.

Dat's face transformed into a deep scowl as his eyes trained on hers again. "Why isn't your head covered?"

His words seemed to punch her in the stomach.

"I'll get you a headscarf." *Mamm* hurried into the utility room off the kitchen.

"Yonnie," Mark called from behind her father. "I'm going to leave."

Priscilla had forgotten Mark was standing there until he spoke, and she longed to run and hide under the table. Why did he have to witness this painful and embarrassing conversation? When her father didn't respond, Mark stayed put. Why didn't he just leave? He'd already said good-bye.

"Who is this?" *Dat* pointed to Ethan.

"My son." Priscilla's voice was soft and shaky. Why did she allow her father to steal her confidence? She forced herself to stand a little taller as she addressed him. Then she turned to Ethan. She had to shield him from her father's festering anger and disapproval.

"Why don't you go use the bathroom in the hallway?" She pointed toward the family room. "Just walk through there. You'll see the door to the bathroom down on the right."

Ethan hesitated, dividing a look between Priscilla and her father. Then he nodded and hurried off.

"Didn't *Mamm* tell you about him? We exchanged letters."

Dat looked toward the utility room. "Your *mamm* didn't tell me she wrote to you. I told her any contact with you is forbidden because you're shunned." His icy voice seemed to bounce off the cabinets before seeping through her skin.

"Here you go." *Mamm* appeared beside her with a light-blue scarf. "Put this over your hair. I kept your dresses, so you can put one on tomorrow." She gave Priscilla a smile that seemed more forced than genuine.

"*Danki*," Priscilla whispered as she covered her hair with the scarf before tying it under her ponytail.

Dat frowned at her mother. "Why didn't you tell me our *dochder* had a *bu*?"

Mamm fingered her apron and looked between Priscilla and *Dat* as she'd always done when *Dat* criticized her. Couldn't *Mamm* ever stand up to him? It was obvious nothing had changed in this house. Anger, hot and explosive, heated her from the inside.

"I knew it would upset you," *Mamm* finally said.

"And you continued to write to Priscilla after I told you not to."

To Priscilla's surprise, *Mamm* lifted her chin. "*Ya*, I did. She's our *dochder*, and Ethan is our *gross-sohn*," she said. "They're our family."

"She's shunned," he repeated before turning his glare back to Priscilla. "Where's your husband?"

"I don't have one, and I left his father." Priscilla folded her arms over her waist, trying to calm her shaking body.

Dat's eyes widened, and she braced herself, awaiting the explosion.

Priscilla's gaze flickered to Mark, and she found his eyes

focused on her. Trepidation detonated in her gut. If only her father had waited to have this conversation until Mark was gone. Now before the next Sunday church service the entire community would buzz with the juicy gossip that Priscilla Allgyer had not only returned, but with a child born out of wedlock.

Mark nodded at her, adjusted his straw hat on his head, and slipped into the family room. She heard the front door shut behind him.

"You came back to *mei haus* with a *kind*, and you're not married?" *Dat*'s voice rose.

"Yonnie," *Mamm* began, her voice trembling. "Please—"

"It's all right, *Mamm*. This was a bad idea." She ran to the front door and yanked it open, hoping she could catch Mark. When she spotted him walking toward one of the barns, she ran to the edge of the porch and leaned on the railing. "Mark!"

He spun and faced her. *"Ya?"*

"Would you please take Ethan and me to a motel?"

He hesitated, but only for a moment. *"Ya*, sure." He pointed toward the barn. "I just need to hitch up my horse."

"Thank you."

"No!" *Mamm* appeared on the porch, her eyes glistening. "Please don't go." She folded her hands as if she were praying. "I just got you back and met Ethan. My heart can't take losing you again."

"I can't stay here if *Dat* is going to criticize Ethan and me." Priscilla pointed to the open door behind her mother as her eyes filled with threatening tears. "I need a healthy and safe environment for my son."

"I understand, but please give me a chance to talk to your *dat*." *Mamm* touched her shoulder.

Ethan appeared in the doorway. "I'm hungry."

Mamm gave Priscilla a hopeful look. "Will you please stay for supper?"

Priscilla hesitated as she glanced toward where Mark stood hitching his horse to his buggy.

"Please," *Mamm* said.

Priscilla glanced at Ethan in the doorway, taking in his sweet face. He looked confused at the idea that they might not be staying. She was grateful he hadn't heard her father's horrible words, but there might be times when she wouldn't be able to shield him. Could she risk that? And could she tolerate her father for the sake of both her mother and her son?

"Just give me a chance to talk to him," *Mamm* whispered. "I'll smooth things over with him, and everything will be fine."

"I'll give him one night," Priscilla said, lowering her own voice. "If he doesn't treat me better, especially in front of Ethan, we're leaving."

"*Danki.*" *Mamm* smiled as she took Priscilla's hands in hers. "I'm so *froh* you're here." Then she turned toward Ethan. "Do you like fried chicken?"

Ethan's face brightened, and he clapped his hands. "Yeah!"

"Will you help me set the table?" *Mamm* asked as she started toward the door.

"Yes," Ethan said.

Mamm touched his shoulder as they walked into the house together.

Priscilla turned toward the barn again.

"Priscilla?" *Mamm* stopped in the doorway. "Are you coming inside?"

"*Ya,*" she said, easily slipping into the language she now realized she'd missed. "In a few minutes. I need to tell Mark we're staying."

After her mother and Ethan disappeared inside the house, Priscilla descended the steps and folded her arms over her middle as she approached Mark. "Thank you for agreeing to help, but I've decided we're staying for now."

"Okay." Mark gave her a little smile. "I guess I'll see you tomorrow."

"*Ya.*" She motioned toward the house as heat pricked at her cheeks and humiliation curled through her. "I'm sorry you had to witness all that back in the *haus.*"

He waved it off. "Don't worry about it." He pulled open his buggy door. "Have a good night."

"You too. Be sure to tell Laura hello for me."

"I will."

As Mark's buggy disappeared down the lane, Priscilla wondered just how fast the rest of the church district would find out she'd come back to the community unmarried and with a child.

TWO

Priscilla stepped into the kitchen just as Ethan set a basket of rolls on the table next to a platter of fried chicken and a bowl of green beans. She noticed a small folding table, set for one, in the far corner of the room.

She ground her teeth and looked at her father, who was sitting in his usual spot at the head of the table with a deep frown lining his face. Just as she'd suspected he would, he was carrying out her shunning as if he were the bishop of their church district. She wouldn't be able to eat with members of her community or exchange money with them. She was now a stranger even in her own home.

She rubbed the bridge of her nose as renewed guilt burned through her. She had no one to blame but herself. The shunning was her fault. She'd made the decision to run away and leave the community.

"Priscilla." *Mamm* smiled as she set a pitcher of water on the table. "Ethan is a great helper."

"*Ya*, he is." Priscilla mussed Ethan's thick, dark hair as he looked up at her. "What can I do to help?"

"I think we're all set." *Mamm*'s smile faded. "I put a table in the corner of the room for you."

15

"I see that." Priscilla lingered by the long table. She was grateful she had explained to Ethan that she might have to eat at a separate table because of religious beliefs about shunning.

"Let's eat," *Dat* said, growling out the words.

Ethan looked up at his *mammi*. "May I sit next to you?"

"I'd like that." *Mamm* touched his cheek and then looked over at Priscilla. "If it's okay with your mother—your *mamm*."

"*Ya*, of course." Priscilla's heart seemed to constrict as her mother gazed down at her son. She sank into the chair at the small folding table and bowed her head in silent prayer. Then she waited for her parents and Ethan to fill their plates before she carried her plate to the table and filled it with food.

"So you've already started school in Baltimore?" *Mamm* asked as she buttered a roll.

"I finished kindergarten," Ethan explained before forking green beans into his mouth.

"Do you like school?" *Mamm* asked.

"Yeah." He looked over at Priscilla. "How long are we staying? Will I go to school here?"

"*Ya*, depending on how long we stay." Priscilla picked up her glass of water.

"Will I go to an Amish school like you did?" Ethan asked.

Priscilla hesitated as she met her mother's curious gaze. "I'll talk to your grandparents about that." She looked at her father. He was still staring down at his plate just as he had since the beginning of the meal. If she and Ethan stayed here, would he continue to treat them as if they were invisible?

"Tell me about your friends in Baltimore," *Mamm* said to Ethan.

"Well, my best friend is Nico," Ethan began as he picked up a drumstick. "He's really great at playing video games." He took a bite of the drumstick, chewed, and swallowed. "This is good."

He looked over at Priscilla. "It's just as good as your fried chicken, Mom."

"Thank you. I use your *mammi*'s recipe." Priscilla pointed at her mother.

Mamm's expression lit up as she turned toward Priscilla. "You do?"

Priscilla smiled. "It's the best."

"*Danki.*" *Mamm* gave her an affectionate look.

Ethan entertained Priscilla's mother with stories about his friends for the remainder of the meal. Then *Mamm* served chocolate cake and coffee. When they'd finished their dessert, Priscilla stood to help her mother clean the kitchen. She piled the dirty plates on the counter and then began to fill one side of the sink with hot, soapy water.

"I'm going to go out and take care of the animals," *Dat* said, still grumbling as he headed for the door.

"Can I help you?" Ethan trotted after him.

Dat stopped and turned, fingering his beard as he looked down at Ethan.

"Please?" Ethan folded his hands. "Please?"

Priscilla looked at her mother, who shook her head as if to tell her to remain calm.

"*Ya.*" *Dat* motioned for Ethan to follow as they headed through the mudroom and out the back door.

As Priscilla returned to washing dishes, she tried to ignore the angry knots in her shoulders. Coming here had been a mistake, but she'd had no choice. She just had to make the best of it.

"Ethan reminds me so much of you," *Mamm* said as she placed a handful of utensils on top of the plates on the counter. "He's so eager to help, talkative, and curious. You were just like him when you were six."

"This was a mistake." The words burst from her lips as she faced her mother.

"What?" *Mamm*'s eyes widened. "No, no, don't say that. It wasn't a mistake."

"*Dat* doesn't want me here." She pointed to the table in the corner. "He's going to keep reminding me of all the mistakes I've made. He'd rather I just left."

"That's not true." *Mamm*'s chestnut eyes glimmered with tears. "We both want you here. Let me work on him."

Priscilla swallowed a snort. "I don't think there's anything you can do to change him. He's just as tough on me as he was before I left." She looked out the small window above the sink as *Dat* and Ethan walked toward the pasture together. "I just hope he treats Ethan better than he treats me. If not, I'll have to go to a motel tomorrow and then find a job and a place to rent."

"He'll be fine." *Mamm* touched her shoulder. "Just give him time to adjust. Your coming home today was a shock. Let him process it."

"I'll give him a few days at most, but if he's still harsh with Ethan and me, we'll leave."

"I'll talk to him tonight, okay?" *Mamm*'s eyes seemed to plead with her.

Priscilla nodded, and her thoughts turned to her dire financial situation. Even if she stayed here for a while, she needed income so she could save some money for a place of her own. "Do you still work as a seamstress and sell quilts?"

Even though her father's horses provided a bountiful livelihood, her mother enjoyed sewing as a side job. Her father had allowed *Mamm* to keep the money and spend it any way she pleased. Priscilla had often wondered if she primarily enjoyed working as a seamstress for the social aspect it provided. Her father had always been such a stoic man.

"*Ya*, of course. Why?"

"Could I help you and split the profits?"

Mamm's face lit up with a bright smile. "*Ya*, that would be nice. I left your sewing machine in your bedroom right where you had it."

"*Danki*." Priscilla moved on to scrubbing pots as she watched her father and Ethan lead a horse into one of the stables. She glanced over her shoulder at her mother. "So Mark Riehl has been working here for a year?"

Mamm stopped wiping down the kitchen table and rested her hand on her hip. "*Ya*, I guess it has been that long."

"Why does he work here when his father has that dairy farm?"

"He was looking for a job, and your *dat* needed the help when Robert left."

"Interesting." Priscilla mulled over the information as she washed utensils. "Why doesn't Mark live in the *daadihaus*?"

"He said he wanted a salary instead of room and board, but sometimes he eats supper with us if he's working late."

Why would Mark need a salary? Had his father's farm fallen on hard times? Or had his older brother taken over the farm and told him to find another job? It just didn't make sense. Both Riehl sons would need to help their father with the chores on a dairy farm that large.

"He's a *gut* worker," *Mamm* continued, oblivious to Priscilla's internal questions. "He's been a blessing to your *dat*."

As Priscilla turned her attention back to the dishes, she imagined Mark sitting at his parents' long kitchen table and telling his family all about her sins. She pressed her lips together. Somehow she'd have to find the courage to blend back into the plain community—at least for now.

—❦—

"Look who finally made it home," Jamie, Mark's older brother, announced from the glider on the back porch of their father's house. His two-and-a-half-year-old son, Calvin, sat beside him and waved as Mark approached.

Mark's father, stepbrother, and brother-in-law laughed as Mark climbed the steps.

"Some of us actually have to work late and then make the trek home." Mark smirked at Jamie. "Unlike you, I can't just roll out of bed and be at work." He leaned down and gave his nephew a high five. "Hi, Cal. How are you?"

Calvin giggled and then leaned against his father. Mark had always thought he was the perfect mixture of his parents, with bright-blond hair from his mother and dark-blue eyes from his father.

"You're the one who made the decision to take the job on Yonnie's farm." Jamie rubbed his clean-shaven chin as he grinned. Although he was married, he hadn't grown the required beard. The bishop in their district made an exception to the rule for married volunteer firemen like Jamie because they had to wear custom-fit face masks. "You could've just stayed here and worked with Roy and me." He leaned forward and looked at their younger stepbrother. He was sitting on a rocking chair at the far end of the porch.

"Leave me out of this." Roy held up his hands. "You know I don't enjoy getting in the middle of your squabbles."

Mark leaned back against the railing. "I guess I missed supper, huh?"

"Cindy saved you a plate," *Dat* said, referring to Mark's younger sister.

"*Gut*, because I'm starved." Mark ran a hand over his flat abdomen. "I worked hard today. Although, if you work for Yonnie Allgyer, you work hard every day. That man is a slave driver."

"Laura was starting to worry that you'd been in an accident," Allen Lambert said from a rocker beside Jamie.

Mark smiled. His twin had been married to Allen more than three and a half years now, but she still worried about him. "I hope you assured her I was fine."

"I did, but she said she wouldn't be satisfied until you got home." Allen pointed toward the front door. "Go on and show her that her twin is healthy and safe."

"I will." Mark gave them a little bow and headed into the house, removing his work boots and straw hat in the mudroom before entering the kitchen.

"*Onkel* Mark!" A little blonde scampered across the kitchen and leapt into Mark's arms. Mark often thought about what a blessing it was when Laura adopted Mollie Faith after marrying her widowed father. Allen's first wife, Savilla, had been one of Laura's best friends. The whole family cherished this small version of her after she suffered a sudden and fatal illness nearly five years ago.

"Hey there, little one." Mark's heart swelled with love as he held her to his chest and kissed her head. "How was your day?"

"*Gut.*" Mollie touched his face and giggled.

"You're going to be five next month. How did you get so big?"

"I just get bigger and bigger!" She held her arms up straight and then giggled again.

He laughed. How he adored his sweet niece.

"You're finally home." Laura walked over and frowned as she looked up at him. "Florence said you didn't call and let her know you were going to be late."

Mark shrugged. "It was unexpected."

"You should have called anyway," Cindy quipped while drying a dish. Who was his twenty-two-year-old sister to tell him what to do? "I checked the voice mail," she added, "and all I found were messages from your girlfriends."

Mark rolled his eyes. "Franey and Ruthann are *not* my girlfriends."

"Have you bothered to tell Franey and Ruthann that?" Laura set her hands on her belly, where a small bump had started to form, revealing she was expecting a child. "At least Sally got *schmaert* and found a man who was willing to commit to just her."

"I've never made any of them promises," Mark responded as he rubbed Mollie's back. "It's their choice to spend time with me."

"*Ya*, but you still have supper with each of them at least once a week," Cindy chimed in again.

"And you told Jamie you tell them to call you because you like their attention," Kayla, Jamie's wife, added as she swept the floor. "It's none of my business, but that sounds like you're leading them on. They probably think you're going to ask one of them to marry you before too long. I'm guessing Franey is almost sure."

"I'm not ready to get married, and I've never said I was." Mark shook his head. "And why does Jamie tell you what I share with him?"

Kayla's cheeks blushed pink as her cornflower-blue eyes widened. She held on to the broom and touched her own belly. It boggled Mark's mind that his twin and Jamie's wife were both due to have a child within a few weeks of each other.

"I'm just kidding." Mark looked down at Mollie Faith, who had her thumb in her mouth as she rested her head on his shoulder. Then he met his twin's gaze. "I can't help it if the *maed* can't resist me."

"You're incorrigible." Laura folded her arms over her chest and rolled her eyes.

"No, sis, I just tell the truth. The *maed* have always loved me. I can't help that God made me irresistible," he said, joking. He looked down at his sweet niece again. "Right, Mollie Faith? You love me."

Mollie's head popped up, and she kissed Mark's cheek. "*Ich liebe dich, Onkel* Mark."

"See? I just have this effect on *maed*." Mark shrugged and then kissed Mollie's head. "I love you too," he whispered into her hair.

"We're twenty-six, Mark. It's time for you to grow up. Besides, you're going to wind up in trouble if you keep leading on Franey and Ruthann. One day one of them is going to get hurt." Laura held out her arms to Mollie. "*Kumm*. Let *Onkel* Mark eat his supper."

"No." Mollie buried her face in the crook of Mark's neck. He grinned.

"Don't encourage her." Laura's bright-blue eyes narrowed. "Mollie Faith. *Kumm*."

"I want to stay with *Onkel* Mark." Mollie Faith wrapped her arms around his neck, and he couldn't stop grinning despite his twin's deepening frown.

"I think she's attached to him." His stepsister, Sarah Jane, chuckled as she set a stack of clean dishes in a cabinet. At least his stepsister, just a year older than Cindy, was nice to him.

Mark looked down at his niece. "Why don't you sit next to me while I eat my supper?"

Mollie nodded, and he set her on a chair before sitting down beside her.

"We kept your supper warm." Laura set a plate with steak, mashed potatoes, and corn in front of him.

"*Danki*." Mark smiled up at his twin before bowing his head for a silent prayer.

"Mark, I'm so glad you finally got home," Florence said when she stepped into the kitchen. "How was your day?"

"Busy," he told his stepmother as he cut up his steak. "It went by quickly." He took a bite and nodded. "This is *appeditlich*," he said after swallowing. "Did you make it?"

"*Ya.*" Florence nodded at Cindy. "Cindy helped."

"*Danki.*"

"I'm going to go sit on the porch." Florence started for the mudroom. "Does anyone want to join me?"

"*Ya,* I will. The kitchen is clean and the dishes are put away." Sarah Jane caught up with her mother, and they disappeared.

"I need to get Calvin home." Kayla set the dustpan and broom in the pantry and then waved as she headed toward the back door as well. "*Gut nacht.*"

"I'm going to go upstairs and read for a while." Cindy wiped her hands on a dish towel as she looked at Laura. "Would you please tell me when you're heading out? I'd like to say good-bye to you, Mollie, and Allen."

"I will. I promise I won't leave without telling you."

"*Danki.*" Cindy left, and then Mark heard her footfalls echoing in the stairwell.

"Boy, I come home and everyone leaves," he quipped.

"You always knew how to clear a room." Laura filled a small plastic cup with water and then pulled a picture book out of a tote bag sitting on the floor by the entrance to the mudroom. She handed them both to Mollie before sitting down across from Mark and looking at him pointedly. "So how was your day? This is me asking now."

Mark wiped his mouth on a paper napkin. "I already said it was fine. Just busy." He spooned some mashed potatoes into his mouth.

"You don't normally work this late, do you?" Laura leaned back in the chair, and he saw her absently touch her abdomen.

"Sometimes I do." He made sure Mollie seemed engrossed in her book. "Did you have an appointment earlier this week?"

"I did." She tilted her head. "You're deflecting my questions."

He smiled. "I'll tell you what happened today if you tell me about your appointment." His smile faded. "I know you've been *naerfich*."

Laura's gaze moved to Mollie, who was flipping through the picture book and humming to herself. Then she looked at Mark again. "Everything is fine." Her words were measured and deliberate.

Mark nodded. *"Gut."*

"I know I shouldn't be nervous, but sometimes it's difficult after two miscarriages." Her eyes shimmered.

"They happened early on." He was careful to keep his tone mild. "Everything is going to be perfect this time. I can feel it."

"Danki." Laura began to draw circles on the tabletop as she frowned.

He could feel her worry as if it were his own. He needed to say something that would make her smile. "If it's a *bu*, are you going to name him Mark after your handsome twin *bruder*?"

"Like I said earlier, you're incorrigible." She groaned, and then there it was—her smile followed by a little laugh. He'd managed to erase her worry and replace it with laughter. Relief filtered through him. He always felt better when his twin was happy.

But then he pressed his lips together. During the ride home tonight, he kept visualizing the pain in Priscilla's eyes when her father criticized her for coming home dressed as an *Englisher* and with a child born out of wedlock. Priscilla's humiliation had been tangible, and it had touched him—more than he ever would have imagined.

"Mark, I've known you since before we were born." Laura pointed at him. "Something is on your mind."

He sighed.

"What is it?" Laura's eyes lit up. "Are you in love? Are you going to ask one of your girlfriends to marry you and you just didn't want us to know yet? Is it Franey?"

He swallowed a groan. "Please, Laura. You need to stop hoping for that. I have no plans to marry. I'm working for Yonnie so I can save money." He pointed toward the back of the house. "You know my goal is to build a *haus* of my own on this property. I'm fine if I never find a *fraa*."

Laura wrinkled her nose as if she smelled something foul. "That's really *bedauerlich*."

"Why?" He touched Mollie's shoulder. "I have *mei bruderskinner*."

Mollie smiled up at him and then looked down at her book. "Who will do your laundry when you move out?"

Mark grinned. "I'll just bring it over here, and Florence will take care of it." He took another bite of steak.

"You're unbelievable," she said as she rubbed her temples.

Mark took a deep breath and moved the rest of his corn around. It was time to tell Laura her friend was home, but he debated how much to tell her. Priscilla's homecoming had been painful, and the story surrounding her son was her business. Would it be a violation of the Allgyer family's trust if Mark told Laura about what happened while he was there tonight? But Laura had been one of Priscilla's closest friends, and Laura was Mark's twin, his closest confidante. They'd always shared their deepest and darkest secrets. He had to tell her the whole truth.

Mark set his fork down and leaned back in his chair as he met his twin's gaze. "Priscilla came home this evening."

Laura clapped her hands over her mouth for a moment before speaking. "Why didn't you tell me as soon as you came home?"

"*Mamm?*" Mollie's blue eyes widened as she looked at Laura. "*Was iss letz?*"

"Nothing is wrong, *mei liewe. Onkel* Mark just told me my dear *freind* came home today. She's been gone a long time." She pointed to Mollie's book. "You can go back to your book, okay?"

Mollie nodded and looked down at the pictures of horses.

"Why did you keep that from me?" Laura frowned. "You know Priscilla was one of my best *freinden*. Priscilla, Savilla, and I were inseparable in school and youth group. I never understood why she left. She seemed okay, as if nothing was bothering her. I knew she argued with her *dat*, but she never made it seem like it was that bad."

"Maybe it was worse than you thought." Mark rubbed the back of his neck.

"What do you mean?"

"Her *mamm* was very *froh* to see her, but her *dat* wasn't welcoming. In fact, he was critical of her."

"Why?" Laura tilted her head. "I know she's shunned for leaving, but why wouldn't he be *froh* to see her?"

"She has a *sohn*. He's six and a half."

"Really?" Priscilla smiled. "That's *wunderbaar*."

"She's not married. She said she left his father, so I think there's a painful story there."

"Oh." Laura's smiled faded. "I'm sorry to hear that."

"*Ya.*" Mark's thoughts swirled as his mind replayed Priscilla's strained reunion with her parents.

"Mark. I can feel your anguish." Laura touched her collarbone. "*Zwillingbopplin.*"

"I know." He set the fork down again. "I just keep thinking that our parents would have welcomed us home no matter what. They would have rejoiced if you or Cindy had come home after so many years, even if you had a *boppli* out of wedlock."

"*Ya,* they'd just be *froh* we came home. *Mamm* would've always supported us. I miss her so much." Laura's eyes sparkled as she patted her middle again.

"I know." Mark's eyes stung as he thought of their mother. "I do too."

"But Yonnie has always been tough. You've told me he's not the easiest man to work for. He expects everything to be perfect, and he lets you know when it isn't."

He grinned. "*Ya*, but he pays well."

"I think he'll come around. Who can resist a *kind*, right?" She nodded toward Mollie. "I fell in love with Mollie the moment I first saw her, right after Savilla had her. I'm so grateful I can be a part of her life."

"I hope you're right, and that Yonnie comes around."

"He will." Laura smiled. "Tell me about Priscilla's *sohn*. I can't wait to see her and meet him."

THREE

ETHAN SNUGGLED INTO THE DOUBLE BED IN THE spare bedroom later that evening. "*Daadi* let me help with the horses, and he said he'll let me help tomorrow too."

"I'm glad you had fun." Maybe her father would continue to make Ethan feel welcome here. After all, he'd already taught him to call him *Daadi*.

"*Daadi* is kind of quiet. He seems sad."

Priscilla suppressed a scowl. *That's one way to describe him.* "He's always been kind of quiet. It's just how he is. Some people like to smile and tell jokes, and other people are quiet and more somber."

"Yeah." Ethan paused as if contemplating something. "It's funny not having lights or air-conditioning. It's kind of like when we went camping with Dad that one time." He pointed to the Coleman lantern on the nightstand next to the bed. "We had to use lanterns too, and there weren't any light switches."

"You're right." Priscilla smiled as she tucked the sheet around him. "It is sort of like camping." She kissed his forehead and then touched his nose. "You get some sleep, okay?"

"Okay. It's hot in here." He pointed to the open window on the far side of the room. "Will it get cooler?"

"Hopefully you'll get a breeze. You'll get used to it eventually." She flipped off the lantern. "Good night."

"How do you say good night in Dutch?"

"*Gut nacht.*" As she crossed the room, she realized it was still decorated the same. Two dressers lined the far wall, and a simple mirror and a shelf with two candles adorned the other wall. Her mother had insisted on having a guest room, although Priscilla never recalled any guests coming to visit and enjoying the pretty room.

"Mom?"

"Yes?" Priscilla stood in the doorway.

"Will Dad visit us here?"

Priscilla's stomach dipped and then spiraled as her thoughts turned to Trent. "I don't know, sweetie. We'll see."

"I miss him."

She pressed her lips together as her shoulders tightened. She'd never told Ethan why it was necessary to leave his father behind. She'd merely explained it was time for Ethan to get to know his grandparents, and then she prayed they'd be accepted. She also prayed Trent would never find them and try to take Ethan away from her.

"I know you do. Don't forget to say your prayers. *Gut nacht,* Ethan."

"*Gut nacht,* Mom."

She began to pull the door closed but stopped when he called her back.

"How do you say I love you in Dutch?" he asked.

She smiled. "*Ich liebe dich.*"

"Okay. *Ich liebe dich,* Mom."

Priscilla's heart seemed to turn over. Was she the mother Ethan deserved? "I love you too. Now get some sleep. You told me your grandfather said you can help with chores again tomorrow."

"I'm glad," he said before rolling over.

She closed his door and crossed the hallway, swallowing back raging emotions as she stepped into her former bedroom. Like the spare room, her bedroom hadn't changed. Her favorite trinkets still lined the long dresser. Her double bed was adorned with the pink and purple log cabin design quilt she'd finished shortly before she made the decision to leave her childhood home in search of a happier one.

She shook her head. She'd been eighteen, not a child. Why had she thought running away would solve her problems?

She opened her closet and found the dresses and aprons she'd left behind. She even found a pair of shoes on the floor.

"I kept everything in case you decided to come back."

Priscilla spun to face her mother. "I didn't hear you walking down the hall."

"I have your prayer covering too." *Mamm* crossed the room and opened the top drawer of the dresser. "I kept it in here."

"Danki." Priscilla touched it. When she left the community, she adapted the *Englisher* way of dressing to blend in, abandoning the few dresses, aprons, and prayer coverings she'd packed. It would feel odd to put on her former clothing, but she felt a strange tug from her former life. Had she missed dressing this way?

"Your *dat* is going to talk to you in the morning."

She looked up into her mother's dark eyes. "About what?"

"His rules for you if you decide to stay."

"I expected that." Priscilla sank onto the corner of the bed. "He wants me to dress Amish, right?"

"Ya, he does, and he wants Ethan to dress Amish too." *Mamm* touched her shoulder. "Please tell me you'll agree to whatever he says. I don't want you and Ethan to leave."

"Ya, I will," she said, realizing she had made the decision to stay despite continued anxiety about being around her father. She

31

forced a smile. "I'll make Ethan some clothes, and I'll see if my dresses still fit."

"They will. You look to be about the same size to me." *Mamm* touched her cheek. "I'm so glad you're here." Her eyes seemed to penetrate Priscilla's soul. "I suspect you wouldn't be unless something happened with Ethan's father. What was it?"

Priscilla swallowed as she debated how much to share. "He changed, and our home became an unsafe environment for Ethan."

Mamm's eyes sparkled with tears. "Did he hurt you?"

"I'm okay." Priscilla squeezed her mother's hand. "Ethan and I will be fine."

Mamm studied her. "Do you want to talk about it?"

Priscilla shook her head as a yawn overtook her. "Maybe later."

"All right. I'm always here."

"*Danki.*" Priscilla's heart seemed to swell. She was grateful for her mother.

"Get some sleep. *Gut nacht.*"

"*Gut nacht.*" Priscilla turned toward the doorway as her mother was leaving. "*Mamm?*"

"*Ya?*" *Mamm* swiveled to face her.

"*Danki* for allowing Ethan and me to stay here."

Mamm's eyes glimmered in the light of the Coleman lantern on her dresser. "Of course you can stay here. You belong here. You're our family. Sleep well." She closed the door as she stepped out into the hallway.

Priscilla walked to the closet and eyed a long-sleeved cranberry-colored dress. Since she'd left home in the summer, she'd left behind her long-sleeved dresses. She pulled the dress off the hanger and yanked off her purple shirt and jeans.

When she turned toward the mirror, her gaze fell on her right bicep and the scars that covered her arm. She touched the discolored and puckered skin, and her mind filled with memories of the night Trent had been so drunk and angry that he'd thrown a beer bottle at her.

Although Trent had never been violent toward Ethan, his drinking had put their son in danger. One day she arrived home from work to find Ethan home alone while Trent had gone out drinking with his buddies. At that moment Priscilla realized she had to get Ethan away from Trent before he wound up hurt.

That was the day she began planning her escape from Trent's drunkenness and abuse.

She closed her eyes to keep her tears at bay. She was strong, and she was determined to keep Ethan safe. She'd gotten away from Trent, and now she had to rebuild her life. If that meant living here and assimilating to the Amish life again, then she'd do it for her son's sake.

Priscilla slipped on the dress and studied her reflection in the mirror. The dress was a little snug, but she could let out the seams. She changed into her favorite nightshirt and shorts and then sat down at her sewing table. She was grateful her mother had left it and all her sewing supplies in her room. She set to work letting out the seams and shortening the sleeves to three-quarter length. Short sleeves were permitted during the summer, but she couldn't risk anyone seeing the scars on her arm. Her mind wandered as she worked, anxiety causing her stomach to roil as she imagined what her father would say to her in the morning.

When the dress was finished, she hung it back in the closet and went to her dresser. She touched the little wooden box where she'd kept her bobby pins since she was a little girl. Then she pulled out her prayer covering and ran her fingers over the organza. Tomorrow she would don her former clothing and try to find her way back into the Amish community. But would they accept her despite her transgressions?

The question lingered in her mind as she turned off the lanterns and climbed into bed. Turning to her side, she closed her eyes.

"Lord, give me strength," she whispered. "Guide me to where Ethan and I belong."

Then she closed her eyes and waited for sleep to find her.

"Gude mariye." Priscilla forced a smile on her lips as she stepped into the kitchen the following morning. The aroma of eggs, bacon, home fries, and fresh-baked bread washed over her, causing her stomach to growl.

"Gude mariye," Mamm echoed as she set a platter of bacon on the table.

Dat barely repeated the greeting from the head of the table.

"You look pretty, Mom," Ethan said as he sat beside her father.

"Danki. That means thank you." Priscilla touched her prayer covering. She'd put on the cranberry-colored dress and a black apron, and then she'd pulled her hair up before donning the prayer covering. The clothing felt oddly comforting. Perhaps she'd missed her former life.

Unwilling to go there, she turned toward her mother. "I'm sorry I didn't come down earlier to help you. What can I do now?"

"Don't worry. It's all done." *Mamm* handed her a plate and then gestured toward the small table in the corner. "Get yourself some food."

"Danki." Priscilla filled her plate and sat down. After a silent prayer, they all began to eat. With her stomach tied up in knots, she merely moved the eggs around as she waited for her father to

speak to her. Would he lay down his rules now? Or make her wait until later in the day?

"Are we going to work on chores after breakfast, *Daadi*?" Ethan asked between bites of home fries.

"*Ya*," *Dat* said. "Mark should be here soon, and you can help us outside."

"Yay!" Ethan cheered. "I saw your horses last night, but what kind are they?"

Dat answered Ethan's questions about the horses and the farm as they finished eating. Priscilla had gathered the empty dishes and was filling one side of the sink with water when her father finally addressed her. She was grateful Ethan had gone out to the porch to wait for him.

"Priscilla, I want to discuss your plans for staying here."

She turned toward him and nodded. "All right."

"If you stay under my roof, you and Ethan will dress Amish and abide by the rules of the *Ordnung*. Ethan will go to our Amish school." *Dat*'s expression could not have been stonier.

"I understand." Priscilla's hands shook as she dried them on a dish towel.

"You will also meet with the bishop and make yourself right with the church."

She swallowed. "I will."

"You'll do it today." *Dat* jammed his finger against the table. "As soon as the kitchen is cleaned up, you will call for a ride and go talk to him. With his agreement, you'll start your classes this Sunday."

"Okay." Priscilla kept back a biting retort. How she despised her father's caustic tone despite her agreeing to his rules.

"And one more thing." He narrowed his eyes. "After you're accepted back as a community member, you will look for a husband."

Her mouth dropped open. "What? Look for a husband?"

"*Ya*. Your *sohn* needs a father, and you need a husband. The sooner you find one, the better. You know how your situation looks to other members of our community. The best thing you can do is make it right. You know what I'm saying."

"No." Priscilla shook her head. "I will live like an Amish woman, and I will make myself right with the church, but I can't allow you to dictate my life beyond that. If that's how you're going to be, I'll find another place to live."

"No!" *Mamm* said. "Don't go."

Priscilla's body shook as she looked at her mother. "I have to go." She hurried up the stairs and into Ethan's room. She opened the closet and pulled out his suitcase before tossing his clothes into it.

Priscilla shook her head as anger and confusion warred inside of her.

"Please stay," *Mamm* pleaded as she stood in the doorway. "Your *dat* only wants what's best for you."

She spun toward her mother. "I can't let him push me to get married. When I'm right with the church, it means I'm forgiven. I can't be forced to marry. Ethan is *mei sohn*, no matter how he came into this world."

"Priscilla, calm down." *Mamm* took a step toward her. "Your *dat* is only thinking about your future. You can stay here and build a life for Ethan. Finding a husband isn't a bad thing."

"No, but it has to be my choice." Priscilla pointed to her chest. "I get to choose who's the best man to help me raise Ethan." What was she thinking? She could never let anyone hurt her again—or hurt Ethan. That was true. But even if she found someone she could trust, what decent man would have her? She would still be damaged goods.

"*Ya*, I know it has to be your choice, and your *dat* knows that.

He never said he would choose a husband for you. Why would he?" *Mamm* touched her arm. "Stop thinking about yourself and think about your *kind*. Where will you go if you leave here? Do you have enough money to provide a *gut* home for him?"

Priscilla's shoulders slumped. She didn't have enough money to rent an apartment, let alone a house.

"Stay here." *Mamm's* voice cracked with emotion. "Just do what your *dat* wants, and I promise everything will be all right."

"Fine." Priscilla released the breath she hadn't realized she'd been holding.

"Go meet with the bishop." *Mamm* nodded toward the doorway. "I'll unpack Ethan's things, and I'll finish cleaning the kitchen. Then I'll start making Ethan clothes."

Priscilla nodded. "All right. I'll go see the bishop, but I'll help you with the chores first."

"Priscilla, I can—"

"No." Priscilla shook her head. "I'll unpack and clean up the kitchen. Then you can start making Ethan's clothes so he's ready for church on Sunday, okay?"

Mamm nodded.

Priscilla hesitated as doubt curled through her. Was making a commitment to the church the right choice? What if Ethan detested living on a farm after he'd been here a few days? Would he adjust to going to a one-room Amish school without the luxuries of electronics or the flexibility of his former clothes?

"Priscilla," *Mamm* said. "You need to do what's best for your *kind*."

"You're right." With her palms sweating, Priscilla headed down the stairs. She sucked in a surprised breath when she met her father at the bottom step. "I'm going to finish cleaning up the kitchen and then meet with the bishop."

"All right. Our driver's phone number is on the desk in the

phone shanty." *Dat* pulled out his wallet and held out a couple of bills. "This should cover the cost of the ride."

"I have a little bit of money."

"Take it." His tone was gruff.

"*Danki,*" she whispered as she took the money from him.

He gave her a curt nod before walking into the hallway.

As Priscilla stepped into the kitchen, she squared her shoulders. She reminded herself again that she was strong. She would find her way, for the sake of her son.

FOUR

"Do you need any help?"

Mark turned toward the entrance to the horse stall as he looked at Ethan. "Hi, Ethan."

"Hi." Ethan raised his hand in a wave. "*Daadi* told me to ask you if you had anything for me to do."

Mark grinned as he leaned on his pitchfork. "I see you're picking up Dutch pretty quickly."

"Yeah, my mom taught me a few words."

"You said you're six, right?"

He stood a little taller. "Six and a half."

"Uh-huh." Mark rubbed his chin. "So you're already in school, then. Don't *Englisher* schools start at five?"

"*Englisher?*" Ethan snickered and shook his head. "What does that mean?"

"An *Englisher* is someone who isn't Amish. So you're essentially an *Englisher*."

"Oh." Ethan nodded slowly. "Yeah, I was in kindergarten last year. My mom just told me I'll start first grade here."

"Oh." *So Priscilla is planning on staying.* "Schools are different here. All the grades are in one classroom with one teacher." Mark lifted his straw hat and wiped his brow with the back of his hand. "I'm sure your school wasn't like that."

"No, it wasn't." Ethan seemed to study him. "Did you go to school with my mom?"

"*Ya*, I did. She was *gut freinden* with my twin sister, Laura."

"You have a twin sister?"

"*Ya*, I do, but we don't look alike. You can tell us apart because she's shorter than I am," Mark said. After a beat, Ethan laughed.

"Do you have any kids, Mark?"

"No, I can't say that I do. Do you?"

Ethan chuckled again. "I'm only six. Of course I don't." He shook his head. "You're funny."

"Well, looks aren't everything." Mark feigned disappointment with a shrug and a phony frown.

Ethan chuckled a third time. "Do you have any other brothers and sisters?"

"*Ya*." Mark leaned against the stall wall and set the pitchfork next to it. "Let's see. There's my older brother, Jamie." He counted everyone off on his fingers. "He's married to Kayla. They have a little boy younger than you named Calvin. He's really cool. You'll like him. Then there's my younger sister, Cindy. And I have two stepbrothers, Walter and Roy, and a stepsister, Sarah Jane. Walter is married, and he has two sons."

"Wow." Ethan's eyes grew wider. "You have a big family. I just have my mom and dad. My dad lives in Baltimore. I don't know when I'll see him again since my mom decided we should come here for a while."

"I'm sorry to hear that." Mark's thoughts spun with questions. Why had Priscilla left his father? And what drove Priscilla from the community eight years ago? Laura said Yonnie and Priscilla argued back then, and he certainly didn't welcome her back. But how bad could their relationship have been? "Do you like the farm?"

"Yeah." Ethan smiled. "The animals are fun. And it's like camping living in a house without electricity."

"It's like camping, huh?" Mark snickered. "That's a great analogy."

Ethan looked toward the entrance of the barn. "My mom went to see someone called the bishop a little while ago. I wonder when she'll be back."

"She went to see the bishop?" Mark felt his eyebrows rise. So Priscilla was going to rejoin the church. That meant she really was back for good.

"Yeah." Ethan tilted his head. "Who is he?"

"Well, have you been to a church before?"

"Uh-huh." Ethan nodded.

"He's like our preacher. He's the head of our church."

"Oh." Ethan looked confused. "Why would my mom go see him?"

Mark folded his arms over his chest as he considered an explanation simple enough for Ethan to understand. "I think she probably went to talk to him about becoming a member of the church again. She'll have to take classes and then be accepted back into the congregation."

"Oh." His brows furrowed. "So she has to ask permission to be a part of the church?"

"*Ya,* sort of."

Ethan nodded as if considering that. "Okay." Then he looked around the horse stall. "Are we going to stand here and talk all day? Or are you going to give me a chore to do?"

"Wow." Mark shook his head and sighed with feigned annoyance. "You're just as demanding as your *daadi.*" Then he held out his pitchfork. "How about I teach you to muck the stalls?"

"Okay." Ethan rubbed his hands together before grabbing the tool. "I'm ready."

41

───⟨×⟩───

Priscilla climbed out of the van and paid her father's driver before walking up the rock path. She was back from meeting with the bishop, and her feet slowed with the weight of uncertainty as she climbed the front porch steps.

Although she'd made the commitment to rejoin the church, anxiety seemed to coil around her insides when she envisioned facing the congregation on Sunday. Would her former friends welcome her back into the fold? Or would they stare at her and her child and whisper about her promiscuity?

"Lord, give me strength," she whispered as she stepped into the foyer and dropped her purse on the bench by the door.

Voices rang out from the kitchen. She stepped through the doorway and found her mother clearing away dishes as her father, Mark, and Ethan sat at the table.

"Mom!" Ethan waved at her. "How was your meeting?"

Leave it to her son to get right to the point. She squared her shoulders and plastered a smile on her face. "It went just fine."

"Are you a member of the church now?"

"Ah. Well, not exactly." Priscilla's cheeks felt as if they'd caught fire as she met her mother's hopeful gaze. "But I will be soon."

"That's great." Ethan grinned.

"Danki." Priscilla turned to her mother. "I can clean up if you have other things to do."

"Are you sure? You must be hungry." *Mamm* pointed to the table. "I made chicken salad, and we have the rolls I picked up at the bakery yesterday. Sit down and eat while I do the dishes."

"No." Priscilla touched her mother's arm. "You go on. I'll clean up after I eat."

"Okay. I'm working on a pair of trousers for Ethan. I'm almost done, and then I can start on a shirt."

"Danki."

Mamm left the kitchen, and Priscilla turned to the table as her father stood.

"It's time to get back to work." *Dat* dropped his napkin on his empty plate. "A couple of customers made appointments to come out this afternoon. I need to get ready for them."

He looked down at his plate and then headed for the door. As he walked past her, Priscilla's heart seemed to falter as she considered her father might never forgive her.

"Daadi, wait for me!" Ethan jumped up and followed his grandfather to the door. "Bye, Mom."

"Bye." Priscilla smiled as she gathered the last of the dishes. She turned to Mark, who was still sitting at the table. "Aren't you going with them?"

"I thought I'd have another sandwich." He plucked a roll from the basket in the center of the table. "Your *mamm* makes the best chicken salad. I think it's because she adds walnuts. They're *appeditlich.*"

She eyed him with suspicion. "I guess that means you eat here often."

He shrugged. "Your mom invites me to join them for lunch every day I'm here. I don't stay for supper often, but I do enjoy her lunches."

Priscilla carried the dishes to the counter.

"You look *schee,*" he said.

She leaned against the counter, squeezed her eyes shut, and swallowed a groan. Was Mark really going to flirt with her? Of course he was. This was how he'd always operated. He'd use compliments, quick wit, and his handsome face to win over the affection of the young girls in their youth group and then lead them on without any promise of commitment. She'd witnessed more than one friend or acquaintance falling under his spell, only to be heartbroken when he moved on to someone else.

But why would he be interested enough in her to flirt? Not only had he never noticed her before, but she certainly couldn't be desirable to him now. She was shunned and had a child from a failed relationship with an *Englisher*.

"What?" Mark asked. "Did I say something wrong?"

"No." She turned back to the table and picked up empty glasses. Mark scooped chicken salad from a bowl onto his roll and then added a piece of lettuce. "Why do you work here?" The question leapt from her lips without any forethought.

He shrugged. "*Mei dat* and I were here running an errand one day about a year ago, and your *dat* mentioned he needed a farmhand. We discussed a salary, and I took the job."

"But why here?"

"Why not here?" He grinned. "It's a great job."

"Why don't you live in the *daadihaus* here on the farm?"

"I want a paycheck so I can save money to build a *haus* on *mei dat's* farm."

Priscilla considered his family, and a twinge of envy poked her. Mark had it all—loving parents and three siblings who would always be his close friends. She'd seen the Riehl family interact at church and whenever she visited Laura, and it was apparent how much they supported each other. She'd often wondered what it would have been like if her parents had given her siblings. Would a couple of brothers have taken off the pressure for her to be the perfect child? She moved to the sink to prepare for washing the dishes.

"How did it really go with the bishop?" His question broke through her thoughts.

"Oh, it was *wunderbaar,*" she tossed over her shoulder. "I'm still shunned, and I need to be under the ban while I take three classes. Only then can I be accepted back into the church. The first class is this Sunday." She scraped crumbs from a dish with more force than necessary. But the chatter of her mother's sewing machine echoed from the second floor above them, and the sound was so familiar it was almost comforting.

"You haven't had lunch, right?" he asked.

"No, I haven't."

"Come eat with me."

She turned toward him and felt her brow pinch.

"Sit." He pointed to the chair across from him. "Please."

"You're going to eat with me?"

"Why not?"

She tilted her head and took in his pleasant expression and sky-blue eyes. What did he hope to gain by being nice to her? Had he told his family about her last night? Had his sisters instructed him to find out all her secrets so they could gossip about them at the next quilting bee? That didn't sound like the Laura she'd known, but she wasn't sure if she could trust anyone now.

His face broke out in his signature grin. "Why are you looking at me like I have an ulterior motive? It's lunch, Priscilla, not an invitation to share a bottle of liquor."

"You know I'm shunned, but you're inviting me to eat with you."

"But you have to eat, right?" He shrugged. "Sit and eat with me."

She hesitated, and then she turned back to the sink and shut off the faucet. It was just lunch, after all, and she would be careful not to share too much about her life in Baltimore.

She took a plate from the cabinet and utensils from the drawer before sitting down across from him. After a prayer, she began building a sandwich. He ate in silence across from her for a few moments.

"Ethan is a hoot," he finally said. "He helped me muck the stalls earlier, and he never stopped talking."

"He does like to talk." She took a bite of her sandwich, chewed, swallowed, and then wiped her mouth with a napkin. "Why are you working here instead of helping your *dat* with his dairy farm?"

"*Mei bruders* are plenty of help."

"*Bruders?*" she asked. "I don't understand. Did your parents have another child after I left?"

He shook his head, and his smile flattened. "No, I have three stepsiblings. Two of them live on the farm."

She gasped, her hand fluttering to her mouth. "You lost your *mamm?*"

His nod was solemn. "Five years ago."

"Mark, I'm so sorry." Tears stung her eyes. "I had no idea."

"It's been tough, but *mei dat* is *froh* again. He met Florence at the library, and they started dating. She has an older *sohn* who's married and took over her farm. Her younger *sohn*, Roy, is twenty-four, and Sarah Jane is twenty-three." He shook his head. "We're just one big, happy family now."

"Is that why you want to build a *haus?* You want some privacy?"

"I guess so. Also, I'm twenty-six and not married, so I think it's time I had my own place." He took a handful of chips and dropped them on his plate before handing her the bag.

"*Danki.*" She shook a pile of chips onto her own plate. "You mentioned Laura has a family now. How many *kinner* does she have?"

"She has a *dochder*, and she's expecting another *kind*."

"What about Jamie?"

"He's married and has a *sohn*. His *fraa* is expecting a *boppli* too."

"Wow." She popped a chip into her mouth while her mind spun with memories of her childhood. While her life was stressful at home, she'd always cherished time spent with her two best friends, Laura and Savilla. "How's Savilla? Is she married?"

Mark stopped chewing, and something unreadable flickered across his face.

"What?" She leaned forward, her curiosity piqued.

"Savilla passed away not long after *mei mamm* died."

Priscilla couldn't stop tears from filling her eyes. She couldn't believe her mother didn't tell her in one of her letters.

"I'm sorry. I didn't mean to upset you." He handed her another napkin.

"It's not your fault." She wiped her eyes and then her nose. "What happened?"

"She died unexpectedly as the result of a heart infection. It was terrible. Her husband, Allen, was just devastated. Their *dochder*, Mollie, was only two months old."

"*Ach.* That's so *bedauerlich.*" Priscilla sniffed.

"After Savilla passed away, her *mamm* helped care for Mollie. But then she broke her leg and hip and Laura took over with Mollie." His expression softened. "Laura and Allen fell in love, and they've been married almost four years now. Laura adopted Mollie, who's a sweetheart." It was apparent from the way he smiled that he was fond of his niece.

Priscilla shook her head as guilt stabbed her heart. Why had she stayed away for so long? Surely Laura needed her when she lost her mother and then Savilla. She wiped away more tears as she imagined Laura mourning her mother and then their best friend. Would Laura ever forgive Priscilla for leaving the way she had and not contacting her for eight years?

"I can't believe it." Priscilla's voice sounded thin and reedy. "Things have changed so much. I've been gone a long time."

"But you're back now." Mark raised his glass of water as if to toast her.

They ate in silence for a few minutes, and she allowed everything Mark told her to sink in. What else had she missed?

"Tell me more about how it went with the bishop." Mark's statement broke through her thoughts.

She shrugged while looking down at her half-eaten sandwich. "It went fine. He seemed *froh* to see me, and he was supportive of my decision to come back to the faith." She moved a chip around on her plate. "He made me feel welcome in his home. I thought he would since he'd always been pleasant, but the meeting wasn't anything unexpected. Like I said, I have to go to the classes on Sundays to relearn our faith. Then I have to confess in front of the congregation."

She tried to sound casual, even though the idea of standing in front of her congregation terrified her to the very depth of her soul. "So after I complete the classes I'll be a member of the community again, and life can go on for Ethan and me."

She looked up, and when she met his gaze, she found tenderness in his eyes that knocked her off balance for a moment. Was he pretending to care? Or did he truly want to be her friend?

"You don't sound so sure," he said.

"What do you mean?"

"Something is bothering you. Is your *dat* forcing you to make yourself right with the church?"

She swallowed. Was she that transparent? Or was he reading her thoughts? Maybe his suspicion was based solely on what he'd heard her father say the day she arrived.

"It's none of my business." He picked up another chip and tossed it into his mouth.

"Did you tell your family I'm back?"

He shook his head as he swallowed. "Only Laura."

She blinked. Her vision of Mark gossiping about her was entirely wrong, unless he wasn't telling her the truth. But she didn't find any evidence of a lie on his face or in his eyes.

"She's really excited that you're back. She can't wait to see you."

"I can't wait to see her," she admitted, ashamed she'd even considered Laura and Cindy gossiping about her. She ran her finger over the wood-grain tabletop as she felt the urge to share more with him. "I didn't come straight home today after I met with the bishop." The words seemed to leap from her mouth as if they craved someone's understanding ear. "I asked *mei dat*'s driver to take me to a coffee shop so I could just sit alone and figure out what I'm doing."

"What do you mean?" He leaned forward, his expression pensive.

"I just keep wondering if coming back here and rejoining the church is the right decision for Ethan. He needs a safe and stable home."

"Why would coming here be wrong, then?"

"What if the community rejects me? Sure, the bishop will tell them I'm a member of the church after I complete the classes, but what if people still treat me like I'm a sinner?"

"That won't happen. You know the entire community will forgive you. Besides, look around you." He gestured around the kitchen. "Your parents are *gut* Christian people. Ethan will have love and guidance here."

"*Ya*, you're right." She nodded, but doubt continued to taunt her. Still, this was too personal of a conversation for her to share with Mark. He wasn't her friend. Why did she feel the need to trust him?

She stood and started picking up their dishes. "I have chores to do, and I'm sure *mei dat* needs you outside. *Danki* for having lunch with me." She carried the dishes to the sink and set them in the water she'd drawn earlier.

When she turned, she almost collided with Mark's chest as he came to stand beside her.

"Here you go." He smiled as he set the utensils and their glasses on the counter. "I'll see you later."

"Danki." She looked up at him and took in his attractive face. Too bad he was a known flirt in her community. Not that she was remotely interested in another relationship.

"Don't doubt your decision to come home. People are going to be *froh* that you're back," he said. "Just wait and see when you go to church this Sunday."

"I hope you're right."

"You know I am." Then he winked before heading to the mudroom.

Priscilla rolled her eyes as she leaned back against the counter. Why would she ever consider Mark Riehl a friend? He had to be the most conceited man and worst flirt she'd ever known.

FIVE

Priscilla's heart pounded as she walked with her parents and Ethan toward the Zook family's house.

"So I have to sit with *Daadi* during church because I'm a *bu*?" Ethan asked.

Priscilla looked down at him. Despite his short haircut, he looked Amish clad in his black trousers, white shirt, and black vest, the Sunday suit all male members of the community wore. "*Ya*, that's right."

Ethan touched *Dat*'s arm. "Where do we sit?"

"In the barn." *Dat* nodded toward the structure. "I'll show you."

Priscilla looked at her father, and when their eyes met, he immediately turned away. She swallowed a sigh. When would he look at her and talk to her as if she were a valuable human being? She turned back to Ethan. Did he notice how her father acted toward her? Was it harmful for Ethan to witness how poorly her father treated her? Would *Dat*'s example influence him to turn out like Trent?

As her thoughts turned to Trent, a shiver danced down her spine despite the humid air, and she absently rubbed her right bicep. She'd tailored two more long-sleeved dresses to give them three-quarter sleeves. Her mother asked why she didn't give them short sleeves, and she'd told her she'd learned to like longer sleeves best. She was relieved when *Mamm* let the subject drop.

She tried to dispel her doubt about moving back home as she smiled at Ethan and rubbed his cheek. "I'll see you after the service. Remember to be quiet and respectful."

"I will."

She squeezed his hand before he and her father took off toward the barn. Then she continued with her mother toward the Zook family's house. She stood up straighter as they approached the back porch.

"You have no reason to be *naerfich*," *Mamm* said as if reading her thoughts. "You have every right to visit with the women before the service."

"I have only a few minutes before I need to meet with the bishop." She fingered the skirt of her dress as she walked behind her mother up the steps.

"You have enough time to see your *freinden*." *Mamm* opened the back door.

Pressure clamped down on Priscilla's lungs as she followed her mother into the mudroom, where voices sounded from the kitchen. She closed her eyes and pressed her lips together for a moment before walking inside with shaking hands. The women in her congregation stood in a circle greeting one another, and she saw a sea of faces, most of them familiar.

"Priscilla!"

She spun as Laura came up behind her and then wrapped her arms around her shoulders.

"Oh, Priscilla." Laura's voice sounded thick. "Mark told me you were back, and I prayed you'd come to church today."

"Laura." Wetness gathered under her eyes. "It's been too long."

"*Ya*, it has." Laura touched her cheek. "You look great."

"You do too." It had always astounded her that Laura shared

coloring more like her older brother, Jamie, than her twin's. Laura had dark-brown hair, and Mark's hair was a lighter shade of brown. But all the Riehl siblings shared the same striking, bright-blue eyes.

"This is *mei dochder*, Mollie. Her *mutter* was Savilla." Laura nodded at the little blonde standing next to her holding a picture book.

Priscilla clicked her tongue as her eyes stung with more tears. "Mark told me what happened. I can't believe it."

"I know. I miss her so much." She touched Mollie's arm. "Mollie, this is *mei freind* Priscilla. Can you say hello?"

"Hi." Mollie waved at her and then hid behind the skirt of Laura's blue dress.

Laura laughed. "She's pretending to be shy."

"She's beautiful." Priscilla smiled at the girl, taking in her baby-blue eyes. She recalled Savilla's chocolate-colored eyes and surmised that Mollie's father must have blue eyes. Priscilla's eyes moved down Laura's body and stopped at her middle.

"I know Mark told you we're expecting." Laura touched her little belly and smiled. "I want to meet your *sohn*. Mark said he's a chatterbox and a *gut* helper."

"*Danki.*" Priscilla's gaze moved to a group of women approaching them.

"You must be Priscilla." A woman with golden-blond hair and blue eyes, and who looked about her age, stepped toward her. She was holding a toddler. "I'm Kayla, and this is *mei sohn*, Calvin."

"Kayla is Jamie's *fraa*," Laura explained before turning to a middle-aged woman. "This is my stepmother, Florence."

"It's nice to meet you," Priscilla said, shaking her hand and taking in Kayla's belly too.

When Priscilla felt a hand on her shoulder, she turned. A young woman smiled at her. "Cindy? Is that you?"

"*Ya*, it's *gut* to see you." Cindy hugged her.

"Oh my goodness. You're taller than I am!"

"Imagine how I feel," Laura quipped. "She's my little *schweschder*, and she towers over me."

"Laura!" *Mamm* joined them. "It's so *gut* to see you."

"Edna," Florence said. "We need to get together to sew again soon. It's been too long."

"*Ya*, it has," *Mamm* said, agreeing. "Did you finish that wedding ring quilt you were working on for that one customer?"

"I did."

As her mother and Florence continued to talk, Priscilla turned back to Laura. "I'm so sorry about your *mamm* and Savilla. If only I'd been here to help you through your grief. I feel terrible for not contacting you."

"I missed you so much, but it was even worse after I lost *mei mamm* and then Savilla." Laura touched Priscilla's hand. "I still can't believe they're both gone." She glanced down at Mollie, who was sitting on the floor and flipping through the pages of her book. "She reminds me of Savilla all the time. She has her smile. When I look in Mollie's eyes, I see Savilla, and it helps me cope with not having her."

Priscilla nodded. "She has her *schee* hair too. I think it's *wunderbaar* that Mollie has you."

"*Danki*." Laura smiled at her. "We have a lot of catching up to do. We need to get together soon."

"*Ya*, we do."

Laura's eyes glimmered. "It's so *gut* to have you back."

Priscilla swallowed against a lump swelling in her throat.

When the clock began to chime, announcing it was nine, Priscilla gestured toward the door. "I have to go meet with the bishop, but I'll see you soon."

"Okay." Laura gave her another quick hug and then whispered in her ear, "Promise me I'll see you soon."

"You will," Priscilla said.

⎯⎯⎯⎯⎯

Mark scanned the congregation as he sat on a backless bench next to Roy in the unmarried men's section of the barn and fingered his hymnal. He spotted Ethan sitting beside Yonnie. When Ethan met his gaze, the boy waved, and Mark grinned in response.

"What are you looking at?" Roy asked.

"Ethan is here." He nodded toward the boy.

"Ethan?" Roy's brown eyebrows shot up.

"He's Yonnie and Edna's grandson. He and his *mamm*, Priscilla, came to live with them this week. I went to school with Priscilla." He explained that Priscilla was best friends with Laura.

"Oh. You haven't mentioned that at home."

No, he hadn't. Mark had shared the news of Priscilla's homecoming with only one person—Laura. Her return seemed so personal, and for some odd reason, he felt the need to shield her from any community gossip.

That was crazy. He and Priscilla had never been good friends. He'd always considered her standoffish and unapproachable. The conversation he'd shared with her on Friday during lunch was the first meaningful discussion they'd ever shared.

The service began, and Mark joined in as the congregation slowly sang the opening hymn. A young man sitting two rows behind him served as the song leader. He began the first syllable of each line, and then the rest of the congregation joined him to finish each line.

Mark tried to concentrate on the hymn, but his thoughts kept turning to Priscilla. He imagined her meeting with the bishop and ministers in one of the upstairs rooms in the Zook house as they reminded her of their beliefs and the history of the Amish church. He remembered her story about visiting the coffee shop and what she'd told him about her doubts. Did she still think the community would reject her and Ethan?

During the last verse of the second hymn, he turned and moved his eyes to the back of the barn just as Priscilla stepped inside and walked up the aisle toward the front. She wore a red dress that had three-quarter sleeves, just like the dress she'd worn on Friday, and it puzzled him. It was a sweltering day, so why hadn't she put on a short-sleeved dress like the rest of the women in the community?

Priscilla kept her eyes focused on the floor of the barn as she made her way to the front row, where she sank onto the bench and then bent forward, her hands covering her face. A lump swelled in his throat. Why did he feel such a deep empathy for her?

The ministers entered the barn and placed their hats on two hay bales, indicating that the service was about to begin. They made their way to the front of the barn and sat in front of Priscilla. The chosen minister began the first sermon, and Mark did his best to concentrate on the words, but his eyes kept finding their way back to Priscilla. She remained frozen in place, her head bent and her hands covering her face as if she were pleading with God to forgive her transgressions. While it was tradition for a shunned member of the church to sit like that, it bothered him to see her that way.

The first sermon ended, and Mark knelt in silent prayer. After the prayers, the deacon read from the Scriptures, and then the hour-long main sermon began. During the second sermon Priscilla sat up, her back ramrod straight as if someone had poured steel down her spine. She kept her focus on the minister.

His gaze wandered toward the unmarried women, and he found Franey Herschberger's hazel eyes focused on him. A sweet smile turned up the corners of her lips. He returned the greeting with a nod. Beside her Ruthann King studied the lap of her pink dress.

While his siblings joked that he was dating them both, he

didn't consider his relationship with either of them serious. They were like special friends, with no promises of a future. The time they spent together was fun. They played board games and ate the delicious food they made for him. They talked for hours, but he'd never kissed either of them or even held their hands.

The arrangement didn't seem to bother Ruthann and Franey. They seemed to enjoy spending time with him and laughing at his jokes. Still, Laura insisted his relationships with them would someday lead to one of the young ladies nursing a broken heart. Mark disagreed. What was wrong with having a little fun?

When it was time for the fifteen-minute prayer, Mark knelt and focused on God. He opened his heart and began to pray.

Lord, danki *for all the blessings in my life. Please keep my family healthy and safe.* Danki *for bringing Priscilla back to the community. I can tell she's struggling with her decision to rejoin the church. Please lead her and guide her heart. Protect her and Ethan and help her rebuild her relationships with her family and* freinden.

After the prayer, the congregation stood for the benediction and sang the closing hymn. Mark's eyes moved back to Priscilla as she sang along with the hymn. Did she still feel like an outcast? If so, could he somehow help her find her way back into the community? Hopefully she would feel God's love wrapped around her like a cozy blanket, helping her feel welcomed back into the church, even if certain individuals should make her feel otherwise.

When the hymn ended, seventy-year-old John Smucker, his church district's bishop, stood and faced the congregation. "And now I invite all the nonmembers of the congregation to please exit and the baptized members to stay for a special meeting."

A murmur spread throughout the congregation as the young, unbaptized members filed out through the barn door, gathering the children as they went.

Priscilla walked to her father and whispered something to him before taking Ethan's hand and leading him toward the barn exit. When she walked past Mark, she met his gaze with a solemn expression. He nodded at her as Ethan gave him another little wave.

After all the nonmembers had left, Mark turned his attention back to the bishop.

"We're having a members-only meeting because one of our *schweschdere* has fallen into sin," John announced to open the meeting. "Priscilla Allgyer left the community eight years ago to live in Baltimore like an *Englisher*. She returned to her family this past Thursday and met with me on Friday. She's repentant, and she wants to return to the church. After her time under the *Meiding*, she can be received back into the church."

John paused a moment, and a soft murmur moved through the congregation once again.

Mark turned to the unmarried women's section and spotted Franey and Ruthann whispering. He pressed his lips together, and his shoulders tightened. He hoped his friends weren't gossiping about Priscilla.

His eyes moved to the married women's section, and when he spotted Edna wiping her eyes, an invisible fist seemed to punch his heart. He could almost feel Edna's joy over her daughter's return. He turned to the married men's section, where Yonnie sat stoically, his expression grave. Was he hiding his feelings? Or was he truly not overjoyed to have his daughter back in his life? He hoped Yonnie was simply talented at masking his emotions.

"The meeting is over," John said, and conversations broke out around the barn.

"Let's set up for lunch," Roy said, patting Mark on the shoulder.

"*Ya*, I'm hungry." Mark smiled as he picked up a bench and helped Roy set it into a stand so it could be used as a table.

"Mark!" Franey appeared beside him and fingered the tie of her prayer covering as she smiled up at him. "I was wondering if you'd like to come over and visit this afternoon. I made a couple of strawberry pies yesterday, and I know you like them a lot." She touched his bicep and tilted her head as her eyes pleaded for a positive response.

Although the strawberry pie was tempting, Mark wanted to spend the afternoon resting. He just wasn't in the mood for company outside of his immediate family.

"*Danki* for the invitation, but I think I'm going to just rest at home," he said with his best smile. "I'd love a rain check, though."

Franey groaned and stuck out her lower lip, an expression Laura referred to as Franey's "wounded puppy dog look" when she'd once witnessed it. Mark bit back a grin at the memory of his twin's comment. Although Franey was the same age as Mark and Laura, she sometimes acted a few years younger. But Franey was pretty with her bright-hazel eyes and medium-blond hair.

"We could set something up for next week." Mark hoped the vague offer of another time would suffice.

"Okay." Franey's smile was back. "I'll see you later." She turned and headed toward the barn exit.

"Why did you turn her down?" Roy asked as he sidled up to him.

Mark shrugged. "I'm just not in the mood."

"You could've told her I'm free this afternoon."

Mark gave a bark of laughter. "She's two years older than you."

"So?" Roy challenged him. "I like strawberry pie."

"I'll keep that in mind." Mark chuckled as they moved to lift another bench. But his thoughts were still with Priscilla.

SIX

"Why can't we stay for lunch?" Ethan asked as he and Priscilla walked to her father's horse and buggy.

"I already told you. I can't share meals with the other members of the church until after my shunning is over." Priscilla opened the buggy's door for him. "I have to complete three classes with the bishop and ministers, before we can stay for lunch."

"What kind of classes?"

"It's sort of like Sunday school at the church we visited in Baltimore. The bishop and ministers are reminding me what our beliefs are."

"So you can't have lunch with everybody after church until your classes are done?"

"That's right."

Ethan rubbed his chin as he frowned. "But I want to eat lunch with *Mammi* and *Daadi*."

"Those are the rules." She pointed to the buggy. "Climb in."

Ethan climbed in and then turned toward her. "How are *Mammi* and *Daadi* going to get home if we take their buggy?"

"They're going to get a ride with one of our neighbors."

"Priscilla!" Cindy called as she rushed after them. "Wait a minute!"

Priscilla turned toward Cindy. "Why aren't you in the member-only meeting?"

"Because I'm not a member."

"What?" Priscilla felt her eyes widen. "But aren't you twenty-two?"

Cindy nodded, the ties of her prayer covering bouncing off the shoulders of her teal dress. "I am, but I haven't joined yet." Her expression clouded as a frown turned down her lips. "I'm sure Mark and Laura told you we lost our *mamm* five years ago."

"*Ya*, Mark did." She touched Cindy's arm. "I'm so sorry. Your *mamm* was a sweet, loving, and kind woman."

"*Danki. Ya*, she was." Cindy took a deep breath. "It's been tough since we lost her, and I just haven't felt like I'm ready to make a commitment to the community. I can't really explain it, but I guess I'm still a little lost without her."

"I understand." Priscilla's heart cracked open with grief at Cindy's loss.

"We didn't get to talk much earlier, and I want to tell you I'm really *froh* you're back. Laura told me she feels like a prayer has been answered. She really missed you."

Priscilla's heart warmed as tears stung her eyes. "*Danki*. That's really sweet of you to tell me that."

Cindy pointed to the buggy. "And I wanted to meet your *sohn*."

"That would be nice." Priscilla smiled as she walked over to the passenger side of the buggy. "Ethan, please come and meet *mei freind*. She's Mark's younger sister."

Ethan hopped out of the buggy and shook Cindy's hand. "Hi. I'm Ethan."

Cindy smiled, her pretty face lighting up. "It's nice to meet you. I'm Cindy Riehl."

"You're tall like Mark." Ethan pointed to Priscilla. "You and Mark are taller than my mom. She's short."

Priscilla and Cindy laughed.

"*Ya*, that is true," Priscilla said. "Most people are taller than I am."

Cindy turned back to Priscilla. "I'll let you get home. I hope I'll see you again soon. Florence sews with your *mamm* often, so maybe I'll see you at a quilting bee."

"That would be nice." Priscilla gave her a quick hug. "*Danki* for coming to talk to me."

"*Gern gschehne*," Cindy said. "Have a *gut* day."

Priscilla and Ethan climbed into the buggy and waved to Cindy as Priscilla guided the horse toward the road. The skill had come back to her immediately. At least her father hadn't questioned her abilities with a horse and buggy.

"The service was so different from our church back in Baltimore," Ethan began. "I didn't know what they were saying, and it was long, but I stayed quiet, just like you said."

"*Gut.*" Priscilla patted his leg. "You were very well behaved."

"You need to teach me a lot more Dutch," Ethan continued. "If you teach me how to speak it, I can understand better. Will the teacher speak Dutch in school?"

"No, they speak English in school."

"Oh good." Ethan glanced out the window. "I can't wait to go to school and meet other kids. Mark told me it will be a one-room schoolhouse. That's different from my school in Baltimore."

Priscilla stared out the windshield as Ethan talked on. Her thoughts spun with her worries about rejoining the community. Laura and the other women in her family had made her feel welcome, which was a relief. Maybe Mark was right. Maybe the members of the community would accept her back as one of their own. Still, she couldn't erase the feeling she got when all the eyes in the church were staring holes into her back during the service. Sitting in front of the bishop and ministers, she'd felt like a sinner on display.

If she didn't feel like she belonged in her own church district, how would she ever feel like she belonged in the community as a whole?

—⁓—

Later that afternoon Priscilla came downstairs and found her parents sitting in the family room in their favorite chairs. *Mamm* was reading what looked like a devotional while *Dat* concentrated on a copy of *The Budget.*

Mamm looked up from her book. "Where's Ethan?"

"He's reading." She pointed to the stairs. "I told him to take a nap, but he said only babies nap."

Mamm snickered. "That sounds like something he'd say."

Priscilla lingered by the bottom step and watched her father as he continued to study the newspaper. Her heart cried for them to work out their differences and somehow build a loving relationship. But how could they if he wouldn't even look at her?

Mamm cleared her throat as she stood. "I'm going to go spend some time with Ethan." *Mamm* gave her an encouraging smile and nodded toward *Dat* before making her way up the stairs.

Priscilla fiddled with the skirt of her dress as she crossed the room and then sat down on the sofa across from *Dat.* She folded her hands in her lap and waited for her father to acknowledge her.

After several moments she took a deep breath. *"Dat."*

"Hmm?" he responded with his eyes still focused on the newspaper.

"Would you please look at me?"

He folded the paper, which rustled in loud protest, and then met her gaze over the top of his reading glasses. "What?"

What did she want to say? As soon as he'd met her gaze, her words evaporated like a puddle on a hot summer day.

With a frown he began to open the paper again.

"Wait." She held up her hand to draw his attention back to her. "I want to know if you're *froh* that I'm starting the classes." How she hated the desperation radiating in her tone. Why was she so eager for his approval?

Because he was her father, and he'd never shown an ounce of satisfaction or pride toward her. All she'd ever wanted was his love.

"That's what you were supposed to do." His voice was flat and emotionless as he opened the paper again. "After all, you're the one who left the community and went to live with an *Englisher*. You got yourself shunned, so now you have to face the consequences."

Her pain and sadness morphed into anger and then surged through her veins, pushing her to her feet. "Why can't you at least acknowledge that I'm trying to fit in again? Why can't you give me a chance to prove I'm going to complete the classes and make you proud?"

His eyes narrowed. "We'll see after the shunning is over. You haven't completed your classes yet or been accepted back into the community."

"So you think I'll fail?" Furious tears filled her eyes.

"I didn't say that."

"No, you didn't say it out loud, but you're thinking it." She pointed to him. "You've always expected me to fail."

"That's not true." He shook his head.

"*Ya*, it is true." Her voice shook. "That's why you wouldn't let me work on the farm with you. You didn't think I could handle training the horses."

"I never said that." He placed the newspaper on the end table beside him. "Training horses is a difficult job, and it's no place for a *maedel*."

"Right." She folded her arms over her middle. "Only *buwe*

should work on a horse farm, and you resented that *Mamm* could only give you a *maedel*."

"You need to stop talking like that." His loud voice echoed throughout the room.

"It's the truth," she continued, her body shaking with boiling emotion. "You were disappointed when the doctors told her she couldn't have any more *kinner* because you wanted an heir. You didn't want me. You wanted a *bu*, so you ignored me. All I could do was learn how to quilt, sew, and cook as well as *Mamm* to prove I wasn't as stupid as you thought I was. But nothing I did mattered, did it?"

"I never said you were stupid."

"No, you didn't, but your constant criticism has shown me over and over that I'm your biggest disappointment."

"I don't think this is an appropriate Sunday discussion."

"Why? Because the truth hurts?" She nearly screamed the words as tears trickled down her cheeks. She brushed them away. She couldn't let him see how much his disapproval cut her to the bone.

"I don't approve of your tone." He stood. "You need to stop this disrespect now."

"No." She pointed to the floor. "It's time for you to listen to me and respect what I have to say. You've never treated me like a *dochder*. You've only ever treated me like an annoyance."

He ran his hand down his face. "If you don't stop talking to me this way, you're going to have to leave. This is *mei haus*, and I won't stand for you to speak to me so disrespectfully."

"Really, *Dat*?" Her voice squeaked. "You'd throw out *mei sohn* and me?"

He hesitated, and then he scrubbed both his hands down his face. Was he restraining himself? Or did he feel guilty for considering putting her and her son out on the street?

When he didn't speak, she shook her head and started for the stairs.

"I give up," she muttered as she headed up to her room. When she reached the top step, she stopped and pulled in a quaking breath. She had to somehow let go of her resentment of her father and push past the pain and anguish his coldness and criticism caused. She had to be strong—not only for herself but for her precious Ethan.

"Priscilla?" Ethan's door opened and *Mamm* stepped out into the hallway. "How did it go?"

The hope in her mother's expression sent guilt spiraling through her. How could she tell her mother that she'd yelled at her father? *Mamm* would never approve of what she'd said. And her father was right—she had been disrespectful to him. But enduring years of his criticism had taken a toll.

"Not well." Priscilla moved past her mother and walked into her bedroom.

"Did you try to talk to him?"

"I did, but it was a disaster." She sank onto the corner of her bed. "He still acts like I'm the biggest disappointment in his life."

"You're not a disappointment." *Mamm* touched her shoulder. "I've been praying for your *dat* to realize he's always been too hard on you. I know God will work on him so he'll realize what a blessing it is that God brought you home. What matters now is that our family is back together."

"Right." Priscilla stiffened, hoping to keep her tears at bay.

Mamm stepped over to the door. "Are you going to come downstairs?"

"No, *danki*." Priscilla forced a yawn. "I think I might take a nap."

"Okay." *Mamm* lingered in the doorway but then disappeared into the hallway.

Priscilla's shoulders hunched as dread threatened to drown her. She wanted so badly to be strong. She had survived Trent's abuse, and she needed to stand firm in this house for her son's sake. She had to tolerate her father until she could save some money and find an affordable place for her and Ethan to live.

SEVEN

Priscilla skidded to a halt when she found Mark standing at the kitchen counter Tuesday afternoon. He was drinking a glass of water.

"Hi." He grinned at her as he placed the glass on the counter.

"Hi." She looked down toward the floor and cleared her throat. She'd done her best to avoid him all day yesterday, seeing him only in passing when he came into the house. She'd hoped to avoid him again today so she wouldn't have to discuss her meeting with the bishop and ministers or how humiliating it had felt to sit in front of the entire congregation with her head bent and face covered. But now she was face-to-face with him, and he had turned that electric smile on her.

"*Wie geht's?*" He swiveled toward her and leaned his elbow on the counter.

"I need to call a driver." She jammed her thumb toward the door to the family room. "I'm out of material, and I'm making a couple of pairs of work trousers for Ethan."

Footsteps sounded in the family room.

"I can take you." Mark stood up straight. "I need to go to the hardware store for supplies."

"Oh no. That's okay. I'll just call a driver." The thought of being stuck in a buggy alone with Mark made her nervously shift her weight on her feet. What would she find to discuss with him during the ride to town and then back home to avoid his delving into her personal life?

"Save me some money and go with Mark," *Dat* chimed in from the doorway.

Priscilla gritted her teeth. Leave it to him to overhear her conversation.

"Let it go," Mark muttered under his breath. "Don't say anything."

Priscilla hesitated, surprised by Mark's interference. Then she nodded. "I'll get my purse," she said before hurrying out of the kitchen.

Mark gave Priscilla a sideways glance as he guided his horse toward the road. She stared out the window with her purse on her lap as if the passing traffic held all the secrets to the perfect life. The only sound was the *clip-clop* of the horse's hooves, the whirr of the buggy wheels, and the roar of passing cars. He was accustomed to his women friends talking his ear off when they spent time together, so the silence between them was unnerving, making his skin itch.

He racked his brain for something to say.

"How was your Sunday afternoon?" he asked.

Priscilla was silent for a moment, but then she turned toward him, her brow pinched. "What?"

"I asked how your Sunday afternoon was."

"Oh." She continued to look surprised. "It was quiet. I took a nap."

He nodded as he turned his attention back to the road.

"How was yours?" she asked.

Aha! He'd managed to start a conversation with her.

"It was *gut*. I just rested and spent time with my family." His glance missed hers as she turned back to the window.

Mark halted the horse at a red light, and out of the corner of his eye, he spotted Priscilla scratching her arm. Today she wore a purple dress that complemented her dark hair and chestnut eyes. Like her other dresses, this one had three-quarter sleeves.

"Why are you wearing longer sleeves when it's close to ninety-five degrees outside?"

An indecipherable expression flashed across her face, and then she shrugged.

"It's just comfortable." She quickly looked toward the passing traffic as if avoiding his eyes.

A horn tooted behind them, and Mark guided the horse through the intersection. A few awkward moments of silence stretched like a great chasm. Mark found himself wishing for a radio to at least fill the dead air with music.

"What do you need from the hardware store?"

Her question stunned him for a moment. "I have a list in my pocket. I need chicken feed and a new hammer since I managed to break one. Let's see. What else? A chisel, some batteries, and a box of nails."

"Oh." She folded her hands in her lap and stared out the windshield.

He tried to think of something else to say, but nothing came to him. Being with her felt awkward, and he'd never felt awkward around a woman before. Why was she different? None of the other young women in their community found him this dull. Was something wrong with him today?

When they reached the parking lot at the hardware store, Mark guided the horse to a hitching post. He tied it up and then turned, surprised to see Priscilla still sitting in the buggy.

He skirted around the buggy and leaned into the passenger window. "What are you doing?"

"I'm going to sit here and wait for you."

"But it's hot out here." He gestured toward the store. "Walk inside with me. I'll buy you a bottle of water."

"Okay," she said, climbing out of the buggy.

They walked side by side toward the store. When they reached the front door, he held it open for her, and she muttered a thank-you as she passed through.

Priscilla walked with him through the aisles as he gathered the items on his list. She lingered a step or two behind him, her arms folded over her waist as he shopped.

"You know, you're giving me a headache," he quipped with a smile.

"What?" Her dark eyebrows pinched together.

"Because you talk so much," he explained, grinning. "You're giving me a horrendous headache."

Her expression relaxed, and then she sighed.

"I'm just kidding." He hesitated, waiting for her smile to light up her face. But it didn't. Instead, she looked away. None of his methods were working on her. Did she truly find him uninteresting? The notion gnawed at his gut.

He made his way down the last aisle and added chicken feed to his cart. As he stepped into the main aisle, he heard someone call his name. Turning, he spotted Rudy Swarey walking toward him. Rudy was Laura's ex-boyfriend.

"Hi, Rudy!" Mark waved to him. "How are you doing?"

"I'm fine." Rudy shook his hand and then turned to Priscilla. "Hi, Priscilla. It's been a long time."

"It's nice to see you." She shook his hand, but her shoulders hunched and her lips flattened. She suddenly seemed skittish and unsure of herself. Was she uncomfortable seeing other members of the community?

"What are you two doing here?" Rudy asked, no doubt surprised to see them together.

Mark pointed to the shopping cart. "I'm just picking up supplies for the farm, and Priscilla needs some material at the fabric shop."

"You're still working for Yonnie?" Rudy asked. He was putting two and two together now.

"*Ya*, I am. I see you're staying busy." Mark gestured around the store. "The store looks great."

"*Danki*. It's going well. We have some new suppliers, and we're able to keep our prices competitive despite the chain stores in town." Rudy gestured toward the front of the store. "If you have everything, why don't I check you out so you can be on your way?"

Mark and Priscilla followed Rudy to the cash register, and Mark paid for the supplies, adding two bottles of water to his purchases. Then they headed out and he loaded up the buggy.

As he climbed in beside Priscilla, he turned toward her. Once again, she stared out the window as if she'd rather be anywhere else in the world. He couldn't take the silence between them any longer.

"Are you upset with me?" He heard the hint of desperation in his voice. What was wrong with him?

She faced him, her eyebrows careening toward her hairline. "Why would I be upset with you?"

"I don't know." He fingered the reins. "You're just so quiet. Did I do something to offend you?"

"No, you haven't done anything. I guess I just don't have much to say." She shook her head. "Let's get to the fabric store so I can get back home and finish making those trousers for Ethan."

"All right." He handed her a bottle of water. "Here. I got this for you."

"*Danki*." She opened it and took a long drink.

"*Gern gschehne.*"

How was he ever going to figure out the puzzle that was Priscilla Allgyer?

—⁓—

The bell on the door chimed as Priscilla and Mark stepped into Herschberger's Fabrics. She gripped her list in her hand and took in the knot of women milling around the large store. Most of them were dressed Amish, but a few Mennonite and *Englishers* were shopping as well.

Priscilla's breath seemed to scorch a hole in her chest as she steeled herself against her growing anxiety at being seen in the community now that the bishop had announced her name during the church's members-only meeting.

"Mark!"

Priscilla turned toward the cashier counter, where Franey stood helping a customer. Her pretty face lit up with a wide smile as she waved at Mark.

"Hi, Franey." Mark returned the smile.

"It's *gut* to see you." Franey looked as if she wanted to leap over the counter.

"Hi, Mark." Sadie Liz, Franey's younger sister, approached them. "What are you doing here?"

Priscilla tamped down the urge to ask Sadie Liz if she were invisible. In all honesty she longed to be invisible these days.

"I'm looking for some material to make a few dresses," Mark said, teasing. "What color do you think would be best for me?"

Sadie Liz giggled. "How about blue to go with your eyes?"

"*Ya*, they are my best feature, aren't they?" he retorted, and then he pointed to a display of patterns. "Would I find the best pattern over there?"

"*Ya*, let me show you." Sadie Liz giggled again as they walked together toward the display.

Priscilla swallowed a groan and headed toward the bolts of material. She picked out what she needed and asked Franey's mother to cut the material for her.

As she took her place in line to pay, she spotted Mark in the corner still chatting with Sadie Liz, who was still giggling. Priscilla rolled her eyes. Did he ever stop flirting? Why were all the women in this community attracted to him as if he wore an invisible magnet?

Several women lined up behind Priscilla as she waited her turn. When she reached the counter, she placed her basket on it and pulled her wallet from her purse.

When Priscilla looked up, Franey's eyes were wide as she shook her head. "I'm sorry, Priscilla, but I can't accept your money."

Humiliation wafted over her as she leaned forward and lowered her voice. "You're joking, right?"

"No, I'm not." Franey's expression was serious, holding no hint of a joke. She also lowered her voice. "You're under the *Meiding*, so I can't take your money."

Whispers erupted behind Priscilla, and her legs began to shake with the weight of humiliation.

"Come on, Franey," Priscilla said, seething as her cheeks burned. "We went to school together, and you know me. I need this material so I can make clothes for *mei sohn*. Please just tell me what I owe you." She opened her wallet and held up a handful of bills.

"I can't. I'm not allowed." Franey pushed the material toward her. "Just take it."

"Please, Franey." Frustrated tears filled Priscilla's eyes as she felt the stares of the women in line behind her burning through her dress and into her clammy skin. "Take my money." Her voice sounded weak and unsure to her own ears.

Hold it together, Priscilla!

"I can't." Franey nodded toward the corner of the store, where her father was stocking shelves. "He won't let me."

A woman behind her clicked her tongue, and Priscilla could imagine her critical thoughts. How could these judgmental women even begin to understand what Priscilla had endured the past few years?

Priscilla's hand trembled as she pushed her wallet back into her purse. She prayed she wouldn't cry in front of Franey and the rest of the people watching her. She couldn't allow them to see her crumble. She was stronger than that!

"Hey, Franey." Mark appeared beside Priscilla and leaned on the counter. "How's your day going?"

"Hi, Mark." Franey's face brightened as she turned toward him. "My day has been fine. How's yours?"

"It's been great." He moved his finger over the counter. "I've been thinking about your offer on Sunday. Do you still have that strawberry pie?"

"I do." Franey nodded with enthusiasm. "I saved some for you."

"*Wunderbaar.* Maybe I could come over one night this week?"

"Of course!" Franey nearly squeaked. "How about Thursday?"

"Great." Mark smiled that electric smile that seemed to make Franey melt.

Priscilla's jaw locked so hard that her whole face ached. Was Mark really going to make a date with Franey now? Unbelievable! Did he think the world revolved around his dating schedule?

Mark pulled his wallet out of his back pocket. "Listen, I really need to get this material. How much do I owe you?"

Franey froze, and her gaze bounced between Priscilla and Mark.

"Come on, Franey." Mark's smile somehow seemed brighter as he nodded toward the long line of women behind them. "I'm certain these ladies are in a hurry, so why don't you just tell me what I owe you."

"Oh. Okay." Franey's smile was back. She added up the material, told Mark the amount, and he paid.

"*Danki* so much. I'll see you Thursday." Mark winked as he took his change from her.

Mortified, Priscilla snatched the bag out of Mark's hand and marched out of the store to his buggy, hoping to leave the accusing stares of the customers behind forever.

—·∽·—

"I don't need you to fight my battles for me," Priscilla said as Mark climbed into the buggy beside her. "I had it all under control." She sat back in the seat and opened her purse.

"No, you didn't." Mark shook his head. "And I'm glad I was there to help you."

"I think you mean you were there to sweet-talk Franey." She pulled out a handful of bills and held them out to him. "Here."

He looked down at the money and then met her gaze. "I don't need your money."

She frowned. "And I don't need your charity. Take it."

He took the money and studied her for a moment, taking in the sadness that seemed to sparkle in her dark eyes.

"Consider the material a gift for Ethan." As he pushed his hand toward her with the money, she flinched before taking it.

"*Danki*," she said as she slipped the bills back into her wallet and then focused on her black purse.

They both remained silent during the ride back to her father's farm, and, once again he longed for a radio.

When they reached one of her father's barns, he halted the horse.

Priscilla turned toward him, her expression more amiable this time.

"*Danki*," she whispered. "I appreciate what you did today."

He opened his mouth to respond, but she was already out of the buggy and marching up the path toward the house.

EIGHT

Priscilla dashed into the downstairs bathroom, closed the door, and leaned against it. Her arms hung at her sides as humiliation and anger gushed out like a raging river. She dissolved into tears. Franey's rejection had torn at her heart and solidified her reasons for being reluctant to return to this community.

After a few moments she leaned on the sink and stared at her image in the mirror. Her eyes were puffy and bloodshot, and tears had streaked her face.

"You're stronger than this," she whispered to her reflection. "And you need to show Ethan that courage."

Leaning over, she filled her hands with cold water and splashed it on her face. She couldn't allow her parents to see her fall apart like this.

As she dried her face on a towel, a new determination blossomed. She'd finish making Ethan's new clothes and then remind her mother about helping with her quilting and sewing business. She'd save all her money and then find a small place to rent and a job that would pay enough for her to live on her own. Once she left her father's house, he couldn't force her to marry an Amish man to support her and her son. She would make her own way. She had to. Her life depended on it.

Priscilla smiled at her reflection. Yes, she would make it on her own without the help of any man, including her father. She would show everyone just how resolute she truly was.

_____ ⟋⟍ _____

"Priscilla." *Mamm* stood in her doorway on Thursday afternoon of the following week.

"*Ya.*" She stopped sewing the quilt she'd been repairing for one of her mother's customers and turned toward her.

"Cindy Riehl left us a message and invited us over for an impromptu quilting bee. She said Laura will be there too." She beckoned toward the hallway. "It starts in a half hour, so let's go."

Priscilla hesitated. There was normally food at quilting bees, and she would have to eat alone, across the room from everyone else, which would humiliate her just as much as she'd been at Franey's store. Everyone would stare at her. She swallowed a groan at the thought.

"*Was iss letz?*" *Mamm*'s brow furrowed.

"I don't know." She nodded toward the quilt. "I promised I'd have this done by the end of the day, and I—"

"So bring it with you and finish it there. You need to get out of this *haus*. You haven't left since you went to the fabric store last week. Let's go. Your *dat* and Mark already agreed to look after Ethan." Before Priscilla could respond, *Mamm* was gone, her footsteps echoing in the hallway.

For a brief moment Priscilla wondered if Mark had asked his sister to invite her to this quilting bee, but she dismissed that notion. Why would Mark worry about Priscilla, especially since she'd avoided him for more than a week? She'd said hello to him a few times, but otherwise she'd steered clear of both her father and him.

"Priscilla!" *Mamm* called from downstairs. "Our driver is here!"

"I'm coming." After gathering the quilt and sewing supplies she'd need, she hurried down the stairs and out to the waiting van.

"I'm so glad you're here." Laura smiled at Priscilla as they sat together on the glider on the Riehls' porch later that afternoon.

After sewing for more than an hour with Laura, Cindy, Florence, Kayla, Sarah Jane, and *Mamm*, Priscilla and Laura had slipped outside to talk alone. Mollie was inside helping Cindy work on a quilt for one of her customers.

"I am too." Priscilla picked up her teacup, sipped from it, and looked out across the meadow toward Jamie's house. "I want to say again that I'm sorry I didn't contact you after I left."

"It's okay."

"No, it's not okay, and I truly regret it." Priscilla touched Laura's hand. "*Danki* for forgiving me for disappearing without a trace. I'm grateful you've welcomed me back into your life."

Laura clicked her tongue and shook her head. "How could I not welcome you back? I've missed you so much. I'm grateful God brought you back to us."

Priscilla looked out across the gorgeous pasture again. She'd forgotten how beautiful the patchwork pastures were in Lancaster County.

Laura paused for a moment. "Tell me about Baltimore."

"What?" Priscilla spun toward Laura.

Laura lifted an eyebrow. "I hit a sore spot? I'm sorry."

"No, it's okay." Priscilla gripped the handle of her cup. "When I left I moved in with my cousin Thelma. She's a few years older than we are, and she left her community when she was nineteen.

We'd been writing letters for some time, and when I told her I was thinking about leaving, she invited me to stay with her."

Laura's eyes rounded, and she touched Priscilla's arm. "I had no idea you were so unhappy. If you'd told Savilla and me, we would've tried to help you."

"*Danki* for that." Guilt felt like a scratchy blanket that wrapped around Priscilla and tightened. "But it's not your fault. I was so confused, and I didn't know what I wanted." She looked down at her tea, too humiliated to admit that her father was the one who had driven her away. "Thelma worked at a restaurant within walking distance of her apartment, and I got a job there too, as a waitress."

"Was that where you met Ethan's *dat*?"

"*Ya.*" Priscilla kept her focus on her cup as she spoke. "He was a frequent customer, and he always asked to be seated in my area. One day he asked me out, and we started dating. About six months later, I moved in with him, and then I got pregnant." She flushed with shame. "Things were *gut* for a while, but then he . . . changed. I knew I had to leave, and that's why I'm here."

Laura rubbed her arm. "And I'm glad you came back no matter what happened."

Priscilla smiled and nodded as relief flooded her. She wasn't ready to share the details of her troubled relationship with Trent.

"What happened to your cousin Thelma?"

"She got married and moved to New Jersey. I haven't heard from her in a couple of months."

"Oh. How are things at home?" Laura asked. "I know you and your *dat* used to argue a lot."

"It's tolerable." Priscilla shrugged. "He insisted I make myself right with the church, which I'm doing. He also insists I need to find a husband, but I'm going to try to be on my own before he can enforce that demand."

"What do you mean?" Laura asked.

Priscilla lowered her voice to be certain her mother wouldn't hear from inside the house. "I'm saving the money I make helping *mei mamm* sew, and I'm going to find a place for Ethan and me. Then I'll find a steady job so I can be on my own. *Mei mamm* doesn't know my plan, so please keep it to yourself."

Laura seemed to search her eyes. "Tell me you're not going to leave the community again."

"I don't know."

Laura's expression clouded with something that looked like worry. She shook her head.

Priscilla needed to change the subject fast. "Tell me about Allen."

"Oh, he's *wunderbaar*." Laura got a faraway look in her eyes as she rubbed her belly and stared off toward the green rolling meadow. "I'm so *froh* with him. He's handsome, kind, and generous. And he's a *gut dat*. He loves Mollie so much, and I know he'll love our second *kind* just as much."

As Laura talked about Allen's carriage business and how hard he worked to support their family, Priscilla tried to imagine having a husband that wonderful. What would life have been like if Trent had married her, worked hard to support their family, and cherished her and Ethan? Heaviness settled over her heart, and she fought back threatening tears.

"Priscilla?" Laura leaned over and touched her shoulder. "Are you okay?"

"*Ya*." She forced a smile. "I was just thinking about how blessed you are. I'm so *froh* you and Allen found each other."

Laura clicked her tongue. "I'm sorry. I didn't mean to brag or sound prideful."

"You didn't." Priscilla shook her head. "I just don't think a *gut* provider and *dat* for Ethan is possible for me."

Laura's eyes were determined. "Don't give up on our community."

Priscilla couldn't stop her snort. "What makes you think any man in the community would want to marry me, even if I was ready to trust another man?"

"Why wouldn't they?"

Priscilla turned toward her. "Laura, I'm shunned for leaving for eight years and then coming back with a *sohn* I had out of wedlock. Why would any man want to be with me?" She pointed to her chest. "I'm damaged."

"No, you're not." Laura shook her head. "You made a mistake, and you're doing what you have to do to make yourself right with the church. You're forgiven."

"I may be forgiven, but my sins won't be forgotten."

Laura sighed. "Stop being so hard on yourself. Give yourself time to readjust in the community. You're *schee* and sweet. Many men would love to have a *fraa* like you."

"*Danki.*" Priscilla shifted on the glider. She didn't believe Laura's insistence that any man would give her a chance after she'd had a child out of wedlock. She needed to change the subject.

"Laura, do you remember the time you, Savilla, and I went to that pond in Ronks in Mark's buggy, and we got stuck in a rainstorm? It was storming so hard we couldn't see out the windshield, so we had to pull over at a 7-Eleven and wait for it to pass. We just sat there and drank Slurpees until the storm passed."

"Oh my goodness!" Laura laughed. "I do remember that. That was so fun. Mark was so angry with me when I got home. He said I should have called and told him we were going to be late." She rolled her eyes. "He always worries about me."

"That's nice, though." Priscilla drained her tea as envy gripped her. What would it have been like if she'd had a brother to worry about her? "How about that time we went to Savilla's *haus* to bake *kichlin,* and we were so wrapped up in our discussion about the cute *buwe* in our youth group that we nearly set the kitchen on fire?"

Laura gave a bark of laughter. *"Ya!"* She wiped her eyes. "Her *mamm* was so upset with us. The kitchen was clogged with smoke!"

They shared more memories of their time with Savilla, and after a while the screen door opened. Cindy stepped onto the porch with Mollie close behind her, holding a tray of cookies.

"We brought you snacks." Mollie held up the tray.

"Ya, you're missing all the refreshments," Cindy added. "May we join you?"

"Of course." Laura patted the chair beside the glider, and Mollie hopped onto it. "We were just getting caught up. *Danki* for the snacks, *mei liewe.*"

As Cindy sat down beside Priscilla, Priscilla smiled. She was thankful for her wonderful friends who had welcomed her home despite her past mistakes.

Mark stepped out of the barn as the blue van parked in front of Yonnie's house. He hurried over just as Edna and Priscilla were climbing out of it. Ever since they'd been to the fabric store, he'd tried to talk to Priscilla, but all his attempts to draw her into a conversation had fallen flat. She gave him only one-word answers to any of his questions, and she still showed no interest in being his friend. It was driving him to the brink of madness.

While Edna paid the driver, Priscilla balanced a large bag containing a quilt, a sewing basket, and a plate of cookies as she walked toward the porch steps.

"Do you need any help?" he asked as he quickened his steps.

"No, *danki*. I'm fine." She teetered, and he grabbed the plate as it slipped from her hands.

"No, huh?" He grinned as he held up the plate.

"Danki." She reached to take it from him.

"Uh-uh." He shook his head. "Allow me." He made a sweeping gesture toward the porch.

She didn't protest.

"Hello, Mark." Edna carried two bags as she moved past them on the steps.

"Hi, Edna."

Edna disappeared into the house, and Priscilla turned toward the row of barns.

"Where's Ethan?" she asked.

"He and your *dat* are talking to a customer in the pasture. I've been working in the barn."

"Oh." She turned toward him, and for the first time in more than a week, she stood still as if she wanted to talk to him.

Relief flooded him. "How was the quilting bee?"

"It was nice. I enjoyed talking with your *schweschdere*." She eyed him with what looked like suspicion. "How was your date with Franey last Thursday night? Did you enjoy her strawberry pie?"

"The pie was *appeditlich*, but it wasn't a date."

"Really?" Her dark eyebrows rose. "The way you were flirting with her, it sure seemed like it would be."

"Wait a minute." He held up his free hand. "I wasn't flirting with her."

"Ha." She started up the steps. "You're unbelievable."

"What does that mean?" He charged forward, following her through the front door and into the kitchen. "I only did that so you could have your material."

"Oh really." She set her bag and sewing basket on the kitchen table and spun toward him. "So you used Franey, then?"

"Well, no." He stopped in the doorway and stared at her, speechless. No one had ever accused him of being a user. The word stung him as if it were an angry wasp.

"Mark, I've seen you in action." She stepped closer to him and wagged a finger just millimeters from his nose. "All you have to do is smile and you have most of the *maed* in our community eating from your hands. You know exactly how much power you have over them." She lifted her chin. "Just admit it. You love the attention, and you use the *maed* to make yourself feel powerful."

"Powerful?" He blinked. "Why would I want to feel powerful?"

"Never mind." She took the plate from his hand. "*Danki* for your help." She set it on the counter before retrieving her bag and sewing basket.

When she walked back to the doorway, he stayed planted where he was.

"Excuse me." When he didn't move, she sighed as she looked up at him. "I have work to do. I need to finish this quilt. I promised the customer she'd have it today."

"Are you angry with me?" He held his breath as he awaited her answer.

"No." Her forehead puckered. "I have no reason to be angry with you." She nodded toward the doorway. "I really need to finish this quilt, though. Please let me through."

He gave her his best smile, certain it would inspire her to stay and talk to him. After all, she was right. That was how he garnered most of the attention from the young ladies in their church district. Surely Priscilla couldn't resist his charms.

But her serious expression didn't melt into a smile. "Mark, I really do have work to do."

Rejection stabbed at his self-esteem. Was she immune to him completely? Or had he lost his touch?

Defeated, he took a step back, and she hurried up the stairs.

Her accusations echoed in his mind. Was he a user? The word made him cringe. Had it been wrong for him to ask Franey to get together with him? He had only wanted to help Priscilla and stop her humiliation. But maybe Priscilla was right. Maybe he had made a mistake.

Even though Priscilla insisted she wasn't angry with him, Mark was certain she didn't approve of him. And for some inexplicable reason, he wanted her approval more than ever. He had to find a way to prove to Priscilla that he was worthy of her friendship.

———

"I had so much fun at the quilting bee today," Kayla said as she sat beside Jamie in the glider that evening.

Jamie nodded as he rocked a sleeping Calvin in his arms.

"That's nice." Mark glanced out across the pasture toward Jamie's house as he sat on a rocker beside his brother. Someday soon his own house would stand beside it. He couldn't wait to walk through his front door after a long day at work and eat supper in his kitchen.

"It was great to see Priscilla again," Kayla continued. "I finally got to talk to her after meeting her at church last week. She's really sweet."

Mark's gaze swung to Kayla at the mention of Priscilla's name. "What did she talk about?"

"She didn't say too much to me." Kayla rubbed Calvin's back. "We mostly talked about sewing. She's really talented. She showed me how she was repairing a quilt for a customer. She sewed for a while, and then she and Laura came out here to talk. I think they wanted to get caught up in private. I didn't want to intrude, so I stayed inside."

Mark tried to hide his disappointment at Kayla's lack of

information. He wanted to know more about Priscilla's life in Baltimore, but it wasn't his business.

Kayla stood. "We should get Calvin home. I'm going to go say good night to everyone." She disappeared into the house, and the screen door clicked shut behind her.

Jamie looked down at his son. "I can't believe Cal is going to be a big *bruder* soon."

Mark smiled. "*Ya*, you're going to have two *kinner*. Can you believe that? We thought you'd never find anyone to marry you."

"At least I had enough sense to settle down."

"Excuse me?"

"You could have any *maedel* you want in this community, but you're still a bachelor." Jamie turned toward him. "What are you waiting for?"

"You know what I want." Mark gestured toward Jamie's house. "I want my own place, and that's my priority right now."

"Why?" Jamie asked. "You have your own room here. Besides, there's more to life than building a *haus*."

"That's easy for you to say." Mark pointed across the meadow. "You have a *schee* three-bedroom *haus* right there."

"You'll have one someday. Get married first, and then build your *haus*."

"No." Mark shook his head. "I'm not ready to get married."

"Why not?"

"Because . . . well . . . I'm just not."

"You know, Mark, it wasn't too long ago that you were giving me a hard time about being almost thirty and not married. You're twenty-six now. What are you waiting for?"

Mark paused and considered the question. "Maybe I haven't found the right *maedel*."

Laughter burst from Jamie's lips, and Calvin moaned and wiggled in his sleep before settling down again.

"What's so funny?" Mark deadpanned.

"You haven't found the right *maedel*? If that's true, then I don't think she exists. You've gained the attention of nearly every *maedel* in Lancaster County."

Priscilla's words from earlier in the day rang through his mind.

All you have to do is smile and you have most of the maed *in our community eating from your hands. You know exactly how much power you have over them. Just admit it. You love the attention, and you use the* maed *to make yourself feel powerful.*

Did his older brother think he was a user too?

Mark stood. "I'm going to bed." He touched Calvin's back. *"Gut nacht,* Cal."

"Did I say something wrong?" Jamie asked as Mark turned to go.

"Why would you say that?" Mark opened the screen door.

"Because you didn't give me a biting remark in response."

Mark tilted his head. "Look, Jamie, when I'm ready to get married, you'll be the first to know."

Jamie shook his head. "I'll be more like the third. First you'll ask your future *fraa,* and then you'll tell your twin."

"Fine. You'll be the third." Mark tapped the doorframe. *"Gut nacht."*

As he stepped into the family room, a question filled his mind. Would he ever feel the urge to be married? If not, he might spend the rest of his life living alone in the house he built on his father's farm. Was that what he wanted?

NINE

"How did your class go?" Laura asked after the service on Sunday.

"It went well." Priscilla shrugged. "You remember how the classes went before we were baptized. They're about the history of our beliefs. Just a refresher." She glanced around the barn as the men began to set up the tables for lunch.

"You have one more class, and then you'll be accepted back into the church." Laura's smile widened.

"*Ya*, I know." Although Priscilla should be relieved that her shunning was almost over, a niggle of worry started at the base of her neck. Was she ready to become a member of the church? Did she even deserve to be a member?

"I'm hungry," Ethan whined as he rubbed his abdomen. "Can't we stay for lunch today?"

"I'm hungry too," Mollie agreed as she stood beside him.

"No, Ethan, you know we can't stay," Priscilla said, trying to keep her temper at bay. "We've discussed this."

Laura bent down and smiled at Ethan. "You'll be able to stay and eat with us soon." Then she stood up straight and touched Priscilla's arm. "I hate that you have to leave."

"Like you said, I'll be helping you serve the noon meal in a couple of weeks." Priscilla's heart seemed to turn over at her friend's words. She looked across the barn and spotted Franey and Ruthann standing with Mark, smiling and gazing up at him as if he were the most interesting person in the room.

"Will he ever pick just one *maedel*?" The question burst from Priscilla's mouth without any forethought. Why did she even care that Mark flirted with more than one young woman—or any women? It wasn't her business. When Mark met her gaze and smiled, Priscilla felt a strange zing of electricity flowing through her veins, taking her by surprise. She quickly turned away, focusing on Laura again.

Laura frowned. "I keep praying he'll choose one and settle down."

"I doubt that will ever happen. Mark has always loved being the center of attention."

Laura chuckled. "That's the truth."

"Priscilla," *Dat* said when he appeared at her side. "You know you can't stay to eat with the rest of the congregation. You need to go."

"*Ya*, I know." Priscilla's mood deflated at her father's stern eyes and curt warning. After he walked away she turned back to Laura. "I'd better go. Take care."

Laura's expression seemed filled with sympathy. She gave Priscilla a quick hug and then touched Ethan's head. "I'll see you both soon."

New humiliation mixed with anger pricked Priscilla's skin as she took Ethan's hand and steered him out of the barn. Why did *Dat* feel the need to remind her she wasn't welcome to stay for lunch? Priscilla didn't need to be reminded that she was shunned and unwelcome at her community's table. He seemed to enjoy shoving her state of affairs down her throat any chance he could. Each night he reminded her to sit at the separate table for supper as if she hadn't eaten her meals there for more than two weeks.

Priscilla swallowed a sigh. She'd always dreamt of having a loving father. So many times she'd witnessed Laura's father hugging her and encouraging her. She even recalled Savilla's father consoling her after she'd fallen and skinned her knee. But Priscilla had no memories of her father showing her affection or telling her that he loved her. She just wanted his love, his emotional support. Why did some fathers dole out love and affection in abundance and others offer only dribs and drabs?

She bit her trembling lower lip as they approached the waiting horse and buggy.

Ethan looked up at her, his eyebrows pinched together. "Are you okay, *Mamm*?"

Priscilla felt her face relax as she took in her son's innocent face. She touched his nose and then smoothed his thick, dark hair. "*Ya*, I'm fine. I was just thinking about all the chores I need to do tomorrow."

"Oh." He smiled. "Can we have peanut butter and jelly sandwiches for lunch?"

She stopped and cupped his cheek. "That sounds *appeditlich*."

"Apple what?" he asked, his nose scrunched as if he smelled something foul.

She laughed at his adorable expression. "*Appeditlich*," she repeated. "It means delicious. We need to work on your Dutch."

"Teach me more words," he said.

"Okay." As they climbed into the buggy, Priscilla did her best to dismiss her frustration about her father. All that mattered was that she and Ethan had each other. She'd never let Ethan wonder if she loved him. She'd be sure to show him every day.

"Ethan?"

"What?" He looked at her.

"Ich liebe dich, mei liewe."

He grinned. "I love you too, *Mamm*."

Her heart swelled with affection for her son. He was the only man she needed in her life.

Mark's eyes lingered on Priscilla as Franey talked about how busy her father's fabric store had been. When Priscilla met his gaze, her cheeks reddened. Then she quickly looked at his twin. Why would she avert her eyes so quickly?

"Did you hear a word I said?"

"Huh?" Mark turned to Franey's narrowed eyes, and he fixed his best grin on his face. "I'm sorry. Go ahead."

"I asked you if you'd like to have supper at *mei haus* this week." Franey jammed her hand on one small hip.

"Oh." Mark rubbed his chin. "I'll have to check my schedule."

"Your schedule?" Ruthann's brow furrowed. "I thought you said you had time for each of us this week."

"Right." He cleared his throat. "I'll let you know." He turned back toward Priscilla just as her father said something to her. When her shoulders hunched, alarm surged through Mark. What was her father saying to make her so upset? The urge to protect her flooded his veins, taking him by surprise. Why would he want to take care of someone who had no interest in even being his friend?

After her father walked away, Priscilla said something to Laura, who hugged her. Then Priscilla and Ethan headed out through the barn doors.

Mark turned his attention back to Ruthann and Franey, but their words were only background noise to his swirling thoughts.

"Mark?" Ruthann asked after a few moments. "Is something wrong?"

"*Ya*. I mean, no." He divided a smile between them. "I really need to start moving the benches, and you should get started serving the meal. I'll talk to you later, okay?"

"Oh," Franey said before sharing a confused look with Ruthann.

"Okay," Ruthann added.

"Let me know about supper, okay?" Franey asked.

Without responding, Mark headed over to Laura. She and Mollie and Cindy were heading toward the barn exit.

"Sis," Mark called, quickening his steps as he approached them. "Laura! Wait a second."

"Hey, Mark!" Roy called from the other side of the barn. "Are you going to help with the benches? Or are you going to chat all afternoon?"

Mark held up his index finger toward his younger brother. "One minute."

Roy shook his head and then said something to Jamie beside him.

Laura and Cindy had spun to face Mark, and Mollie yanked on Laura's hand.

"We need to go serve the meal," Laura said. "What do you need?"

"I want to talk to you."

"I'm hungry!" Mollie whined.

Cindy took Mollie's hand. "I'll take her to the kitchen and feed her."

"*Danki*," Laura said with a sigh. "I'll be right there." As Cindy and Mollie walked away, she pivoted back to Mark. "What's this about?"

Mark gestured for Laura to follow him to a corner.

"What did you and Priscilla discuss before she left?"

Laura raised her eyebrows. "Just girl stuff. Why?"

"She seemed upset when her *dat* spoke to her, and I was wondering what happened. What did he say?"

Laura grinned as she leaned forward. "Why are you suddenly so interested in Priscilla?" She wagged a finger at him. "Do you like her?"

"Sure I do. She's our *freind*, right?"

"Uh-huh." Laura shook her head. "It's more than that. You really like her."

He swallowed a groan. "Please, sis. We're not sixteen anymore."

Laura studied him, and he could almost hear her thoughts clicking through her mind. She was drawing conclusions about his interest in Priscilla, and that sent annoyance hurling through him.

"If you're so interested in what Priscilla's *dat* said to her, you can ask her yourself."

"Fine." He gave her a curt nod. "I will."

<hr />

Priscilla yawned as she descended the stairs the following afternoon. Her eyes were tired from staring at her sewing machine all day. She'd finished two sewing projects for customers and had started a third when she decided she needed a break.

She'd skipped lunch, and her stomach felt hollow as it growled. A turkey sandwich and a couple of her mother's peanut butter cookies would hit the spot.

When her shoe hit the bottom step, she turned toward the kitchen and stopped in her tracks. Mark came around the stairwell. She gripped the banister as she looked up at him. She'd hoped to avoid another awkward conversation with him today, but he always seemed to have a sixth sense about when she was on her way to the kitchen. How did he manage to anticipate her every move?

"Hi." He smiled. *"Wie geht's?"*

"I'm fine." She did her best to sound chipper despite her rising anxiety. "How are you?"

"I can tell you're not fine." His gaze was penetrating, and she hugged her arms to her chest.

Was she so transparent to everyone? Or to only him?

"What's bothering you?" he asked.

"I'm just busy. I had hoped to finish four sewing projects today. I'm only on the third one, and I'll have to start supper in another couple of hours." She started toward the kitchen door-way. "I'm on a quick break to eat some lunch."

"Nope, that's not it. You looked unhappy after church yesterday."

"What do you mean?" She squinted her eyes as she tried to recall what he might be talking about.

"I saw your *dat* say something to you before you and Ethan left the barn. You looked upset. What happened?"

"It was nothing." She went to step toward the kitchen, and as if predicting her attempt to flee, he slipped in front of her and leaned against the doorframe.

"Really, Mark?" She jammed her hands onto her hips. "You're going to block me from walking into the kitchen, just like that day you blocked me from getting out of it?"

"I do what I have to, to make you talk to me." He tilted his chin, and he somehow looked taller and more attractive than usual. It was as if his blue eyes were brighter and his jaw was more chiseled.

What was it about Mark that made him so desirable when he'd never shown any interest in her?

Then his mouth turned up in that electric smile, the one that reduced women like Franey, Sadie Liz, and Ruthann to giggling nitwits.

But it wouldn't work on Priscilla. She'd already been fooled by one attractive man's deception, and she would never fall for that again. Trent had seduced her, and then he'd betrayed her.

Lifting her chin, she stood taller and looked up at him. "Does that usually work for you?"

He blinked as if he was surprised. "Does what work for me?"

"The flirting." She gestured at his face. "The cocky attitude and smile."

He shrugged. "*Ya,* I guess it does."

"Well, I'm immune to your charms, Mark, so you can knock it off." She pointed toward the kitchen. "Please move out of my way."

"Not until you tell me what happened yesterday."

"Fine. I'll tell you." She gestured widely. "I was talking to Laura, and *mei dat* came over and reminded me I had to go. As if I would forget I'm not welcome at meals. He reminds me here every day when he points to my sad little table in the corner. But this time he had to embarrass me in front of *mei freind* and the entire congregation." She pointed at him. "There. Are you *froh* now? You know how pathetic my life is."

His smile faded, and his face clouded. Bitterness, resentment, and hurt boiled in her belly at the tenderness and concern she saw in his eyes. How could it be real? Trusting him would be a mistake, and he'd already gotten her to reveal too much personal information.

"I'm hungry," she muttered. "Would you please let me by?"

He took a step to the side, and she slipped past him. As she began to make her sandwich, she felt his eyes still watching her every move from the doorway. She tried to ignore him despite her flaming cheeks. She finished making her sandwich and put away the supplies before grabbing a few cookies from the jar on the counter.

"Why didn't you eat lunch with your family and me today?" he finally asked after several moments.

"Because I don't like having to eat at another table." She immediately regretted revealing another truth to him. How did he always manage to pull her deepest feelings out of her? She kept her eyes focused on her lunch to avoid his gaze.

"I'll eat with you." He walked over to the table and dropped into a seat.

"I appreciate your concern, but I don't need your pity. I'm just fine on my own."

He flinched, and she tried to ignore the guilt chewing on her stomach.

"I just want to be your *freind*, Priscilla."

"*Danki*, but I'm fine. Really."

He opened his mouth to speak but then closed it as if he thought better of wasting more breath on her.

She bit back a grin. She'd reduced Mark Riehl to silence, something she'd been certain was impossible.

She gathered her lunch and headed up the stairs to her bedroom to eat alone.

───── ❧ ─────

Mark stowed his horse and buggy, and then he headed up the path to his father's house. Confusion weighed heavily on his shoulders. For the past two days, he'd continued to try to encourage Priscilla to talk to him, but she either responded to his questions with one-word answers or ignored him. Nothing had changed.

Bewilderment was his constant companion, and he was at the end of his rope. It was apparent that no matter how supportive and kind he tried to be to Priscilla, she didn't want to be his friend. A sane person would most likely have given up by now, but he couldn't convince himself to give up on her. It was as if an invisible force pulled him to her, and he couldn't rest until she gave him a chance to prove he could be a genuine and trusted friend to her.

As he stepped into the mudroom, voices echoed from the kitchen. He paused, ran his hand down his face, plastered a smile on his lips, and then marched into the kitchen where his entire family sat around the table, including Laura and her family. The aroma of pork chops filled his senses, causing his stomach to growl as he crossed to the sink and washed his hands.

"The prodigal *sohn* has returned," Jamie announced.

"No, he's the prodigal twin," Allen quipped, and everyone laughed.

"How was your day, Mark?" Florence asked.

"*Gut.*" He faced the table as he dried his hands with a paper towel. "I didn't realize everyone was going to be here for supper tonight."

"I told you this morning, but you never listen to me," Cindy responded.

"What?" He held his hand to his ear. "Did you say something, Cindy?"

"Ugh." Cindy groaned, rolling her eyes.

"He's incorrigible," Laura chimed in. "I tell him that all the time."

"No, he isn't." Mollie shook her head as she sat beside Laura. "He's *mei zwillingboppli onkel.*"

"That's right." Mark crossed the room as everyone laughed. He stopped by Mollie's chair and kissed her head. "Did you save this seat for me?" He patted the back of the empty chair beside her.

"*Ya*, of course." Mollie grinned up at him, and his heart seemed to swell. He adored her.

"She wouldn't let anyone else sit there," Sarah Jane said. "Jamie tried."

"*Ya*, he did." Roy laughed. "Mark is clearly the favorite *onkel*."

"Well, I am the best-looking *onkel*," Mark said, joking as he sank into the chair beside Mollie. Then he leaned over and rubbed his nose against hers as she giggled.

Everyone groaned, and Mark bowed his head in silent prayer before filling his plate high with food from the platters at the center of the table. Florence had made breaded pork chops, mashed potatoes, broccoli, and rolls. His stomach gurgled with delight as he buttered a roll. It was still warm. He hadn't realized how hungry he was until he breathed in the delicious aromas.

While he ate, he tried to concentrate on the conversations swirling around him, but his thoughts kept turning to Priscilla. Why was it that most of the single young women in the community enjoyed his company but Priscilla repeatedly pushed him away? What was he doing wrong?

"Are you done?"

"What?" Mark looked up as Cindy stared down at him.

She raised her eyebrow before gesturing around the table. "Everyone else is done, and the men have already gone outside to talk. You've been sitting here moving around the mashed potatoes on your plate for almost five minutes. *Was iss letz?*"

"Nothing, nothing." He took a drink from his glass of water.

Cindy didn't look convinced. "You're never quiet during supper, Mark."

"That's for sure," Laura chimed in from the sink, where she was scrubbing a pot.

"You normally guide the conversation," Kayla added as she dried a dish.

Mark tried to think of something witty to say in response, but he came up empty. Maybe there *was* something wrong with him!

"I'm done. *Danki.*" He pushed back his chair and turned to Mollie as she struggled to sweep the floor. "That broom is twice your size. Do you need help?"

"No, *danki.* I've got it." She pushed the ties of her prayer covering over her shoulders and then stuck out her tongue as if concentrating on her task.

He grinned as he stood. "*Danki* for supper, Florence. It was *appeditlich.*"

"I'm glad you liked it." Florence gathered up his utensils and Cindy took his plate.

He looked at Laura as he started toward the mudroom. She was studying him. By the expression on her face, he was certain she was going to try to get him alone to ask him what was wrong. How was he going to explain that for the first time in his life, he had no idea how to get a woman to pay attention to him?

Leaning against the back porch railing in front of Jamie, he tried to join the men's discussion about how quickly the harvest season would arrive. But he was lost in thought when Laura stepped onto the porch holding Mollie's hand.

"We should get going," she told Allen. "It's almost Mollie's bedtime."

"Time flies when you're having fun." Allen stood and scooped Mollie into his arms. "Say *gut nacht,* Mollie."

Mollie reached for Mark, and he pulled her into his own arms for a hug.

"*Gut nacht, Onkel* Mark," she said before kissing his cheek. "*Ich liebe dich.*"

Mark melted at the sound of her little voice. "*Ich liebe dich, mei liewe.*" After another quick hug he handed Mollie back to her father.

As Mollie addressed each of her uncles and grandfather, Laura rested her hand on his forearm. "I want to talk to you." She nodded toward the steps. "Walk with me."

Mark complied, following her toward the barn.

"*Was iss letz*?" she asked.

"Nothing." He shrugged as he glanced out toward Jamie's house.

She stopped and spun toward him. "You know I can feel your worries, right?" She touched her collarbone.

"*Ya*, I know." He stuffed his hands in his pockets and looked at the sunset. The sky was streaked with such intense reds and oranges, it looked like fire.

"You were so quiet at supper that I wondered if someone else had taken your place."

When he laughed she grinned.

"There's my twin." She tilted her head. "So what is it? Are you tired of Yonnie's moods and ready to quit the horse business?"

"No, that's not it." He glanced out toward the pasture. "I'm just worried about Priscilla."

"Did something happen to her?"

"No, no. She's fine. It's just that I've tried to be her *freind*, and she won't talk to me. I can see the sadness in her eyes, and I want to help her. But every time I try to get her to talk, she rebuffs me." He looked down and kicked a stone with his toe. "I've tried really hard to show her that my friendship is genuine."

Keeping his gaze focused on the ground, he shared how he'd convinced Franey to sell him the material Priscilla needed and then how Priscilla had avoided him ever since.

"I just don't get it, sis. It's like she has no interest in talking to me. I feel like I bore her, and I've never had anyone react to me that way. I have no idea what to do." When he looked up, Laura grinned at him. "Why is this so funny?"

"You don't just like Priscilla. You care about her." She jammed a finger into his chest.

He shook his head. "Not in the way you're implying."

"*Ya*, you do." She clapped her hands. "It finally happened!"

"What finally happened?"

"You're falling in love."

"No, no, no." He held up his hands. "I'm not—"

"My prayers have been answered! You're finally going to get married."

"Whoa. Sis, you've got it all wrong."

"No, I'm exactly right." She rubbed her middle as she spoke. "You can't stop thinking about her, and you can't stand that she won't give you the time of day. That's love, Mark."

He groaned and looked at the emerging moon. Why had he confided in her? He wanted advice, not an incorrect analysis of his feelings. "I don't like her like that. I'm just worried about her. Can you help her?"

Laura tapped her chin with her finger and then snapped her fingers. "I think she still feels she won't be included and loved by the community, and that's what's weighing on her. Why don't I invite her over for supper one night? I know we're just one family, but that should help."

"But the shunning isn't over for another two weeks."

She waved off his words. "I'm not worried about that. She's welcome at my table."

He nodded slowly. "But you know you're breaking the rules, right? You're not supposed to eat at the table with her until the shunning is over."

Laura raised her eyebrows. "Are you going to tell the bishop?"

He shook his head. "No."

"Then I think we'll be fine. *Ya*, I'm breaking the rules, but I'm doing it for my best *freind*. I think most people in the community would understand."

"Okay." He nodded as the idea took root. "That just might work."

"*Ya*, it will work." She clapped her hands. "I'm so *froh*. You've finally met your match." When he frowned she touched his arm. "Your secret is safe with me."

"Laura," Allen called from the driveway. "We need to get going."

"I'll be right there," she called back. "I'll see you soon, Mark."

"*Danki*," he said before she hurried down the path to her family.

As Laura climbed into their buggy, hope lit in Mark's chest. His twin would fix this.

TEN

"I HAD SO MUCH FUN TODAY," ETHAN SAID AS HE SWEPT the kitchen floor. "Mark and I mucked the stalls, and then he let me help him fix the henhouse."

"You're a *gut* helper." Priscilla looked over her shoulder at him as she stacked clean dishes in a cabinet.

"That's nice," *Mamm* said as she wiped off the table. "You like Mark, don't you?"

"Oh *ya*." Ethan bent and swept the crumbs into the dustpan. "He's really nice to me."

Priscilla bit back the bitter taste of guilt as she remembered how she'd avoided Mark earlier in the week. It had been two days since she'd rejected his invitation to eat lunch with him. He'd seemed to still want to talk to her when he approached her in the kitchen on Tuesday and then again out on the porch on Wednesday. But she'd dismissed him both times.

Why did he continue to try to win her over with friendship? Most men would have given up by now. What did he hope to accomplish by befriending her? She wasn't worthy of his constant attempts, but he didn't seem to be planning on giving up anytime soon.

"There! All done." Ethan dumped the crumbs into the trash can and then set the dustpan and broom in the utility room.

"Are you ready for your bath?" *Mamm* asked.

"*Ya.*" Ethan started toward the stairs.

"I'll get him ready if you want to finish the kitchen," *Mamm* said, offering her help.

"*Ya,* that would be fine. *Danki.*"

Priscilla finished stowing the utensils and wiping down the counters.

Once the kitchen was clean, she went into the family room. Her father was sitting in his favorite chair reading *The Budget.* She wiped her palms down her apron as her stomach seemed to flip.

How she longed for her father's approval, for his love. She still felt like a stranger in the home where she'd been born.

Her thoughts turned to the small swing set *Dat* and Mark set up for Ethan last week. She'd watched Ethan play on the swings and slide more than once since then, and the smile on his face had made her happy. It was clear *Dat* loved his grandson, which was a step in the right direction. Perhaps she could use the swing set as a bridge to a truce.

Taking a deep breath, she squared her shoulders. "*Dat.*" Her voice trembled as she took a step toward him.

He peered at her over his reading glasses, his lips making a flat line.

She stared at him, her words caught in her throat and her thoughts a jumbled mess.

When he looked back down at the newspaper, her shoulders tightened with anger.

"I want to thank you for building the swing set for Ethan," she began. "He really enjoys it."

Dat mumbled something that sounded like "*gut*" while keeping his eyes on his newspaper.

"*Dat,* look at me," she pleaded. She nearly faltered at the thread of desperation in her voice.

He kept his focus on the newspaper as if she were invisible.

"Don't ignore me," she insisted. "I'm your *dochder*."

His eyes snapped to hers, and his face clouded with a scowl. "You stopped being *mei dochder* the day you left this community."

His words speared her, like a knife piercing her heart.

He returned to reading as if he hadn't just inflicted pain.

"Did you ever consider that you could be the reason I left?" she snapped. Swallowing back a burning knot of sobs, she fled up the stairs. When she reached her bedroom, she stepped inside, closed the door, and wilted against it as tears streamed from her eyes.

_____

"There's a voice mail message for you."

Priscilla looked up from her sewing machine the following morning. She faced her mother in the doorway as dread washed over her, locking her muscles. Had Trent found them?

"Why are you looking at me like that? You should go listen to it." *Mamm* nodded toward the hallway. "You're going to be excited."

"Who is it?" Priscilla held her breath.

"Laura."

"What did she say?"

"Just go listen to it." *Mamm* grinned and then disappeared from the doorway.

Breathing a sigh of relief, Priscilla finished the stitches on the quilt she'd been repairing and then headed outside.

She breathed in the humid air as she descended the back porch steps and trekked toward her father's office in the largest barn. She looked over at the pasture and spotted Mark leaning forward on the split-rail fence as he stood beside Ethan and gestured toward where her father was training a horse. Mark smiled as he said something to Ethan, who nodded in response, his face serious as if he were concentrating on what Mark told him.

Ethan looked over his shoulder at Priscilla, and his face broke into a smile as he waved. "Hi, *Mamm!*"

"Hi, Ethan!" Priscilla waved in response.

Ethan stood up straighter and pointed to Mark. "Mark is teaching me about horse training!"

Mark glanced at her, smiled, and shrugged. "Your *dat* is really the expert. I'm still a student."

"That's nice. *Danki*, Mark." She smiled.

Something in Mark's smile changed, and it seemed more genuine and tender. She took in his attractive face, tall stature, and broad shoulders, and heat infused her cheeks. He truly was a striking man, and she appreciated his kindness and patience toward her son. If only her life were different, maybe she could consider him a trusted friend. But how could she trust another man? She couldn't take that risk with Ethan or with her heart.

Mark nodded before he and Ethan turned back to the pasture, and she hurried into the barn, its aromas greeting her as she walked to the office. She picked up the phone's receiver, dialed the voice mail number, entered the code, and retrieved Laura's message.

"Hi." Laura's voice sounded through the receiver. "This is Laura Lambert. I'm calling for Priscilla. Priscilla, I want to invite you and Ethan to join my family and me for supper tomorrow night. It will be a lot of fun, and we'd love for you to come. We'd like to eat around five thirty. I hope to see you both there. Let me know if that works. *Danki!*" She left her phone number, and then the line went dead.

Priscilla sank onto a stool as she considered her response. While she'd love to join Laura and her family for supper, she also didn't want to be subjected to eating at a separate table. Laura hadn't isolated her at the quilting bee, but a family dinner would be different. How embarrassing would it be to go to supper at a friend's house and be ostracized because she was still shunned? No, now wasn't the time to socialize with friends. As much as she wanted to spend time with Laura, she'd have to wait.

She dialed the number and, feeling like a coward, hoped to get voice mail so she wouldn't have to hear the disappointment in her friend's voice when she turned down her invitation.

After a couple of rings, Allen's voice came through the phone. "You've reached the Bird-in-Hand Carriage Shop. We sell, restore, and repair buggies. The shop is open Monday through Friday, eight to five, and Saturdays, eight to noon. Please leave a message, and I will call you back as soon as I can. Thank you."

After the beep Priscilla began to speak. "Hi, this message is for Laura. This is Priscilla. Thank you so much for your invitation, but we're not going to make it for supper tomorrow night." She picked up a pencil and absently drew circles on a notepad. "I'm backed up with sewing projects, and I need to get them completed so the customers can have them. *Danki* for inviting me, but maybe Ethan and I can come another time. Talk to you soon. Bye!"

When she walked by the pasture, Ethan and Mark waved again. She entered the house, climbed the stairs, and took her place at the sewing machine.

She was finishing up the quilt repair when *Mamm* came and sat on the chair beside her table.

"Did you call Laura back?" *Mamm* asked.

"*Ya.*" Priscilla turned toward her. "I turned her down and said maybe some other time."

"Why?" *Mamm*'s eyes searched hers for an explanation.

"I don't want to go to Laura's *haus* and feel like an outsider." She shrugged and looked down at the quilt.

"An outsider? What do you mean?"

"I don't want to go to supper with her entire family and have to eat at a separate table. I know that's the rule, but it's humiliating for me. It's bad enough Ethan and I can't stay for lunch after the services. Being singled out there would be even worse." Priscilla turned and began sewing again.

"Wait." *Mamm* placed her hand on Priscilla's shoulder, prompting her to stop working and turn toward her. "Laura wouldn't invite you over just to exclude you. You should go. You need to get out of this *haus* and be with your *freinden*."

"No, not until the shunning is over."

"But Priscilla, you need to—"

"Please, *Mamm*." Priscilla held up her hand to stop her from speaking. "I'm fine." She gestured toward the pile of sewing projects stacked on her dresser. "I'm busy, and I'm *froh*. I'll worry about seeing *mei freinden* after I'm caught up on my projects and I can sit at the same table to eat with them. Okay?"

Mamm nodded, but she continued to study her.

Priscilla's stomach tightened as she anticipated a lecture from her mother. She turned her attention back to the quilt and hoped *Mamm* would leave without instructing her on how to live her life.

"What happened with Trent?"

Priscilla stilled at the question, her eyes trained on the quilt as her stomach soured.

"When I asked you the first night you were back if he'd hurt you, you said you were okay. I told you I'm ready to listen if you want to talk, but you haven't opened up to me. I'm worried about you. What happened?"

Priscilla's hand flew to her bicep as she considered her response. "He was loving and attentive when I first met him, but he changed, especially after I had Ethan."

"How did he change?" *Mamm* prodded.

Priscilla rubbed the back of her neck as she considered her

words. "He had a short temper, and he expected me to work harder and make more money while he stayed home and drank. He couldn't keep a job, and I had to take care of everything. I grew tired of his moods."

Mamm clicked her tongue and shook her head. "He should have been taking care of you and Ethan. Was he cruel to Ethan?"

"He never physically hurt him, but he yelled at him."

"I'm sorry to hear that. I'm glad you were strong enough to leave him and come home to us." *Mamm* rubbed her back. "Just don't let Trent's behavior hold you back from moving on with your life. Don't let Trent define your relationships with others."

Priscilla nodded. "Okay."

Mamm stood. "I'm going to get back to work. Let me know if you need any help."

"I will." Priscilla forced a smile as she looked up at her. *"Danki, Mamm."*

After her mother left the room, Priscilla turned her attention back to the quilt and tried not to allow her thoughts to linger on Trent.

─── ☙ ───

Mark tried to keep his focus on his work as he hammered a nail into the barn door, but his thoughts kept drifting to how pretty Priscilla looked in the rose-colored dress she was wearing when he saw her walking from the house to the barn. He'd been mesmerized when she smiled at him and waved. Was she going to give their friendship a chance?

"Mark?"

He tented his eyes with his hand and looked up at Edna standing over him.

"Hi, Edna." He set the hammer on the ground and stood, wiping his hands down his dusty trousers. *"Wie geht's?"*

"I need your help."

"What can I do for you?"

Edna glanced toward the house and then looked up at him. "Laura left Priscilla a message inviting her and Ethan to supper tomorrow, and Priscilla refuses to go. She says she doesn't want to feel like an outsider with her *freinden*."

Disappointment pulled at his lips. His sister's plan wasn't going to go as smoothly as he'd anticipated. "How would Laura make her feel like an outsider?"

"She says she doesn't want to have to sit at a separate table during supper and feel ostracized."

"Laura would never do that."

"I know." Edna folded her hands as if she were praying. "Would you please convince her to go?"

Mark couldn't stop a smile. "What makes you think I have the power to change her mind?"

"I just have a feeling she might listen to you. Would you please talk to her?"

"Ya." Mark shrugged. "I'll give it try."

"Danki." Edna patted his arm. "You're a *gut* man."

As Edna walked away, Mark racked his brain for a new approach that would convince Priscilla to go to his sister's house tomorrow night.

—❦—

"Did you have a *gut* day?" Priscilla sat on the edge of Ethan's bed and tucked the sheet under his arms later that evening.

"Ya." Ethan nodded. "Mark told me all about training horses, and *Daadi* says he's going to teach me how to do it when I'm

112

bigger. Are we going to stay here long enough for *Daadi* to teach me how to train horses?"

"*Ya*, I was thinking that we might stay here longer than we planned. Would you like that?" Priscilla pushed a strand of his thick, dark hair off his forehead and kissed it. She hoped her father would keep that promise and maintain a close and healthy relationship with Ethan.

"Yeah, it would be fun to stay longer. I think Dad would love to see the horses, though," Ethan continued. "Do you think we can invite him to come visit us?" He patted the empty side of the bed beside him. "He could sleep with me if you want."

Priscilla's belly churned as a wall of panic at the thought of seeing Trent slid into her. "I guess we'll see."

"Please, *Mamm*?" Ethan whined.

"I'll have to think about it." She touched his nose to distract him. "Get some sleep. Don't forget to say your prayers."

"*Gut nacht, Mamm. Ich liebe dich.*"

She rubbed his arm. "You're doing well with your Dutch." She stood. "Good night, and I love you too." She stepped out of his room and closed the door behind her.

Someday she'd explain why she had to take him away from his father. When she did, maybe her son would understand and forgive her.

ELEVEN

MEMORIES OF HAPPIER TIMES SPENT PREPARING MEALS with her mother rained down on Priscilla as she flipped through a cookbook. She paused when she reached her mother's recipe for chicken and dumplings. She already had the chicken thawed. That had always been her father's favorite meal. If she made it, would he thank her? Would he acknowledge that she was a good cook?

She bit her lower lip as she read the directions. She had to check the pantry and make sure she had—

"When will you be ready to go?"

Priscilla spun toward the doorway where Mark stood. "Go where?"

"To *mei schweschder's haus*."

She shook her head. "I'm not going."

"*Ya*, you are going. So get ready." He jammed his thumb toward the front door. "I want to leave in about an hour, after I've cleaned up. Meet me outside."

So Mark is going to be there. She looked down at the cookbook. "I'm going to make supper here, so just go without me."

"No, you're going with me. We have to be there at five thirty."

"No, I'm not." She shook her head again. "I already left Laura a message telling her that I'm not."

"Well I told her that you are."

"She understands I have things to do." She opened the pantry door and waited to hear his footsteps heading away from her, but instead his footsteps came closer.

"Priscilla," he said. "Priscilla, please look at me."

Out of the corner of her eye, she saw him reach for her, and without thinking, she flinched, blocking her face as his hand came closer.

"What have I done to scare you?" His voice was next to her ear, and heat cascaded throughout her body.

"Nothing." She ignored him and moved a few items around on the pantry shelf.

"That's the second time you've flinched from me." His voice changed, and it seemed to hold an edge of earnestness she'd never heard from him before. "Why are you so skittish?"

"I'm fine. You just caught me off guard." She could hear the thickness in her voice as she waved him off.

"I'm sorry. I didn't mean to startle you." He was still speaking close to her ear, and his nearness sent more warmth pouring through her.

What was wrong with her?

She looked at the floor and tamped down the sudden urge to tell him the truth—to unload all the dark, painful secrets she'd carried for the past few years.

No! Don't trust him! He's a user! He'll only hurt you!

"It's okay. I'm fine. Really, I am," she whispered as a swelling knot of anguish grew into what felt like a lump of ice in her chest. "I really need to get back to my cooking."

After a beat, his footsteps started out of the pantry. Her hands trembled as she returned to searching for all the ingredients she needed.

"Your *mamm* asked me to take you and Ethan to Laura's, so

I'm going to." His voice sounded from the family room. "Can you both be ready in an hour?"

Priscilla sagged as all the fight drained out of her. "Fine. We'll be ready."

"*Danki*, Priscilla."

She nodded while keeping her eyes focused on the pantry shelves. After the front door clicked closed, she covered her mouth with her hand and swallowed her surging anxiety. The anxiety wasn't so much about how she'd be treated at Laura's anymore. It was about how she was going to navigate a life where Mark Riehl appeared at every turn.

Priscilla gripped a plate of cookies as Mark knocked on Laura's back door. She glanced around the property, taking in the big brick farmhouse and the large three-bay workshop. Laura had a good life with Allen, the kind of life Priscilla knew she'd never have.

The back door swung open, revealing Laura with a bright smile turning up her lips.

"You made it!" Laura hugged her twin and then pulled Priscilla in for a tender embrace. "It's so *gut* to see you." She shook Ethan's hand. "How are you?"

"Fine. *Danki*." Ethan smiled up at her.

"Come in." Laura beckoned Priscilla to follow her into the house.

Mark smiled as he made a sweeping gesture, indicating that Priscilla should go first.

Priscilla's heart stuttered as she made her way through the mudroom and into the large kitchen where Cindy and Kayla worked at the counter and the men already sat around the table.

"Priscilla!" Cindy called. "I'm glad you came."

"How are you?" Kayla asked.

"I'm doing well. *Danki.*" Priscilla smiled as relief uncoiled the knots in her shoulders. She took a deep breath. It felt so good to be part of a community again. How she'd missed having real friends. She looked up at Mark and smiled. Her mother and Mark had been right—she needed this tonight.

"*Onkel* Mark!" Mark swept Mollie into his arms, and she wrapped her arms around his neck.

"How's my girl?" Mark asked before kissing her head.

"Ethan." Jamie patted the chair beside him. "Come sit with me. How are you?"

As Ethan sat down beside Jamie, Priscilla turned to the other women. "Can I help you with anything?"

"*Ya.*" Laura pointed to a cabinet. "Would you like to put glasses on the table?"

"Of course." Priscilla set the plate of cookies on the counter. "I brought some chocolate chip *kichlin* to share."

"I love chocolate chip," Mollie announced as Mark set her on the floor.

"That's great." Priscilla grinned as she reached for the glasses.

"Mollie," Ethan called. "Come sit by me."

"Okay!" Mollie scampered across the kitchen and hopped onto a chair.

"They get along great," Laura whispered as she rested her hand on Priscilla's arm. "I'm so glad you decided to come."

Priscilla smiled. "I am too." And she was.

———— ⚬✕⚬ ————

"How are your sewing projects going?" Laura asked as she sat beside Priscilla during supper. "You sounded busy when you left me the voice mail message yesterday."

"They're going well." Priscilla glanced over at Laura. "I finished four projects between yesterday and today."

"I'm so glad you finished them so you could have supper with us tonight," Kayla chimed in from Priscilla's other side as she turned to Calvin and handed him a roll. He was squirming in a booster seat.

"Danki." She looked across the table where Mark had ended up next to Ethan and Mollie.

Ethan scooped a spoonful of peas into his mouth before whispering something to Mollie, who smiled.

"This is delicious, Laura," Priscilla said.

Laura looked toward her husband sitting at the other end of the table. She grinned. "Allen just loves my hamburger casserole. Right, *mei liewe?*"

"What's that?" Allen raised his eyebrows.

"You just love my hamburger casserole, right?" Her grin widened as if there was an unspoken private joke passing between them. "He loves casseroles."

"That's right." Allen raised his glass to her. "Your casseroles are my favorites."

Envy became a heavy rock in the pit of Priscilla's belly. She'd never have that kind of connection with a man.

"What kind of sewing or mending repairs do you do for your customers?" Kayla asked.

"I do just about anything," Priscilla said. "I've repaired a few quilts, shortened trousers, and even altered a wedding gown for a young woman who's going to wear her grandmother's."

"Wow!" Laura said. "That sounds like difficult work."

"Not really." Priscilla looked over at Cindy, who sat by Jamie. "You're an expert seamstress, right?"

Cindy shook her head and blushed. "Not really."

"She's being modest," Laura said. "Cindy is the best seamstress in the family."

"I learned everything from *Mamm*." Cindy looked down at her plate.

"*Ya*, you did." Laura nodded.

A hush fell over the sisters, and Priscilla's heart felt the pain of their loss.

Priscilla turned to Kayla. "How have you been feeling?"

"*Gut*." Kayla nodded. "I had a doctor's appointment yesterday, and everything looks great."

The family talked about the new additions coming to their family for the remainder of supper. When they were finished eating, Priscilla helped Laura bring two apple pies and a shoofly pie to the table while Kayla made coffee.

"Oh, I am stuffed," Mark said as he leaned back in the chair and rubbed his flat waist. "Sis, you make the best pies."

"*Danki*." Laura stacked the empty dessert plates. "I'm so glad you all could come."

"*Mamm*, may I show Ethan my swing set?" Mollie asked.

"*Ya*, of course." Laura waved her off. "Have fun."

Mollie looked at Mark. "*Onkel* Mark, would you please go with us?"

"Of course." Mark stood, and Mollie took his hand. "Let me guess. You want me to push you on the swing."

"Yay!" Mollie sang as she, Mark, and Ethan headed toward the mudroom.

"Ready to go sit on the porch?" Allen asked Jamie as they stood.

"*Ya*, let's go."

"Take your *sohn*," Kayla instructed as she began filling one side of the sink with hot water.

"*Ya, Mamm*," Jamie said, teasing her as he removed the tray from Calvin's booster seat and wiped his face with a wet cloth Kayla handed him.

Priscilla joined Kayla at the sink and dried dishes, making small talk about recipes as they worked. When she spotted movement outside the kitchen window, she peered out to where Mark pushed both Ethan and Mollie on the swings, one with each hand. He talked and laughed, and Priscilla shook her head as a smile turned up the corners of her lips. The children loved Mark, and he loved them.

Why hadn't Mark settled down with one of the eager women in the community? Priscilla had to admit he would make a wonderful father—and a handsome one too.

She swallowed a groan and returned to drying the dishes. Was she becoming one of his eager *maed*? She hoped not! What good would that do?

But the question haunted her as she worked. She couldn't allow herself to fall for Mark Riehl. Giving her heart to any man, especially him, would only lead to disaster.

—◌⋆◌—

"You seemed like you had fun tonight." Mark peeked at Priscilla as he guided his horse down Laura's driveway.

"*Ya*, I did." She gave him a half shrug and then turned toward him and smiled. "*Danki* for making me go." The smile lit up her whole face and made her even more attractive.

"*Gern gschehne.*" He turned back toward the road, and they rode in silence for several minutes. When snores sounded from the back of the buggy, he glanced at her again. "Did Ethan fall asleep?"

She looked over her shoulder and then grinned. "*Ya*, he did. You wore him out on the swings."

"No, those *kinner* wore me out. My arms are sore."

She seemed to relax in the seat, and a comfortable silence sat between them.

After several moments she turned to him once again. "Why haven't you married?"

The question stunned him silent for a beat. "I don't know. I guess I've never found the right *maedel*."

"But you flirt all the time. Do you have feelings for any of the *maed* you attract?"

Once again her question caught him off guard, and Priscilla waited as he took a moment to consider his response. "They're all nice, and I consider them *mei freinden*, but I don't want to marry any of them."

"Do you ever want to get married?"

He halted the horse at a red light and then smirked at her. "Are you proposing to me? Because I have to be honest with you. I really like you, but I'm not sure I'm ready to make a commitment to you. I mean, maybe we should at least go on a date first."

"Mark Riehl, you're hopeless."

He laughed as he guided the horse through the intersection. "I'm just *froh* you had fun tonight. You seemed at ease with my family, and I was grateful to see that."

"Did you plan this evening for me?"

He paused as dread exploded like buckshot. *Caught, red-handed!* "No."

Out of the corner of his eyes, he spotted her wagging a finger at him.

"You hesitated."

"Look," he began, his words measured, "I just wanted you to see that you're not an outsider."

"What do you mean?"

"You act like you think you don't belong to this community, but you do. I think coming back here was the best choice you could've made for both you and Ethan."

"That's easy for you to say, but you don't know everything about me." Her voice was soft as she looked out the window.

"Priscilla, you can talk to me if you need someone to listen." He held his breath, hoping she'd share whatever was bothering her. But she didn't. She kept facing the road as headlights zoomed past them.

He sighed. They were back to square one. Why hadn't he kept his mouth shut instead of trying to tell her how much the community cared about her? Perhaps he should mind his own business. But that seemed impossible when he cared about her and Ethan too.

The *clip-clop* of horse hooves and the sound of passing cars filled the buggy once again as he did his best to analyze her feelings for him. It seemed that one moment she trusted him and liked him as a friend, but then the next he was invisible and insignificant. If only he could convince her that he wanted to be her friend, maybe she would trust him.

"Why do you dislike me?" His question broke through the suffocating silence.

She swiveled toward him. "I don't dislike you. I just don't know why you keep expecting us to be such *gut freinden*. I'm not the kind of *maedel* you seek out. When we were younger you were interested only in the *schee maed*, the exciting *maed*. You never noticed me when we were younger, so I don't expect you to particularly notice me now."

"Are you kidding?" He snorted. "I noticed you. You're *mei schweschder's* best *freind*."

She blew out a heavy sigh that seemed to bubble up from her toes. "That's not what I mean."

"So what do you mean, then?" He longed to understand her, but her words just confused him.

"Just forget it, okay? It doesn't matter."

"It matters to me."

She turned toward him, her pretty lips turned into a frown. "I'm not the kind of *maedel* you like. Why would you waste your time on me?"

"Waste my time on you?" He shook his head.

"That's what I said. I've always been part of the background, not the kind of *maedel* you wanted to—and still want to—spend time with, like Franey and Ruthann. Why don't we leave it that way, okay? It will keep life uncomplicated." She waved him off, as if he didn't matter.

The gesture gutted him. So she didn't want to be his friend. He had to let it go, but the dismissal burned him like a hot knife to his soul. He kept his eyes focused on the road ahead as he guided the horse onto the road leading to her father's farm.

Mark clamped his teeth together so hard that his jaw throbbed as the farm's driveway came into view. Confusion churned in his stomach. He wanted to be Priscilla's friend, but all his efforts were met with a polite dismissal. What could he possibly do to earn her friendship?

And why was he so determined to win her over? Why couldn't he just let it go?

When he halted the horse near the house, she turned toward him, her eyes seeming to glitter with sadness.

"*Danki* for taking me to Laura's tonight," she said, her voice thick. Then she leaned over the seat and shook Ethan. "Get up. We're home."

"Okay." Ethan yawned and rubbed his eyes. "*Gut nacht,* Mark."

"*Gut nacht.*" He opened his mouth to ask her what he could do to close the great chasm that seemed to continually widen between them, but Priscilla had already climbed out of the buggy and started toward the house.

There had to be a way to earn her trust. He'd try harder, and maybe, just maybe, she'd give him another chance.

TWELVE

MARK'S THOUGHTS SWIRLED LIKE A TORNADO AS he sat next to Roy in the barn during the service. As the congregation sang the last hymn, the humid August air felt like a constricting blanket hovering over him.

Today was the day Priscilla would be forgiven and rejoin the congregation. Her shunning would be over, and she would be welcomed back as a sister in the faith. It was a momentous day, and he longed to be by her side after the service to welcome her personally. But he was certain he wouldn't be the first person she'd seek after her acceptance.

He'd spent the entire service staring at the back of Priscilla's prayer covering and analyzing the past week. He'd tried different approaches for trying to encourage her to open up to him, but none of his lame conversations had resulted in more than a half-hearted smile or the one-word responses he couldn't get used to. Still, each rejection had made him more determined to win her friendship. He wasn't going to give up, no matter how many times she dismissed him with an uninterested wave of her hand.

When the hymn ended, the bishop stood and faced the congregation. "And now I invite all the nonmembers to please exit and the baptized members to stay for a special meeting."

A murmur spread over the barn as the children and nonmembers of the church exited. When Priscilla stood, her gaze moved toward the unmarried men's section, and her eyes flickered over to his. He tried to smile at her, but she looked down and then headed out of the barn, her eyes focused on the barn floor.

Roy leaned over and whispered, "This is it. She's going to be a member again."

"I know." Mark nodded. "I'm glad for her."

Roy's eyes narrowed as he studied Mark for a moment. "Do you have feelings for Priscilla?"

"What?" Mark sat up straighter. "Why would you say that?"

"I don't know." Roy tapped his clean-shaven chin. "You just seem totally focused on her when she's around."

"That's ridiculous." Mark turned his attention back to the bishop.

"As you know, Priscilla Allgyer has returned to the community after eight years. She moved to Baltimore to live like an *Englisher,* but as of today, she has completed her time under the *Meiding,* and she is ready to be received back into the church."

John paused and looked around the congregation. "She told me she's ready to confess. The ministers and I agree if you vote to accept Priscilla today, we're going to immediately welcome her back into the fold. Now I need to know if each of you agrees she's repentant and ready to be received back into the church." John pointed to the side of the barn where the men sat. Then he pointed to the minister. "I will ask the men, and Abner will ask the women."

Mark sat up taller as John walked over to his section of the barn. On the opposite side of the barn, Abner went to the women. Mark heard each woman take turns saying *"Ya,"* and he silently asked God to encourage every member to echo that response.

"Do you believe Priscilla Allgyer is repentant and ready to be received back into the church?" John asked the unmarried men.

"*Ya,*" Mark said when it was his turn.

"*Ya,*" Roy echoed.

Each man after Mark gave the same response, and the muscles in his back eased.

When John moved to the married men's section, he again asked if they agreed. Each of the men responded with "*Ya.*"

Mark swallowed a deep breath of relief.

Then John moved to the center of the barn. "We will invite our *schweschder* back in to confess now."

Mark gripped the bench and sucked in a deep breath. He prayed Priscilla would be strong as she stood in front of their congregation to repent for her sins.

Priscilla wrung her hands as she stood at one corner of the barn and watched the children play on Mary Glick's elaborate wooden swing set. Ethan and Mollie swung next to each other while teenage girls leaned on a nearby fence and talked.

Priscilla's heart felt a mixture of fear, excitement, and relief. She was finally going to be accepted back into the church. But uncertainty still plagued her. Was she making the right choice for Ethan's future? Did he belong in this community after being born in the *Englisher* life?

It's only temporary! I'll be out of here and on my own soon, and then I can go back to the Englisher *life!*

Maybe this wasn't about Ethan as much as it was about her.

Closing her eyes, she opened her heart in prayer.

God, please lead me down the path you've chosen for me. Help me figure out what's best for mei kind. *Is he supposed to remain in this community? Is this the right choice for Ethan's future? Help me make the right choice and be a* gut mutter. *I'm so confused, and I never know if I'm doing the best I can for* mei sohn, *even though I try. Help me, God. I need you more than ever—not just for Ethan's sake, but for mine too.*

"Priscilla."

She jumped with a start at the sound of her name.

"I'm sorry." Cindy came up behind her. "I didn't mean to startle you. I wanted to see if you're okay. You looked pretty terrified when you walked out of the barn."

"That's an accurate description for how I feel right now."

"Everything will be fine." Cindy rubbed her arm. "You made it through the hard part. Now the bishop will tell you you're forgiven, and you can stay for the noon meal and shop at Amish stores."

"I know." Priscilla looked out toward the swing set again. It seemed like only yesterday that she was playing on a swing set without a care in the world. How had her life become so complicated?

"Do you want to talk about whatever is bothering you?"

Priscilla turned toward Cindy's pretty face. "Do you ever wonder where you belong?"

Cindy nodded. "All the time. Why do you think I haven't joined the church?" She fingered her white apron. "When *mei mamm* died I felt like I was lost, just floating through life without a destination. I thought it would get easier with time, but it's been five years and I still feel like I'm straddling a line between the Amish church and the outside world. It's not that I don't want to be Amish, but I'm not sure I belong here."

Priscilla studied Cindy's bright-blue eyes. How was it that she was only twenty-two years old but understood how Priscilla felt?

Cindy gave her a sheepish smile. "You're looking at me like I'm *narrisch*."

"No." Priscilla shook her head. "I understand exactly how you feel."

"But you came back, so I thought you figured out you belonged here." Cindy pointed to the ground. "If you didn't feel that way, why are you confessing?"

Priscilla shook her head. "It's not that simple." She gestured toward the swing set. "I had to find the safest home for *mei sohn*. Coming home was my only option."

Cindy seemed to contemplate her words for a moment. "What would you have done if you hadn't had Ethan to consider?"

"I don't know."

"So how do you know if you truly belong here?"

"I don't."

"I see." Cindy looked past her. "Jamie and Laura are settled and *froh*, and I believe Mark will settle down soon, even though he says he's not interested in getting married. Sometimes I think I'll be alone for the rest of my life. I keep waiting to wake up and realize I'm in the right place, but it hasn't happened. I've prayed about it, but I don't think God is ready to answer me."

"You're so young, Cindy. It will happen for you."

Cindy smiled at her. *"Danki."*

Just then the bishop came around the corner, his brow furrowed and his frown serious. "We're ready for you. You can repent now."

"Okay." Priscilla smoothed her hands down her apron and cleared her throat.

John's expression was serious but also caring. "Priscilla, are you ready?"

"I think so." Panic chewed at her insides, and she stood on shaky legs. Where was the courageous woman who had packed all her worldly possessions and snuck out of the townhouse she rented while Trent was out with his friends?

John gestured toward the barn doors. "Let's go. The congregation is waiting."

She squared her shoulders and followed the bishop, her steps bogged down with the heavy apprehension pressing her heart.

When she reached the barn's entrance, her lungs seemed to seize. Would the congregation accept her confession as she knelt before them? Would they believe her intentions were sincere?

John stood inside the barn and swiveled toward her. "Are you going to come in?"

Unable to speak, she nodded. She followed him up the center aisle, between the sections with unmarried men and unmarried women. When her eyes locked with Mark's, her hands trembled. The intensity in his gaze caught her off guard, stealing her breath for a moment. While she'd tried her best to ignore and dismiss Mark since they'd had supper at Laura's house, she sensed a tiny flare of what felt like attraction for him growing. Why was she wasting her time thinking about Mark Riehl? He would never love a woman as plain as she was.

She looked toward her father, and when she met his impassive expression, dismay stirred inside her once again. No, this wouldn't be as simple as confessing. The congregation wouldn't be satisfied with her honesty. How could the whole community forgive her if her own father, who was supposed to love her, couldn't even do it?

"Our *schweschder* Priscilla has completed her instruction classes, and she is ready to repent for her sins." John's words slammed Priscilla back to reality as they stood in front of the congregation. John's wife, Naomi, came to stand beside him as he turned to Priscilla.

"Please go down on your knees," John instructed her.

As she knelt, Priscilla's stomach clenched, and bile rose in her throat.

Please, God, give me strength.

"Priscilla," John announced. "Are you truly repentant and sorry?"

"*Ya.*" Her voice quavered with anxiety as she felt the weight of the congregation members' stares. Were they all silently judging how she'd spent the last eight years?

"Is it still your desire to join the church again?"

"*Ya.*" Her voice was tiny and unsure, sounding more like a terrified little girl than a grown woman.

"Do you promise to renounce the world and the devil?"

"*Ya.*" Her hands shook, and her body shuddered like a leaf in a windstorm. Was she strong enough to do this? Did she deserve to be a member of the church after all the mistakes she'd made? Was this right when deep in her heart she was just contemplating leaving once she had the resources she'd need?

"In the name of Jesus," John continued, "I give you my hand."

She clasped his right hand with hers, and he helped her up. She took a shaky breath as her eyes stung with tears and, keeping with tradition, Naomi kissed her cheek.

"Priscilla," John continued, "stand up and be a faithful member of the church."

Priscilla nodded.

"I am *froh* that Priscilla has made the decision to come back to the church," John said. "I know I can speak for her parents and say they are *froh* and grateful God led her home. Today is a joyous day."

Priscilla glanced at her mother and found her wiping her eyes. When she looked at her father, his expression remained grave, his lips pressed in a thin line. Her thoughts turned to his cruel words from the night he said she was no longer his daughter. Would this day change his mind?

"It's always a blessing when one of our *bruders* or *schweschdere* makes the decision to return. We welcome Priscilla back into our congregation." John smiled at her. "We welcome you back into the fold."

Priscilla wiped away her tears and nodded. *"Danki."*

"The meeting is over," John announced.

Priscilla folded her shaky arms across her waist while a flurry of conversation started around the congregation and the men began converting the benches into tables for the noon meal.

"I'm so *froh*." *Mamm's* voice sounded thick with emotion as she came up from behind Priscilla and pulled her into a hug. "My prayers have truly been answered."

"Danki," Priscilla whispered into her mother's neck as tears pricked her eyes.

Laura hugged her next. "Welcome back. I know I keep telling you this, but I'm so very thankful God brought you back."

"Danki." Priscilla wiped at the tears streaming down her cheeks. *"Danki* for welcoming me. I'm so grateful for you."

"We're so *froh* you're back," Florence said before she, Sarah Jane, and Kayla took turns hugging her.

"It's time to go help the other women." Sarah Jane gestured toward the barn exit, and her mother started toward it.

As Florence and Sarah Jane walked away, Laura looped her arm around Priscilla and smiled at her. "Promise me you won't leave again."

Priscilla opened her mouth to agree, but then she held back the words. It was a sin to lie, and she did still feel the pull of the *Englisher* community. Yet if she left and then returned, she'd have to go through the same process—the shunning and meetings with the bishop and ministers. Could she endure all that again?

"Come on," Kayla said. "The others are expecting us."

Priscilla followed her friends to the door. When she strode past Mark, Jamie, and Roy lifting a bench, her eyes met Mark's, and an unexpected tremor shimmied down her back. He nodded at her, and she quickened her steps.

"Laura is so *froh* Priscilla is back," Allen said as he sat across from Mark during lunch. "She was in tears last night talking about what a blessing today is for her and the rest of the community."

"*Ya*, it is." Jamie lifted a pretzel from his plate. "Kayla said something similar on the way here this morning."

Mark cleared his throat and glanced toward the other side of the barn where Priscilla filled coffee cups and smiled at the men seated along the long table. She looked gorgeous in the hunter-green dress she wore today. He'd longed to pull her into his arms and hug her, just as his twin had done after the members-only meeting.

What was wrong with him?

Jamie leaned toward him. "You're awfully quiet. What's on your mind?"

"Nothing." Mark forced his lips into a smile. "I'm just tired. It was a long week at the farm. We're training some horses, and Yonnie asked me to repaint one of the barns. I feel like I can't get caught up." He shrugged and swiped a pretzel from his plate. "You know how it is."

"*Ya*, I do." Jamie nodded toward Roy, who was engrossed in a conversation with their *dat* and Allen. "Roy and I have been working on a few projects too. They never seem to go as quickly as you imagine."

"*Kaffi?*"

Mark craned his neck and glanced over his shoulder as Priscilla appeared holding a carafe. Her chestnut eyes focused on him, and his mouth dried as they stared at each other. For a moment it felt as if the rest of the congregation faded away and they were the only two people in the barn. His heart hammered, and his pulse spiked. What was happening to him?

"Would you like some *kaffi*?" she repeated, breaking their connection.

"*Ya, danki.*" He handed her his cup, and she filled it.

After she filled the cups of the men surrounding him, Mark angled his body and watched her move down the line. He studied her beautiful profile and admired how her eyes sparkled and her rosy lips curved up as she worked her way toward the end of the table.

When he realized he'd been staring at her too long, Mark swiveled around and picked up his coffee cup. He glanced beside him and found Jamie watching him. His eyebrows were lifted, and his expression flickered with something that resembled surprise—or maybe curiosity.

Jamie had caught him watching Priscilla, but Roy, Allen, and *Dat* were still engrossed in a conversation about Allen's carriage business. A thread of relief wove its way through Mark.

As he sipped his coffee, Mark braced himself, waiting for Jamie to make a biting comment, but Jamie remained silent for a beat.

"So, Priscilla, huh?" Jamie picked up another pretzel and popped it into his mouth.

"What do you mean?"

"Please, Mark." Jamie grinned. "I'm not blind."

"You're not blind to what?"

"You've finally fallen in love."

"Love?" Mark shook his head. "No, no, no. That's not it at all."

"So what is it?"

"I'm determined to be her *freind* because I think she really needs one. I've tried everything, but it's not working. She won't talk to me, and I don't know what to do to fix it." He turned toward her as she filled another cup. He couldn't stand the irritating distance between them. It was slowly chipping away at his insides.

Jamie's lips twitched.

"Why is that funny?" Mark's irritation flared.

"Mark, let me tell you something." Jamie leaned toward him. "The only *maedel* who could make me so insane that I'd nearly lose my mind was Kayla. If you're frustrated because Priscilla won't talk to you, then you're in love." He nodded toward Priscilla. "Find a way to tell her how you feel about her."

"How I feel about her?" Mark blinked as he struggled to comprehend Jamie's hidden meaning.

Jamie pointed at Mark's chest. "You're crazy about her. You're just too blinded by frustration to see it. But trust me, little *bruder*, it's written all over your face."

"Mark," Roy began, "when are you going to start building that *haus* you keep talking about? Your room is bigger than mine, and *Dat* just said I can have it when you move out—unless Cindy wants it."

"What?" Mark placed his hand over his heart as if he'd been stabbed. "You're trying to kick me out? What kind of *bruder* are you?"

As everyone laughed at his joke, Mark pretended to join in, but his mind remained stuck on Jamie's words. He needed to construct a plan to convince Priscilla to talk to him. If she would just open up to him, maybe he could sort through all his confusing feelings for her.

—⟶⟵—

Priscilla hated how her body trembled as she approached her father in the family room later that afternoon. Her first attempt to navigate through their painful and rocky relationship and find a peaceful solution had failed. But now that she was accepted back into the church, she hoped she could make some headway toward a normal, loving, father-daughter relationship with him.

"*Dat.*"

"What do you need?" He kept his eyes trained on his newspaper.

She looked toward the windows and spotted her mother and Ethan sitting together on the glider on the front porch. Then she squared her shoulders and lifted her chin. She wouldn't allow her father to get to her. "You haven't said anything about how I've made myself right with the church. I thought you'd be *froh.*"

"I am." He peered at her over his reading glasses. "Now you need to find a husband."

She bit her lower lip to stop the furious words that threatened to escape. She longed to give him a piece of her mind, explaining that she didn't need a husband for redemption. She was already forgiven by God and the church, but she stifled her rant. Arguing with him hadn't helped before, and she was certain she'd come up empty again today.

"Is there anything else?" he asked.

"No, that's it." She turned toward the front door, and the urge to flee gripped her again. She'd already saved up a good amount of money, but it still wasn't enough to pay the first month's rent on an apartment in a nice area, let alone put down a deposit.

As she stepped onto the porch, she found *Mamm* sitting with her arm around Ethan as he leaned against her shoulder. Guilt squashed her anger. She didn't want to hurt her mother again, but she also didn't want to live in a home where her father made her feel unwanted and unworthy of his love.

"Isn't it nice out here?" *Mamm* asked as Priscilla sank onto the rocker beside them.

"*Ya*, it is." Priscilla moved the chair back and forth. She would give her father more time to forgive her, but if he continued to hurt her, she'd find another place to live as soon as she had enough resources. She couldn't live in a place that continued to break her heart.

THIRTEEN

IRRITATION BUILT IN MARK'S GUT AS HE STOOD BY the barn door and looked toward the back porch. Priscilla was hanging a load of laundry. He swiped his hand over his sweaty brow and ground his teeth as he took in her serene expression. She was clipping a pair of Ethan's trousers onto the clothesline that spanned the distance between the porch and one of her father's barns.

Despite the stifling August heat, she wore another longer-sleeved dress today, this one blue. He hadn't seen her wear a short-sleeved dress since she arrived at her parents' house nearly two months ago, and it puzzled him.

He'd been trying so hard to talk to her, going as far as offering her a bouquet of wildflowers he'd picked in her father's meadow and an ice cream sundae he'd picked up while in town one day for supplies. Not one of his tactics had earned him any more than a smile or a murmured "*Danki.*" She still refused to have an in-depth discussion or treat him like a trusted friend. Instead, she continued to avert her eyes whenever he approached her and frown at him when he offered a silly joke.

But Mark wasn't a quitter. He'd try until he ran out of words. For some unknown reason, he couldn't give up on Priscilla.

He started up the path to the house, glancing over his shoulder once to make sure Yonnie and Ethan were still in the pasture talking to the bishop, John Smucker. John had come to discuss purchasing a horse for his teenage grandson.

Only a few clouds dotted the sky, but the smell of threatening rain filled his nostrils.

When he reached the porch, he stopped and gazed up at Priscilla. She gave him a sideways glance and then hung another pair of Ethan's trousers.

"Can we talk?" he asked.

She shrugged. "Sure."

"I've been trying to pull you into a conversation for weeks now. Would you please give me a chance?"

"*Ya*, of course you can talk to me." She kept her focus on the wash instead of meeting his eyes, and it caused his frustration to burn hotter.

"Look at me."

She looked at him, her eyes hesitant. Did she really not trust him?

"Why can't we be *freinden*?" He blew out a sigh.

"We are *freinden*. I never said we weren't."

He gave a wry bark of laughter. "That's pretty funny, because you're much more attentive toward your other *freinden* than you are to me."

She folded her arms over her waist and studied him as if he were a confusing puzzle. "Mark, I don't know what you want from me."

"I just want to be a real *freind*—someone you trust and talk to about meaningful things."

"You are *mei freind*." She turned her back to him and dug in her laundry basket, indicating the discussion was over.

Her dismissal sent white-hot fury roaring through Mark's veins, and he saw red.

That does it!

"You know what, Priscilla?" His voice was louder than he'd anticipated, and he heard the tremble in it.

She turned toward him, her brow pinched as she studied him.

"I officially give up," he continued, his voice growing louder. "If my friendship isn't *gut* enough, then so be it. I don't need your friendship anyway. I have plenty of *freinden* who treat me with dignity and respect."

Then he spun on his heels and stalked into the barn. Grabbing a pitchfork, he began to muck the first stall, slamming the tool through the hay to ease the wrath that bit into his back and shoulders.

Confusion and anger swarmed through Priscilla as she tossed the pair of Ethan's trousers she held in her hands back into the basket. Why was Mark angry with her for not being the friend he'd expected her to be? She didn't owe him anything. In fact, she had done her best to be pleasant to him, although she wasn't about to encourage him. Was he upset that she didn't follow him around and fight for his attention like Franey and Ruthann did?

She had to find out why he felt he had the right to talk to her that way when she hadn't done anything wrong.

She hurried down the back porch steps and stalked toward the barn. When she stepped inside, she marched over to where he mucked a stall and pointed her finger toward his face.

"Why did you just yell at me?" she demanded. "Are you angry I don't follow you around and compete with the eager *maed* in our church district for your attention? Besides, you're the one who always has to be the center of attention. I just want to be left alone."

"Really?" He tossed the pitchfork against the stall wall with a clatter and smirked at her. "If you wanted to be left alone, you wouldn't be living with your parents. You'd be off on your own."

"I have no choice. I had nowhere to go. I'm stuck here until I can earn enough money to rent a place for Ethan and me."

He blanched. "So you're going to leave? You're going to break your *mutter*'s heart again? Do you know how selfish that is?"

"Selfish?" His words shot across her nerves like shards of glass, cutting and fraying them. "You don't know anything about me. And I don't owe you an explanation for the choices I've made."

"Then why are you standing here trying to prove to me that you're not selfish?" His gorgeous eyes challenged her, and a heartbeat passed as they stared at each other.

"Forget it," she muttered.

When she turned to leave, she tripped on a stone, stumbled, and staggered forward as she tried to right herself. Losing her footing, she slammed into the barn wall, pain radiating from her shoulder to her elbow. She shut her eyes and took deep, cleansing breaths to avoid yelping at the pain.

"Priscilla!" he called as he hurried over to her. "Are you all right?"

"*Ya.*" Her face burned with a mixture of embarrassment and frustration. She tried to move away from the wall, but she couldn't. Her right sleeve was snagged.

"Wait." He reached for her. "Let me see."

"I'm fine."

He blew out a sigh, his eyes narrowed. "For one second, would you not be so stubborn?"

"Fine."

"*Danki.*"

He leaned forward and touched her sleeve, and his nearness sent her senses spinning. She breathed in his scent—earth and soap mixed with sandalwood. The aroma sent heat coursing through her veins. She closed her eyes and took a trembling breath. What was wrong with her? This was Mark, the man who could have any woman he wanted in their community and would never give her the time of day, at least as anything more than a friend. And she didn't even want him as more than a superficial friend. She had to protect the wall she'd erected between them.

"I can't get it." He jiggled her sleeve. "It's stuck on a nail."

"Let me." She gave her arm one hard yank, and the sound of ripping fabric filled the air as her arm broke free. She teetered and fell backward into a sitting position. She looked down at her arm and then blew out a puff of air when she found it was bare. The ugly, purple, puckered skin was exposed for the world to see, her sleeve hanging tattered by her side.

"Priscilla." Her name left his lips in a murmur that sounded almost reverent as he dropped to his knees beside her. "Who did this to you?" He cradled her battered bicep in his hands as he examined it.

"Please don't touch me," she hissed through her teeth. She tried to dislodge her arm from his hands, but he kept her cemented in place.

He moved his fingers over the scars with a gentle touch, like the whisper of butterfly wings. She stopped breathing and tears stung her eyes.

"Did he do this to you? Ethan's father?" he asked again.

She sniffed and then tried once again to remove her arm from his grasp.

"Please tell me the truth."

She shook her head and looked down at the barn floor. "Just let me go."

"No, I want to know the truth once and for all." He looked down at her arm once again and moved his finger over the scar.

His touch almost drove her crazy as shivers moved up and down her entire body. "Did he hurt you often?"

She shook her head. "Only when he was drunk."

"What?" The expression in his eyes was fierce as they met hers. "How often was he drunk?"

"He wasn't like that when I first met him." She shook her head again, trying to breathe normally. "When I left here I lived with my cousin Thelma and got a job in a diner near her apartment. Trent was one of my regular customers. He liked me, and he used to ask to sit in my section."

She looked down at the floor. "He asked me out, and we started dating. After a while I moved in with him. In the beginning he was kind and attentive, and I enjoyed how he made me feel. When I was with him, I felt loved. I got pregnant with Ethan, and I thought he was going to marry me. I thought we were going to be a family, and that was what I wanted. That was what I craved." She kept her eyes focused downward.

"The day after he hurt me he apologized and brought me flowers. He promised he'd never do it again, and I believed him because I was blinded by my love for him. But he hit me again only a week later. I wanted to leave him, but I was terrified, and I had nowhere to go. I was stuck with a boyfriend who hit me, but I had a *kind* to protect."

A weight lifted off her shoulders as she finally shared her deepest and darkest secret. And then she shattered, like spun glass. A choked sob escaped her lips, and her tears broke free.

"*Ach*, Priscilla." Mark pulled her against him and wrapped his arms around her as she sobbed into his chest. "It's okay. You're safe now. I won't let him hurt you ever again." He whispered his gentle words into her prayer covering, and they were a balm to her battered soul.

him? But his empathy seemed so genuine. Now
thing to him but another eager *maedel* fighting for
ention.

felt cherished and safe in his strong arms, and it
hat she'd craved for years. The feeling had been
most like a dream. What would it be like to have
r life who really cared about her and loved her?

she thinking? Mark Riehl wasn't capable of loving
just one woman. Even if he were, she was kidding
believed she could be the one woman for him.

pushed the notion away and changed into a fresh
looked at her reflection in the mirror, she touched
vering, and that familiar apprehension rolled over
r and the bishop had caught Mark and her in an inti-
sation, which was forbidden for unmarried couples.
would most likely punish her, and the bishop could
er and Mark. Her heart couldn't stand the idea of
ized during another shunning and then confessing in
congregation yet again.

n even worse punishment occurred to her, rocking
ore. What if her father demanded that she and Ethan
eaving them homeless and destitute? What would she

She held on to him, and for the first time in so long she felt
safe and protected, and she didn't want to let go. When her tears
finally stopped, she sat back and wiped her face.

"When did he do this?" He touched her arm.

"About six months ago." The memory came on so fast, it left
her head spinning. "When I got home from work, he grabbed my
purse and pulled out my tips. It had been a slow night, and he was
furious I hadn't brought home more money." She shivered as she
remembered the maliciousness in Trent's dark eyes. "He started
screaming at me. He was drunk, more drunk than I'd seen him in
a long time. I told him to go sober up, and he threw a beer bottle
at my head. The bottle missed me, but it hit the wall and exploded
just above me. Glass landed in my arm, and I had deep gashes. He
wouldn't let me go to the hospital."

A muscle ticked along Mark's jaw.

She looked down at her arm. "I bandaged it up as well as I
could, and it healed like this. Now I'm disfigured, and I can't ever
wear short sleeves." She shook her head as a hole opened in her
heart and sadness flooded in. "I made so many mistakes. If only I
hadn't gotten involved with him."

She looked up into Mark's blue eyes. "But I don't regret having Ethan. He's *mei sohn*, my heart." She placed one palm over her
chest. "If I could have changed anything, it would be that he had
to live with that monster." Her lower lip trembled.

"Stop blaming yourself." Mark cupped her chin with his
hands and leaned down, his mouth close to hers. "Trent was the
evil one, not you."

She nodded as she lost herself in his eyes.

"No one has the right to hit you. No one." He leaned even
closer, only a fraction of an inch from her mouth. "And I will never
let anyone hurt you again."

The intensity in his eyes stole her breath, and for a moment she was certain he was going to kiss her. She stilled, waiting for the feel of his lips against hers.

"Mark! Priscilla!" *Dat* bellowed. "What's going on here?"

As Mark jumped to his feet, Priscilla covered her bare arm with her opposite hand.

Her father and the bishop stood at the entrance to the barn, and their stern stares seemed to burn a hole through her.

Mark held out his hand, and she took it before he lifted her to her feet as if she weighed nothing. When he released her hand, she fought the urge to grab his hand once again. She yearned for the strength and solace his touch had provided.

A heavy ball of dread invaded Priscilla's body as she hugged one arm to her waist. She glanced at Mark, who stood up straight and swallowed, his Adam's apple bobbing.

"What's going on here?" *Dat* repeated as he turned his menacing glare on Mark. "What were you doing to *mei dochder*?"

"Nothing inappropriate was going on here." Mark held up his hand. "We were just talking."

Her father sneered as he glanced at the bishop and then back at Mark. "Nothing inappropriate? I'm not blind, Mark. What do you think you're doing? You're here to work, not this."

"We weren't doing anything inappropriate." Mark's voice remained calm and even, and she marveled at his confidence. "I would never disrespect Priscilla or you, Yonnie. You know me."

"What do you have to say for yourself, Priscilla?" *Dat* demanded.

"Mark is telling the truth." She despised the tremor in her voice. "We were only talking."

"You were talking while sitting close together on the floor of the barn." He pointed to her arm. "With a ripped dress!"

"It was innocent, Yonnie," Mark insisted.

"Go get changed," *Dat* barked at Priscilla, his eyes steely.

With her eyes focu
almost ran to the house
and a rumble of thunde
a forecast of rain for tod

As she climbed the
worry and fear. Would t
be worse and more humi
munity say about her if t
things with Mark Riehl in

Oh no.

She did a mental head
started up the stairs. How
her heart out to Mark? She'
anyone what Trent had don
up, the truth flowed out of h

Priscilla crossed her be
panes were peppered with ra
she looked out toward the ba
echoed in her mind. She glan
her scar. Her heart seemed to
as she recalled the gentleness o
eyes. The attraction between M
surely he was an expert at creati

Priscilla cupped her hands
the electricity that had sparked
to the depth of her soul that he
wanted him to kiss her! She'd hel
contact, but her father and the
before their lips could collide.

Swallowing a groan, she dropp
She was doomed. Although she'd t
to his charms, she'd let Mark into he

herself to trust
she would be n
his precious at

Yet she'd
was exactly w
wonderful, al
someone in h

What wa
and caring fo
herself if she

Priscilla
dress. As she
her prayer c
her. Her fath
mate conver
Her father
shun both
being ostra
front of the

Then
her to her
move out,
do then?

FOURTEEN

"She's telling the truth." Mark glared at Yonnie as Priscilla ran out of the barn. Fury was a bitter taste in his mouth. "We weren't doing anything wrong. We were having a private conversation."

Yonnie shook his head and turned to the bishop. "It looked inappropriate to me. There's no telling what would've happened if we hadn't decided to walk in here."

Mark took a step toward him, his hands balled into fists at his sides as his heart hammered against his rib cage. "Yonnie, nothing inappropriate would've happened if you hadn't walked in. I would never take advantage of Priscilla that way. I'm more honorable than that, and you can trust me around Priscilla." He nodded toward the barn exit. "You need to have faith in your *dochder*. She may have made mistakes in the past, but we've all had lapses in judgment. Stop using her past against her."

While John's expression remained impassive, Yonnie's grave expression suddenly brightened with a strange gleam in his eyes.

Mark gritted his teeth as confusion and suspicion mixed with his burning anger. Rain beat a steady cadence on the barn roof above them.

Yonnie turned to the bishop. "Why don't we take our discussion outside, John?"

"*Ya.*" John started for the door.

Yonnie leaned toward Mark and lowered his voice. "I suggest you remember who owns this farm. If you want to keep this job, you'll mind your own business when it comes to my relationship with my family. Now, if you know what's best for you, you'll get back to work."

Mark took a deep, shaky breath as Yonnie followed John out of the barn. Once his boss was gone, Mark turned toward a wall and kicked it with all his might. Pain exploded in his foot, and he hopped and grunted in response.

When he came to a stop, he leaned back against the wall and scrubbed his hand down his face as his thoughts spun.

What had just happened?

In less than an hour, he'd gone from being frustrated with Priscilla to longing to console her and take away all the pain her ex-boyfriend had caused her. And then he found himself caught up in holding her, touching her, and being close to her. And if Yonnie and John hadn't walked in, he would've kissed her.

He groaned and stared up at the barn ceiling as thunder rolled. How could he have allowed himself to lose all control with her? What was it about Priscilla that brought out his most confusing and fervent emotions?

He padded over to the barn exit and looked out toward the doorway of another barn where Yonnie stood speaking to John out of the rain. His arms flailed about as if he were engrossed in a heated discussion. Was he complaining about Priscilla and calling her cruel names?

This is your fault! If you hadn't held her in your arms and almost kissed her, this never would have happened.

The voice crept in from the back of Mark's mind, leaving guilt and regret in its wake. He turned toward the house and fought the urge to walk in there and ask to speak to Priscilla alone to apologize.

But that would only make things worse for the two of them. He had to wait for the situation to defuse before he could speak to her. The plan was simple, but the idea of staying away from Priscilla felt like pure torture.

What was happening to him?

Stepping back into the barn, Mark picked up his pitchfork. Yonnie had told him to get to work, and he didn't want to risk losing this job. As he began to muck the stalls, Priscilla's words about how Trent had treated her echoed through his mind, causing him to work harder and faster. He had to burn off some steam before he drove himself crazy.

As he continued to work, the scars on Priscilla's arm and the tears in her gorgeous eyes haunted him. He would do everything in his power to be the friend she deserved, no matter how she tried to reject him. He couldn't give up on her. Her father and her ex-boyfriend had failed her, but he would never fail her. No matter what the cost.

─ C×D ─

Priscilla jumped with a start as a clap of thunder ripped through the air. She pulled the last pair of her father's trousers from the clothesline and placed them in the basket as the unexpected rainstorm continued to drum the roof and splatter on the porch. She'd have to hang the clothes on a line in the utility room.

When she heard footsteps, she turned and sucked in a deep breath as her father and the bishop came up on the porch. She gripped Ethan's shirt in her hands and pressed her lips together. Now she'd learn her fate after the incident in the barn.

The strangely satisfied look displayed on her father's face sent alarm slithering through her veins.

"We'd like to speak with you inside the *haus*, Priscilla." *Dat* pointed to the door. "Now."

"Ya, Dat." She hurried inside to the utility room with the basket of clothes she'd have to deal with later. She peeked out the window and spotted Ethan sitting on the porch playing with a toy car. He looked so happy, so adjusted to this new life. But her decision to open her heart to Mark in the barn may have changed everything. She had to be strong now for Ethan's sake.

She went into the family room, glad to hear her mother still at her sewing machine upstairs. Her father and the bishop stood by their wood-burning stove.

"I've discussed this at length with John, and we've decided you need to marry Mark." *Dat* said the words as if they were mundane and not life changing, earth shattering.

"What?" Priscilla divided a look between her father and the bishop as her pulse galloped. Had she heard her father correctly? He expected her to marry Mark?

No, no, no, no! He was the last person she'd ever marry!

"You need to marry Mark," *Dat* repeated. "Your behavior in the barn suggests that you and Mark have been involved in an intimate relationship for some time, and this is both sinful and disappointing. The only way to make this right is to marry him as soon as possible." He turned to the bishop. "Right, John?"

"Ya." John gave a curt nod. "You and Mark can decide on the wedding date. And there should be no more physical contact between you until you're married."

"But we haven't had any—"

Dat shot Priscilla an icy glare, and she stopped speaking.

"It's settled, then. You'll marry him." *Dat* turned to John. *"Danki."*

John nodded. "I'm going to go talk to Mark." Then he turned and disappeared through the front door.

"What's going on?" *Mamm* came down the stairs, her dark eyes wide.

"John and I caught Priscilla and Mark kissing in the barn." *Dat* folded his arms over his wide chest. "John and I spoke and agreed she should marry him as soon as possible."

Mamm blinked, and her gaze settled on Priscilla. "Is that true? Were you kissing Mark?"

"No." Priscilla grasped the edges of her apron, and she felt a surge of confidence that seemed to rise from deep within her battered soul. "It's not true at all. We were talking, and he was sitting close to me. *Dat* has decided to use this as an excuse." She glared at her father. "This is just what you wanted. You wanted me to find a husband, and since I haven't, you arranged one for me. You want me to marry so I'm no longer an embarrassment."

"Mark is perfect for you." He gestured out the window. "He can have half of my business. I'll give you both land and even build you a *haus*. You can live in the *daadihaus* until your new *haus* is built."

Disgust roiled in Priscilla's stomach as she studied her father. *Dat is getting what he wants. And although Mark might do this to avoid being shunned, he won't want to turn down every man's dream—land, a successful business, and a* haus.

Mamm stepped over and touched Priscilla's arm. "Mark is a *gut* man, and he cares about you and Ethan. He will be a *gut* husband and *gut* provider."

"That's all that matters, right?" Priscilla yanked her arm away from her mother's grasp. "No one cares how I feel or what I want." She wagged a finger at her father. "It's all about what's best for you. Now everyone will see Priscilla as a *gut* woman. I've confessed my sins and I'm forgiven. And now I just have to legitimize *mei sohn*."

"If you want to stay here, you need to marry him." *Dat* barked the words at her. "If not, then you and Mark will be shunned for your inappropriate behavior. You both know we have a strict rule of no touching before marriage, and I can't take another shunning in my family."

Priscilla's knees wobbled as she realized the truth. She was trapped in this situation. She had to do what her father and the bishop said. She couldn't allow her father to evict her and Ethan. They'd have to go to a homeless shelter because she couldn't ask anyone in the community—not even Laura—to take them in if she was shunned again. She had to succumb to their demands, even if it meant marrying a man she hadn't chosen, a man who would never have chosen her. She had to make this work for her son's sake.

Priscilla turned back to her father. "What makes you think Mark will agree to this?"

"Trust me," *Dat* said, insistent. "He will."

—⟡—

Mark's arms and back ached as he set the pitchfork aside and started toward the barn exit. He had mucked all the stalls in record time. His stomach growled, indicating it was time for him to head home for supper, but he longed to stay and talk to Priscilla. He needed to know that she was okay, but he had to force himself to leave.

Tomorrow was Friday. Maybe her father would realize he'd been wrong about what he'd witnessed in the barn and would allow Mark to talk to Priscilla.

"Mark." John Smucker appeared in the barn doorway. "I need to speak with you."

"John, I didn't realize you were still here." Hope sparked

within Mark. This was his chance to make things right! "I want to talk to you too. What you saw earlier wasn't what it seemed. We were only talking, and I would never have tried to do anything inappropriate with Priscilla. She's *mei freind*, and I care about her."

"I realize that." John fingered his long, graying beard. "It's apparent how you feel about her, which is why you need to marry her."

"Marry her?" Mark took a step back as if the words had punched him.

"*Ya*. The damage has been done, and only you can make things right." John's tone was even, despite the weight of his words. "It's what's best for her and the *kind*. Only you can repair her reputation."

Renewed fury boiled through Mark's veins. "Whose idea was it for Priscilla to marry me?"

John paused as if caught off guard by the question. "Well, Yonnie and I agreed on it."

"Really?" Mark lifted his chin. "Did Yonnie suggest it to you?"

"That's not important."

"*Ya*, it *is* important." Mark's voice rose. "And rather than keeping this innocent incident to yourself and counseling Yonnie to do the same, you're going to go along with what he wants?" He stared at the bishop for a few moments as the truth dawned on him. "Tell me you're not blind. Tell me you see what's really going on here, John. Yonnie treats Priscilla terribly, and he's forcing her to marry me as some sort of punishment."

John's look became steely. "You've got it all wrong. Yonnie is a *gut daed*, and he's only doing what's right. Priscilla needs a stern hand because of her past behavior."

"Priscilla's sins were forgiven when she repented."

John's eyes narrowed as he studied Mark for a moment. "Mark, it's obvious you care for Priscilla, which means you'll do what needs to be done. If not, then you'll both be shunned for the inappropriate and intimate behavior before marriage I saw with my own eyes. Besides, you've earned yourself quite a reputation with the young women in this community. I think this marriage will be *gut* for you too."

"My reputation?" Mark exclaimed. "Are you serious?"

"*Ya,* I am. Everyone knows you enjoy the company of the *maed* in the community, and you're nearing thirty. I think it would be a *gut* decision for you to finally settle down." He paused. "It's up to you what happens now. How would your *dat* feel if you were shunned?"

Mark's throat constricted. He couldn't allow the bishop and Yonnie to humiliate Priscilla again, but was he ready to get married?

"What's your choice?" John asked.

"I'll speak to Priscilla, and we'll decide together."

"Fine, then. But Yonnie and I have already spoken with her, and I believe she sees what's right. I need to get home to *mei fraa.* I'm sure supper is ready." John nodded and started toward the door. "Tell your *dat* hello for me."

John disappeared from the barn, and Mark stilled as if his boots were glued to the barn floor.

Shock rippled through him as all his hopes and dreams dissolved. He felt as if he were dreaming. This couldn't really be happening! How could his entire future be decided for him in a matter of a few hours? He felt as if he couldn't breathe as the bishop's words echoed through his mind. If he married Priscilla, he'd never build a house on his father's farm. He'd never come home to his own kitchen, his own bedroom. He'd never have the freedom he'd envisioned in that little house he'd hoped to build next to Jamie's. Instead, he would have a wife and a child to support, which meant he'd have to consider their wants and needs before his. Was he ready to be responsible for a family?

But if he wasn't ready, then he and Priscilla would be shunned. Priscilla had already told him she wanted to leave the community, and another shunning would be just the catalyst to shove her away. His lungs constricted at the thought of her leaving their community forever.

Closing his eyes, he sent a fervent prayer up to God.

God, please lead me down the right path. I'm at a crossroads, and I'm so confused I feel like I can't breathe. I feel like the world is closing in on me. I have to make the right decision or I could jeopardize the lives of two other people. I don't want to force Priscilla to marry me, and I'm not sure I'm even ready to be married. But I also can't stand the thought of losing her. Show me your will. Show me the way.

With a deep, shaky breath, he stepped out of the barn. The rain had stopped, but dark clouds still dotted the sky and the smell of rain remained in the air. He strode through the mud and up the back porch steps, and then he knocked on the storm door. The door opened and Yonnie stepped out on the porch.

"I thought you were gone," Yonnie said. "It's almost six."

Mark jammed his hands in his pockets to stop himself from wiping the smug expression off his boss's face.

Calm down! You don't want to be shunned!

"I want to talk to Priscilla. Is she available?"

"She's making supper with her *mutter.*" Yonnie lifted his chin. "What do you want to discuss?"

"You know what I want to discuss, Yonnie." Mark fought to keep his voice calm despite his raging anger. "It's about our future."

"I'd like to discuss that with you, actually." Yonnie nodded toward the barns. "If you agree to marry *mei dochder,* I'll give you half my business, plus half my land, and I'll build you any size *haus* you want."

Mark pressed his lips together as his stomach soured.

This is bribery! This is more sinful than if I'd kissed his dochder in the barn!

"What do you think, Mark?" Yonnie held up his hands. "I think that's a fair payment for marrying my *dochder*."

"Priscilla can't be bought and sold like one of your horses," Mark said, seething as his entire body vibrated with sudden, white-hot anger. "I'm not going to force her to marry me. I'm going to let her make that decision."

"Fine." Yonnie pointed toward the door behind him. "Would you like to come in?"

"No." Mark shook his head. "I'd like to speak to her out here. In private."

"I'll get her for you."

Mark spun toward the porch railing and leaned forward on it while he waited. His thoughts were moving so fast that he felt queasy. There had to be a way to stop this ridiculous mandate. But how?

When the door clicked open, he glanced over his shoulder at Priscilla. She fingered her black apron as she gave him a shaky smile.

"Hi." He stood up and faced her.

"Hi." She pushed the ties of her prayer covering over her shoulder. "I guess the bishop spoke to you."

"*Ya.*" He lifted his straw hat and pushed back his thick hair. "I wanted to talk to you about it in private. I think that if we talked to the bishop, we could—"

She put her finger to her lips as if to shush him and then pointed to the open windows behind her. "*Kumm.*" She reached for his arm and then pulled her hand back. "This way."

He followed her down the porch steps, and then they walked side by side on the path leading to the *daadihaus*, the small, one-story brick house just past the empty swing set.

They walked up the porch steps, and she sank onto a glider and nodded toward the spot beside her.

"How are you?" he asked as he sat down and angled his body toward her.

She shrugged. "I guess I'm okay."

"I'm sorry." He heard the quaver in his own voice. "This is all my fault."

"No, it's not." She shook her head. "It's my fault."

"No, if I hadn't been kneeling on the barn floor so close to you, then we never would've wound up in this mess."

She looked up at him, and her lower lip trembled. "No, *mei dat* would've found another way to make you marry me. He wants the stigma of his *dochder*'s illegitimate *sohn* taken off his family."

Mark glowered and shook his head. "What if we go talk to the bishop? He's always been a reasonable man. If we explain exactly what happened and I take the blame, then maybe he'll change his mind." He jammed a finger into his chest. "He can shun me since I'm the one who got too close." *And almost kissed you.*

Her expression grew grave. "I have no choice. I'm trapped, and there's no way out unless I want to be homeless. *Mei dat* won't let me stay unless I marry you. I don't have enough money saved to find a place to rent, and I can't afford day care for Ethan if I have to work outside of school hours. You're my only option for giving *mei sohn* a decent home. He's innocent in all of this. He didn't choose this life." She looked out toward her father's house. "I guess marrying you is better than being out on the street or living in a shelter."

Mark flinched at her biting words, but then he worked to make his expression serene.

"I should have realized when I decided to come home that *mei dat* would punish me for sinning." She looked over at him. "Would you rather go through with the marriage or be shunned?"

He frowned as disgust rolled through him. "I can't allow your *dat* to throw you and Ethan out on the street, and I can't stomach the idea of you both living in a shelter. What if I talk to Jamie and Laura? They both have plenty of room in their homes. What if you and Ethan lived there?"

She gave him a sad smile. "That's sweet, but it would never work. I'd still be shunned, and so would you."

"But isn't that better than having to marry me?"

She sighed and turned away from him. "I think we're both trapped unless you want to be shunned. But if you're shunned, *mei dat* can't pay you until the shunning is over."

Mark snorted. "He'd probably fire me anyway. I'd have to go back home and work on *mei dat's* farm."

"But that's not what you want."

"I don't want you and Ethan to be homeless. I don't think we have a choice."

They were silent for a moment, and he longed to hear her thoughts.

"What about your girlfriends?"

"Girlfriends?" He raised an eyebrow as he angled his body toward her again.

"You know." She gave him a sardonic smile as she counted them off on her fingers. "Let's see. Franey and Ruthann. And Sadie Liz seemed to really like you that day at the fabric store."

"I've told you, they're *not* my girlfriends."

"Do they know that?"

"You sound like *mei schweschdere*." He had to change the subject. "Priscilla, we can make this work if we have to. We've known each other our entire lives. Surely we can find a way to live together."

"*Ya.*" She nodded. "I guess it could be worse. At least you're not a stranger."

Mark tried to pretend the insult didn't cut him to the quick. "All right. I guess it's settled, then."

She sighed. "*Ya*, I guess so."

"So." Mark smiled. "Will you marry me?"

She rolled her eyes and then laughed, and he enjoyed the sound. "You already know the answer to that question."

"Are you going to tell Ethan?"

She pursed her lips. "*Ya*, but I need to find the best way to tell him."

"Now we need to meet with the bishop and pick a date, right?"

She nodded.

"We can go see him tomorrow after I get here in the morning."

She nodded again, and then they stared at each other. Once again, he longed to know what she was thinking. Was she disappointed, scared, anxious? Did she care about him at all?

She stood. "I guess I should get inside and help serve supper."

"*Ya*, and I need to get home."

Mark followed her down the porch steps, and they walked side by side up the path toward her parents' house.

When they reached the house, she looked up at him once again. "*Gut nacht.*"

"*Gut nacht,*" he echoed. He started toward the barn and then spun toward her once again. "Priscilla!"

She pivoted toward him, her eyes questioning his.

"For what it's worth, I'm sorry for all of this," he said.

She seemed to wilt a little, her slight shoulders hunching. "It's not your fault. I'm sorry you've been tangled up in my mess."

He smiled at her. "We'll get through it."

She nodded. "Be safe going home."

"I will." But he wasn't planning on heading home right away. He was going to go see Laura and beg her to help him make sense of this crazy day.

FIFTEEN

MARK HALTED HIS HORSE AT HIS TWIN SISTER'S back porch, and then he jumped out and tied the mare to the fence before loping up the steps. His mind had raced with bewilderment and anger as he'd made the trek to her house.

When he reached the back door, he knocked and then glanced up at the now cloudless sky, taking deep breaths to calm his zooming heart.

The screen door clicked open, and Allen smiled at him. "Mark. Laura had a feeling you might stop by. Come in." He made a sweeping gesture. "We were just finishing supper. Are you hungry?"

"*Ya*. I mean no." The thought of eating caused Mark's sour stomach to roil even more. "I was wondering if I could talk to Laura."

"Of course. Come on in."

"Who is it?" Laura called from the kitchen.

"Your twin," Allen responded.

"*Onkel* Mark!" Mollie called.

As Mark stepped into the mudroom, Mollie slid around the corner and skidded into him, her little arms outstretched. He grinned as he knelt and hugged her.

"Hey, Mollie girl." He kissed the top of her blond hair. "How's my big girl? I can't believe you're five now."

"I'm *gut*." She smiled up at him, and he touched her nose before hanging his straw hat on a peg by the door. "I love the doll you gave me for my birthday last week. *Mamm* is going to make me clothes for her. I named her Savilla after my other *mamm*."

Mark's lungs squeezed, but he kept a smile on his face. "That's really nice."

He followed her into the kitchen, and the aroma of country-fried steak and baked potatoes wafted over him, causing his stomach to growl.

"Mark." Laura stood up from her chair at the table. Her face clouded with a frown, and her eyes narrowed. "Something is wrong. You've been on my mind all afternoon." She pointed to the tray of steak in the center of the table. "That's why I made your favorite meal."

"I need to talk to you." He rubbed the back of his head.

"It's serious." Her tone was grave as she turned to Allen. "Would you please give Mollie a bath?"

Allen looked at each of them and then nodded. "*Ya*, of course." He turned to Mollie. "Let's go, kiddo. It's bath time."

"But I want to see *Onkel* Mark." She threaded her fingers with Mark's and held on tight.

"You can see him after your bath." Allen's face seemed to question if that were true, and Mark nodded. "You can play in the tub for a while, and then we'll come back down."

Mollie considered this and then nodded. "Okay." She looked up at Mark again. "Don't leave before I see you. Pinky promise?" She held up her pinky, and he threaded his own with it.

"Of course I won't." Mark leaned down and whispered in her ear. "I would never leave before saying good night to my twin niece."

Her smile brightened, apparently pleased. Then she scampered over to Allen and took his hand before he steered her through the family room toward the stairs.

Laura touched his arm. "Have you eaten?"

Mark shook his head. "I came right here after leaving Yonnie's."

"Sit." She pulled out her chair and pointed to the seat. "I'll get you a plate."

He pinched the bridge of his nose as the beginning of a headache stabbed at the back of his eyes. He had to sort through the events of the day and figure out how to explain it all to Laura. But how could he even explain it when he was so confused? It all felt like a bad dream—more like a nightmare.

Laura cleared away the used plates and utensils. After placing them in the sink, she set a glass of water, a clean plate, and utensils in front of him, and then she sat down beside him. "You need to eat."

He shook his head. "I don't think I can."

Her blue eyes shimmered. "I've never seen you like this." She swallowed. "At least, not since we lost *Mamm*. What happened today?"

He rested his elbow on the table. "I'm still trying to make sense of it." He turned toward the platter of steak again.

"Eat." She pushed the dish toward him.

After a silent prayer, he filled his plate with steak, a baked potato, and string beans. He ate a bite of the steak and nodded. "You still make the best country-fried steak."

"*Danki.*" Her expression grew impatient. "Now, tell me what happened."

Between bites he shared his story, starting with the discussion he and Priscilla had in the barn earlier and ending with their conversation on the porch of the *daadihaus*. He told her every detail, not holding back anything despite his swelling guilt and frustration. When he finished speaking, he angled his body toward his twin and held his breath, awaiting her sage assessment and advice.

When she stared at him wide-eyed, he placed his fork beside his plate and gave her a palm up. "Well, sis? What do you have to say?"

"I-I don't know." She shook her head. "I'm a little overwhelmed. I'm trying to get my brain around the fact that Trent hurt Priscilla, you almost kissed her in the barn, and the bishop and her *dat* are forcing you two to get married. It's a lot to take in, Mark."

He gave her a grave nod. "I know."

"When I asked her about Trent, she didn't share that he'd hurt her. She just said she had to leave."

"Really?" Mark asked. "You're her best *freind* and she didn't tell you?"

"No, but she confided in you."

Mark puzzled over that for a moment. Why would Priscilla trust him and not Laura? Of course, he'd seen the evidence when the sleeve of her dress ripped. That made the difference. She couldn't hide that scar from him any longer.

"I could feel your confusion and anger all day." She touched her collarbone. "But I never in my wildest dreams imagined you would tell me this." She pressed her lips together, opened her mouth, and then closed it again.

"What?" He leaned forward. "Don't hold back. What were you going to say?"

"I'm surprised John is being so forceful about this. When Rudy's *mamm* talked to him about how I was staying over here to take care of Mollie, John was reasonable. He told Allen I shouldn't stay here, and he trusted Allen and me to make the right decision." She rubbed her belly as she settled back in her chair. "I guess he feels that it would be best for the community if Priscilla is married. It's *bedauerlich* to hear that, but I guess I can see his point of view. I just think it should be Priscilla's choice and your choice who you want to marry."

"Exactly. He also said it would be *gut* for my reputation if I were married since I seem to enjoy spending time with the young women in our community. I know the family teases me, but I never thought other people were judging me because I like to have more than one female *freind*." Mark nearly spat the word. "And not only are Yonnie and John blackmailing me with the threat of shunning, but Yonnie is trying to bribe me as well by offering me half of his business, land, and a *haus*. It's not right."

"No, it's not. I'm very disappointed in Yonnie." She looked down at the table.

"So what do you think I should do?"

Her gaze snapped to his. "What do you *want* to do?"

"I can't let Yonnie throw Priscilla and Ethan out on the street, and I can't allow John to shun her again and ruin her name in the community. She's been through enough."

"Huh." A smile seemed to tug at the corner of her lips.

"What?" He groaned. "Please just say what you're thinking."

"I find it interesting that you're thinking only of Priscilla. You haven't said much about how this will affect you."

"That's not an answer I was hoping you'd give me. What do you think I should do?"

"I don't know." Laura shook her head. "This is your decision."

"You're not helping." Mark rubbed at his eyes as his headache flared. "I need your advice. I need you to be *Mamm* and tell me what to do."

"I miss her so much."

"I know. I do too." Mark slumped in his chair. "She would

know what I should do." He picked up his fork and moved the remaining string beans around on his plate. "I can't stop thinking about the pain in Priscilla's eyes when she told me what Trent had done to her. I've never been so angry in all my life. I wanted him to feel that same pain, but I also wanted to take her pain away. I've never felt anything like that."

Laura snapped her fingers. "I was right! You *are* in love with her."

"What?" Mark shook his head. "No, no, no. Just because I care about her doesn't mean I'm in love with her."

She smiled. "You love her, Mark. Just admit it."

He sighed. "I came over here to get your help, sis. This isn't helping."

She glanced toward the doorway. "You want my honest opinion?"

He rolled his eyes. "You're really going to ask me that?"

"Fine, fine." She waved him off. "I think you should pray about it and then follow your heart. If you truly care about Priscilla and you can see yourself building a life with her, then you should marry her."

"You think I'm capable of being a *gut* husband?"

"Why not?"

"Sis, no one knows me better than you do. You know just how spoiled, self-centered, and cocky I am. How can I possibly be capable of taking care of a *fraa* and a *sohn*?"

She gave him a cheeky grin. "*Ya*, but you've got me as your twin, so at least you have something going for you."

He guffawed. "That's something I would've said. I'm proud of you." His smile faded. "But seriously. I'll let Priscilla down from day one. This will never work. She's better off without me."

A pleasant smile curved up his twin's lips as she touched his bicep. "That is the most humble statement I've ever heard you make. If you keep striving every day to be a *gut* husband and *dat*, then you will be."

He stared at her.

She pushed back her chair and stood. "You need to finish your meal. I have a surprise for you."

"What?"

"I made your favorite dessert too." She opened the refrigerator and pulled out a chocolate cake.

"That's *wunderbaar*. You just made my day so much better. *Danki*, sis."

"I *said* you were on my mind today." With a smile she carried the cake to the table. "We can have it when Allen and Mollie come back down." Then she returned to the counter where she gathered a knife, four cake plates, and forks. "Mark, just open your heart to God, and he'll lead you down the right path for you and Priscilla. He did the same for Allen and me."

Mark nodded as he chewed another piece of steak. He swallowed and took a drink of water. "If I marry her, I want you to promise to keep all this a secret. I don't want anyone to know we were forced to marry. I don't want to risk her reputation in any way. I need to protect her and Ethan from the gossips in this community."

Laura gave him a knowing smile. "You know your secret is safe with me."

"*Danki.*" He was so grateful for his twin.

"I need to talk to you about something." Priscilla tucked Ethan's sheet around him.

"Okay." Ethan's dark eyes focused on her with interest. "What is it?"

"Mark and I have decided to get married."

"Oh." Ethan nodded. "So that means he'll live with us, right?"

"That's exactly right. We're going to stay in the *daadihaus* until we build another *haus.*"

"Will he be *mei daed*?"

"*Ya*, he'll be your stepfather. Do you know what that means?"

He nodded. "My best friend, Nico, has a stepfather. So he has two fathers."

"Right." She rubbed his arm. "How do you feel about that?"

Ethan shrugged. "It's okay." He paused for a minute as if contemplating something. "Can I call Mark *Dat* since he'll be my Amish dad?"

"*Ya*, I think that would be fine." She smiled as relief flooded her. He seemed to be taking it better than she thought he would.

"My friend Sammi back in Baltimore said people fall in love and then they get married. Does that mean that you and Mark are in love?"

"Ah, well, no, not exactly." Priscilla rubbed at a knot in her shoulder. "Mark and I are friends—*freinden*. Sometimes *freinden* decide to get married." She stilled, hoping her son would accept that answer.

"Okay." He nodded again. "So if two people really like each other, they can get married."

"Right."

"And that means you, me, and Mark will live in a *haus* together just like a family?"

Priscilla smiled as an unexpected warmth rolled through her. "That's exactly right."

"Nico has a half brother and a half sister. Will I get a brother and sister too? A *bruder* and *schweschder*?"

Her stomach lurched at the unexpected question. How was she going to address the intimacy issue with Mark? They weren't in love, but would he still expect her to fulfill her wifely duties? She shivered at the notion.

"Are you okay, *Mamm*?"

"*Ya*, I just don't know the answer to that question. I guess we'll see."

"Okay." He snuggled down under the sheet and yawned. "*Gut nacht.*"

"*Gut nacht.* I love you." She kissed his forehead and then stepped out of his room, closing the door behind her.

As she walked into her bedroom, Ethan's question rolled around in her head, and the muscles in her shoulders tightened. Tomorrow she and Mark would visit the bishop and decide on a wedding date. Then her new life with Mark Riehl would be set in motion.

She dropped onto her chair and stared at her sewing machine, which she'd believed would be her ticket to freedom from the Amish community. But now she was trapped here and heading into a marriage she'd never wanted. When she married Mark she'd be yoked to him for the rest of her life since divorce wasn't permitted. She'd be forced to marry a man she didn't love, which meant the marriage would be a sham. She'd never know what it was like to fall in love with a man who loved her in return.

Could she stomach seeing Mark every day, thinking of everything she'd given up to marry him? Would she resent him, and would that resentment morph into hate? If so, would Ethan sense her animosity toward his stepfather? How could that be healthy for her son?

Marrying Mark also meant she'd have to give up any chance to leave the community. Unless she was strong enough to leave and never look back, the decision to marry Mark would keep her trapped on her father's farm and stuck to Mark's side for eternity. This was a path she'd never envisioned or wanted. But how could she not offer her son the safety and security of a real home?

She held back threatening tears and ran her finger over the cool metal machine. Tomorrow she would have to choose a color and begin creating her wedding dress and the dresses for her attendants. And after they were married, she'd have to pack up her things and move into the *daadihaus* with Mark. How would she ever survive this?

With prayer.

The answer came from deep in her heart. She closed her eyes and opened herself to God.

I don't know why you've chosen this path for me, but I have to trust that you're in control. Please help me make the best decisions for Ethan, and please guide Mark to make the best decision for him. I'm scared, but I know you'll keep Ethan and me safe.

Then she got ready for bed, climbed in, snuffed out the lantern, and stared at the ceiling.

SIXTEEN

"DID YOU CHANGE YOUR MIND?" PRISCILLA TURNED toward Mark as he guided the horse out of her father's driveway and wiped her sweaty palms down the skirt of her rose-colored dress.

"Change my mind about what?" Mark kept his gaze focused on the road ahead.

"About marrying me? Did you decide to be shunned instead?"

"No." He shook his head without taking his eyes off the windshield. "I'm not going to back out on you."

"Oh." She chewed on her lower lip. "So you're going to go through with it?"

"*Ya*, if you are." He peeked over at her.

"I was planning on it. Did you tell your family last night?"

"I told only Laura. I went to see her after I left here."

"Oh." Priscilla's stomach writhed as she envisioned Mark telling Laura he was going to marry her. "Did you tell her what happened yesterday?"

He nodded, still looking straight ahead.

"Did you tell her *everything*?"

"*Ya*, I did." He gave her a sideways glance. "We can trust Laura."

As his words echoed through her mind, she found herself stuck on the word *we*. She and Mark were a couple now. But would he think of Priscilla before he thought of the other women he'd been seeing in the community? Could he ever truly love and cherish her the way a husband should? Did she want him to?

"I mean it," he added. "Laura and I have always shared our deepest secrets. She won't tell anyone about the bishop insisting we marry or be shunned. When we tell the rest of the community, they only need to know that I asked you to marry me. The rest is our business."

"Okay." She nodded. "What did she say about what happened?"

"She was surprised John was so forceful with his demand for us to marry. She said she was disappointed in him and your *dat*."

"And she's not disappointed in me?"

Mark halted the horse at a red light and angled his body toward her. "Why would she be disappointed in you?"

"Because you're her *bruder*, and you're being forced to marry me."

"Laura would never blame you for any of this." The tenderness in his eyes hummed through her. "You're her best *freind*. Why would she be disappointed in you?"

"Because this wasn't your choice. You're her twin, her closest relative, and your future has been decided for you."

"Laura has been pressuring me to settle down for a long time. She'd be the last person to be upset about it. Besides, like I said, you're her best *freind*. She told me to pray about it last night and then follow my heart."

"And?" Priscilla held her breath.

"I prayed about it, and, well, here I am. We're on our way to see the bishop and make plans for the wedding."

They rode in silence for several minutes. Priscilla's thoughts swirled in her mind. She was going to marry Mark Riehl. Never in her wildest dreams did she imagine she'd become Priscilla Riehl.

"Did you tell Ethan?"

The question took her by surprise. When she looked at Mark, she found him studying her as the horse sat at another red light.

"*Ya*, I did."

"And . . . ?"

"He took it well." She smiled. "He wants to know if he can call you *Dat* since you'll be his Amish dad."

A cryptic emotion flashed in his eyes. Was it affection, fondness, surprise, or something else?

"Would that be okay with you?" she asked.

"*Ya.*" His voice sounded thick. "That would be just fine."

When a horn tooted behind them, Mark guided the horse through the intersection and turned onto the road that led to John Smucker's dairy farm.

Tiny balls of anxiety formed in Priscilla's belly as Mark guided the horse up the short driveway to the *daadihaus* located behind the main farmhouse where John's son lived with his family. She gathered all her courage from deep within her. She could go through with this for her son.

"Are you ready?" Mark asked as he halted the horse.

"I think so." She climbed out of the buggy and met him by his horse as he tied it to the fence. "Have you given any thought to a date?"

He smiled. "I assumed you'd be in charge of that. You just tell me what date and time, and I'll be there."

She nodded. "All right. I was thinking the fourth Thursday in September. That gives me five weeks to make dresses and all the preparations."

"That sounds *gut* to me." He made a sweeping gesture toward the front steps. "I'll follow you."

Priscilla's heart thudded so fast she thought it might rip through her rib cage as she climbed the steps and knocked on the door. Mark stood directly behind her, his body heat mixing with hers. Why did his nearness drive her crazy?

The door swung open and Naomi, John's wife, smiled at her. "Priscilla. Mark. It's so nice to see you."

"Hi, Naomi." Priscilla forced her lips into a smile. "We were wondering if we could speak with John."

"Oh. Was he expecting you?" Naomi's gaze bounced between them.

"No, not really," Mark chimed in. "Does he have a few minutes to talk?"

"*Ya*, of course." Naomi motioned for them to enter. "Please have a seat. I'll tell him you're here."

Priscilla stepped into the small cottage and scanned the room, finding a small sitting area with a sofa, two wing chairs, two end tables with propane lamps, and a coffee table.

Mark moved past her and touched her arm. "We can sit." He sank onto the sofa and patted the cushion beside him.

She swallowed and then sat down beside him. When her leg brushed his, she felt a flutter in her chest as her pulse took on wings. Had she lost her mind?

"Priscilla. Mark." John stepped into the family room and gave them a big smile, as if this were a joyous occasion. "How nice to see you."

Priscilla swallowed the acidic words that threatened to leap from her tongue. He was the bishop, and he could convince the other ministers to shun her. She had to keep her tongue in check.

"Hi, John." Mark stood and shook his head. "Do you have a few minutes to talk?"

The sounds of dishes clinking and water running came from

the kitchen. Was Naomi truly cleaning up? Or was it an excuse to listen in on their conversation with her husband?

John sat on a wing chair across from them and smiled. "What brings you here today?"

Priscilla gave Mark a sideways glance, and Mark's expression seemed to warn her to not say anything acerbic.

"We've decided to get married." Mark gestured toward her. "Priscilla has picked a date, so we'd like to discuss arrangements."

"That's *wunderbaar.*" John clasped his hands together and sat forward. "I think you've made the best choice."

Priscilla held back a frown.

Mark's expression grew serious, and he lowered his voice. "We want everyone to know that we came to the decision to marry on our own. I don't want any rumors floating around that we were forced into this decision. Do you understand?"

Priscilla's eyes rounded as appreciation snuffed out her anger. Was Mark defending her reputation?

"*Ya,* of course." John's expression was solemn. "Our conversation yesterday has been kept confidential. I haven't shared it with anyone."

Priscilla felt her body relax slightly.

John's expression suddenly brightened. "What date have you chosen?"

For the next ten minutes, Mark and John discussed their wedding plans while Priscilla listened, her head swimming with the gravity of it all. This was really going to happen. She hadn't dreamed the bishop's ultimatum. She was going to marry Mark Riehl and live with him in the *daadihaus* on her parents' farm. She was trapped in a life she'd considered leaving after she earned enough money.

How was she going to adjust to being someone's lawful wife? Would the marriage really work? Could she and Mark build a harmonious life together? What if they didn't get along? Would it be a healthy environment for Ethan?

But more than that, she couldn't envision herself living with another man. How was she going to ever trust Mark after the way Trent treated her? Would Mark one day turn to drinking alcohol and hitting her the way Trent had? The Amish didn't permit divorce, so she would be stuck with this marriage for the rest of her life, no matter what. Was she prepared to make this life commitment to a man she didn't even love?

Her head ached and her neck stiffened as she considered the reality of what was happening.

"Priscilla?"

"Ya?" She turned to Mark. He was studying her.

"Do you have any other questions for John?" Mark's brow furrowed as if he were asking her if she was okay.

"No, *danki.*" She smoothed her hands down the skirt of her dress. "I think we're all set."

"Fantastic." John stood, and they followed suit. He leaned forward and lowered his voice as he shook Mark's hand again. "You've made the right decision, and I'm convinced you won't regret it."

I pray you're right. Priscilla shook his hand. *"Danki."*

Priscilla was in a daze as she climbed into Mark's buggy to start their journey back to her father's farm. She had to gain control of this situation.

"We need to set some ground rules," she blurted as Mark guided his horse toward the road.

"Ground rules?" He raised an eyebrow.

"Ya." She sat up taller as unexpected confidence surged past her inner turmoil. "This is going to be a marriage in name only. We're going to live like two *freinden,* not husband and *fraa.*"

He nodded slowly as if understanding her implications. "Agreed."

"When *mei daadi* built the *daadihaus, mei mammi* had two requests. She wanted a fireplace and hearth like ones she'd seen at an *Englisher* bed and breakfast, and she wanted an extra bedroom as a sewing room. After she died my parents put a spare double bed in that room. I'll sleep there with Ethan." She clasped her hands together while awaiting his response. Would he agree to her not being with him at night?

"Okay." He kept his eyes focused ahead. "I respect that."

"*Gut.*" Her heartbeat slowed to a more normal pace. "So I guess now we have to tell our families?"

"*Ya,* I guess so." His gaze flickered to hers. "Yours first?"

"*Ya,* although since they both already know everything, I'm sure the conversation will be mostly about wedding plans— especially in front of Ethan." She sucked in a deep breath. "How's your family going to take the news?"

"They're going to be surprised." His words were slow, measured.

"Will they approve of me?"

He halted the horse at a red light and faced her. "Sweetheart, they're going to be so shocked and delighted that I'm settling down that they will shower you with love and affection." He smiled. "And, *ya,* they already approve of you. You're one of Laura's dearest *freinden.* You're already family."

She rubbed her forehead. What if she let his family down? What if she let Laura down?

─ ⌘ ─

"So we have five weeks to make your dresses." *Mamm* clapped her hands as a bright smile spread across her lips. "How many attendants will you have?"

Priscilla drew a blank. She turned to Mark as he sat beside her at her parents' kitchen table. When they arrived home, her mother already had lunch prepared for them—platters of rolls, lettuce, lunch meat, and cheese sat by a bowl of macaroni salad and jars of condiments. She'd begun peppering Priscilla with wedding questions as soon as she and Mark walked in the door.

"We haven't talked about attendants yet." Priscilla set her ham sandwich on her plate and turned toward Mark. "I suppose you'd like to have your *bruders*?"

Mark nodded and swallowed. "Jamie, Roy, and Walter." He looked over at Ethan. "And Ethan too."

"So I could have Laura, Cindy, and Sarah Jane." She turned to her mother. "We need to make four dresses."

"What color?" *Mamm* asked.

"Red," Mark said.

Priscilla spun toward him. "Red?"

He pointed toward her. "It looks great on you with your dark hair."

Priscilla studied him, confusion filling her mind. He'd noticed what color looked best on her?

"I think you look good in red too!" Ethan said between bites of macaroni salad.

"They're right," *Mamm* said. "So we need to get to the store."

"Let me ask his *schweschdere* first," Priscilla said.

"They'll say *ya*," Mark chimed in.

"Have you told your family yet?" *Mamm* said.

"Only Laura," Mark said. "And she was supportive. We should go to *mei dat*'s for supper tonight and tell them."

"*Ya*, you should," *Mamm* said. "You know how news flies through this community. Once it gets out, everyone will know. You want your family to hear it from you."

"That's a *gut* point." Mark took a drink of water from his glass.

"Can I come?" Ethan asked.

"Of course you can," Mark said. "You're family too."

Priscilla's stomach churned as she imagined facing Mark's large family when he told them they were going to get married. Would they believe she and Mark had fallen in love in only two months? Or would they see right through Mark's façade?

"We need to start working on the biggest barn," *Dat* said. "We'll want it to be clean and painted for the ceremony. Some of the floorboards need to be replaced as well."

Priscilla's gaze snapped to her father's face as he looked across the table at Mark. Her father was smiling, and while he was admitting the barn wasn't already in perfect shape too. Was he happy that she was getting married? Or was he happy he'd gotten his way? It was probably a mixture of both. She frowned.

"I'll help paint the barn." Ethan held up his hand as if he were volunteering at school.

"And we should plant flowers," *Mamm* added. "We should plant your favorites, Priscilla—daisies."

"I love the idea." Priscilla smiled. "I've missed working in the garden. I couldn't do that when we lived in Baltimore. It's my favorite hobby."

"I'll help!" Ethan's expression brightened.

"*Danki*, Ethan," Priscilla said.

"We need to get to the nursery too, then. I have to make a list." *Mamm* took a notepad and pen from the counter and began writing a shopping list, announcing each item they'd need for the wedding.

"We have to clean out the *daadihaus* too," *Dat* added. "We should probably paint the inside. When do you think you'll move in, Mark?"

"I don't know. Maybe the night before the wedding?" Mark asked.

"No, that will be too chaotic." *Dat* shook his head. "How about a couple of weeks before the wedding?"

"That sounds *gut*." Mark picked up his turkey sandwich. "What do we need for the *haus*?"

"It's furnished," *Dat* said. "It just needs to be cleaned."

Priscilla's lunch suddenly felt like a lead ball in the pit of her stomach. Everything was happening so fast. When was it all going to slow down?

The conversation swirling around her faded as she stared down at her plate and imagined her life marching by. She was about to embark on a new journey—a new but loveless marriage in a new home. How was she going to cope?

She turned toward Mark and took in his handsome profile— his chiseled cheekbones, strong jaw, and bright-blue eyes. He would be her husband, living with Ethan and her, but he would never truly love her. Further, he'd never have the opportunity to fall in love with anyone else. She was robbing him of his future just as much as he was stealing hers. Maybe she should've agreed to be shunned.

Her gaze moved to Ethan as he grinned at Mark. She had to agree to marry Mark for Ethan. He deserved a safe home, and Mark would be a good provider and role model for her son.

She could do this. After all, she'd survived living with Trent for almost seven years.

"We have a lot of work to do." *Mamm* beamed as she looked around the table. "This will be a family effort. We'll get it all done in time." She turned her smile to Priscilla and whispered, "I'm so *froh*. You made the right decision."

Priscilla forced a smile. If only she had the same confidence in her future.

SEVENTEEN

"WE HAVE AN ANNOUNCEMENT TO MAKE." MARK glanced around the full table in his father's kitchen that evening. He was standing near his *daed*, Priscilla at his side.

For some reason, he had decided to wait until they were finished eating before he told everyone the reason he'd called and requested a last-minute family supper. They'd been patient as they shared the delicious chicken and egg noodles Florence made, but he could tell they were all bursting with curiosity—especially since he'd invited Priscilla and Ethan to join them.

Poor Ethan had squirmed in his chair the whole meal, dying to tell his secret. But Priscilla had given him strict instructions to keep quiet.

Now the whole family was staring at Mark. He turned toward his fiancée, and her brown eyes widened with something that looked like fear sparkling in them. He looped his arm around her shoulders and yanked her to him, causing her to stumble awkwardly before grabbing his waist to right herself.

"Priscilla and I are getting married." His voice sounded too loud and slightly wobbly.

The room went silent and someone muttered, "What?"

"Yeah! Mark's going to be my stepdad!" Ethan said.

Then Florence stood and clapped. "That's *wunderbaar!*" She hurried over and hugged Mark and then Priscilla. "Oh, what a blessing! When is the wedding?"

Priscilla shared the date, her voice quiet and unsure.

"Oh my goodness!" Kayla jumped up from her seat. "That's not too far off." She turned to Laura and Cindy. "We need to help Priscilla get ready. There's so much to do."

The women gathered around Priscilla. After each one took a turn hugging her, they immediately began to discuss wedding plans. Mark stole a glance at Ethan. He and Mollie seemed fascinated by the commotion among all the adults.

Dat and Jamie appeared beside Mark. They shared a confused look and then turned to face him.

"Is this a joke?" *Dat* whispered, and Mark shook his head, his throat suddenly dry.

"This is a shock." Jamie eyed him with suspicion. "You sure acted like you weren't ready to get married the last time we talked."

Dat patted Mark's back. "I never saw this coming. You really kept it quiet that you were dating."

"Well, you know how it is." Mark grinned and hoped he sounded convincing. "We couldn't wait. I was just so excited that she came back to the community, and I couldn't wait to ask after she became a member again."

Priscilla turned toward Mark and gave him a look that said, *Knock it off,* before turning back to his sisters. "We're going to keep it small, only family and *freinden,* but I'd love for you three to be my attendants."

Cindy squinted her eyes as she studied Priscilla. "Why are you going to keep it small? Everyone is so *froh* you're back."

"*Danki,*" Priscilla began, "but I'm not sure *everyone* is glad I'm back."

"Why would you say that?" Sarah Jane asked.

When a wry smile turned up Priscilla's pretty lips, Mark braced himself for her sardonic comment.

"Well, I don't think the other young *maed* from my youth group will be cheering when they learn Mark asked me to marry him instead of any of them." Priscilla turned toward Mark. "I might have some hecklers."

Laura and Jamie burst out laughing, and Mark glowered at them.

"What are you going to tell Franey and Ruthann?" Laura asked.

"I think they'll be fine," Mark said.

Cindy shook her head. "I'm not so sure. Franey seems pretty determined to be your *fraa*."

"Let's celebrate!" Florence moved to the counter and picked up a chocolate cake.

"Oh," Mark said, nearly groaning. "My favorite."

Jamie smacked Mark's back and then leaned up close to his ear. "We're going to talk later. Come by *mei haus* after you take Priscilla and Ethan home. I'll wait up for you." Then he walked over to the chair where Calvin sat on a booster seat and patted his head before sitting down beside him.

Mark swallowed. How was he going to convince his older brother that this marriage was genuine?

He turned to Priscilla as she continued to discuss plans with the women in his family. She looked beautiful with her cheeks flushed pink and her eyes sparkling in the light of the Coleman lanterns hanging above them. His heart swelled when he imagined living with her in the *daadihaus*. Could they make this marriage work? Would she ever have any affection for him?

Oh no. Was he falling for her? He couldn't allow himself to feel anything but friendship for her. Her heart wasn't in this marriage, and her ground rules proved how disconnected she felt from him. She didn't want to truly be with him, and she'd never give him her whole heart. She didn't desire to have children with him. She'd made it apparent that she craved only the stability of the marriage for the sake of her son.

Was she only biding her time until she could afford to move out? When he gave her access to his bank account, would she take his money and leave him alone in the *daadihaus*? What would he do then? He'd never be permitted to remarry while Priscilla was still alive.

"Who wants *kuche*?" Florence announced as she set two chocolate cakes on the table.

"Eat some *kuche*," Laura whispered in Mark's ear. "Everything is going to be fine."

Hoping his sister was right, Mark sat down, looked up at Priscilla, and patted the seat beside him. She sat down, and he smiled as his family continued to embrace his future wife.

It seemed that his family would accept his announcement as genuine—as long as he could convince Jamie that it was.

─⟲⟳─

"What's on your mind?"

Priscilla swiped her hand down her face and contemplated how to put all her churning thoughts into words as Mark guided the buggy back to her father's farm later that evening.

She glanced into the back of the buggy where Ethan slept and thought about Mark's family. They had seemed surprised but supportive of their decision to marry.

Soon she'd be a member of the Riehl family, and her heart warmed at the idea. Even Ethan seemed to fit in as he played with Mollie and Calvin. But if marrying Mark was so right, why did it feel so wrong? She wouldn't have a real marriage, but it would be the next best thing. Didn't that make it acceptable in God's eyes? Wasn't this what God wanted her to do for her son?

"I can smell the smoke from your thoughts all the way over here." Mark grinned at her. "Why don't you just share what's bothering you?"

"Nothing. I was just thinking about how your family is so supportive."

He snickered. "Yeah, they sure are. Sometimes they're too interested in my business."

"That's because they love you. You're blessed to have their love and support."

His smile faded as he gave her a sideways glance, but he remained silent.

She shifted in the seat. "I am wondering why you didn't tell your family the truth."

"The truth about what?"

"About why we're getting married. They can't possibly believe we're in love."

Mark rubbed his chin as if considering his answer. "I didn't think they needed to know."

"Because you're embarrassed. You don't want them to know the bishop found us sitting close together in the barn, right?"

"No. Because we didn't do anything wrong. They don't need to think we were having an inappropriate relationship. Like I told you earlier, only Laura knows, and I intend to keep it that way."

Was he truly protecting her reputation? Or his own? The question took hold of her mind as they approached her father's farm.

But was it fair to expect him to keep it a secret if her family knew the truth? No, it wasn't. He was in this as much as she was.

She turned toward him. "Mark, if you want to tell your family the truth, then you should. I trust you to explain what happened, and I trust your family too."

He raised his eyebrows. "Okay. But I don't think I will."

When Mark halted the horse in front of her father's porch, Priscilla woke Ethan, and they all climbed out of the buggy.

Mark walked them to the steps, and after saying good night to Mark, Ethan hurried into the house.

Priscilla looked up at Mark, and a fist-size ball of unease formed under her ribs. "So I guess I'll see you tomorrow . . . and then at church."

"I have to run some preplanned errands for the farm all day tomorrow, but I'll pick up you and Ethan for the service on Sunday."

"Why?"

"We're engaged now, so we should ride to and from church together."

"Right. We have to make sure everyone believes this is real."

"So I'll see you Sunday." He started down the steps.

"Mark," she called after him, and he spun toward her. "Are you ready for the community to find out about us?"

He rested his hand on the railing. "*Ya*, I am. Are you?"

"*Ya*." She nodded. "*Gut nacht*."

"*Gut nacht*." He strode down the steps.

As his horse and buggy started down the driveway, she glanced around her father's vast property. Of course Mark was ready for the community to find out he was marrying Priscilla. After all, he hadn't turned down her father's offer of half his successful horse breeding and training business and land. He was set financially for life. Besides that—and not wanting to be shunned—why else would he want to marry her?

But was his desire for acceptance and wealth enough to sustain a commitment to her for a lifetime?

The question lingered in her mind as she stepped into the house. She locked the front door and then walked into the kitchen, where a yellow lantern glowed. She stepped into the doorway and expected to find her mother there, but she bristled as her gaze collided with her father's.

"How did his family take your wedding announcement?" *Dat* lifted a glass of water and took a drink.

"Fine." She folded her arms over her waist. "They actually believe we're in love."

The twinkle in her father's eyes caused the angry knots in her shoulders to tighten.

"Everything will work out just fine." *Dat* stood and set the glass on the counter. "Mark will have the *haus* he's always wanted and eventually my farm. You'll have a husband, and Ethan will have a proper *dat*. Plus, my farm will finally have an heir since Ethan is here."

She shook her head as irritation churned in her stomach. "Have you ever considered what I want?" She jammed her finger into her collarbone. "You act as if my opinion doesn't matter. You never once have thought about my happiness."

His eyes narrowed. "That's not true. I'm doing what's best for you and *mei gross-sohn*." He pointed toward the ceiling. "Your *bu* needs a *gut* role model for a *dat*. Mark Riehl is a *gut*, solid Christian man."

"But shouldn't marriage be based on mutual love and respect?" Her voice thinned. "Didn't you marry *Mamm* because you loved her?"

He waved off her comment. "Love and respect will come later."

"What if it doesn't?" She raised her arms for emphasis. "What if I'm trapped in a loveless marriage for the rest of my life? Doesn't that matter?"

"What matters is that you and your *sohn* have a *gut*, stable home." He took a step toward her, his lips forming a deep scowl. "Isn't that better than living on the street?"

"I don't know." She shook her head. "I thought my happiness mattered for something."

"Maybe you should have thought of that before you ran off and got pregnant," he snapped.

His words were a kick to her stomach, and she gasped as if the statement had caused her physical pain. Reeling from the cruelty in his dark eyes, she left the kitchen and mounted the stairs.

She stopped short in the hallway when she heard her mother's voice. It sounded as if *Mamm* was reading Ethan a story in his room. Priscilla leaned back against the wall and closed her eyes.

"Please, God," she whispered. "Give me strength. Help me find my way through this confusing mess."

Then she fought back threatening tears and stepped into her son's room. She'd get through this somehow—for him.

⁓◌⁓

Mark stowed his horse and buggy in his father's barn and then headed down the path to Jamie's house. He found his older brother sitting on his porch, a lantern on the floor illuminating him as he rested his elbows on his thighs and leaned forward. A look of suspicion had overtaken his face.

"I was wondering if you were going to stand me up," Jamie said as Mark climbed the porch steps. "Just weeks ago you told me you weren't ready to get married. You also told me I'd be the third to know when you got engaged. How could you not let me know you were planning to make this announcement?"

"I'm sorry to disappoint you." Mark dropped into the rocker beside Jamie and gave it a gentle push. "I wanted to tell everyone at the same time."

Jamie turned toward him, raising a dark eyebrow. "So what's really going on here, little *bruder*?"

Mark brushed his hands down his thighs and stared out toward the dark pasture. How was he going to lie to his older brother? But he made a promise to Priscilla, and he intended to keep that promise. She was going to be his wife, and their marriage needed a good, solid foundation based on trust.

Who was he kidding? This was a marriage of convenience, arranged as punishment, thanks to the bishop.

"Wow. I've never seen you be so secretive. This must be a *gut* story."

"No, not really." Mark plastered a smile on his face. "Priscilla and I have fallen in love. I wasn't expecting it, but it just happened."

Jamie's loud laughter sliced through the air.

Mark swallowed a groan.

"You fell in love?" Jamie wiped his eyes. "Please, Mark. How gullible do you think I am?"

Mark sighed and tipped his head back. Why hadn't he just gone straight home and to bed?

"What really happened?"

Mark gripped the arms of the chair.

Jamie's smile faded. "You know you can trust me, right?"

Mark nodded. "*Ya*, I do know that, but I made a promise."

"Wait a minute." Jamie's expression grew more serious. "Is she—do you *have* to get married?"

"What?" Mark sat up straight. "No, no, no. It's nothing like that." He shook his head. "This is why I don't want to tell you the truth. I'm afraid people are going to make assumptions about her and about us that aren't true. I want people to believe that she came back after all these years, we fell in love, I proposed to her, and she said *ya*."

"So if that's not what happened, what is the truth, Mark?"

"I'll tell you the truth, but you and Laura are the only ones who'll know, other than Priscilla's parents and the bishop. I want it to stay between us. Do you understand?"

Jamie nodded. "*Ya*, I do. Now tell me."

Settling back against the rocking chair, Mark explained how Priscilla's father and the bishop had found them when she opened up to him in the barn. He explained the bishop's ultimatum, their decision to marry, and their meeting with John.

When he finished speaking, Mark moved the rocker back and forth and stared out toward the pasture again, his stomach in knots while he waited for his brother's opinion of it all.

"Wow."

"Really?" Mark deadpanned. "All you can say is 'wow'?"

Jamie held up his hand. "Give me a minute to process this."

Mark rubbed his temples as that familiar stress headache began behind his eyes.

"Do you love her?" Jamie asked.

Mark hesitated. "She's a *gut freind*."

"You shouldn't marry her if you don't love her. It will never work if you don't have that foundation of love."

"I can't confess to something I didn't do, and she shouldn't have to either. Plus, Yonnie offered me land and half the business, I'll have a place of my own, and our siblings will have more room in the *haus*. It just makes sense."

"I understand, but that's not a reason to get married."

"It's a great reason." Mark pointed to the porch floor. "I'll have stability, and so will Priscilla and Ethan."

"You need to really think about this. Marriage is for life. You and Priscilla will resent each other if you marry for the wrong reasons. You deserve happiness too."

Mark shook his head. "You don't understand. I've already made the commitment to Priscilla, and we've spoken to John. I can't go back on my decision. I can't disappoint Priscilla like that.

All the men in her life have let her down. Her father treats her terribly, and Ethan's father abused her. If I change my mind, I'll be just as bad as they are."

"Mark, please just listen to me." Jamie leaned forward and held up his hand as if to calm Mark. "You will regret this. You need to talk to the bishop again. Tell him you think there should be another solution other than shunning or getting married. You and Priscilla weren't doing anything inappropriate in the barn, and this has all been blown out of proportion. Make him understand that this isn't right."

"I think it's more complicated than that. I think Yonnie pressured the bishop to make us get married. I think he's embarrassed by Priscilla and he wants to legitimize Ethan." He glowered. "He only cares about how Priscilla looks to the community."

A strange expression flickered over Jamie's face as he was silent.

"What are you thinking?" Mark asked.

"Nothing."

"Jamie, just say it. I can feel your criticism."

"It's not criticism. I think you care about her more than you're willing to admit."

"No, I don't. I care about her like I care about a *freind*. I just think this can be *gut* for both of us. She needs a husband as well as a father for Ethan. Besides, like I said, I'm getting land and a business."

"It might sound like a *gut* idea, but if you're marrying her for what Yonnie will give you, the marriage is going to fail."

Anger whipped through Mark. "That's easy for you to say. You have it all right here." He gestured toward the house. "You have the farm, Kayla, Calvin, and a *boppli* on the way."

"I thought you didn't want those things," Jamie said, challenging him.

Mark pressed his lips together. Jamie was right. When did Mark start wanting those things?

They sat in silence for a beat.

"Did you pray about it?" Jamie suddenly asked.

"*Ya*, I did last night."

"What was the answer?"

"The answer was *ya*, that I should marry her. Will you support me?"

"Of course I will." Jamie smiled. "And I think Priscilla is perfect for you."

"What makes you say that?"

"When she teased you about Franey and Ruthann tonight, I could tell she's not intimidated by you. She's not afraid to challenge you or speak her mind. Kayla is the same way with me. She challenges me just about every day. In my opinion that makes Priscilla a *gut* match for you. I just hope you two can find your way together."

A tangle of emotions expanded deep within Mark. "I do too."

EIGHTEEN

"So Mark." Ethan leaned over Mark's buggy seat Sunday morning. "When you marry *mei mamm*, does that mean Mollie and Calvin will be my cousins?"

Mark tilted his head while keeping his eyes focused on the road ahead. "*Ya*, I guess they will be your cousins."

"Awesome. I've never had cousins before."

"Sit down," Priscilla scolded him. "Stop hanging over the seat like that."

Ethan sat back, but he kept his attention on Mark. "Mom says we're going to live in the *daadihaus* until *Daadi* builds us a bigger *haus*, and you'll be my stepdad."

"Right." Mark gave Priscilla a sideways grin.

"I'm sorry," she muttered as her cheeks heated. "We talked about this again last night, and he has a lot of questions for you."

"It's fine. This is a big adjustment." Mark looked over his shoulder at Ethan. "What do you want to ask me?"

"Can I call you *Dat* since you'll be my Amish dad?" Ethan tapped his chin. "Or should I call you Mark since you're not my dad yet?"

"You can call me whatever you want, but just don't call me late for dinner." Mark grinned, and Ethan hooted with laughter.

"Oh, Mark." Priscilla shook her head, but she couldn't stop herself from chuckling.

"In all seriousness," Mark began with a sentimental smile, "you can call me *Dat* or Mark. It's up to you."

Ethan rubbed his chin. "I think I'll go with Mark for now and then *Dat* after you marry *mei mamm*."

"That sounds *gut* to me." Mark glanced over at Priscilla and winked.

The gesture touched Priscilla's heart.

Don't allow him to lead you on. He'll never truly love you!

The voice startled her and cooled the warmth.

When they arrived at the Yoders' farm for the church service, Ethan hopped out of the back of the buggy.

"*Daadi* is here," he announced as he ran around to Priscilla's door. "He said I can sit with him again today."

Priscilla nodded. "Okay."

"See you later!" Ethan waved as he hurried off.

Priscilla climbed out of the buggy and watched Ethan meet her father near the barn. Then she turned to Mark as he sidled up to her. "I find it fascinating that *mei dat* isn't *froh* to have me back, but he loves *mei sohn*."

Mark nodded toward her father. "You know how he is. Just give God time to melt his heart."

She turned toward him and studied his pleasant expression. "Are you sure you don't want to change your mind about this?"

"About what?"

"About us." She gestured between them. "This marriage. Becoming a stepfather and husband."

His expression hardened. "No, I don't want to change my mind. Do you?"

She hesitated and then said, "No."

He pursed his lips, his blue eyes gleaming in the morning light. "What are you thinking right now?"

"The community is going to be shocked when they find out you're marrying me."

"So?" Mark shrugged. "Let them be shocked. It's our business."

She laughed. "No, that's not how gossip works."

"Gossip is a sin."

"*Ya*, but it's alive and well."

He took a step toward her and lowered his voice. "Are you okay?"

The tenderness and concern she found in his face touched her deep in her soul. Was it genuine? No, it couldn't be—at least not beyond being a friend. He was just trying to convince her this relationship would somehow last.

"*Ya*, I will be."

"*Gut*." He rubbed her arm, and the sudden, unexpected contact caused her to flinch. "I'm sorry," he said. "I just wanted to tell you it will be fine. I'll see you after the service."

"Okay." She drew in a deep breath and watched him saunter to the barn, where he greeted the men in his family.

"Priscilla!" *Mamm* waved as she walked over to her. "It's a *schee* day, *ya*?" She pointed to the cloudless, bright-blue sky.

"*Ya*, it is."

"Let's go inside." *Mamm* gestured toward the house.

Priscilla strode beside *Mamm* and entered the kitchen, where the women in the congregation were gathered in a circle greeting one another.

Her mother walked over to Florence, and when Priscilla's gaze fell on Laura, Sarah Jane, Cindy, and Kayla, she waved and walked over to them.

"*Gude mariye*," Priscilla said. "How are—"

"There she is!" Florence announced. "There's Mark's bride!"

All conversation around the kitchen ceased, and Priscilla saw every set of eyes focus on her. She felt as though their curiosity was burning into her skin. She tried to swallow against her suddenly arid throat as she hugged her arms around her waist.

Florence smiled and held her hand to her chest. "I'm just so grateful Mark is finally going to settle down."

Priscilla stilled as a flush crawled up her neck to her face. *Oh no, no. Please be quiet, Florence!*

"Mark Riehl is getting married?" a voice asked.

"Really?" someone across the room said. "Mark is going to settle down?"

Priscilla longed to crawl under the kitchen table and hide from the inquisitive crowd of women.

"That's right," Florence continued. "They're getting married in five weeks."

"It's fine." Laura's voice was close to Priscilla's ear. "Once the announcement is out, it will get easier."

Priscilla met her best friend's kind eyes. "You think so?"

"Of course." Laura rubbed her arm.

When Priscilla turned to her right, she found Franey's eyes wide and glistening as she studied her. Then Franey turned and made a hasty exit out the back door.

Embarrassment spread through Priscilla as a group of women huddled around her.

"Congratulations," Ruthann said as she hugged Priscilla. "I always hoped Mark would pick me, but I never really felt his heart was in our friendship." She smiled, but her dark eyes were wet with unshed tears.

"*Danki*," Priscilla said as shock surged through her.

"How did you get Mark Riehl to want to settle down?" a woman who looked to be her mother's age asked.

"You must have stolen his heart quickly," another quipped.

"Did you date when you were teenagers?" a third asked. "I don't recall that he dated you."

"Your wedding is coming quickly. You have to get started on your dresses soon," a fourth said.

Priscilla took a deep breath and began trying to respond to the questions as quickly as they were thrown at her.

Mark nodded at a couple of friends as he made his way through the knot of people milling around the barn after the service. His mind had been swimming with thoughts of his upcoming wedding as he tried but failed to concentrate on the sermons.

His eyes had also kept gravitating to the unmarried women's section, where Priscilla sat between Cindy and Sarah Jane. She looked radiant today in her pink dress, yet she also seemed lost in thought as she stared down at her lap. Had she been focused on their upcoming nuptials too?

He stepped out of the barn and walked the path toward the house while recalling their conversation in the buggy this morning. He'd enjoyed his conversation with Ethan. For the first time in his life, he looked forward to becoming a father. He hoped and prayed he'd be a good one—like his father and Jamie were.

Why was he changing so quickly? He felt like a new man, a different person since he'd decided to get married.

"Is it true?"

Mark spun and came face-to-face with Franey. Her pretty face featured a deep frown as her eyes trained on his.

"Is it true?" she repeated as she took a step toward him.

"Is what true?" Who was he kidding? He knew exactly what she wanted to know.

"You're marrying her, aren't you?" Her voice shook as her lower lip quivered.

Oh no. Please don't cry. Not here.

He nodded. "*Ya*, I've asked Priscilla to marry me."

"Why?" Her eyes glittered. "I've waited five years for you. Five years!" Her voice broke as tears spilled down her pink cheeks.

"*Ach*, no." Guilt, hot and searing, sliced through Mark as he pointed to the far corner outside the barn, away from the curious crowd that turned toward them. "Why don't we walk over there?"

"Why?" Franey's voice grew louder. "You don't want everyone to hear how you've hurt me?"

Mark's shoulders hunched.

"Five years, Mark!" She nearly spat the words at him. "I've invited you over for hundreds of meals. I've sat on my father's porch and talked to you for hours. I've welcomed you into my home. Yet she's back barely two months, and you propose to *her*. What does she have that I don't? Am I not *schee* enough? Am I not *schmaert* enough? What is it, Mark? What's wrong with me?"

"It's not that at all. There's nothing wrong with you." He reached for her arm, and she stepped away from him. "Franey. *Kumm*." He took her arm and steered her away from the barn door as questioning eyes locked on them. "It's not you. You're a *wunderbaar maedel*, and you'll make a husband very *froh* someday."

She gave a cry. "Apparently not. I thought you cared about me. I was blind."

"I do care about you—as a *freind*."

She groaned and wiped at her tears.

"Franey, listen. I never meant to hurt you." He tried to smile. "I'll cherish the time we've had together. This wasn't anything I planned. Love is just unpredictable sometimes. Priscilla and I have a deep connection I never expected."

"I thought we had a connection."

"Look, I'm sorry."

"How could you?" Her eyes narrowed. "How could you lead me on like that for so long?"

"I didn't lead you on."

"*Ya*, you did." She pointed at him. "You called me twice a week and you even invited yourself over some nights. Why would I not think someday you'd propose to me?" Then she turned her finger toward herself. "I knew you were seeing Ruthann too, but I thought you and I had something special."

"I never made you any promises." But Mark did a mental head slap. Laura was right. What he'd done was wrong.

"No, you didn't make me any promises, but you kept me hanging on for years. You acted like you liked me."

"You're right, and I'm sorry."

"No, *I'm sorry* I ever believed in you." Franey shook her head. "I meant nothing to you. I was just someone to pass the time with until you met your true love."

"No, you're a *freind*, a *gut freind*."

She shook her head, and then her expression darkened. "You know, I had a feeling something was going on between you and Priscilla the day you brought her to the fabric store."

He blinked. "Why would you say that?"

"It was the way you acted when you purchased the fabric for her. I should have known then that you had fallen in love with her."

Mark tried to hide his surprise at her comment.

"You were seeing her before her shunning was over?"

He shook his head. "No, of course not."

"Well, it doesn't matter now." She lifted her chin. "I wish you many blessings in your marriage." She pushed past him and headed back into the barn.

Mark leaned his back against the barn wall and rubbed his forehead. How could he have been so blind? Why had he allowed his relationship with Franey to get so complicated? Guilt was a snake slithering around his insides.

Closing his eyes, he blew out a deep breath.

—ᘓᕽᘔ—

Priscilla's heart pounded as she stood on the back porch of the house. Mark and Franey were standing close together and talking by the corner of the barn. She couldn't hear what they were saying, but it was obvious that the conversation was emotional and intense.

Mark reached for Franey's arm and leaned in closer to her, and Priscilla tried to swallow back the jealousy that rolled through her. So he *did* still have feelings for Franey. Would he cheat on Priscilla with Franey after they were married?

Acid churned in her stomach. Priscilla wanted a marriage in name only, but she cared if he had feelings for Franey because she didn't want any more humiliation than she'd already had to endure since she returned. How would it look to the community if they found out Mark was seeing Franey behind her back? They'd both be shunned.

Another thought gripped Priscilla. What if Mark told Franey the truth about their marriage? Surely Franey would tell her friends, and then the entire community would know Mark was marrying her not only to avoid being shunned, but to get half of her father's business and some of his land. That was worse than his having an affair.

"Priscilla?"

"*Ya?*" Priscilla turned toward Cindy's curious expression.

"Could you please help me serve the *kaffi?*" Cindy held up a carafe.

"Of course." Priscilla plastered a smile on her face.

"Are you all right?" Cindy asked.

"*Ya*, I'm fine." Priscilla stepped into the house. "Do you want me to take this carafe or fill a second one?" As she busied herself with the task of helping to serve the food, her worries about Mark and Franey taunted her.

_◦◦◦_

"Have you thought about table decorations?" *Mamm* asked as she and Priscilla sat on the back porch later that evening.

"No, not really." Priscilla pushed the glider to life with her toe as she looked toward the swing set where Ethan was going down the slide.

"What's on your mind?"

"Nothing." Priscilla shrugged and cradled her mug of warm tea in her hands.

"Priscilla, I can tell when you're upset. It might help if you talk about it."

"It's *gegisch*, really." Priscilla averted her eyes by studying her plain white mug.

"Why don't you let me be the judge of that?"

Priscilla sighed. "I saw Mark talking to Franey today. They were having what looked like an intimate conversation outside the barn before we had lunch. And, well, it bothered me."

"Why did it bother you? Mark is marrying you, not Franey."

Priscilla pressed her lips together. "You know the truth of why he's marrying me. He's avoiding being shunned. And he's also going to be well off, thanks to *Dat*'s business and land."

Mamm looked unconvinced. "I think he cares about you."

Priscilla gave a sardonic smile. "*Mamm*, I hope you realize nothing happened in the barn that day when *Dat* and John say they 'found' us doing 'inappropriate' things." She made air quotes with her fingers. "We were talking. That's it. Mark and I weren't dating in secret. He doesn't love me."

"But you're *freinden*." *Mamm* patted her leg. "That's a great foundation for a *gut* marriage."

Priscilla clicked her tongue. "We're not close *freinden*. We're just acquaintances trapped together now."

"That's not what I see." *Mamm* gave her a knowing smile. "He cares about you."

"No, he doesn't." *But if only he did . . .*

"Just give it time. It will all work out. The Lord works in mysterious ways."

As Priscilla took a sip of tea, she longed for her mother to be right. But instead, she was certain their marriage was headed for disaster.

NINETEEN

"Sis." Mark approached the van as Laura climbed out of it the following Thursday afternoon. "I didn't know you were planning to visit today."

"Hi. I came to help Priscilla with her dresses for the wedding. She doesn't have long to make them." Laura balanced a cake saver in her hands as she hoisted her purse onto her shoulder.

"Give me that." Mark took the container, and she paid the driver. "That's nice that you offered to help her."

"That's what family is for, right?" Laura smiled up at him. "I'm so glad you're marrying Priscilla. You're going to be perfect for each other."

"*Ya*, we are." He gave a wry smile. "Where's my favorite niece?"

"She's playing at Irma Mae's today. I thought it would be easier if she went there so I could concentrate on helping Priscilla." She pointed to the cake saver. "I just might have brought over a chocolate *kuche* for you."

"Really?" He grinned. "For me?"

"Maybe. But you have to promise me something."

"I'll do anything for your chocolate *kuche*." He shrugged as they walked up the porch steps.

"You have to be extra nice to Priscilla and supportive of her while she makes the wedding plans. You know how stressful wedding planning can be. You've seen me go through it."

He opened the front door, and she stepped through. "Okay."

"Danki." She smiled up at him. "You seem different since you made the decision to get married."

"Oh. Do I?" He lifted his chin and posed. "Am I more handsome? Funnier? Less resistible?"

"Ugh." She swatted his arm, and he could feel her irritation. "You're hopeless."

"That's why you love me. Priscilla is probably upstairs since I hear the sewing machine going. Her *mamm* is in the utility room doing laundry." He pointed toward the kitchen. "Would you like me to put the *kuche* in there for you?"

"Ya. Danki." She gave him a little wave. "I'll see you later."

As Mark set the cake carrier on the counter, his twin's words rattled through his brain.

I'm so glad you're marrying Priscilla. You're going to be perfect for each other.

He shook his head. How could his twin be so blind? This marriage was doomed to fail, but he'd make the best of it. At least Ethan seemed to like him. Ethan was a blessing for certain.

"I'm here to help." Laura slowly sat down in a chair across from Priscilla and rested her hands on her belly, which looked like it already protruded a little more than it had the day before. "Put me to work."

"I'm so *froh* you're here." Priscilla pointed to the notebook on her bed. "I have everyone's measurements there. Do you want to start cutting out Cindy's dress?"

"I'd love to."

Priscilla gathered supplies for Laura and then returned to working on her own dress.

"How are things going for you?" Laura asked. When Priscilla met her gaze, Laura added, "With your *dat*?"

Priscilla shrugged. "Okay, I guess. He still doesn't talk to me much at all, but he's kind to Ethan, which I appreciate."

Laura seemed to study her, and Priscilla looked down at the dress.

"Did Mark tell you I know the truth about why you're getting married?"

"*Ya.*" Priscilla nodded, keeping her eyes focused on the dress. Was Laura going to try to talk Priscilla out of marrying her twin? If she succeeded, what would she say now that the announcement had been made to the community? How could she ever face the bishop again?

"I'm not upset, Priscilla."

"Really?" Priscilla looked up, shocked to find her best friend's smile.

"Why would I be upset? I've been praying for years that Mark would settle down, and he's finally going to. You're a blessing."

"A blessing?" Priscilla shook herself. Had she heard Laura right? "How is being forced to marry me a blessing?"

Laura set the scissors on the desk beside the sewing table. "God has a reason for everything that happens, and he has the perfect plan for each of us. There's a reason why your *dat* and the bishop found you both in the barn."

Priscilla grimaced. "It sounds so bad when you say it that way."

Laura chuckled. "Mark told me what happened, and I know it was innocent."

But I wanted him to kiss me . . .

Priscilla dismissed the unwelcomed thought. "But I'm ruining his life."

"What?" Laura shook her head. "No, you're not. You're forcing him to grow up, and it's about time."

"We should get back to work." Priscilla turned her attention to the dress, and they worked in silence for several minutes.

"You know," Laura began, breaking through the quiet, "Mark is a *gut* man, and he'll take *gut* care of you and Ethan."

Priscilla glanced at her.

"He uses humor and arrogance as a defense mechanism. Deep down, he's just as humble as Jamie. And he's a hard worker."

Priscilla nodded. "I've seen how hard he works here, and he's very kind to Ethan."

Priscilla's thoughts swirled as they turned their attention back to their work.

"I think he cares about Franey," Priscilla blurted.

"What?" Laura's forehead furrowed.

"I saw them talking at church yesterday." Priscilla described their body language. "It was intense."

Laura shook her head. "I don't think he cares about her as anything more than a *freind*. When he told me he was going to marry you, he didn't mention Franey or Ruthann. He talked only about you."

Priscilla was unconvinced.

"What are you thinking right now?" Laura asked.

"I'm wondering how we're going to adjust to living together. How can we be a *gut* example for *mei sohn* if we don't love each other?"

"Give it time. It will all be fine. Just pray about it and ask God to guide your heart and give you patience."

Priscilla nodded and turned back to her sewing machine.

"So what are you considering for table decorations?" Laura

asked. "I was at the market yesterday, and I saw the most gorgeous red candles that would match this material."

They talked about the wedding, and then Laura gave her updates about people they'd both known in school and youth group.

Later they took a break and had cake with her mother and Ethan in the kitchen before Priscilla walked Laura outside to call her driver.

"I had a great time," Laura said as they stood in the driveway waiting for the van.

"I did too." Priscilla hugged her. "*Danki* for helping with the dresses."

"*Gern gschehne.*" Laura grinned. "Soon we'll be *schweschdere.*"

Mark jogged up behind them, his dark trousers and gray shirt speckled with white paint, evidence that he'd been working in the *daadihaus.* "You're leaving, sis?"

"*Ya.* I need to get home and start supper. Irma Mae is going to bring Mollie home soon." Laura pointed to the house. "I left you chocolate *kuche.*"

"*Danki.*" He rubbed his hands together.

Laura turned toward Priscilla. "I have to warn you. You'll probably find yourself baking a lot of chocolate *kuche* after you're married."

"Please." Mark gave Priscilla an adorable smile. "I promise I'll work hard to earn it."

Laura snickered as her driver steered his van up the rock driveway. "I'll see you two soon."

"*Danki* again," Priscilla said. "I'll return the *kuche* saver."

"No hurry." Laura climbed into the van and waved before it headed down the driveway.

"Well, back to work," Mark said when the van was out of sight. "The *daadihaus* isn't going to paint itself." He turned and started up the path to the small house.

"Mark," Priscilla called after him, and he spun toward her. "Would you like to stay for supper?"

He studied her for a moment, and then his lips curved into a smile. "Only if I can have a piece of *mei schweschder's kuche*."

"Of course."

"Great. Then I'll stay."

As he strode toward the house, she tried to imagine their marriage. Would it ever be filled with laughter and love as well as chocolate cakes?

No. A marriage had to be built on a foundation of love. How could love come later? That wasn't how it worked.

With a frown, Priscilla walked back into the house and tried to put the negative thoughts out of her mind, but they lingered there, mocking her as she returned to her sewing project.

"Was *mei schweschder* any help today?" Mark asked as he sat on a rocking chair beside hers on the front porch later that evening.

"*Ya*, she started on Cindy's dress while I worked on mine."

"*Gut*." Mark looked off toward the row of barns, and she longed to read his thoughts.

They had chatted about the wedding and Ethan's day at school during supper, and then he'd helped her father and Ethan take care of the animals while she and her mother cleaned the kitchen.

"How is the painting at the *daadihaus* coming along?" she asked.

"I'm almost done with the first coat." He rested his hands on the arms of the chair. "I'm hoping to finish the second coat before the end of the week. The walls look *gut*."

"Great." She moved the chair back and forth as her thoughts

turned to Franey. While she longed to ask him what they had discussed on Sunday, she didn't want to seem clingy or reveal the jealousy she'd felt. Instead, she stared out toward the barns and hoped he'd say something to kill the awkwardness between them.

"What's bothering you?" he finally asked.

She strangled a moan. That wasn't what she'd hoped he'd say. "Nothing." She forced a smile. "I was thinking about the *daadihaus*."

"No, you weren't." He swiveled toward her and smiled. "You were thinking about something much more interesting than my painting skills." He sat up a little taller. "By the way, I am talented with a paintbrush, in case you were wondering."

Her thoughts moved to Laura's comment earlier that day. Did Mark use humor and arrogance as a defense mechanism? No, she doubted it. He truly believed he was talented and handsome, and he was right.

"*Gut nacht*, Mark." Ethan appeared in the doorway, looking proud. "I said that right, didn't I?"

"You certainly did." Mark grinned at him.

"*Mammi* said I have to take a bath. I'll see you tomorrow when I get home from school." Ethan waved and then disappeared into the house, the storm door clicking shut behind him.

"I need to get going. *Danki* again for supper." Mark stood and held out his hand. Not sure what else to do, she gently shook it. When his skin touched hers, she felt an electrical current zing up her arm. Had she imagined it? If not, had he felt it too?

"*Gern gschehne*." Priscilla stood as Mark started down the steps, surprised she was reluctant to let him go.

TWENTY

A WEEK LATER THE RUMBLE OF A TRUCK ENGINE sounded nearby, and Mark stepped out of the largest barn. The September sun warmed his arms as he walked toward the faded red, late-model Chevrolet pickup bouncing up the driveway.

Confusion sparked as Mark quickened his steps to catch up with the driver. Mark didn't recall Yonnie's mentioning that a customer had made an appointment to come see a horse. In fact, Yonnie and Edna had gone to town for supplies an hour ago, and already home from school, Ethan had tagged along for the promise of ice cream. Yonnie never would have left the farm if he were expecting a customer.

When Mark reached the truck, he tapped on the window.

A man who looked about Mark's age lowered the window and nodded. "Hi." He had dark hair and eyes, and he seemed nervous as he cleared his throat.

"May I help you?" Mark asked.

"Is this the Allgyer family farm?"

"*Ya.*" Mark pointed behind the truck. "The name is on the sign. Are you looking for a horse?"

"No." The man shook his head. "I'm trying to find Priscilla Allgyer. Does she live here by any chance?"

A dark foreboding grabbed Mark by the shoulders. "She might."

"Well, if she does, thank goodness!" The man slapped his hands together. "I've been searching for months. All I knew was her last name and that her father was Amish and sold horses. I can't believe I finally found her. Do you know how many Allgyers there are around here?" He gave a chuckle that sounded forced as he pointed at Mark. "Sure you do, since you're obviously Amish."

"What do you want?" Mark barked the question as alarm burrowed into his gut.

"I need to see her." Trent climbed out of the truck and stood next to it.

"Who are you?"

"I'm Trent Parker." Trent held out his hand in an offer of a handshake, but Mark remained in place, unmoving. "I was hoping to see her. Is she home?"

Mark stiffened as his eyes narrowed. "What are you doing here?" He ground out the words. "You have no right to come here. You're not welcome."

Trent held up his hands as if in surrender. "I'm just here to apologize."

"Don't bother." Mark pointed in the direction of the road. "You need to leave, or I'm going to call the police and have you escorted off this property."

Trent shook his head. "I won't leave until I see Priscilla and my son."

"You don't have the right to call Ethan your son." Mark gripped the truck's door handle. "You need to leave now. I mean it."

"Trent!" Priscilla jogged over to the truck from the house. "What are you doing here?"

Mark's body quaked as he turned toward her. "I just told him to leave. Stay away from him."

"No." She shook her head as she reached for Mark's arm. "Just give me a minute to talk to him."

"Please don't." Mark took her arm and gently steered her away from the truck. "I saw what he did to you. I will not allow him to hurt you again."

"I'm fine." She placed her hands on his biceps as she stared up into his eyes. "I will stand right here and talk to him, but I want you to leave, okay?"

He shook his head. "I can't bring myself to leave you alone with him."

"Mark." She spoke slowly as if he didn't understand the language. "I promise you I will be fine. He's not going to hurt me here, especially in front of you." She nodded toward the barn. "Just go back to work. I'll be only a few minutes, and then I'll make him leave. I'll yell for you if I feel threatened, okay?" She touched his hand, and he enjoyed the feel of her soft skin against his. "I need you to trust me on this."

"Fine." He gave her a curt nod and then glanced past her to where Trent had climbed out of the truck. "If he hurts you . . ."

"Go. I promise you I will be fine."

With fury pumping through his veins, Mark headed toward the barn. When he reached the barn door, he turned, crossed his arms over his chest, and watched Priscilla approach Trent.

He stood ready to jump into action if Trent even reached for her.

—❧—

"What are you doing here?" Priscilla hated the thread of worry in her voice. She couldn't let Trent know how nervous he made her. At least she wasn't as afraid as she thought she'd be if he ever showed up on the farm. Mark's presence made the difference.

211

"I'm here to apologize." He pointed toward her scarred arm. "I'm sorry for everything that happened. I got help, and I stopped drinking. I want to tell you and Ethan that I'm ready to be a family. I'm better, and I will be the father and boyfriend you both deserve."

If only he'd said those words months ago.

No! How could she ever trust him after the way he'd treated her? She deserved better, didn't she?

She shook her head. "It's too late."

"No, it's not." He took a step toward her, and she stepped back, away from him. "I want to make it up to you. I have a steady job now, and I'm looking for a better place for us to live. I'm ready to provide for you. If you and Ethan come with me, you won't even have to work. You can go back to school or stay home. It's up to you." His desperation covered her like a silky, slimy substance.

"No." She lifted her chin and made her voice strong and forceful. "We're not going anywhere with you."

Trent looked around the farm. "Is Ethan in the house?"

"He's not here."

Trent's dark eyes seemed to study her. "You look different. You seem more confident."

She nodded. "I am."

"And you're Amish now, huh?" He grinned. "You looked better in jeans and T-shirts. That bonnet looks uncomfortable. I like your hair down."

"It's a prayer covering." She touched the ties. "You need to go. You've said what you came to say. Get out of here before Mark calls the police." She glanced past him to where Mark stood watch by the barn, his expression unmoving. She'd never seen him look so serious or so angry. It sent uneasiness swirling through all the cells in her body.

Trent turned and stared at Mark. "Is he your new boyfriend?"

He'd raised his voice as Mark took a few steps toward them. Did Trent want Mark to hear?

"He's a family friend." She matched her tone and volume to his, not wanting him to believe he was gaining the upper hand.

Trent studied her for a moment, and her skin felt as if it were crawling. "Where's Ethan?"

"He got home from school early today, so he went to the store with my parents."

"When will he be back?" Trent asked.

"I don't know."

"I want to see him." Trent's expression softened as he lowered his voice. "Please. I really want to see him. I've missed you both so much."

"You should have considered that before you did this to me." She pushed up her sleeve, revealing the puckered skin. "And before you neglected our son. You need to go now."

"But I want to see Ethan."

She shook her head. "Now is not a good time."

"If now isn't a good time, then when is?"

"I don't know." She shrugged. "Let me think about it. I'll call you."

Trent's eyes narrowed, and his jaw tightened. "I have a right to see him. He's my son."

"No, you don't, actually." She lifted her chin again as a sudden surge of confidence swept through her. "Remember how you disappeared just before Ethan was born? You weren't at the birth, and I didn't know if you were ever coming back. Your name isn't even on the birth certificate. That means you have no legal rights to him at all." She pointed to herself. "Besides, if you were so concerned about your son, you would have treated me with respect."

"I've changed. I'll make up for my mistakes." Trent held up his hands. "I told you. I got help and found a decent job."

"Good for you." She nearly spat the words at him.

He pulled his wallet from the back pocket of his jeans. "What if I gave you money? How much do you want?"

"You can't be serious!" Anger flooded her. "You want to buy your way into your son's heart?"

"No." He pulled out a wad of bills. "But I owe you for child support. How much do you want?"

"I don't want any of your money."

"Sure you do." Trent held out the cash, desperation lining his face. "How much?"

"You need to go." Mark sidled up to him.

Priscilla had been so focused on Trent that she hadn't even noticed Mark as he approached.

"You need to go right now." Mark opened the truck door and gestured for Trent to climb in. "Does Priscilla have your number?"

Trent nodded as he put the money back in his wallet. "My number hasn't changed."

Mark nodded. "Good. She'll call you if she decides to allow you to see Ethan. Now go before I make you go."

Trent climbed into the truck and slammed the door. Then he looked between Priscilla and Mark, his gaze finally landing on Mark. "You'd better watch out for her. She's not stable. She'll turn on you too." Then he started the engine and drove away.

Once the truck was out of sight, Priscilla released the breath she'd been holding.

Mark turned toward her, his eyes narrowed. "*Freind?* You told him I'm your *freind*?" Bitterness and frustration radiated off him in waves.

"Mark, please." She held up her hands. "I didn't want him to know any of my personal life."

"Why?" His scowl deepened. "Do I embarrass you?"

"No." She shook her head. "That's not it at all."

"Why didn't you tell him we're engaged?" He gestured toward the road. "Do you still love him?"

She paused, considering her feelings for Trent Parker. "No, but it's complicated."

"You hesitated." He wagged a finger at her. "So you do love him. You love the man who hit you, cut you, and scarred you."

"No, it's not that, but we have a *kind* together. We'll always be tied by Ethan. That's why I couldn't just send him away. You have to understand—"

He held up his hand. "Save it."

As Mark stomped off toward the barn, Priscilla felt frozen between two men and two worlds.

—⸙—

Mark's arms and shoulders throbbed with pain as he hammered another new board into the barn floor with all his might. His jaw ached as he continued to clench it.

The vision of Priscilla talking to Trent filled his mind as anger, raw and raging, drowned him. Why did she tell him Mark was only her friend? Was she hoping Trent would offer to take her and Ethan with him? If he had, would she have gone? Didn't their friendship and her promise to marry Mark mean anything to her?

"Mark!" Ethan scampered into the barn. "I brought you a present. I hope you like chocolate peanut butter ice cream." He stood tall as he held out a little bag.

The anger seemed to dissolve as Mark looked down at the little boy's proud smile. "*Danki.* That's my favorite flavor." He set the hammer and nails on the floor.

"I thought so. Here. Take it." Ethan shook the bag. "It might be melting."

Mark took the bag and opened it. He found a cup of ice cream with a lid and a spoon. "*Danki* for thinking of me."

"Of course I thought of you." Ethan scanned the barn. "Can I help you with the boards? You can show me how."

"You don't have to." Mark took a bite of ice cream, and it melted in his mouth.

"I thought I saw my dad's truck earlier." Ethan picked up the hammer as he spoke. "We were driving toward the farm, and I saw a red truck that looked just like my dad's. It was ahead of us, so I couldn't see who was driving it."

Mark stilled for a moment and then took another bite.

"I told *Mammi* and *Daadi* that it looked like his truck, but they didn't say anything." Ethan swung the hammer around.

"Don't do that," Mark said, warning him. "You might hit yourself in the head or drop it on your foot. Trust me. It hurts when you do that."

Ethan stopped swinging the hammer. "I was thinking about my dad. I wonder if he misses me. It's been a long time since I've talked to him."

"Do you miss him?" Mark took another bite of ice cream.

"Yeah, sometimes I do." Ethan nodded.

"Do you want to go back and live with him?" Mark knew he was probably overstepping his bounds, but he so wanted the boy to say no.

Ethan shook his head. "No, I like it here with you, *Mammi*, and *Daadi*."

"Why don't you want to live with him?"

"Because he's not nice to *mei mamm*. I don't like how he . . . talks to her." Ethan set the hammer on the floor and then looked at Mark again. "Will you be nice to her when we live with you?"

Mark nodded, hoping with all his heart that Ethan had never

seen his father physically abuse his mother. He didn't think so. "I promise I'll always be nice to your *mamm*."

"Good." Ethan picked up two nails. "Show me how to put the new boards on the floor."

"Let me finish my *appeditlich* ice cream first." Mark held up the spoon. "You want a taste?"

"I already tasted it." Ethan smirked.

"Did you really?"

"No, but I made you believe me!" Ethan cackled.

Mark grinned and pointed the spoon at him. "That was a *gut* one. You're learning." Then he poked Ethan's arm. He prayed Priscilla would never take Ethan away from him.

─◦⌘◦─

Priscilla stood by the entrance to her father's large barn. She fingered the skirt of her green dress and chewed her lower lip as she watched Mark kneel on the floor and hammer a new board into place.

His face was lined with frustration and maybe sadness as he worked. The pain in his eyes had haunted her as she and her mother planted flowers in the remaining hour or so before they had to start making their evening meal. She'd hoped he would come out of the barn and talk to her, but she hadn't seen him. The distance between them was tearing her apart, and she'd felt worse and worse as she'd made a meat loaf.

"Mark." Her words were muffled by the loud banging of the hammer echoing through the empty barn. "Mark!"

He stopped working, sat back on his heels, and looked up at her. His handsome face hardened with a frown as he lifted his straw hat and wiped his hand over his brow.

"Are you hungry?" She took a step into the barn. "It's almost suppertime."

"No, Ethan brought me ice cream a little while ago." He turned back to the floor and picked up more nails.

"Wait. I want to talk to you."

His shoulders hunched as he stared down at the floor.

"Please look at me." She walked over to him.

He kept his eyes focused on the floor. "What do you want?"

"I want to apologize and explain myself."

"There's nothing to explain. It's obvious you still love Trent, despite all he did to you." He looked up at her, and the disappointment in his eyes sent guilt spiraling through her.

"That's not true." Her voice sounded strained to her own ears. "When I met Trent, I was lonely, and I was desperate for someone to care about me. I was never *gut* enough in *mei daed*'s eyes, and Trent was the first man who paid attention to me. When we were in youth group, the *buwe* always looked at Laura and Savilla, but none of them gave me a second look. Maybe because I've always been so short or maybe because I wasn't as outgoing and *schee* as your *schweschder* and Savilla. It was as though I was invisible next to them."

Mark's eyebrows drew together as he scowled. "That wasn't true."

"No, it was true. I never felt special, and aside from *mei mammi* and *mei mamm*, I'd never felt anyone love me."

"I'm sure your *dat* loves you, even though he doesn't always treat you well."

She frowned. *You have no idea.*

"He does, Priscilla. He's your *daed*." Mark stood and brushed the dust off his dark trousers. "I know that with the bishop's help, he's forcing you to marry me, but you have to give him time. He's—"

She waved off his comment. "Please, let me finish. Trent

showed up at a time when I was at my lowest and feeling hopeless. He knew what to say to convince me that he cared about me, and I quickly fell for it."

Mark's expression darkened as his eyes locked with hers.

"I felt affection for him, but looking back, I'm not sure it was ever true love. He said he would take care of me, and I was too weak to take care of myself. And then I had Ethan. No matter what, I'll always be connected to Trent because of Ethan."

"Do you want to go back to Trent?" Mark asked, his voice sounding thin and reedy.

Priscilla was almost certain she heard a hint of worry in Mark's voice. Was he jealous of Trent? No, that couldn't be possible. Why would Mark be jealous of Trent when he didn't love her?

"No." She shook her head. "I would never go back to Trent. I don't love him, and I could never trust him after what he did to me." She opened her mouth and then closed it.

"What are you not telling me?"

"I don't know what to do. I don't trust him around Ethan, but he is Ethan's father."

"I don't want him around Ethan at all. If you're asking for my opinion, my answer is no." Mark's concern for Ethan warmed her heart. "Why don't you want Trent to know you're going to marry me?"

"I don't want him to know anything about my life since he's not a part of it anymore."

Mark looked unconvinced.

"That information felt too personal." She reached for him and then pulled her hand back. "I'm not embarrassed by you, Mark. I'm sorry if I hurt you."

He studied her for a moment, and then his frown waned. "I'm not perfect, but I will never hurt you or Ethan."

Her chest swelled with affection at the comment. He was burrowing in, digging in deep, and carving out a piece of her heart. But she didn't feel worthy of a man as good as he was.

"Danki." She looked deep into his blue eyes. Had he forgiven her? "Why don't you come in and eat something? Ice cream is not a healthy meal, and you skipped lunch earlier because you were working so hard."

"No." He shook his head and pointed toward the far end of the barn. "I have plenty of boards to replace. I'll eat something later."

"Okay." She studied his face, hoping he would smile at her. A smile would let her know everything was okay.

But he didn't smile as he picked up the hammer and set to work. She watched him for a few beats and then headed back to the house.

TWENTY-ONE

"How's the sewing going?" Mark leaned against the doorframe of Priscilla's bedroom on Tuesday afternoon of the following week.

She looked up, and her breath stalled in her lungs. Mark's eyes seemed to be a brighter shade of blue, and he somehow seemed taller and more attractive. How did he do that?

She longed to tell him to leave so she could hold back her growing attraction to him. That was the reason she'd been using their conversation about Trent as an excuse to act cool around him.

"I'm sorry." He stepped inside her room and grinned. "Did I startle you?"

"No." She shook her head. "I'm just surprised to see you."

"Why?" He laughed. "You know I work here." He walked over and pointed to the half-finished dress on her sewing table. "So how's it going?"

"Pretty well." She shrugged. "I finished my second one yesterday." She held up the dress. "This will be Sarah Jane's."

"Nice." He touched the material. "You're talented."

"*Danki.*" She hoped he couldn't see her blushing. "Do you need something?"

"That's what I came to ask you." He sat on the chair across from her. "I have to go out for supplies. Do you need anything?"

She paused, and then said, "Would you mind stopping at the Bird-in-Hand Bake Shop?"

His eyes lit up, as if he were happy for the task. "No, not at all. What do you need?"

"I've been craving a large pretzel. Ethan likes them too."

"Okay." He nodded toward her sewing table. "Anything else? Like material or something else you need for the dresses?"

Her eyes moved to her material. She was running low, but did she want to risk sending him to Franey's store without her?

"What is it?" He leaned forward, resting his forearms on his thighs. "I can find it if you write it down. I'm not a complete moron. Just a partial one."

She turned toward him, and his smile widened. "Are you certain you're only partial?"

To her surprise, he laughed.

"What do you need?" he asked again.

"Material and a few more spools of thread. And a few other things. I need to make Ethan a new pair of church trousers since he fell and ripped his only pair." She picked up her notepad and began writing a list. "Everything will be on here."

"Okay." When she was done, he took the list and stood. "I'll be back soon with pretzels and supplies."

"*Danki.*"

He started toward the door.

"Mark."

"*Ya?*" He faced her in the doorway.

"Are you having second thoughts?"

"No, but if you keep asking me, I might develop some."

She gaped at him.

He laughed, and relief threaded through her.

"I'm kidding, so stop looking so worried." He waved at her. "I'll be back soon."

As he disappeared from the doorway, she hoped she hadn't made a mistake sending him off to Franey's father's store alone.

———⟨⟩———

Mark stepped into the fabric store and glanced at the front counter.

When Sadie Liz spotted him, she lifted her hand and waved. "Hi, Mark! I'll be right with you." Then she turned back to the customer in front of her.

Mark wandered around, glancing at Priscilla's list and wondering how he was going to find all the items without help. Asking Priscilla if she needed anything had seemed like a great idea, but he was lost here. He'd rather pick up groceries than try to find his way around a fabric store.

But he'd had an ulterior motive when he went upstairs to check on her earlier today. Priscilla hadn't spoken to him longer than a few minutes since she'd asked him to stay for supper last Thursday and he'd declined. After their conversation in the barn, she'd been cool again, and the atmosphere between them had been strained. It was his fault. He'd had no real reason to assume she would ever go back to Trent.

But the damage had been done. Just yesterday he walked up on the porch while she hung out laundry and chatted about how nice the *daadihaus* looked with the fresh coats of paint. But she only nodded in response. The day before, he'd mentioned how excited Cindy and Sarah Jane were about the wedding, and Priscilla only smiled.

He'd never before had to work so hard to get a woman to talk to him, and this was the woman he was going to marry. That was why he'd used the offer of running errands as a lame excuse to spend a little bit of time with her. He was grateful she hadn't just given him a one-word response—"No."

"How may I help you?" Sadie Liz appeared beside him with a wide smile on her face.

"I need to get these supplies for Priscilla, but I have no idea where to begin." He handed her the list.

Sadie Liz examined the list and then nodded. "I can find all of this for you. I'll be back in a jiffy."

"*Danki.*" Mark spun the display of patterns a few times and then walked over to a wall of quilts.

After a few minutes he walked toward the back. When he heard Franey say his name, he stilled and listened to the conversation taking place in the next aisle.

"Oh *ya,*" Sadie Liz said just loud enough for him to hear. "Mark is so handsome. He could have married any *maedel* in our community."

"That's true," Franey said with a sigh. "I thought for certain he was going to choose me."

"Why do you think he chose Priscilla?" Sadie Liz asked.

A beat went by, and Mark held his breath.

"Go ahead," Sadie Liz encouraged her. "Say what you're thinking. I can tell you want to."

"Well, she already had one *kind* with a man," Franey said. "Maybe they're expecting one together."

"You think she's pregnant?" Sadie Liz exclaimed.

Mark's blood boiled. Clenching his fists at his side, he forced a pleasant expression on his face and headed to the counter at the front of the store. Anger and disappointment swirled in his gut as he waited for Sadie Liz to appear with Priscilla's supplies.

When Franey emerged from a nearby aisle, she smiled, and he nodded a response as he shoved his hands into his pockets.

"Hi, Mark," Franey called as she approached.

"Hello." He hoped he sounded pleasant.

"I have all your supplies," she said as she stepped behind the counter. "You had quite a list."

"Well, Priscilla is busy working on the dresses for the wedding, and Ethan needs a new pair of church trousers." He pulled his wallet from his back pocket as she began ringing up the items.

Sadie Liz appeared beside Franey and began putting the items into bags.

"How's your day going?" Franey asked him.

"Fine. It's been busy." He rested his wallet on the counter. "There's a lot to do on Yonnie's farm. I just finished painting the *daadihaus* earlier this week. Now I'm cleaning the barn and replacing its rotten floor boards for the wedding."

"Oh." Franey's smile grew tight. She rang the last item and told him the price.

Mark handed her the money, and she gave him his change. "Well, I'd better get back to the farm." He smiled. "Priscilla is expecting me to bring her supplies and then a pretzel. She and Ethan love pretzels, and I'm *froh* to bring my future *fraa* the things she loves."

Franey's smile faded.

Sadie Liz nodded. "Oh, I'm certain you are."

"*Danki* for your help." Mark slipped his wallet into his back pocket.

"*Gern gschehne.*" Franey gave him a little wave.

"See you at church," Sadie Liz said.

Mark turned to go, and then he stopped and faced them. "Oh, and by the way, Priscilla and I *are* expecting."

The two women's eyes grew so wide he feared they might fall out of their heads.

"Well, aren't we all *expecting* a cold winter?" He narrowed his eyes. "You do know it's a sin to spread rumors, right? Especially when they're not true."

Franey's mouth dropped open.

Before they had a chance to respond, he stalked out of the store.

"Danki!" Ethan announced as Mark handed him the large pretzel in the kitchen. "This is the perfect afterschool snack."

"Gern gschehne." Mark placed the two bags of supplies on the counter.

"Danki so much." Priscilla came up behind him. "How much do I owe you?"

Mark rolled his eyes. "Please. We're going to share a bank account soon."

"I guess that's true." She turned to Ethan as he sat at the table and ate the pretzel. "How is it?"

"Wunderbaar," he responded with a mouthful.

"You need to swallow before you talk."

Ethan nodded and continued chewing.

"Here's yours." Mark handed her a large pretzel in a wrapper. "I hope it's still warm."

She took the pretzel and smiled. *"Ya,* it is. *Danki."*

He nodded, and she noted the tightness around his mouth. Something was bothering him. Had he seen Franey and regretted his decision to marry Priscilla?

"Is everything okay?" She braced herself for his response and possible rejection.

He nodded. *"Ya."*

"Did you see Franey at the store?"

A strange expression flashed over his features, and it stole her breath for a moment.

"*Ya*. She sends her regards." He jammed his thumb toward the door. "I need to finish unloading the supplies from my buggy. I'll see you later."

"Do you need help?" Ethan asked, his mouth full again.

"Ethan!" Priscilla snapped.

Ethan's shoulders hunched, and he looked down.

"No, but *danki*, Ethan. I've got it." Mark disappeared out the door, leaving her with doubts he'd told her everything there was to tell.

TWENTY-TWO

MARK TOOK A PAPERBACK FROM HIS BOOKSHELF AND ran his fingers over the cover the following Monday night. It was the last book *Mamm* gave him before she died. His eyes stung as he turned it over in his hand. She'd stopped at her favorite bookstore before grocery shopping one day, and when she saw the mystery novel sitting on the end of a display, she thought of Mark. She passed away only a week later, before he'd had a chance to start reading it.

He'd held on to the book since the day she gave it to him, but he couldn't bring himself to even open it. It was as if reading it would somehow erase her memory. It was a silly notion, but he couldn't push it out of his mind.

A knock drew his attention to the doorway of his bedroom where he found Cindy standing with an unsure expression on her face.

"May I come in?" She bit her lower lip.

"*Ya*, of course." He dropped the book into a nearby box. "I was just packing."

"I can't believe you're moving out tomorrow." She gestured at the sea of boxes.

"*Ya*, I know." He grinned. "I bet you thought this day would never come."

"No, I knew it was coming. You've been talking about building your own *haus* for a long time, and I had a feeling you'd wind up getting married first."

"Huh." He set two more books from the shelf into the box. "Why did you assume I'd get married first?"

She shrugged and picked up a softball from one of the boxes. "It was just a feeling I had. I guess since you kept saying you'd never get married, I assumed God had a different plan for you. It seems like his plans always take us by surprise."

"What do you mean?" Mark sat on his desk and faced her.

"It's difficult to explain." She turned the ball over in her hands as she spoke. "Jamie wasn't expecting to meet Kayla and fall in love with her when he did, and then Laura fell in love with Allen when she was trying to make things work with Rudy. God seems to know what's best for us when we think we already have it all figured out."

He nodded as her words soaked through his mind. "What about you?"

"What about me?" Her cheeks flushed. Cindy never seemed to enjoy being the center of attention.

"What do you think God has in store for you?"

"I don't know." She shook her head and looked down at one of his boxes as if avoiding his eyes. She dropped the softball into the box and then turned to the box of books beside it.

"Do you think you'll fall in love and get married like the rest of us, Cindy?"

"I don't know."

"Why not?"

She kept her eyes focused as she fished through the contents of the box.

"Cindy?" He stood. *"Was iss letz?"*

"Nothing's wrong." She looked at him and offered a forced

smile. "I'm just *froh* for you and Priscilla. You're a great couple, and you'll be *gut* together." Her fake smile disappeared. "I'm going to miss you. I'm going to be the last Riehl sibling here."

He sighed. "I know, but I won't be far, and neither is Laura. Jamie and Kayla are just down the path too. We're still family, and we'll see each other all the time." He studied her blue eyes, which seemed to sparkle in the glow of his lanterns. Was she going to cry? His shoulders tightened. He needed to lighten the mood—quick!

"Besides, you get my room since Roy decided to stay in his." He made a sweeping gesture. "You'll finally have your own space, and it's much bigger than the room you share with Sarah Jane."

She shook her head. "It won't be the same without you here." She swiped her fingers over her eyes. "You and Priscilla better come and visit often."

"We will." He paused for a beat as the question he'd longed to ask for years surfaced in his mind. "Do you think you'll ever join the church?"

Her eyes rounded for a fraction of a moment and then returned to normal size. "I don't know."

"It's because we lost her, right?"

She took a step back toward the door. "I should let you finish packing."

"Wait." He reached for her arm. "I didn't mean to upset you. Please don't leave."

She stilled, but her eyes seemed to glimmer with uneasiness.

"I miss *Mamm* too. She's always in the back of my thoughts," Mark admitted. "But you need to remember that she'd want us to move on."

"How?" Cindy's voice was tiny, as if she were six years old again.

"I don't know." He shrugged. "I guess we just keep praying for

strength and then put one foot in front of the other. Our fa has changed and grown, but we're still here. I'm going to m Priscilla, but I'm still your *bruder*. Just like Jamie and Laura still your siblings. You're never going to lose us."

"How do you know that?" A single tear traced down her pi cheek. "We lost *Mamm*."

Mark winced as if she'd rammed a stake into his heart. " know, Cindy, but you can't live in fear. We have to just live." He touched her arm. "I'll be only a phone call away, okay?"

She nodded.

"Come here." He gave her a quick hug. "You're still my favorite youngest *schweschder*."

She laughed. "I'm your only youngest *schweschder*."

"Exactly." He grinned, grateful to see her smile.

She moved toward the door and then turned back. *"Gut nacht."*

"Gut nacht." He lifted his chin as if to wave. "Take *gut* care of my room."

"I will."

As she disappeared into the hallway, Mark hoped Cindy would someday feel comfortable enough to join the church and settle down. It broke his heart to see her still clinging to their mother's memory, but he understood the depth of her grief.

Only God could heal his baby sister's heart, and he prayed that someday soon God would.

―――⟳―――

"For a single guy, you sure have a lot of stuff," Jamie quipped as he set a box on the floor of the small living area of the *daadihaus* the following day.

"I don't have that much stuff. You just like to whine." Mark

glanced around the room, taking in the sofa sitting in front of the fireplace hearth.

Across the room was a small kitchen area, including a table with four chairs. The two bedrooms, a utility room, and a bathroom were all just off the living area. This tiny house would be the home he'd share with Priscilla and Ethan until he and Yonnie began building a larger house. Somehow it already felt like home, which didn't make any sense. Perhaps it was because this would be *his* house. His first house with his new wife.

Mark swallowed against his suddenly parched mouth.

"You're going to be a husband and a *dat* in a little more than two weeks." Jamie looped his arm around Mark's shoulders. "Are you ready for this, little *bruder*?"

Mark rubbed his chin as anxiety filtered through him. "Sure I am. How hard can it be?"

Jamie's laugh was loud, and it annoyed Mark. He shook off his older brother's arm and stepped away from him.

"Can you two quit hugging and get the door?" Roy called as he stood outside the screen door with another box.

"Whoops! Sorry!" Mark rushed over and opened the door. "*Danki*."

"Where does this go?" Roy scooted past him.

"The bedroom." Mark skirted around him and opened the door to the larger bedroom with two dressers. A nightstand sat beside a queen-size bed. He had to ask Priscilla if she had sheets the right size since his sheets would only fit the bed in the other bedroom.

He kneaded the back of his neck as he surveyed the boxes scattered on the floor.

"Is there anything else in the trailer?" Jamie asked.

"No, that's about it." Roy held out his arms. "Do you want us to help you unpack?"

"Are you guys hungry?" Priscilla appeared in the bedroom doorway. She looked beautiful in her gray dress. She scanned the room. "You have a lot of stuff, Mark."

"See?" Jamie exclaimed.

"Don't encourage him," Mark snapped, and they all laughed.

"Come on." She beckoned them. "I made BLTs." Then she disappeared from the bedroom, and Mark heard the screen door close behind her.

"Let's unpack after we eat." Roy rubbed his flat abdomen. "I'm hungry." He headed out the door.

"I am too." Jamie followed him.

Mark sat on the corner of the bed, and it creaked under his weight. Tonight he would spend his first night in this house, a house that would be considered his.

His life was about to change. He shivered. Was he ready to be a husband and father? Did he have the strength and courage to care for a family?

"Hey, Mark!" Roy bellowed from outside. "I'm going to eat your BLT!"

"I'll be right there," Mark called.

He glanced around the bedroom one last time before heading out to meet his younger brother.

Priscilla bit into her BLT sandwich as she sat across from where Mark was sitting between his brothers.

Everyone laughed as Jamie shared a story about a cow named Sassy that learned how to open the gate and trot down the street to visit the neighbor's German shepherd.

"I think she believes she's a dog," Roy chimed in.

"*Ya*, I agree." Jamie chuckled.

Dat and *Mamm* laughed, and Priscilla smiled. It was good to see her father smile.

Priscilla's gaze locked with Mark's, and when he smiled, heat crawled up her neck to her cheeks. She'd never felt that kind of intensity when she was with Trent. Did it mean her feelings for Mark were more genuine and deep? No, that wasn't possible. She didn't know Mark as well as she knew Trent. She was only imagining the depth of her feelings for him.

"I have to meet this cow," Priscilla told Mark. "Would you please take me over to your *dat*'s farm sometime?"

"Sure." Mark picked up his glass of water. "That would be fun. I think Ethan would enjoy meeting Sassy too."

"How's the move going, Mark?" *Mamm* reached for another roll from a platter in the center of the long table.

"He has a lot of stuff," Roy quipped.

Mark groaned. "I'm so tired of hearing that. As if you didn't have a hundred boxes when you moved into *mei dat*'s *haus*."

"That wasn't just my stuff," Roy retorted. "If you remember, *mei mamm* and *schweschder* moved in too."

"So Cindy and Sarah Jane will have their own rooms now, right?" Priscilla asked.

Mark nodded. "Cindy is going to take my room. She's moving in today. That's why *mei dat* stayed home. He's helping her."

"She must be excited to have her own room," *Mamm* said.

Mark's expression darkened as he and Jamie shared a look.

"Oh. Did I say something wrong?" *Mamm* said.

"No." Mark shook his head. "Cindy just has conflicting feelings. I think she misses Jamie and Laura, and now I'm leaving . . ."

Priscilla's eyes stung as she thought of Mark's mom.

"Oh, I understand." *Mamm*'s expression was solemn. "I know you've all had a tough time since you lost your *mamm*. I'm sorry."

Mark looked down at his plate, and an awkward silence filled the kitchen. Priscilla longed to push back her chair, hurry around the table, and hug Mark to take away his pain.

Where had that come from?

"So," Jamie suddenly said, "are we going to help you unpack your boxes and organize your clothes too?"

Mark lifted an eyebrow. "You really want to organize my sock drawer?"

"Well, it's better than mucking stalls," Roy responded.

Everyone laughed, and the tension in the air dissolved.

When the bacon, lettuce, and tomato platters were empty, Priscilla and *Mamm* hopped up from the table and began clearing it.

"I made a chocolate *kuche* too," Priscilla announced as she filled one side of the sink with soapy water.

"You did?" Mark's face lit up. "For me?"

"Well, it's for everyone, Mark." She gave him a feigned pointed look. "You have to share."

He stuck out his lower lip. "Next time, just make one for me."

"If you eat the whole cake by yourself, you'll get fat," Roy said, and everyone laughed again.

"Let me help you." Mark stood. "I'll put on the *kaffi*."

"No, sit." Priscilla waved him off.

"I'm capable of putting on *kaffi*." He came up behind and reached over her head for the percolator.

"I can do it." She turned and bumped into his chest. She breathed in his familiar scent—earth and soap mixed with sandalwood—and his nearness sent a shivery wave over her skin.

Behind him, her father and Jamie became engrossed in a conversation. Trying to concentrate on anything but Mark, she caught something about training horses and how perhaps the techniques could help with the unruly cow.

Mark leaned down to her. "You need to realize I'm not going

to sit on my rear end and let you wait on me." His voice was close to her ear, and heat flooded her senses. "Got it?"

Unable to speak, she nodded.

"Gut." His lips twitched. "So show me where the *kaffi* is."

"Okay." She pointed to the cabinet, and he withdrew the can before setting up the percolator.

As she turned toward the counter to get the cake saver, she looked at her mother, who gave her a knowing smile. Priscilla felt her brow furrow. What was *Mamm's* expression supposed to mean?

"So about that *kuche.*" Mark rubbed his hands together. "Let's see if it's as *gut* as Laura's."

"What?" Priscilla snapped, and he laughed.

"If it's not, then you'll have to make me another one." Mark took the cake saver and set it on the table.

"We'll see about that." She smiled as she gathered plates, utensils, and a knife to cut the cake.

As she set everything on the table, her thoughts moved to Trent once again. She couldn't recall a time when she'd felt so comfortable joking around with him the way she and Mark teased each other. Perhaps this marriage would be easier than she'd imagined.

Still, doubt made her ask a question she couldn't let go. How would they adjust to living together if they weren't in love?

Priscilla balanced a plate of chocolate chip cookies as she descended the porch steps and walked toward the *daadihaus* later that evening. Above her the sunset painted the sky in canary yellow and tangerine.

Ethan's laugh filled the air as she started up the path. Priscilla turned and spotted Mark and Ethan playing catch with a softball.

"That's right." Mark pointed. "Just toss it a little higher."

Ethan stuck out his tongue as if in deep concentration before tossing it to Mark, who caught it with ease.

"Perfect!" Mark smiled, and it lit up his handsome face. "*Gut* job. Try it again." He tossed it back, and Ethan caught it. "Great! You're getting the hang of this."

Priscilla's heart felt like it tripped over itself. She couldn't recall a time when Trent had showed Ethan how to play any sport, aside from sitting in front of a video game console.

"Cookies!" Ethan announced when he spotted Priscilla. "Are those the oatmeal raisin ones you made earlier?"

"Oh no." Mark shook his head as he held up the ball. "She made those for me." He pointed to himself.

"No." Ethan laughed. "She made them for me."

"Actually," Priscilla chimed in, "I made them for everyone, but you have to wash your hands before you can have any." She waved toward the *daadihaus*. "Go on. Wash your hands."

Ethan jogged through the grass and into the house as Mark sidled up to her.

"Just admit it." He swiped a cookie from the plate. "You made them for me."

"You need to wash your hands." She swatted his arm, and he laughed before taking a bite.

"Oh, Priscilla." He groaned. "These are fantastic. You can make them for me every day for the next twenty years."

"Remember what Roy said." She wagged a finger at him. "You'll get fat."

"I don't care. I'll be fat and *froh*." He took another bite.

She couldn't stop her laugh. "That's nice of you to teach Ethan how to play catch."

"He said he likes school, but he's a little intimidated with how much softball they play. You remember how much softball we played in school." He slowed when they reached the porch steps. "I thought I'd give him a few pointers on throwing and catching. We'll work on hitting the ball later. I don't want him to feel embarrassed."

She smiled as Mark went inside, and appreciation filled her. Mark truly cared about her son.

"I want a cookie!" Ethan charged out of the house and grabbed one from the plate.

"Slow down." Priscilla said, warning him. "You'll get a stomach-ache."

Ethan took a bite and then pointed toward the field behind her parents' house. "*Daadi* said that's where he's going to build our *haus*."

Priscilla nodded and turned to Mark when he came back and took another cookie from the platter. She tried to imagine a two-story brick house standing behind her parents' house. It seemed like a foreign concept. When she left, she never imagined coming home and living on her parents' farm.

"Do you want to see my room?" Ethan grabbed her arm.

"What?" Priscilla asked.

"We talked about living in the *daadihaus* earlier," Mark explained. "He helped me finish unpacking."

"Oh," she said before Ethan yanked her toward the porch steps, causing her to teeter.

"Don't knock your *mamm* over," Mark said with a smile. "I don't want her to drop *mei kichlin*."

"They're not all yours," Ethan said, and Mark laughed.

Priscilla followed Ethan into the house, and she spotted a mountain of empty boxes sitting by the hearth.

"I'm going to take all those out tomorrow," Mark said, appearing behind her. "I was just storing them there overnight."

Ethan pulled her into the spare bedroom, which included

a double bed, a dresser, and a nightstand. "This is going to be my room."

"Wow." She forced a smile while wondering how to tell him he wasn't going to sleep alone here. "It's very nice."

"When can I move in?" The smile on his face was as wide as she'd ever seen there.

"Not until after the wedding."

"Oh." His smile faded.

"It's only a couple of weeks away, though." Priscilla held out the plate of cookies. "Why don't you take another one?"

"Okay." Ethan swiped a cookie from the plate and then headed back outside.

"If you'd like to see more of the other bedroom, too, go ahead," Mark told her.

Priscilla put the tray of cookies on the kitchen counter and then stepped into Mark's room. The bed was made with the blue sheets she'd given him, along with a gray, white, and blue lone star quilt. She ran her fingers over the quilt, silently marveling at the beauty and skill sewn into it. Who had made this for him—perhaps his mother or grandmother?

"Cindy gave it to me last Christmas."

She gasped and turned toward the doorway.

"I didn't mean to startle you." Mark stepped into the room.

"It's so *schee*." She touched the quilt again. "She's talented."

"She is."

Priscilla's gaze moved to the corner of the room, where she spotted a box with pieces of wood sticking out of it. She stepped over and picked up a flat piece of wood with a carving of a tree on it. She ran her fingers over the tree and silently marveled at the detail. The tree had leaves and a complete root system under the trunk. It was beautiful.

"I meant to leave that box in *mei dat*'s attic," Mark said. "I'm going to take it over there when I go back."

She looked up at Mark. "Did you make this?"

He shrugged. "*Ya*. It's not very *gut*."

"It *is* very *gut*." She took in his sheepish expression. "When did you start carving wood?"

"I've always done it as sort of a hobby. *Mei daadi* showed me how when I was little. He gave me a set of tools before he passed away, but I've lost a few of the chisels. One of these days I might buy another set, but I really don't have time to carve anymore."

She looked down at the box and flipped through more of his creations, finding a carved picture of a barn and one of a bird. Each one was so detailed, they were lifelike.

"These are incredible. You're so talented." She ran her fingers over the image, as admiration for him rolled through her. "You need to make time to keep doing this. Don't take the box to your *dat*'s."

"Why?"

"These are great. You should keep them, and maybe someday you can teach Ethan how to carve. I think he'd like that."

"Okay."

She set the carvings back into the box and then turned toward him.

He sank onto the corner of the bed and ran his hand over the quilt. "*Danki* for the sheets."

"It's no big deal. I'm glad I found a set that fit this bed." She glanced around the room and suddenly wondered where she would keep her clothes. Would she change in Ethan's room or in here? No, in the bathroom. She trembled at the thought of their wedding night. She'd already told him she would sleep in Ethan's room, but would he insist otherwise?

"What's on your mind?" he asked.

She hoped her expression wouldn't betray her private thoughts as she met his curious eyes.

"You can have this room," he said. "The sofa isn't all that uncomfortable."

"I don't expect you to sleep on the sofa after working hard on the farm all day." She shook her head. "I just have to figure out how to tell Ethan that I'm staying with him." *And then pray he doesn't tell everyone I'm not sleeping with his stepfather.*

"That's why it would be easier if I slept on the sofa and then got up before he did."

She shook her head. "You deserve the bed in here. I'll make do until our new *haus* is built."

He lifted his eyebrows. "Have you always been this stubborn?"

"You know the answer to that." She looked out the window to avoid getting lost in the depths of his gorgeous blue eyes. "I'll just have a talk with Ethan the night before the wedding and explain to him that sometimes *freinden* get married and have separate bedrooms." She hoped Ethan wouldn't ask why she didn't have a separate bedroom when they lived with Trent.

"If that's what you want." Mark sounded resigned.

No, it wasn't what she wanted in a marriage, but it would have to work. Doubt threatened to drown her.

"Mark," she began as she turned to him. "Are you sure—?"

"Really, Priscilla?" He stood. "Do you know how furious *mei bruders* will be if I have to ask them to move all this back to *mei dat's haus*? You heard how much they complained about all my stuff."

She laughed.

His expression became tender. "You have a great smile. I wish I could make you smile more."

She gaped as he turned and left the bedroom.

TWENTY-THREE

T HE NEXT DAY MARK HEARD THE PHONE RINGING
in Yonnie's office as he stepped into the barn. He hurried in and
picked up the receiver.

"Allgyer's Belgian and Dutch Harness Horses," he began.
"This is Mark. How may I help you?"

"I'm trying to reach Priscilla Allgyer," a woman's voice said.
"Do I have the right number?"

"*Ya*, you do. May I ask who's calling?"

"My name is Tammy Larson, and I'm a social worker at
Lancaster General Hospital." The woman hesitated, and dread
pooled in the pit of Mark's gut. "I have her son, Ethan, here."

"What?" Mark gripped the receiver with such force that he
thought it might break in his hand. "Why is Ethan there?"

"May I ask your relationship to the child?"

"I'm going to be his stepfather," Mark explained. "I'm engaged
to his mother. My name is Mark Riehl."

"You're Mark," she said, recognition sounding in her voice.
"Ethan mentioned you. Ethan has been in an accident, but he's
going to be okay."

"I don't understand." Mark heard his voice echo around the
room as it raised a notch. "How was he in an accident?"

"Ethan was walking home from school, and a Mr. Parker, who says he's Ethan's father, convinced him to get into his truck with him."

"Trent." Mark spat out the name as fury burned through his veins.

"Mr. Parker has admitted he'd been drinking. He hit a parked car. Someone called an ambulance, and it brought them both here."

"How is Ethan?" Mark asked, his anger mixing with worry for the boy.

"He's sore." She hesitated. "He seems to have hurt his arm, and I think he's going to need some stitches. Also, I think he'll be bruised from the seat belt. Is his mother home?"

"Yes, she is," Mark said. "Tell Ethan we'll be there as soon as we can."

"Thank you," Tammy said.

Without another word, Mark hung up the phone and ran toward the house.

———— ❦ ————

"Priscilla!" Mark yelled.

Priscilla stilled, and the sewing machine stopped. She took in the frantic thread in Mark's voice as his boots clomped their way up the stairs to her bedroom.

"What?" She jumped up from her sewing table and met him in the hallway.

"We have to go." His eyes were wide as he worked to catch his breath. "We have to leave now."

"Where are we going?" She searched his face for an explanation as her heart began to thump. Something was wrong.

"Everything is going to be fine, but we have to leave for the hospital. Your *dat*'s driver is on his way."

"I don't understand. Why are we going to the hospital?"

He hesitated.

"Tell me!" she begged him.

"Ethan is fine, but he was in an accident." His words were measured.

"What?" Her voice broke as her pulse galloped with fear. "What happened?"

"Just come with me." He took her hand and tugged her toward the stairs.

"Tell me what happened." She squeezed his hand and yanked him back.

"I'll tell you in the car." Mark held on to her hand and led her down the stairs.

Tears began to pour from her eyes as visions of horrible accidents swirled through her mind. Had he been hurt on the playground or been hit by a car while walking home from school? The possibilities were endless, and the anticipation was quickly eating away at her soul.

"What happened to Ethan?" Priscilla demanded when they reached the bottom step. She tugged at his hand and pulled him toward her. "Mark, tell me!"

Mamm appeared in the kitchen doorway, her dark eyes wide with concern. "What's going on?"

"Ethan is fine," Mark began slowly, "but he was in an accident, and a social worker called from the hospital. Your driver should be here soon to take us there."

Mamm clutched her chest. "What happened?"

Mark took a deep breath, and his body shook. He was visibly upset, and that knowledge sent alarm spiraling through Priscilla. She gripped his hand tighter.

"Apparently Trent lured Ethan into his truck when he saw Ethan walking home from school." Mark's expression grew stony as Priscilla gasped. "Trent had been drinking, and he hit a parked car. Ethan is fine according to the social worker, although he's going to be sore. She said he might have hurt his arm and he needs some stitches. He's also bruised from the seat belt, but he's okay." He peered out the window. "Warren is here. Let's go." He nudged Priscilla toward the door.

"I'm coming with you," *Mamm* insisted. "Let me just tell your *dat*."

———✦———

Priscilla hurried into the hospital room behind the nurse, her heart feeling as if it might beat out of her rib cage. She'd spent the drive to the hospital vacillating between fury at Trent and worry for Ethan's well-being.

When they finally arrived at the hospital, she had practically run to the front desk and asked for Ethan. She was grateful that a nurse took her, Mark, and her mother back to see him immediately instead of forcing them to worry in the waiting room.

She blew out a puff of air when she found Ethan sitting on the edge of an exam table, staring up at cartoons on a television set as a young woman sat in a nearby chair. His right arm was in a sling, and a large bandage, stained with bright-red dots, covered his little forehead.

"*Mamm!*" Ethan exclaimed.

"Ethan!" Priscilla hurried over to him. "How are you?"

"My arm hurts, and my head hurts too."

"I'm Tammy, the one who called you," the young woman said as she walked over and shook Priscilla's hand. She looked to be in her midtwenties. "You must be Miss Allgyer."

"*Ya.*" She pointed to Mark. "This is my fiancé, Mark, and my mother, Edna."

Tammy said hello to them.

Mark shook her hand. Then his expression clouded with a frown. "Where's Trent?"

"He's in another room." Tammy nodded toward the doorway. "He's receiving treatment, and the police are going to interview him. They'd like to talk to you as well, Miss Allgyer."

"What happened?" Priscilla turned toward Ethan.

Ethan grimaced. "I was walking home with *mei freinden*, and Dad pulled up next to us. He said he had permission from you to pick me up and take me out for ice cream."

Mark came to stand beside Priscilla, and she could feel the rage coming off him in waves.

Priscilla shook her head. "I never gave him permission to pick you up." Her voice vibrated with anger. She felt a hand on her back and turned toward Mark, who gave her a reassuring expression, as if to calm her.

"I didn't know," Ethan said, his voice cracking. "I thought it was okay."

"It's not your fault." Mark's voice remained even despite his deep frown. "Go on."

"Well, Dad seemed kind of weird," Ethan continued. "His words sounded funny, like they used to sometimes. I asked him if he was okay, and he said he was."

"He was drunk," Priscilla whispered.

"Well, he smelled funny like when he used to drink beer. Then he couldn't drive very well. He was swerving, like this." Ethan pretended he was steering a car with his left hand, and he leaned a little to the right, grimaced, and then leaned to the left. "I started getting scared because he wasn't staying on the right side of the road." His lower lip quivered, and his dark eyes filled with tears.

"It's okay." Priscilla rubbed his back, her heart breaking when he sniffed. "Keep going." She glanced at Mark, and he shook his head. Beside him, *Mamm* sat in a chair and wiped her eyes with a tissue.

"And then he hit a car," Ethan continued, his voice shaking. "The crash was so loud, and I was so scared. My arm hit the door hard, and then the window broke and glass flew into my head."

Ethan shouldn't have even been in a truck without a child's seat to restrain him, let alone in a front seat. When he dissolved in tears, Priscilla gathered him into her arms and fought back her own tears.

"It's okay, Ethan," Priscilla whispered into his dark hair. "You're safe now, and I won't let anyone hurt you again."

"I won't either." Mark was beside her in an instant, and he patted Ethan's left arm. "I'll keep you safe."

Priscilla looked up into Mark's sky-blue eyes and felt such appreciation. He was the father Ethan needed, no matter how make-believe their marriage was.

Mark turned to Tammy. "Will the police charge Trent?"

Tammy nodded toward the doorway. "Could I please speak to you outside?"

Mark gave her a nod, and then turned to Priscilla. "I'm going to step outside with her."

"I want to come with you," she said.

"Go." *Mamm* stepped over to her with a box of tissues. "I'll stay with him." She stood beside Ethan and wiped his eyes with a tissue. "You're safe now, Ethan. We're with you, okay?"

Ethan nodded. "Yeah. I know."

Priscilla walked out into the hallway with Mark and Tammy. Tammy pulled the curtain closed, giving Ethan privacy and blocking his view of them. Then she pointed to a treatment room across the hall. A tall police officer stood outside of it.

"The police are going to ask if you want to bring charges

against Mr. Parker," Tammy said as she looked at Priscilla. "No matter what, he'll be charged with driving under the influence and child endangerment. Pardon me for asking this, but does he have any legal rights to Ethan?"

"No." Priscilla shook her head. "His name isn't even on Ethan's birth certificate."

"Okay. I'm glad to hear that because of his past behavior. In my opinion Mr. Parker is not a safe person. He should never be alone with Ethan."

"How do you know about his past behavior?" Priscilla asked.

"Ethan admitted he's aware that his father drinks and that he's been violent with you. He told me what Mr. Parker did to your arm."

Priscilla gaped. "I never told him about my arm, and I always try to keep it covered."

Tammy offered her a sad smile. "Miss Allgyer, children are more observant than you realize. He probably heard a conversation, saw your arm at some point, and then connected the dots. Plus, he mentioned to me that Mr. Parker made you cry often. He's aware of what went on in your home."

Priscilla nodded as a crippling guilt rained down on her. Her attempts to protect Ethan from his father's abusive behavior had failed.

"It's up to you if you want to bring charges against him since he didn't have permission to take Ethan," Tammy continued. "He has no legal right to the child, and it's evident that he's been abusive to you and harmful to Ethan."

Priscilla nodded as confusion nearly overcame her. Should she ask the police to charge Trent even though it was against her church's beliefs to bring charges against someone? But this was her son. Trent had clearly put Ethan in danger, and the consequences could have been much worse. What if Trent had hit another vehicle head-on? Ethan could have been hurt much worse or even . . .

She swallowed a sob as it bubbled up in her throat.

"Hey." Mark's voice was close to her ear. "I want to talk to you before we see Trent."

"Okay." She took a deep breath and pulled herself together.

Mark turned to Tammy. "I need a minute with Priscilla before we see Trent."

"Okay." Tammy nodded and motioned to the treatment room across the hallway, where the police officer continued to stand guard.

"As I indicated, Mr. Parker is in there," she said. "I'll give you a few minutes to talk to him. Also, the doctor needs your permission to treat Ethan. She wants to take an X-ray of his arm to be sure he has no fractures, and she also needs to stitch his forehead. I'll get her for you."

"Thank you," Priscilla said before she walked away. Then she turned to Mark. The seriousness in his expression caught her off guard for a moment. His face had contorted into a deep frown, and his blue eyes shined as if they were full of tears. His posture was straight, and his hands were balled into fists. He looked as if he might snap into a rage or cry at any second. She'd never seen him so emotional. "What do you want to discuss?"

"Tammy said it's your choice if you want to bring additional charges against him." Mark glanced around the hallway and then lowered his voice. "What if you tell Trent you won't press charges if he promises to stay away from us from now on, and if he doesn't try to stop me from adopting Ethan?"

Speechless, Priscilla stared up at Mark for a moment. "You want to adopt Ethan?"

"*Ya*, if you'll allow me to." His expression held what looked like hope or longing. "I meant it when I told Ethan I would protect him. I want to be his father, for real."

Her heartbeat sputtered. "*Ya*, he needs you." *And I do too.*

"*Gut.*" His gaze moved to the treatment room where Trent was and then back to her. "Do you want me to do the talking? Or do you want to handle it?"

She swallowed. "I think we can both talk. We'll see how it goes."

"Are you okay?" His gaze seemed affectionate as he touched her cheek. She leaned into the gentle caress and pulled strength from him.

"*Ya*, I think I will be. I'm glad you're here." The words tumbled out of her mouth without any forethought.

"I promise we'll get through this," he said.

Mark threaded his fingers with hers, and together they walked to the treatment room. Priscilla squared her shoulders as they approached the officer, who held up his hand to stop them.

"May I help you?" the officer asked.

"My name is Priscilla Allgyer. I'm Ethan Allgyer's mother." Priscilla motioned toward Mark. "This is my fiancé, Mark Riehl. I want to speak to Trent Parker about what he did to my son."

The officer looked between Priscilla and Mark and then nodded. "Go ahead."

"Thank you." Mark released her hand and then touched her back. "We won't be long."

Priscilla pushed back the curtain and stood up taller as her gaze fell on Trent. He sat on another exam table with a bandage above his right eye. An angry, purplish bruise trailed down the right side of his face.

Trent looked at her and Mark, and his lips pursed. He hit a button on a remote control, muting the sound on the television, and then he turned toward them. "I guess you're here to yell at me." He blew out a deep sigh. "I was wrong, and I'm sorry."

Priscilla marched over to him as fury boiled inside her. "That's all you have to say?" She gestured widely. "You lied to my son, told him you had permission to take him, and promised him ice cream. And then you drove drunk with him in your truck and hit a parked vehicle?" Her voice rose. "Now he needs an X-ray on his arm because it could be broken, and he needs stitches on his forehead. There's no excuse for this! I'm thankful he's here to tell me the story."

"I have the right to see him." Trent's eyes narrowed. "He's my son too."

"No, you have no legal right to him," Priscilla snapped. "You're not legally his father. He doesn't have a legal father."

"But that will change soon enough." Mark joined her at the bed, his expression grave.

Trent divided a look between Priscilla and Mark. "What does that mean?"

"It means we have a proposition for you," Mark said. "You're in a lot of trouble. Not only did you drink and drive, but you hurt a young, innocent boy. The social worker told Priscilla she has a right to bring more charges against you."

"Is that so?" Trent snorted. "How can you charge me?"

"You didn't have permission to take Ethan. The police know you've been abusive in the past to both Ethan and Priscilla, and apparently, that's enough to charge you with kidnapping and child endangerment." Mark turned to Priscilla. "Do you want to tell him?"

Priscilla nodded. "If you agree to stay away from Ethan and us from now on, and you don't challenge Mark's plan to adopt Ethan, we won't press charges."

Trent swallowed and then paused for a moment as if

contemplating their offer. Then his eyes focused on Priscilla. "So I guess this means you're marrying this guy?"

"*Ya*, I am." She raised her chin. "We're getting married next week. Mark wants to adopt Ethan, and he'll be the best father Ethan could ever ask for. You're a danger to my son, and I want you to stay away from him."

Trent's expression fell. "I did make a huge mistake. I never should have gotten behind the wheel today." He looked toward the television, and his eyes seemed to mist over. "Can I write to him later? Maybe in a few years?"

Priscilla looked at Mark. "What do you think?"

Mark shrugged. "You can keep the letters for him, and then Ethan can decide when he's older if he wants to read them and respond." His eyes narrowed. "But Trent can't have any other contact with him. No phone calls and no visits."

Priscilla nodded. "I agree." She turned back to Trent. "Will you agree to this?"

"Yeah." Trent nodded. "I won't stand in Mark's way to adopt him."

"Thank you." A weight lifted off Priscilla, and she touched Mark's arm. "We'll be in touch."

"All right," Trent said.

Priscilla and Mark started toward the doorway.

"Priscilla," Trent called, and she looked over her shoulder at him. "For what it's worth, I am sorry."

"Maybe so, but you'll never have another chance to do something like this again," Mark snapped before pushing back the curtain and gesturing for Priscilla to step through the doorway first.

As she and Mark stepped out into the hallway, she could feel to the depth of her bones that Mark would be the father Ethan needed and deserved.

—⟨∞⟩—

"How's Ethan?" *Dat* asked as Priscilla stepped into the kitchen later that evening. He was sitting at the table eating a cookie with a glass of milk.

"He's fine. He's sleeping," she said as she filled a glass with water. "Like *Mamm* told you, he didn't break his arm, but he sprained it, and he has to wear the sling for a couple of weeks. He says the stitches in his forehead are tender, but the doctor said the pain should subside in a few days. He's going to be sore for a while, but all in all, it could have been much worse. I'm grateful God protected him."

Every bone in her body ached after spending the rest of the afternoon at the hospital. She was grateful to have Ethan home and fed. After a bath and a story, he'd fallen asleep.

She was also grateful he'd at least worn a seat belt, and she was even more grateful to have Mark with her during the harrowing experience. He never left her side when they met with the social worker and police or when they brought Ethan home. He'd stayed until Ethan finished his supper, and then he'd gone to the *daadihaus* and promised to see him the next morning.

As soon as they were married, they'd obtain the paperwork for Mark to adopt Ethan. Then they would be a family for real. The notion sent a strange heat through her. Mark seemed to truly love her son.

"How could you allow that to happen to Ethan?"

Priscilla spun toward her father. "What?"

"How could you allow Trent to put Ethan in danger like that?"

"Why are you blaming me for Trent's behavior?" She set her glass on the counter and then stared at him with disbelief. "Trent is the one who lured Ethan into his truck with the promise of ice cream. He lied to Ethan and told him I approved of the visit. I don't see how that's my fault."

Something inside her shattered, and she rolled up the sleeve of her dress to reveal her ugly scars. "Would you like to see what Trent did to me?" She stepped over to him and held out her arm. "He did this one night when he was drinking. He didn't think I'd brought home enough money in tips, and he threw a beer bottle at me."

Dat's eyes rounded as his mouth dropped open.

"Would you like to know why I finally left him?" she asked, her voice sounding more confident than she felt.

He nodded.

"I decided it was time to get *mei sohn* away from him when I came home from work and found Ethan alone. Trent had gone out drinking with his buddies." She pulled her sleeve down over her arm. "That was when I knew it was time to leave, before Trent's behavior became even more erratic and Ethan was in even more danger. So tell me how Trent's behavior is somehow my fault. I was the one who got Ethan away from him."

She took a deep breath as her confidence blossomed and surged through her. "Do you know why I left here and wound up with Trent?"

"Because you couldn't stand to be Amish," *Dat* scoffed.

"No. It was because of you." She wiped away a furious tear. "It was because of how you constantly criticized me and belittled me. I thought I had to get away from here before you broke me. But you didn't break me, and neither did Trent. Neither of you was able to suffocate my spirit despite everything you put me through."

Dat blinked.

She nodded in the direction of the *daadihaus.* "Did Mark tell you he's going to adopt Ethan?"

Dat shook his head. "He didn't."

"*Ya*, he is. He's going to be Ethan's legal father. Trent's name isn't on Ethan's birth certificate, so he has no legal right to him. Still, we told Trent that if he agreed to stay away from us forever and not interfere with the adoption, we won't press charges against him."

"That was a *gut* decision," *Dat* said, and Priscilla bit back her shock at his compliment.

"I thought so too." She set her glass in the sink. "I'm going to bed. *Gut nacht.*"

Before her father could respond, Priscilla dragged herself up the stairs to her bedroom. The weight of her fatigue pressed down on her shoulders as she changed into a nightgown and crawled into bed.

As the events of the terrifying day echoed through her thoughts, she opened her heart and prayed.

Thank you, God, for keeping Ethan safe. Please continue to keep him safe in the days to come.

Then she closed her eyes and allowed exhaustion to pull her into a deep sleep.

TWENTY-FOUR

MARK PUSHED THE PORCH SWING INTO MOTION WITH his toe and breathed in the warm September evening air a week later. Tomorrow his life would change forever. He'd become a married man, and Priscilla would take his name. Soon after that Ethan would officially be his son. Just a short time ago, he'd told Jamie he wasn't ready for marriage or children, and now he would have both.

How had life changed so quickly?

When a horse and buggy came up the driveway, Mark stopped the swing. Were Priscilla or her parents expecting company?

The horse halted, and when his father climbed out of the buggy, Mark felt alarmed. Did *Dat* need help? But why would he come all the way over here when Roy and Jamie both lived on his farm?

Mark hurried down the porch steps and up the path, thankfully noting that his father didn't look worried or upset. "Hi, *Dat*. Do you need something?"

"*Ya*, I need to visit you." *Dat* smiled as he tied the horse to a hitching post.

"Oh." Mark pointed toward the *daadihaus*. "Come on over."

"Great." *Dat* patted Mark on the shoulder as they walked together. "You look *gut*."

"*Danki.*" Mark raised a curious eyebrow. "You haven't seen *mei haus* yet. Come on in."

They climbed the steps together, and Mark welcomed *Dat* into his home.

"So this is it." Mark gestured around the small family room. "This is the *schtupp* and the kitchen." He pointed to the doors. "We have two bedrooms and a small bathroom. And there's a utility room over there for the wringer washer. Yonnie is going to build us a bigger *haus*. He said we can break ground in the spring."

"This is *schee.*" *Dat* walked over to the hearth and touched one of the candles Priscilla had put there as a decoration last week. "A fireplace."

"*Ya.* Priscilla said her *mammi* wanted one." Mark smiled as he thought of the surprise gift he planned to give her tomorrow after the wedding.

"Very nice and homey." *Dat* smiled at him. "It's a *schee* night. Why don't we sit on the porch?"

"Okay." Mark gestured toward the kitchen. "Would you like a glass of water?"

"No, *danki.* I'm fine."

On the porch Mark sat on the swing and *Dat* sat beside him in a rocking chair.

"How's Ethan doing?" *Dat* asked.

Mark's body tensed as he recalled the ordeal Ethan endured the week before. "He's better. The stitches were removed from his forehead on Monday, and the doctor said the scar won't be noticeable. His arm is much better. He wants to stop using the sling, but the doctor says he'll need to wear it at least another week. His bruises are looking better, and he seems to be okay emotionally."

Mark paused before going on. "We've talked about it, and he understands that he didn't do anything wrong. Trent was wrong to lie to get him into the truck, and to drink and then get behind the wheel." He gritted his teeth. "I can't fathom how Trent thought that was okay."

Dat shook his head. "Sometimes people make really stupid decisions. We just have to pray Trent gets the help he needs and never hurts anyone again."

"Ya." Mark nodded and settled back on the swing. A comfortable silence fell between them for a few moments.

"It's not supposed to rain before Sunday," *Dat* finally said. "I think tomorrow is going to be the perfect fall day."

Mark turned toward his father as curiosity gripped him. "Okay, *Dat*. Why are you really here?"

Dat smiled as he looked over at him. "I was surprised when you announced you were getting married. I was certain you'd be a bachelor until you were at least forty."

Mark guffawed. "So you didn't think I'd marry one of my eager *maed*, as Priscilla calls them?"

Dat shook his head. "I knew all along they weren't the *maed* for you."

"Okay." Mark nodded. "And Priscilla?"

Dat leveled his gaze, the humor evaporating from his face. "I know the truth."

"Jamie told you." Mark frowned.

Dat nodded.

Mark sighed as his shoulders deflated. "I should have known," he muttered. Why had he trusted his older brother? He should have trusted only his twin.

"Don't be angry with Jamie. I had suspected something more was going on. I asked him, and he told me the truth." *Dat*'s expression filled with concern. "I wish you had told me."

"So you think I'm making a mistake, and you came over here to try to talk me out of it."

"No, but I'm concerned."

"Why?" Mark hated the thread of doubt that still coiled low in his gut.

"Do you love her?"

Mark rested his elbows on his thighs as he threaded his fingers together. "I'm not sure."

"*Sohn*, I'm not going to lie to you or sugarcoat it," *Dat* began. "Marriage takes patience and compromise. Some days are easier than others. Your *mamm* and I had some challenging times. When the farm had a tough year and money was tight, we took our frustrations out on each other. Some days we hardly spoke, and your *mamm* was so angry with me that she locked herself in our bedroom while she cried."

Dat got a faraway look in his eyes, as if he were clearly seeing those days with Mark's mother. "At times we argued about the *kinner*. She'd tell me I was too tough on you and your *bruder*, and then I'd tell her she spoiled you both." He turned toward Mark and smiled. "Do you remember the time you and Jamie went fishing and came home soaked and covered in mud?"

Mark laughed. "*Ya*, I do. I think I was eight and Jamie was twelve. I had fallen into the pond, and Jamie came in after me. He was afraid I was going to drown."

"You two came into the *haus* and got mud all over the kitchen. Your *mamm* was furious about the mess." *Dat* grinned. "She was even angrier with me because I laughed."

They both broke into cackles, and Mark wiped at his wet eyes.

"Oh, we had some *gut* times." *Dat* sighed. "And we had some tough times, but we got through it because we loved and respected each other." He shook his head. "Florence and I are older, and we've both been married before. So we're more patient than you young folks tend to be. But we disagree at times too."

Mark looked toward Yonnie's house as he tried to imagine what his marriage would be like.

"You have to learn to compromise," *Dat* continued. "A *gut* marriage takes work. The marriage will be *froh* only if you respect Priscilla and are patient with her. Sometimes you won't agree." He paused. "Normally I would have told you all this shortly after you announced your engagement, *sohn*, but I think my suspicions held me back. When Jamie told me the truth today, I decided to come. You and Priscilla have a unique challenge."

Mark rubbed his chin, which would soon be covered in a sprouting beard.

Dat wagged a fat finger at him. "The most important advice is don't go to bed angry. If you do that, your anger will fester overnight, and it will be much worse the next day. Believe me."

"Okay."

Dat's expression softened. "And cherish Priscilla. Show her how much you care about her and Ethan."

Mark heaved a sigh as he worked to memorize all his father's advice.

Leaning over, *Dat* rubbed his shoulder. "You're a *gut* man with a *gut* heart. You'll be a *wunderbaar* husband and *dat*. Just give yourself time to adjust. And remember, all that matters at the end of the day is love."

Mark nodded.

Dat stood. "Well, I suppose I should let you get some sleep."

Mark walked his father to his horse and buggy. "*Danki* for coming to see me."

Dat shook his hand. "I'm proud of you, Mark."

"Why?"

Dat leaned against the buggy. "John was wrong to force you to marry Priscilla when you hadn't done anything wrong."

Mark nodded.

"But Jamie told me you couldn't allow Priscilla to go through more humiliation. You're standing up for what you feel is right, and you're putting Priscilla's reputation and well-being above your own. That shows how mature and selfless you are, and that will make you an even better husband and *daed*." *Dat* gave him a quick hug. "I'm proud of all of *mei kinner*, and your *mamm* would be too."

Tears stung Mark's eyes as he thought of his mother.

"*Gut nacht*," *Dat* said. "I'll see you tomorrow."

"*Gut nacht*."

As his father's buggy disappeared down the driveway, Mark wondered how he would ever live up to the task of being the husband and father *Dat* was certain he could be.

Priscilla pulled up her green window shade and peered toward the *daadihaus*. When she spotted Mark and his father sitting on the porch and laughing in the waning light of evening, she smiled. Had Vernon come to wish Mark well the night before the wedding?

She watched them for a few moments. And then she climbed into bed. She needed to get some extra sleep—if that were even possible. She stared at her dark ceiling, and her heart raced as she imagined the wedding tomorrow. The past five weeks had rushed by at lightning speed.

Although she'd wanted to keep the wedding small, it seemed their entire church district would be there, and of course everyone would stare at her and Mark as they sat at the front of her father's barn. The benches had been delivered on Monday, and Mark, Ethan, and her father finished setting them out last night. The food was prepared and the table decorations were made. Now she just had to make it through the actual wedding.

How was she going to go through the ceremony without trembling?

Her thoughts moved to the pair at the *daadihaus*. She was going to marry Mark Riehl. He'd always been the handsomest boy at school and youth group, and she was going to be his wife. How had that happened?

Rolling to her side, she groaned. She wasn't ready for this, but she didn't have a choice. It seemed she hadn't had a choice in any decision since she'd come back to this community.

"I can do this," she whispered. "I can be strong for Ethan."

She tried to imagine Ethan and Mark together, playing softball and talking on the porch. This was the right decision for her son. Mark would be the father Ethan needed. But what kind of husband would he be to Priscilla?

The question echoed in her mind, but she couldn't expect more than friendship from Mark when she'd made it clear he couldn't expect more than friendship from her.

"I don't think I can do this." Priscilla sat on the corner of her bed and hugged her middle as her stomach soured. She looked up at her mother and shook her head. Tears pricked at her eyes. "I can't."

"You can, and you will." *Mamm's* dark eyes narrowed. "More than a hundred people are in the barn right now. This wedding is going to happen. It's time for you to stand up and go marry Mark Riehl as you planned and promised."

Priscilla's lip quivered. She'd spent nearly the entire night staring at the ceiling and trying to imagine her life with Mark. It all felt surreal—and wrong.

"I can't do it." Priscilla's voice vibrated with her anguish. "I'd rather be shunned. I just can't do it. I can't live a lie."

"It's not a lie. He's already moved into the *daadihaus*, and yesterday I heard your *dat* and him discussing plans for your new *haus*." *Mamm* motioned for her to stand. "Get up. The bishop is going to wonder where you've gone. Do you want rumors to start in the community?"

Priscilla gave a humorless laugh. "You don't think they already have?"

Footsteps echoed in the stairwell, and Priscilla braced herself. Was her father coming to yell at her? She'd cry for sure if he did.

"Priscilla?" Laura looked beautiful as she stood in the doorway clad in the red dress Priscilla made for her. She touched her extending abdomen as she studied Priscilla. "Are you okay?"

"*Ya.*" Priscilla sniffed.

"She's *naerfich*," *Mamm* said, and Priscilla shot her a look.

"Laura, I don't think I can do it." Priscilla shook her head. "I can't be the *fraa* Mark needs or deserves."

Laura clicked her tongue as she sat down beside her and took her hand. "*Ya*, you can, and you will. Mark is blessed to have you."

Priscilla shook her head and rubbed her eyes with her free hand. "No, he's not. I'm a mess, and he should have a better *fraa*."

Looping her arm around Priscilla's shoulders, Laura pulled her in for a hug. "You and Mark are going to have a *wunderbaar* marriage."

"Not if Priscilla refuses to leave her bedroom," *Mamm* snapped before pointing at the clock. "You need to get out to the barn now." She waved her arms in the air and hurried out of the room, muttering something about giving up.

"Priscilla, listen to me," Laura began. "We're all *naerfich* on our wedding day. I saw Mark earlier, and he looked just as nervous as you do."

"Really?" Priscilla looked up at her.

"*Ya.*" Laura smiled and rubbed her back.

"Were you nervous when you married Allen?"

"Oh *ya*." Laura gave a little laugh. "I was a mess, but Cindy and Mark calmed me down."

That knowledge eased something inside of Priscilla.

"Everything will be fine." Laura stood and held out her hand. "Come on. Let's go before the bishop comes looking for you."

Taking a deep breath, Priscilla stood and allowed Laura to thread her fingers with hers. Then she headed toward the stairs and her future as Priscilla Riehl.

TWENTY-FIVE

Priscilla folded her hands, trying to stop them from shaking as she sat at the front of her father's barn. The stale air was nearly unbearable, causing beads of sweat to pool on her temples. She'd do anything for a breeze. If only the barn had windows.

She swiped her hand across her forehead before resting it on the lap of her red dress. Then she glanced across the aisle to where Mark sat next to his attendants—Ethan, Jamie, Walter, and Roy. Mark wore his Sunday best—a crisp white shirt, black vest, black trousers, and black suspenders.

They'd sung a hymn, and then the minister launched into a thirty-minute sermon based on Old Testament stories of marriages. Mark's bright-blue eyes were fixed on the minister as if he were hanging on his every word.

Priscilla, however, couldn't focus or stop her body from trembling. She felt as if she were stuck in a dream. Today her name would change, and she would move into the *daadihaus* later this evening.

Everything in her life was about to change.

She smoothed her quaking hand over the skirt of her red dress as her thoughts turned to the uncertainty of what her future would hold. Was it possible she and Mark could develop affection for each other? Or would their marriage forever remain one of convenience—merely giving Mark a stable future and her a place in the community?

Priscilla shifted in her seat, and the overwhelming awareness of eyes studying her overtook her senses. Glancing to the side, her gaze collided with Mark's. His lips turned up in a tender smile, and she tried to mirror the gesture, but she couldn't. Mark seemed happy, but that could be a ruse. After all, his twin sister said he used humor and arrogance to mask his insecurity. Why had she ever trusted his smiles?

Yet her relationship with Mark had changed from being distant to forging a close friendship. She *had* gained a level of trust in him, and she was so grateful that he loved her son. But they had no foundation of love or trust necessary for a real marriage between them, and they couldn't force those either.

It had seemed to make sense to marry Mark to avoid shunning and to give her son a home, but now reality hit her like a ton of hay bales crashing down from the loft in one of her father's barns. She had to stop this wedding. She had to stand up and tell the bishop that she changed her mind and would face the shunning instead.

And allow Dat *to kick you and Ethan out of his house and off his land forever?*

The voice came from the very back of her brain. No, she couldn't allow that. And she couldn't break her promise to Mark either.

She glanced over at Ethan as he sat beside Mark. Her son looked happy and proud. Was he proud to be part of the Riehl family? He was gaining a stepfather who seemed to cherish him and cousins who loved him. Maybe this was the best choice.

Oh, she was losing her mind! When would she stop feeling so off-kilter?

Laura touched her arm, and Priscilla looked up at her. Laura lifted her eyebrow as if asking if she was okay, and Priscilla nodded. Looking satisfied, Laura turned back toward the minister. Thankfully, he continued to talk, oblivious to their silent conversation.

Beside Laura, Cindy and Sarah Jane looked beautiful in their matching red dresses. They would all be her new sisters.

Priscilla glanced at Mark again when she thought she felt his stare, and he gave her another smile. This time she smiled in return, but her smile faded as fear washed over her once again. She had to make this marriage work for her son's sake, but she didn't know how to be Mark's wife. She only knew how to be Ethan's mother. She breathed around the razor-edged knot of anguish that lodged in her throat.

When the sermon was over, Priscilla bowed her head as the rest of the congregation knelt for silent prayer. When the prayer ended, the bishop stood and began to preach the main sermon. His words were only white noise as the undercurrent of worries that had been rippling inside her continued to grab her attention. She'd packed all her and Ethan's belongings yesterday, and her father and Mark carried the boxes and suitcases to the *daadihaus*, leaving behind only what she and Ethan needed for today.

She still didn't know how she was going to explain to Ethan why she was sleeping in his room.

Suddenly the sermon was over, and Priscilla's body began to shudder anew. She tried to swallow, her throat feeling like sandpaper rubbing together. She glanced up just as the bishop looked between her and Mark. It was time for her to stand with this man so they could declare their desire to be married. She didn't know if she was strong enough to go through with this after all. If she backed out now, would Mark and his family ever forgive her?

Would *Dat*?

"Now here are two in one faith," the bishop said. "Priscilla Elizabeth Allgyer and Mark Abraham Riehl." The bishop asked the congregation if they knew any scriptural reason for the couple not to be married. After a short pause he continued. "If it is your desire to be married, you may in the name of the Lord come forth."

Priscilla turned toward Mark as fear crawled onto her shoulders and dug its claws into her. With a smile, Mark held out his hand. She took it, and he lifted her to her feet. His hand was warm and strong, and when she swayed with dizzying doubt, he held her fast. She peeked up at him as he watched the bishop intently. His face was serious as they took their vows.

Priscilla's heart pounded as the bishop read "A Prayer for Those About to Be Married" from an Amish prayer book called the *Christenpflict*.

Priscilla and Mark sat down for another sermon and another prayer, and she willed herself to concentrate on anything but her doubts. She was safe. Ethan was safe. Their families and the community would be satisfied. That was all that mattered.

After the bishop recited the Lord's Prayer, the congregation stood, and the three-hour service ended with the singing of another hymn.

And then it was official—Priscilla and Mark were married. She thought she might choke on the lump forming in her throat.

The men began rearranging furniture while the women prepared to set out the wedding dinner. Priscilla tried to remember what they were serving. Oh yes. Chicken with stuffing, mashed potatoes with gravy, pepper cabbage, cooked cream of celery, cookies, pie, fruit, Jell-O salad . . . Maybe if she concentrated on the mundane, she'd be okay.

Priscilla stood, and Mark held out his hand again.

"Are you ready?" he asked.

Priscilla stared at him before blinking. Mark Riehl was now

her husband and partner—forever. There was no going back. No changing her mind. She was stuck with Mark, and he was stuck with her. The idea stole her breath.

When will this feel real?

"Are you ready?" His smile drooped as he repeated the question, his hand still held out to her.

"I don't—"

"Priscilla!" Laura came from behind her and hugged her. "Congratulations!"

Cindy was next to offer a hug. "I'm so *froh mei bruder* has finally settled down."

Priscilla glanced at Mark. He was engrossed in a conversation with Jamie and Allen as his father stood beside him and laughed.

Mamm arrived and hugged her as she whispered in her ear. "You made the right decision. You'll be *froh* with Mark. Trust me."

"Welcome to the Riehl family," Kayla said as she squeezed Priscilla's arm. "They are a blessing."

"But no one can spell your name when you're in the *Englisher* world. Just wait until you see a doctor. They think it's spelled R-E-A-L," Florence said. Everyone around her laughed.

"Let's eat!" Ethan said.

Priscilla forced a smile as Ethan tried to tug her toward the food the women were beginning to deliver to the tables. She felt as if she were spinning out of control, and she was ready for the world to slow down and let her off.

⎯⎯⌒⌒⎯⎯

"Congratulations, *sohn*." *Dat* patted Mark's back.

"*Danki*." Mark glanced at Priscilla, who looked stunning in her red dress as she spoke to his sisters. She was his wife. He had a wife! And a son!

"Pretty soon you'll be welcoming a little one too." Jamie smacked Mark on the back.

"What?" Mark looked at his older brother, and everyone laughed.

"You'll have a *boppli* too," Jamie said, explaining slowly as if Mark were a dolt.

"I knew what you meant," Mark said, grousing.

"Don't worry." Allen's smile widened. "*Kinner* are fantastic. I thank God every day for my Mollie." His gaze turned to where Laura stood holding the little girl's hand. "*Kinner* are a blessing. Don't let anyone tell you any differently."

Mark's heart warmed at the thought of having a child with Priscilla. But then he remembered Priscilla's rules from the day they'd met with the bishop.

This is going to be a marriage in name only. We're going to live like two freinden, *not husband and* fraa.

He swallowed back his gripping regret. Any hope for having a real marriage fizzled.

"Don't look so terrified." Allen chuckled. "You'll be a great *dat.*"

"Sure he will." Jamie looped his arm around Mark's shoulder. "If I can be a *dat*, then anyone can."

"Oh, it's not so bad." Walter, his stepbrother, joined their circle. "You just have to have patience and remember that as much as you want to send your *kinner* back, you can't."

Everyone chuckled.

"That's the truth," *Dat* chimed in. "There are days when you'd like to."

Mark laughed and then glanced over at Priscilla. She'd looked terrified during the wedding, and he'd longed to hold her hand and comfort her. He'd prayed she'd relax. Hopefully tonight he could talk to her and promise her that everything would be okay.

While his brothers continued to make jokes, his mind wandered to how he'd stayed awake for hours last night mulling over his father's wise words. He'd concluded that he would do his best to be patient with both Priscilla and Ethan. He'd allow Priscilla to take the lead in their relationship. He'd let her come to him for affection when—and if—she was ready. Until then he'd bide his time and be the best friend he could be without crossing any intimacy lines—even if that meant her having her own bedroom when they moved into the new house next year.

As much as he loathed the idea of living like two friends, he couldn't force her to do anything. He wouldn't abuse her the way Trent had. He would respect her, just as his father advised.

While this marriage hadn't been their choice, he'd do everything possible to make it work. He just prayed Priscilla would do the same.

—ↄ⌀ↄ—

"Gut nacht!" Priscilla waved as Laura and her family climbed into a van.

As the vehicle bounced down the driveway, Priscilla cupped one hand to her mouth to stifle a yawn. The day had been long, and she was ready for bed.

"Ethan is fast asleep," *Mamm* said as she came down the path from the *daadihaus*. She held a Coleman lantern in her hand. "He was worn out from playing with his cousins."

"Ya, he was." Priscilla hugged her sweater to her chest. The night air had cooled as soon as the sun set. "Cindy, Sarah Jane, and I cleaned up most of the food from the barn."

"We'll finish it tomorrow." *Mamm* waved off her worry. "Go on to bed. I'll see you in the morning." She looked past Priscilla and smiled. "There's your husband."

Priscilla's heart seemed to trip over itself at the word *husband.* How long would it take to get used to that? She spun as Mark approached with a lantern from the direction of the barn where the wedding had been held. Still clad in his Sunday clothes, he was more handsome than ever.

Priscilla suddenly remembered the surprise she'd planned for him. She turned to her mother. "Did you leave the package on the counter in the kitchen?"

"Just as you asked." *Mamm* nodded.

"*Danki,*" Priscilla said before turning back toward Mark.

"I was looking for you." Mark waved at her mother. "Are you and Yonnie heading in?"

"*Ya,* we'll finish cleaning up tomorrow." *Mamm* winked at her. "*Gut nacht.*"

Priscilla swallowed a gasp as her mother turned and left.

"Well, I guess we'll turn in." Mark made a sweeping gesture toward the path leading to the *daadihaus.*

Priscilla fell into step beside him as she searched for something to say.

"I meant to tell you earlier that you look beautiful," he said.

She looked up at him.

He laughed. "Why do you look so stunned? You know red is my favorite color on you."

"*Danki.*" She fingered her dress. "Your family was a tremendous help at cleaning up."

"You mean *our* family." He bumped her with his elbow. "They're your family too now."

"I know, but it will take me awhile to get used to that." They headed up the porch steps, and he reached around her to open the door. She stilled as his arm brushed hers, sending shivers dancing up her arm to her shoulder.

He wrenched open the door, and she stepped through. She

pressed her lips together as he closed and locked both the storm door and front door.

"It was a lovely day," she said.

"*Ya*, it was." He turned to face her. "I have a surprise for you."

"Really?" she asked. "I have one for you."

"Okay." He laughed. "You go first."

She crossed to the kitchen counter, picked up the package, and handed it to him.

"What's this?" He turned it over in his hands.

"It's a wedding gift." She shrugged. "It's not much. Just a little something."

"Wow. I never expected this." He opened the package, and then he blew out a puff of air as he stared at the case that held a twelve-piece wood carving chisel set. "Priscilla. You shouldn't have."

"I wanted to get you something, and you mentioned that you'd lost a few of your *daadi*'s chisels." She bit her lower lip. "I hope you like it."

"I love it." He met her gaze and smiled. "*Danki.*"

"*Gern gschehne.*" As she looked into his eyes, something unspoken seemed to pass between them. She sucked in a breath as her body tingled. Did Mark feel it too?

"Your gift." He made a sweeping gesture toward the hearth. "I hope you like it."

She spun, and then she cupped her hand to her mouth again as she took in a beautiful rocking chair sitting by the sofa. "Mark!"

She crossed the room and ran her fingers over the smooth wood. Happy tears filled her eyes.

"Where did you get this?" she asked.

"One of Jamie's firefighter *freinden* makes and repairs furniture, and his *dat* has a store. His name is Leon. I went to town one day to the hardware store, and I stopped in to see him. He had this chair there, and I thought it would be perfect for you to sit by the fire when it gets cold."

"*Danki.*"

"Try it out." He sat on the sofa and gestured toward the rocker.

She sank into it and pushed it into motion. Leaning back, she smiled. "It's perfect. I love it."

"I'm so glad."

They stared at each other as awkwardness permeated the air around them.

Finally, he patted the arm of the sofa. "I'll sleep here. Just let me get my clothes out of the bedroom." He stood and started toward the larger bedroom.

"No." She jumped up from the chair, trailed after him, and pulled him back. "Let me get my clothes, and I'll sleep with Ethan, like we've already discussed."

"Priscilla, I don't feel right letting you sleep with Ethan. It's better if I just sleep on the sofa until we have a bigger *haus.*"

"There's no discussion." She grabbed a lantern from the kitchen counter and headed into the bedroom, where she retrieved her nightgown, slippers, and robe. When she walked back out to the family room, she saw Mark had remained in the same spot as if his shoes were glued to the floor.

She walked over to him and smiled. *"Gut nacht."*

His expression clouded with something that looked like intensity, and her heart hammered. He reached over and cupped his hand to her cheek, and her breath stalled in her lungs. Was he going to kiss her? Her mouth dried.

"I just want you to know," he began, his voice low and husky, sending an unfamiliar tremor through her, "that I'm in this marriage one hundred percent. I'm grateful you're allowing me to adopt Ethan and give him my name. I'll take care of you and Ethan, and I'll do my best to be the husband you deserve."

"Danki." She nodded and held her breath, waiting for his kiss.

"You don't have to thank me." He let his hand drop to his side. *"Gut nacht,* Priscilla." Then he moved past her into the bedroom, the door clicking shut behind him.

Priscilla worked to catch her breath. Her cheeks heated as she covered her forehead with her hand. She'd been certain he was going to kiss her, and she'd wanted him to!

Was this wrong? They weren't in love. Kissing would turn into more, and her heart wasn't prepared to give itself to Mark. How could she when she didn't love him and he didn't love her? Allowing herself to become attached to him would only lead to disaster and heartache.

Forcing herself to push away her confusing feelings, she headed into the bathroom to get ready for bed.

After changing into her nightgown, she gathered her things and tiptoed into Ethan's room before carefully climbing into bed. Ethan rolled onto his stomach, and his soft snores sounded through the darkness.

She moved onto her side and tried to ignore a sudden yearning for her husband.

TWENTY-SIX

PRISCILLA SANK ONTO THE BACKLESS BENCH BETWEEN Laura and Kayla on Sunday morning. Today's service was held at the King family's farm, and Priscilla glanced around at the married women in her section. It felt surreal to sit with these other women when only a couple of weeks ago she had been with Cindy, Sarah Jane, and the rest of the unmarried women.

"So how's married life?" Laura bumped Priscilla's arm with her shoulder. "You seem *froh*. Is everything going well?"

"*Ya.*" Priscilla shrugged. "It's fine."

Laura and Kayla shared a look.

"What?" Priscilla asked.

"You just look really *froh*." Kayla smiled. "I'm glad for you. Mark is a *gut* man, and he'll take *gut* care of you and Ethan."

Priscilla turned toward the rows of married men and found Mark sitting between Ethan and Jamie. She took in his serene face. The past couple of days had been comfortable as they settled into a routine. Mark seemed satisfied with her cooking, and he'd been patient with Ethan, helping him get ready for school Friday morning and allowing him to help with chores when he arrived home and yesterday.

So far her new life had been just fine—better than she'd

expected. But still, something was missing, something she and Mark would never have: a true marriage with love and affection at its core.

Priscilla studied Mark as he turned his attention to his brother beside him. He was even more attractive than usual dressed in his Sunday clothes. Priscilla admitted to herself that she could watch him from afar for hours, but she pulled her attention away and looked down at her apron. She had to find a way to remove these thoughts from her mind.

"*Was iss letz?*" Laura whispered in her ear.

"Nothing." Priscilla sat up straight and lifted the hymnal beside her from the bench. "I'm just preparing my mind for worship."

"Is everything *really* going okay?" Laura asked.

Priscilla glanced to her right. Kayla was speaking to a woman beside her.

"*Ya*, of course." How could she possibly reveal to Mark's twin that she longed for intimacy with him? This was too personal and embarrassing to say out loud.

"I'll listen if you ever need someone to talk to, okay?" Laura said, her blue eyes full of concern.

"I appreciate that. *Danki*." Priscilla fingered her hymnal and then glanced down at Laura's belly. "How are you feeling?"

"Oh, okay." Laura smiled. "I'm just really tired all the time." She nodded toward Kayla. "I can't believe we're both due in a couple of months. It's gone so quickly. Right, Kayla?"

Kayla laughed and shook her head. "No, it feels like I've been pregnant for three years."

They all chuckled.

"It's almost over." Laura smiled. "And then I'll have mine too." She rubbed her belly.

"Have you discussed names?" Priscilla asked.

"*Ya,* we have."

As Laura shared their top choices for names, Priscilla settled into her seat. She was ready to worship God and allow her worries to dissolve.

The service began with a hymn, and Priscilla redirected her thoughts to the present. She joined in as the congregation slowly sang the opening hymn. During the last verse of the second hymn, Priscilla's gaze moved to the back of the barn just as the ministers returned from choosing who would preach. They placed their hats on two hay bales, indicating that the service was about to begin.

As the chosen minister began the first sermon, Priscilla folded her hands in her lap and studied them, but her thoughts turned to Mark and their new life together. She tried her best to keep her focus on the minister, but her stare moved toward the men across the aisle. Mark sat with his head bowed, looking at his lap.

Was he thinking about their first couple of days as husband and wife? Did he already regret his decision to marry her?

Or did he feel the same invisible magnet she felt pulling her to him, causing her to long for a true marriage?

While the minister continued to talk in German, Priscilla lost herself in thoughts of the past couple of months. She'd gone from being shunned to being engaged at lightning speed. Now she was a married woman, joined to a man she'd never considered as a husband. How had her life become so out of control? But she'd never again be in control of her own decisions. Now her husband would make all the decisions for her and her son.

She looked at Kayla's belly and felt a sudden tug. Would she ever have another child? Would she ever give Ethan a brother or sister?

Stop torturing yourself! You told Mark you wanted a marriage without intimacy, and he seems more okay with that than ever.

Priscilla redirected her thoughts to the sermon, taking in the message and concentrating on God. She wondered what God had in store for her, despite what she and Mark currently felt. Did he want her and Mark to have a real marriage? Should she initiate intimacy? No, of course not! If Mark ever wanted to kiss her, he would. It was up to him to initiate any intimacy between them.

The first sermon ended, and Priscilla knelt in silent prayer between her sisters-in-law. She needed God to guide her heart and give her strength. Closing her eyes, she began to pray.

God, I'm still confused. I felt you leading me toward this marriage with Mark, but it still doesn't feel right. Are we supposed to live like two freinden, *instead of husband and* fraa? *I thought we were, but if that's true, why do I feel like something is missing in our marriage? I can't make Mark love me, but I find myself longing for him to kiss me and tell me he loves me. Who am I supposed to be? Am I supposed to be truly his* fraa, *or am I supposed to be married to him in name only? Please show me what my role should be as Priscilla Riehl.*

After the prayers, the deacon read from the Scriptures, and then the hour-long main sermon began. Priscilla looked at Mark once again and found him watching her, his gorgeous blue eyes intense. He nodded, and she smiled in response. She hoped her growing feelings for him weren't written on her face. She couldn't allow him to know if her feelings weren't reciprocated. The rejection would be too painful to endure.

Relief flooded Priscilla when the fifteen-minute kneeling prayer was over. The congregation stood for the benediction and sang the closing hymn. While she sang, her eyes moved to Mark again. She wondered if he could feel her watching him.

Laura touched Priscilla's and Kayla's hands. "I'm ready to serve if you are."

"*Ya,* I am," Kayla said.

With one more glance toward Mark, who was now talking

to Jamie and Ethan, Priscilla followed her sisters-in-law out of the barn.

As she walked up the path to the house, she heard someone call her name. She turned and stopped as Franey hurried after her. Jealousy bubbled up in her throat.

"Could I please talk to you for a moment?" Franey wrung her hands. Was she nervous?

"Of course." Priscilla nodded toward a nearby tree, her curiosity piqued.

"I didn't get a chance to congratulate you at the wedding." Franey gestured toward her. "So congratulations on your marriage."

"*Danki.*" Priscilla folded her arms over her middle and studied her. "What did you really want to say to me?"

Franey cleared her throat and glanced toward the barn before meeting her gaze again. She *was* nervous, and Priscilla almost smiled. How the tables had turned!

"I owe you an apology."

"An apology for what?"

"I said some terrible things when I found out Mark had proposed to you, and I'm embarrassed now. I was jealous, and jealousy is a sin."

Surprised, Priscilla tamped down her own jealousy. "What did you say?"

"It was the day Mark came to the store to buy supplies for you. I was angry. I had thought for years that Mark cared about me, so I was upset when he decided to marry you." Franey swallowed and her eyes gleamed with tears. "After I'd waited patiently for five years, I thought it wouldn't be much longer before he asked me to marry him." She paused and cleared her throat.

"When Sadie Liz came to the back of the store to say Mark was there, we talked about you. Sadie Liz said she didn't know why

Mark had asked you to marry him, and I said that you already had a *kind*, so maybe you were expecting one together." She looked away as her cheeks grew pink.

Priscilla felt her eyes narrow. "How could you make an assumption like that?"

Franey wiped at her eyes as she turned to look at her. "I never should have said that. It was cruel and heartless. And Mark overheard it. He defended you and made me realize I was terrible to say that about you. And I'm very sorry. I hope you can forgive me."

"Mark defended me?"

Franey nodded. *"Ya."*

"How?"

Franey shook her head. "After he paid for your supplies, he told me it was a sin to spread rumors, so I knew he'd heard me." She wiped away a tear. "I'm so sorry. I was terrible. Mark chose you, and I'm *froh* for you both. I really am."

Priscilla nodded as Franey's words soaked through her. Mark had defended her? No one had *ever* defended her until Mark did when her father and John Smucker accused her of inappropriate behavior. And now she was learning Mark had defended her again.

Appreciation swirled through her.

"Do you forgive me?" Franey asked.

"*Ya*, of course I do. *Danki* for being honest."

"*Gern gschehne.*" Franey gave her an awkward hug and then scurried to the house.

As Priscilla glanced toward the barn, she smiled. Maybe Mark did truly care about her. Maybe they did have the seeds of a real marriage.

Her heart soared. She couldn't wait to thank him later.

Priscilla stood on the porch of the *daadihaus* later that afternoon. She rested her hand on the railing as she watched Mark and her father exit the barn together after stowing the buggies.

As Mark came up the path toward her, he smiled and waved. She took in his attractive face and bright, intelligent eyes as Franey's words from earlier filtered through her mind. How did she manage to marry such a good man?

It's a marriage of convenience.

Her smile faded away like ashes on the wind as the words taunted her.

"What's on your mind?" Mark jogged up the steps and came to stand beside her.

"Franey told me something earlier."

"Oh?" His eyebrows rose. "What did she say?"

"She told me what you said to her in the fabric store."

"What do you mean?" He leaned back against the porch railing.

She repeated the conversation as his eyes widened. "You defended me. No one had ever done that for me until you did that day in the barn with my father and the bishop, and now you've done it again."

"Of course I defended you." He stood up straight. "You're *mei fraa*, and I'll always defend you. I hope you'll do the same for me."

"*Danki.*"

His smile returned. He crossed the porch and opened the storm door. "Is any of the chocolate *kuche* left?"

"Only if you haven't finished it."

"Let's have a piece. I'll put on some *kaffi*." He disappeared into the house.

A pang of guilt flashed through Priscilla as she stood on the porch. She didn't deserve a husband as good as Mark, but someday soon he'd realize he needed more than he'd ever want from her.

TWENTY-SEVEN

"COME ON, ETHAN," MARK CALLED FROM THE PORCH. "You're going to be late for school."

Ethan grabbed his lunch box and dashed out the front door.

Mark glanced past him at Priscilla, who smiled and shook her head. She was beautiful today, just as beautiful as every day since they'd married exactly a month ago. There was something in her eyes too. Maybe he was imagining it, but she seemed more at ease this morning and less timid with him.

"Let's go!" Ethan called as he hurried down the path toward the driveway. "*Mei freinden* will be waiting for me, and they don't like it when I'm late."

Mark took longer strides to catch up with him as the cool October breeze wafted over them. "How do you like school these days?"

"It's *gut*." Ethan nodded. "*Mei freinden* and the teacher are nice."

"*Gut*. What's your favorite subject?" Mark asked.

"Math."

"Really?"

"*Ya*." They hurried down the driveway to where his group of friends always met him so they could walk together to school.

When the group of children came into view, Ethan quickened his steps.

"Hey, wait a minute," Mark said.

Ethan stopped and spun.

"Where's my high five?" Mark asked.

"Oh! Sorry!" Ethan giggled as he gave Mark a high five. Then he ran off.

"Have a *gut* day," Mark called after him.

"Thanks, *Dat*!" Ethan tossed over his shoulder with a little wave.

Mark's smile widened at the name. He enjoyed it when Ethan called him *Dat*. He relished being someone's father.

Mark walked back up the driveway and breathed in the crisp air. He smiled as the *daadihaus* came into view.

The past month had been better than he'd expected as he, Priscilla, and Ethan settled into a routine. He enjoyed walking Ethan to meet his friends in the morning and then working with Yonnie during the day. He ate lunch with Priscilla and then returned to chores in the afternoon. Ethan joined him after he returned from school, and then they worked together until supper.

Everything was comfortable—until they went to bed at night. Priscilla continued to sleep in Ethan's room. This shouldn't have surprised Mark since she'd made it clear the day they met with the bishop to schedule the wedding that she wasn't going to consider this a real marriage. He'd had second thoughts on their wedding day when he realized he'd love to have a child with Priscilla, but then he'd accepted her decision. Hadn't he?

So why did it still bother him so much?

He dismissed the question and jogged up the porch steps. He smiled at the fall flowers Priscilla had planted in front of their little house. Just as she'd told him, it was apparent that she loved to work in a garden.

When he stepped into the kitchen, he found Priscilla setting clean dishes into a cabinet.

She looked over her shoulder at him. "Did Ethan make it in time to meet his *freinden*?"

"*Ya*, he did." Mark leaned his hip against the counter beside her. "He told me his favorite subject is math."

She smiled. "That's great."

"I know. He's *schmaert*, like his *mamm*."

She shook her head.

"What?" Mark said. "You were brilliant when you married me."

She groaned and rolled her eyes as he laughed.

"Let's do something fun today," he said.

"Like what?"

"I don't know." He clapped his hands as an idea filled his mind. "Why don't we go on a picnic?"

"A picnic? On a Thursday?" She studied him as if he were crazy. "I have a pile of laundry waiting for me, and you have chores to do. We don't have time for a picnic."

"Come on." He spun her toward him and rested his hands on her shoulders as she peered up at him. "Let's forget our chores for one day."

"What makes you think *mei dat* will let you take a day off?"

"I don't know. Let's just do it." He stared down at her, his eyes locking with hers. His heart kicked as he ran his finger down her soft cheek.

Her eyes widened as she stared up at him. Something unspoken passed between them, and the air around them felt electrified. He was certain to the very depth of his marrow that she felt the attraction too.

This was it. He was going to kiss his wife.

"Priscilla," he whispered as he leaned down.

She sucked in a breath and then stepped away from him. "I need to get started on the laundry."

"What?" He shook himself.

She swiveled away from him and hurriedly disappeared into the utility room.

Mark leaned against the counter and held his breath while working to slow his racing heartbeat. He'd almost kissed her. He had been so close, but then she'd run off.

Face it. She really doesn't want to be more than freinden.

He closed his eyes and took deep breaths until his pulse slowed to a normal rate. Then he headed out the front door, disappointment weighing down his strides as he hurried off to complete his chores.

—⁂—

Priscilla leaned against the utility room door as she drew shallow breaths to slow her racing heart. When Mark spun her to face him and rested his hands on her shoulders, she was certain she was dreaming. But then he'd run his finger down her cheek and whispered her name, and she knew exactly what he was doing. He was going to kiss her.

At first, she'd wanted it. In fact, she'd craved his touch. But then she remembered that Mark wasn't in love with her, and she wasn't the woman he'd wanted. She couldn't allow him to worm his way into her heart only to reject her later when he realized he was disappointed in her. They needed to keep living as friends before they made a mistake they'd both regret.

When Priscilla thought about Mark and Ethan, she admitted the past month had been wonderful. She'd enjoyed witnessing how their relationship was growing as the adoption process progressed. Ethan had started calling Mark *Dat*, and it was obvious Mark enjoyed it because of the smile he wore every time Ethan said it.

Priscilla couldn't jeopardize that by allowing Mark to take their relationship to a deeper level. She had to keep it platonic, no matter how difficult that was.

When she heard the front door click shut, indicating that Mark had gone outside, Priscilla retrieved a laundry basket from the shelf in the utility room and then stepped into the bathroom to gather dirty laundry from the hamper.

Soon she was running clothes through the wringer washer, and her thoughts wandered as she worked. She was grateful Ethan had not only made an easy transition to an Amish school shortly after they'd arrived, but now to living in the *daadihaus*. He had also accepted that Priscilla wanted to sleep in his room until the new house was built. She explained she and Mark preferred sleeping in separate bedrooms, and Ethan never asked any questions, not even when she told him that fact should be just between them. She and Mark didn't need the world to know their marriage wasn't . . . traditional.

As she washed a pair of Mark's trousers, she thought about how her heart had raced when he touched her. She didn't recall feeling that kind of excitement when Trent touched her or kissed her. Did that mean her feelings were deeper for Mark than they'd been in the beginning with Trent?

She dismissed the thought. She couldn't allow herself to fall for Mark. It would never work. Remaining friends was the best solution.

If only she could convince her heart to believe that too.

———⌇———

"How's it going?"

Mark turned toward the barn entrance and found his older brother standing in the doorway. A van he hadn't heard coming sat in the driveway.

"What are you doing here?" Mark leaned the pitchfork against the stall wall and wiped his hands down his trousers.

"Well that's a nice hello." Jamie grinned. "I was out picking up supplies and thought I'd stop by."

Mark shook his hand. "It's *gut* to see you."

"You too." Jamie seemed to study him. "Is something on your mind?"

"No." Mark shook his head and tried to smile, despite the disappointment still eating at him. He'd spent all morning doing hard labor to try to dispel the frustration his wife's rejection had caused him, but it still clung to him like a scratchy wool sweater. "How's Kayla?"

"She's doing well." Jamie's face lit up. "She had a doctor's appointment yesterday, and the due date in a few weeks still seems right."

"Aren't babies early sometimes?" Mark waved him off. "You should be at home."

"It's fine." Jamie shook his head. "Calvin was a week later than expected, and my driver has a cell phone handy. Kayla will call me if she needs me, and I can be there quickly." He leaned back against the barn wall. "How are things with you? How's married life?"

Mark snorted and kicked a stone with the toe of his shoe.

"Uh-oh." Jamie's smile drooped. "What's going on?"

Mark hesitated. Should he be honest with his brother? He longed to keep his confusing feelings to himself, but maybe Jamie could offer some helpful advice. "I was hoping that somehow Priscilla and I could have a real marriage instead of just a marriage in name only. But it's impossible."

"I don't understand." Jamie's brow furrowed.

Mark shared how Priscilla had made it clear long before their wedding that they would never have a real marriage, and how she slept in Ethan's room and shied away from any affection he tried to give her. He ended with telling him what happened earlier.

"She won't even let you kiss her?" Jamie asked.

"No, but I know she cares about me, and I feel like she wants me to kiss her." Mark swallowed as the reality hit him. "I thought I could be okay with this, but it's starting to get to me. I adore Ethan, and I wouldn't mind having a few more *kinner* running around. In fact, I'd love to have more *kinner*, but we'll never have them. This is more difficult than I thought it would be when I agreed to live only as *freinden*."

Jamie folded his arms over his wide chest and pressed his lips together.

"What are you thinking?" Mark asked, hoping his brother held the answers.

"You've never had this problem before, have you?"

Mark rolled his eyes. "That's all you have to say? You want to rub my nose in my failure?"

"No, no. It's not that. I'm just surprised." Jamie grinned. "You're asking me for advice after all those years you taunted me and told me to get married. How does that feel?"

"Forget it." Mark walked over to the stall and picked up the pitchfork. "*Danki* for stopping by."

"Hold on." Jamie followed him. "I'm sorry."

Mark glared at him.

"I'm just a little stunned." Jamie paused. "I think you should give her time. Don't give up on her. Let her come to you. I have a feeling she will."

Mark nodded as hope lit within him. "Okay." He set the pitchfork against the barn wall. "So let her kiss me first, then?"

Jamie shrugged. "Or at least let her give you the cues that she's ready. You'll know when it's time."

"That makes sense." Mark smiled. *"Danki.* Would you like some lunch?"

"Do you think Priscilla will mind?"

"No, but will Kayla worry about you if you're gone too long?"

"She'll be fine."

"All right," Mark said, teasing. "But I don't want to hear about it if you get into trouble."

___⌒x⌒___

Priscilla climbed out of the shower and dried off before dressing in her warmest nightgown. Now that it was November, the temperature had dropped, and she shivered as she pulled on her pink terrycloth robe. She stared at her reflection in the bright-yellow light of the lantern and then combed her waist-length, dark-brown hair.

After brushing her teeth she opened the bathroom door and was greeted by the pop and hiss of the fire in the fireplace. Her eyes adjusted in the dark, and she spotted Mark sitting on the sofa, staring into the flames.

Regret settled over her as she recalled the two weeks since she'd rejected Mark when he'd tried to kiss her. He seemed to be pulling away from her ever since that day, and she had longed to go back in time and replay that event with a different ending. But the thought of allowing Mark to kiss her also frightened her. What if a kiss wasn't all she'd imagined? What if a kiss turned into more and she wasn't ready for it? Would he have stopped if she'd asked him to slow down?

"Come sit by me." Mark had seen her, and his voice was gentle. "There's a seat by the hearth for you."

"Okay." She crossed the room, and instead of sitting in the rocking chair, she sat down on the sofa beside him. She stared into the fire as its heat surrounded her like a soft blanket.

"I see why your *mammi* wanted a fireplace." Mark shifted on the sofa, moving away from her. "It's not only warm but soothing after a long day."

"It is." She looked toward Ethan's bedroom door.

"He's asleep," Mark said as if reading her thoughts. "I checked on him while you were in the shower."

"I can't believe Thanksgiving is in three weeks."

"I know." Mark rested his elbow on the sofa arm. "Florence wants to know if we're coming over for a meal."

"Do you want to?" She turned toward him. His handsome face was lit by the glow of the fire, making his chiseled features, coupled with his sprouting light-brown beard, even more striking.

"It's up to you." Mark shrugged. "Your parents could come too. Florence loves being surrounded by family."

"I'll ask *mei mamm* if she and *Dat* would like to have Thanksgiving dinner at your *dat's haus*."

"Okay."

A hush fell over the room, and Priscilla felt a tug on her scalp. When she turned, she was surprised to see Mark fiddling with a strand of her hair.

"What are you doing?" she asked, trying not to laugh.

"Sorry." He grinned. "I just wanted to touch your hair. It seemed to be taunting me when it hit my hand."

She suddenly felt the wall around her heart crumbling as she looked into her husband's kind eyes. She longed to let him in and tell him everything about her past. She *needed* to let him in. Was it time to trust him?

"Are you all right?" He anchored a tendril of hair behind her ear.

"*Ya.*" She nodded. "I want to tell you something."

"Okay."

"It's about Trent."

A muscle tensed in his jaw. "Go on."

"I didn't tell you everything when we were in the barn that day," she said, her voice trembling. "When Trent lost his job, he changed. He became angry and agitated." She took a ragged breath.

"Take your time." Mark moved his fingers across her back and over her shoulder, and his touch gave her the strength to go on.

"I kept working. In fact, I took double shifts and filled in for my coworkers to try to keep food on our table and pay our rent. One night I came home and found Ethan sleeping on the sofa. I think he was about three years old. Trent was drunk and sitting in his recliner. There were dirty dishes in the sink and the trash was overflowing."

Her voice sounded foreign to her own ears, too shaky and high-pitched. "I was furious, and I told him I was tired of both working and taking care of the *haus*. I said it was time for him to do his part. That was the first time he hit me. He smacked me so hard I fell backward and hit my head on the wall. I'd never been so afraid in my life."

Mark blew out a deep breath and then pinched the bridge of his nose. "How dare he hurt you like that." He pulled her against his chest, and she rested her head on his shoulder.

"He was volatile, and I never knew what would set him off. I felt like I was walking on eggshells every time I walked into the room."

Mark kissed the top of her head. "I'm so sorry."

She stared into the fire as she spoke. "Trent never hit Ethan, but he used to yell at him. The day I realized I had to get Ethan away from him was the day I came home from work and found

Ethan alone. Trent had gone out drinking with his buddies. He'd chosen alcohol over our *sohn*'s safety."

Her lower lip quivered. "I couldn't believe he had done that. That was when I decided I had to leave. I couldn't stay there and give him the chance to hurt Ethan."

She took a trembling breath. "I knew if I stayed, not only was Trent likely to endanger Ethan again, but he could turn his violence on him too. I couldn't put *mei sohn* in danger. It's my job to protect him. I can take it, but I can't let someone hurt *mei kind*. If I had been a better *mutter*, I would have escaped with Ethan before I finally snuck out one day when Trent was out with his buddies. But I was afraid. I should have been stronger and left sooner.

"That was when I came home and found you here." Tears splattered down her cheeks as sobs racked her body.

"Shh. It's okay." Mark pulled her against him, and she cried onto his shoulder, soaking his white T-shirt. "You're safe now. You and Ethan never have to deal with Trent again. I'll never let anyone hurt you. I promise you. I'll protect you and Ethan for the rest of my life."

She sniffed as she rested her cheek against his shoulder. *"Danki."*

"Why are you thanking me?" He looked down at her. "I haven't done anything."

"You're wrong. You've done everything. You've given Ethan and me a safe home."

"I'm *froh* to do it." He released her from the hug, and she remained beside him.

They stared at each other, and her breath hitched. She suddenly felt closer to him than she'd felt to anyone in her life. Mark had become important to her. He had become her closest confidant.

"I should get to bed." He stood and then gestured toward the fire. "I put a big log on it, and it should last awhile. I'll set my alarm and check on it in the middle of the night so we don't freeze." He started toward his bedroom. When he reached the door, he turned and faced her. *"Gut nacht."*

"Gut nacht," she said before he disappeared into his bedroom, leaving her alone by the hearth.

TWENTY-EIGHT

MARK HUMMED TO HIMSELF AS HE FINISHED FEED-
ing the horses. He thought about how Priscilla had seemed to
warm up to him in the month since she told him about leaving
Trent. Jamie's plan of allowing her to come to him seemed to be
working.

Last week Priscilla, Ethan, her parents, and Mark had eaten
Thanksgiving dinner at his father's house with the rest of his
family. Priscilla had seemed to enjoy being there, and she'd
smiled and laughed as the Riehl siblings told stories about their
childhood.

She had also taken his hand when they walked to his buggy,
and after they arrived home and put Ethan to bed, they had sat in
front of the hearth and talked until late into the night.

They still hadn't kissed, but they were slowly getting closer
and acting more like a couple.

If only she'd allow him to kiss her, but he was determined to
let her come to him first.

When Mark heard Yonnie's phone ring, he jogged into the
office and picked up the receiver.

"Allgyer's Belgian and Dutch Harness Horses," Mark said.
"This is Mark."

"Mark!" His stepmother's voice was loud in his ear. "It's Florence."

"*Mamm*," Mark said as alarm gripped him. *"Was iss letz?"*

"Kayla is having her *boppli*," Florence gushed. "The midwife is at their *haus* now."

"Really?" Mark realized he was grinning. "That's *wunderbaar*. Would you please call me after the *boppli* is born?"

"Of course."

"Danki." Mark hung up the phone and jogged to the house to tell Priscilla the news.

───❧───

"Priscilla!"

"Ya?" Priscilla looked up from her sewing machine when she heard someone running toward her former bedroom. Her mother had been happy to let her use it until she had her own sewing room in her new house.

Mark burst through the doorway, leaned against the wall, and panted to catch his breath. "Kayla is having her *boppli*."

"Really?" She jumped up and closed the distance between them. "She's in labor right now?"

"Ya. Florence is going to call back after the *boppli* is born." He gave a little chuckle. *"Mei bruder* is going to have two *kinner* before the day is over." He scrubbed his hand over his short beard. "I can't believe how much life has changed this year. I'm married now, and *mei bruder* is going to have his second *kind*. It seems like just yesterday that Jamie and I were kids, fishing together at the pond."

She studied him, admiring how his beard made him look even more handsome and mature. What would it be like to have a child with him?

That will never happen. Let that dream go, Priscilla! Just because you and Mark are getting closer as friends doesn't mean he'll ever love you.

She looked away and cleared her throat. "Let me know when Florence calls you back."

"I will. We can go visit them in a few days after things settle down."

"That sounds *gut*." She went back to work as Mark disappeared into the hallway.

As Priscilla, Mark, and Ethan climbed Jamie's porch steps three days later, Priscilla held a gift bag containing diapers and the pink baby blanket she'd made for her new niece. Despite a cold breeze, Jamie sat out on the porch with his father, Roy, and Allen.

"Congratulations." Mark shook Jamie's gloved hand. "How does it feel to have two *kinner*?"

"I'm not sure yet." Jamie's eyes widened. "Ask me in another month."

Everyone laughed.

"Congratulations." Priscilla shook his hand, and Ethan followed suit.

"Is Mollie here?" Ethan asked.

"*Ya*." Allen pointed toward the front door. "She's playing in the *schtupp* with Calvin. Cindy, Sarah Jane, and her *mammi* are there too. You should go join them."

Ethan looked up at Priscilla. "Is it okay?"

"Of course," Priscilla told him.

"Laura is upstairs with Kayla," Allen said.

"*Danki*." Priscilla looked at Mark. "I'm going to go see them."

"I'll be out here," Mark told her before sitting in a rocking chair next to his older brother.

Priscilla climbed the stairs and found her way to the nursery, where Laura sat in a rocker feeding the newborn a bottle.

"Hi," Kayla said as Priscilla stepped into the room.

"Congratulations." Priscilla handed her the bag. "I brought you a little something."

Kayla opened the bag and pulled out the pack of diapers and pink blanket. "Oh, *danki*." She hugged Priscilla.

"*Gern gschehne.*"

"Give me your coat," Kayla said, and Priscilla slipped it off. Kayla set it on the changing table.

"How is she?" Priscilla asked, leaning down to see the baby's little face and shock of golden-blond hair, just like Kayla's and Calvin's.

"She's precious." Laura held her up. "This is Alice Dorothy."

Priscilla smiled as she looked between Laura and Kayla. "Dorothy after your *mamm*?" she asked Laura.

"*Ya.*" Laura eyes grew bright with tears.

"That's beautiful." Priscilla's eyes stung with her own threatening tears.

"Would you like to hold her?" Laura held up the baby.

"I'd love to." Priscilla took the baby and the bottle as Laura stood.

"Sit." Laura gestured toward the chair.

"*Danki.*" Priscilla sat down, and Laura slipped a burp cloth onto Priscilla's shoulder. As she fed Alice, the baby made little grunting noises and stared up at her.

An overwhelming sense of longing and regret swallowed Priscilla whole as the reality of her pretend marriage gripped her. She would never experience having a baby with Mark. She'd never pick out names with him or see his reaction as he held his child in his arms for the first time. They would never watch their child learn to walk or speak or give them hugs.

She craved those things and more. She wanted to have all of them with Mark, and only Mark. She couldn't imagine being another man's wife. She enjoyed sharing a home with him and eating her meals with him. She cherished his smile, his laugh, his sense of humor. She loved how he interacted with Ethan. He was a good man, a wonderful father, and a fantastic husband.

He had become important to her. He was her first thought in the morning and her last thought before she fell asleep.

And then it hit her. She'd fallen in love with Mark. She truly loved him to the depth of her soul.

An ache opened in her chest and spread until she had what felt like a gaping hole in her heart. Tears, hot and swift, flowed down her cheeks.

"Priscilla." Laura touched her arm. "Are you okay?"

"*Was iss letz?*" Kayla asked.

Priscilla tried to catch her breath.

"It's okay." Kayla's voice was caring. "You'll have one soon. Sometimes it takes time to get pregnant."

"That's right." Laura smiled. "I've had two miscarriages since Allen and I got married, but everything has turned out fine so far with this one." She touched her protruding belly. "I'm due in the next few weeks. You'll be next. Just pray about it."

"No, no, I won't be." Priscilla held Alice out toward Kayla. "Please take her. I'm sorry."

Kayla took her baby, and Priscilla started for the door. Her hurt ran so deep that she feared she might drown in it.

"Wait." Laura took her arm and stopped her. "Talk to us."

"What's going on?" Kayla asked, her blue eyes wide.

"She doesn't know?" Priscilla asked Laura.

Laura shook her head. "I never told her."

"What don't I know?" A thread of annoyance sounded in Kayla's voice.

"My marriage is a sham. We got married to avoid being shunned." Priscilla quickly shared the events that led to her marriage to Mark, and Kayla listened with her eyes wide. "We don't live as a married couple. We've never even kissed, and I stay in Ethan's room at night." She pointed to Alice. "I'll never have the joy of having a *boppli* with Mark."

"This is all a joke, right?" Kayla's gaze bounced between Laura and Priscilla.

"Why would I joke about this?" Priscilla asked before wiping her eyes and blowing her nose with a tissue.

"Because Mark adopted Ethan, and you two are obviously in love." Kayla sank into the rocking chair. "I can see it when you're together."

"What?" Priscilla asked.

"Just last week at Thanksgiving dinner, I noticed how you and Mark smile at each other, and I saw you holding hands when you walked out to his buggy together." Kayla lifted Alice to her shoulder and rubbed her back. "You love each other."

Priscilla shook her head. "We're just *freinden* who got married. He married me so he wouldn't be shunned. And he wanted half of *mei dat*'s business and a *haus* too."

"That's not true." Laura's expression was serious. "He wanted to save your reputation. When he told me he was going to marry you, he never mentioned his own needs or wants. He talked only about doing what was right for you."

Priscilla shook her head as irritation overtook her. "I can't believe that."

"It's true," Laura said, insisting.

"No. Mark told me he wasn't ready to get married. He puts on a show in front of your family so he can convince you he's *froh*."

"No, Kayla is right," Laura said. "*Mei bruder* never would have asked to adopt Ethan if he didn't love both of you. He *is* in love with you. He's just too dense to realize it and tell you how he truly feels."

Priscilla shook her head as her eyes filled with fresh tears. "He doesn't love me. Except for gaining land and a business, his life is ruined. I ruined it by trapping him."

"Priscilla, listen to me." Laura placed her hands on Priscilla's biceps. "Mark loves you. He's never acted this way about any other *maedel*, and he's had a group of them following him since he was sixteen. *Mei bruder* would lay down his life for you and Ethan. His feelings are real." She touched her collarbone. "I can tell because we're twins. We feel things for each other."

Priscilla cleared her throat and mopped her face. "I'm sorry. I didn't mean to get so emotional."

"It's okay." Laura released her arms and smiled. "Trust me. Everything will be fine."

Priscilla wanted to believe her, but she couldn't. Yet she knew one thing for certain—she couldn't stand another day in a loveless marriage. She had to find a way out before she suffocated from her growing loneliness and disappointment.

"Where's my new niece?" Mark asked as he stepped into the nursery.

"She's right here." Laura walked over and held up the baby.

"Aww." Mark touched her little head. "Look at you." He glanced at Priscilla as she stood in the corner with Kayla. Her eyes looked red and puffy. Had she been crying? His shoulders tightened at the thought.

"Do you want to hold her?" Laura held her toward Mark.

"No, no." Mark shook his head.

"You won't break her." Kayla chuckled. "You held Calvin."

"*Ya*, but Calvin is a *bu*. I might break a *maedel*."

Laura rolled her eyes. "Just take her."

"All right." Mark held out his arms, and Laura situated the baby in them. He gazed down at her, taking in her little pink nose and pretty blue eyes. When he heard a sniff, he looked across the room and found Priscilla wiping her eyes. "Are you okay?"

"*Ya*." Priscilla gave him a watery smile. "*Bopplin* make me cry." She ripped a tissue out of a nearby box and blotted her eyes.

"Would you like to come downstairs with me?" Kayla asked Priscilla. "I have a *kuche* to share, and we can make *kaffi* too."

"*Ya*." Priscilla seemed to jump at the chance to leave the room. She followed Kayla into the hallway without giving Mark a second look.

Something was wrong. He could feel it in his bones.

Once they were gone, he looked at Laura. "What's going on?"

Laura's expression clouded. "You need to ask your *fraa*."

Laura's eerie warning haunted Mark throughout the evening as they visited with Jamie, Kayla, and the rest of their family. Priscilla seemed to avoid Mark's gaze as they ate cake and drank coffee in the kitchen. While she spoke to the women at the table, she gave him those same one-word responses to any questions he asked her. He couldn't fathom what he'd done wrong, but he had to find out before the worry ate him from the inside out.

When they finally climbed into the buggy to go home, he was determined to get her to talk to him.

She shivered and covered herself with a quilt as Mark guided the buggy toward the road.

"Are you okay?" Mark asked, lowering his voice as he gave her a quick glance. He didn't want Ethan to worry about her too.

"*Ya.*"

"You don't look okay," Mark continued. "You've been quiet all evening."

"I'm just tired."

"It seems like more than that," he said, prodding her.

"It's not." She kept her gaze fixed on the road ahead.

Frustration coursed through him. She was upset about something, and he needed to know what it was so he could fix it. Ethan started chatting about one of Mollie's toys, but an awkward silence remained between Mark and Priscilla.

When they entered the house, he set to building a fire while Priscilla got Ethan ready for bed. When Ethan was down for the night, she disappeared into the bathroom for a while. She emerged a while later dressed in her nightgown and robe with a scarf shielding her beautiful, thick, dark hair.

"Did you have a *gut* time tonight?" Mark walked over to her.

"*Ya*, I did." She looked down at her slippers. "Did you?"

"Look at me." He slipped his finger under her chin and lifted her face so she had to gaze into his eyes. "Talk to me. Something is bothering you. I can feel it."

"I'm fine." Her voice was hoarse, as if she'd screamed for hours. "I'm just really tired, okay? Please let me go to bed."

The desperation in her voice nearly sliced him in two.

"Okay." He studied her eyes, finding pain there. "You know you can talk to me, right?"

She nodded, but she didn't look convinced.

"I'll always listen, no matter how painful it is for me to hear."

Her lower lip trembled, and she pulled away from him. "*Gut nacht.*" She slipped through Ethan's bedroom door and closed it behind her.

Mark sank onto the sofa and stared at the fire. He turned toward her bedroom door and considered going in and demanding that she speak to him. But he didn't want to frighten her or Ethan. He couldn't lose her trust or risk her thinking he would become abusive like Trent.

Still, he longed to know what was in her heart. He wanted to help her.

Deep in his soul he feared she was building a new wall to keep him away, even after they'd come so far.

TWENTY-NINE

PRISCILLA STARED UP AT THE CEILING AS ETHAN'S soft snores filled the room. She tried to sleep, but her thoughts roared through her mind like a cyclone. Laura and Kayla were so wrong, and she couldn't live like this anymore. She had to leave. She had to give Mark his freedom. But how? Where would she go?

She had some money saved. If her mother loaned her more, she could find a place to live and a job. She could work as a waitress or a seamstress to support herself and Ethan, and then she could pay her mother back.

Anticipation buzzed like wings of hummingbirds. That might work. She just had to talk to her mother.

She turned toward Ethan. He was fast asleep. She could sneak out now and see if her mother was awake. Some nights her mother couldn't sleep and sat in the family room to read for a while. She prayed that was the case tonight.

She grabbed the lantern off the nightstand and slowly cracked the door. When she found the sofa empty, she pushed the door open, slipped on her boots, pulled on her coat, and set out into the cold night air.

She spotted a light on in her mother's kitchen and walked faster. She climbed the porch steps and knocked on the door.

When the door opened, her mother's eyes widened as she pushed open the storm door. "What are you doing here?"

"I need to talk to you. May I come in?"

"Ya." Mamm waved her in, and they sat down at the kitchen table together. "What's going on?"

"I was wondering if I could borrow some money from you."

"Why?" *Mamm* eyed her with suspicion.

"I can't live a lie anymore. My marriage is a sham. There's no love and no intimacy. Today I met Kayla's new *boppli*, and I realized that this pretend marriage is slowly killing me." When her eyes filled with tears, Priscilla grabbed a paper napkin from the holder in the center of the table. "I can't stay with Mark without being his *fraa* for real. I know you have money saved up from your seamstress jobs. May I please borrow it so I can take Ethan somewhere and give him a stable home?"

"You want to take Ethan away from us and Mark?" *Mamm's* eyes filled with tears.

"We can visit you." Priscilla reached across the table and touched her mother's arm. The pain in her eyes stabbed at her heart. "We won't leave forever. I could never do that to you again. I just can't stand to be here. It hurts me every day to live with Mark in a fake marriage."

"You love him," *Mamm* said.

"Ya." Priscilla nodded as tears sprinkled down her cheeks. "I do, but he doesn't love me, and it's breaking me in two."

"Why do you think leaving him will make it better?"

"If I leave, he can have the life he wants. He never wanted to marry, but he can have his *haus* and his business, and I won't be in his way," Priscilla said. "I don't belong here. I have to go. Will you help me?"

"So that's it, Priscilla?" *Dat's* voice boomed from the doorway. "You're just going to leave again?"

_⌒×⌒_

Mark heard the front door click shut, and he rolled over in bed. Was he dreaming, or had someone just walked into his house?

He sat up and rubbed his eyes. He turned on the lantern on his nightstand and pulled on a long-sleeved shirt and a pair of trousers. He stepped out into the family room and stilled. Only the pop and crackle of the fire in the fireplace filled the little house. He walked to the second bedroom door and pushed it open. He held up the lantern. Only one person was lying in the bed.

Priscilla is gone!

Panic gripped him as he slipped his feet into a pair of boots and hurried out the door and up the path. Cold air smacked his cheeks. Lights on in Edna's kitchen alerted him that someone was awake. He hoped Priscilla was there and that she hadn't left him to go back to Trent.

There it was. The fear he'd tried to forget but never could.

Mark climbed the back steps and opened the door. Yonnie's angry voice filled Mark's ears as he stepped into the house.

"So that's it, Priscilla?" Yonnie bellowed. "You're going to just leave again? You're going to walk out on your husband, and you're going to break your *mamm*'s heart again, and be shunned again?"

Mark stepped through the mudroom to the kitchen doorway as his pulse pounded in his ears. All his nightmares were coming true. Priscilla was going to leave him. She didn't love him. How could she even care about him at all if she was willing to leave him for a man who'd hurt her and endangered Ethan? Maybe he didn't know her as well as he'd thought. His heart splintered into a million painful shards.

"You want to know what you are, Priscilla?" Yonnie continued, circling the kitchen table so his back was to Mark. "You're nothing but a harlot."

"Yonnie, stop! That's not true!" Edna yelled. "You need to stop treating her this way! She's our *dochder*. Don't push her away. I can't lose her again!"

Mark's blood boiled as he walked up behind Yonnie.

"You're going to lose the best thing that has ever happened to you," Yonnie said. "You don't deserve Mark. You're blessed to be here with us. You're fortunate that he even agreed to marry you after what you did."

"I don't deserve to be treated this way," Priscilla said, seething as she stood. "You have no right to talk to me like this, and I won't stand for it any longer. I came here looking for help, not more criticism."

Then the truth hit Mark between the eyes. Priscilla had two abusers in her life—Trent and her father. This was why she left the community eight years ago. She'd gone to escape this verbal abuse, which was worse than he'd ever heard or imagined. She told him that day in the barn that she'd fallen for Trent because she was desperate for someone to love her. But he hadn't realized that desperation came not just from a lack of love from her father, but from how horribly Yonnie had treated her.

Mark had to put a stop to this now! He had to be the one man who treated Priscilla with respect and cherished her. He had to save her from this endless cycle of abuse. He had to get her out of this toxic environment for good.

"Stop it!" Mark yelled as his red, burning hot anger erupted like a volcano.

Yonnie spun and faced him, his face twisted into a scowl. But he took a step back as Mark came into the kitchen.

Mark's body quaked as he shook his finger at Yonnie. "You have no right to treat her that way. She's not a harlot. She's your *dochder*, Ethan's *mamm*, and *mei fraa*. She's not fortunate that I married her." He jammed the finger into his own chest. "I'm fortunate that she agreed to marry *me*. I don't deserve a woman as kind, sweet, and lovely as she is. And you don't deserve to even call her your *dochder*."

He pushed past Yonnie and made his way to Priscilla. She wiped tears from her face as she stared at him.

"Let's go, Priscilla." Mark motioned for her to follow him.

She hesitated. "Where are we going?"

"I'm getting you out of here for *gut*," Mark said. "He's never going to treat you this badly again."

"Just wait a minute," Yonnie said. "I was talking to her. You have no right—"

"Actually, Yonnie, I do have a right to take her from here." Mark walked over to him. "I'm her husband, and I will not allow you to abuse her any longer."

Priscilla went to Mark, and he threaded his fingers in hers. They started toward the mudroom, and then he stopped and turned toward Yonnie, who stared after them, wide-eyed.

"Oh, one more thing, Yonnie," Mark said. "I do remember that you own this farm and you're my employer. Consider this my resignation. We're leaving tonight, and we're not coming back."

Priscilla felt as if her head was spinning as Mark held on to her hand and pulled her down her parents' back porch steps.

"Wait." She stopped and yanked him back to her. "Where are we going?"

"I was thinking of taking you to Jamie's, but they have a new *boppli*. We'll go to Laura's. She has room for us." He started down the path. "We'll pack enough clothes for overnight and come back for more in the daylight."

She opened her mouth to protest, but then she closed it again.

When they arrived at the *daadihaus*, she quickly dressed and then filled a bag with clothes for all of them while Mark gathered Ethan in his arms and covered him with a quilt. Then they hurried through the cold to the stable.

Mark hitched up the horse and buggy, and they started on their journey to Laura's house.

They rode in silence for several minutes as Priscilla stared out the window. Only Ethan's breathing filled the buggy as her father's cruel words echoed in her mind and tears filled her eyes once again.

"I'm sorry he did that to you." Mark's voice was compassionate. "He's always talked to you that way?"

"*Ya.*" She swiped her hand over her eyes.

"Is that why you left years ago?"

"*Ya.*" She shivered as her memories turned to the night that had driven her away from her childhood home. "I had been out with the youth, and we stayed out past our usual ten o'clock. When I got home it was after eleven, and he was waiting for me at the door. He accused me of being out all night, drinking and being promiscuous, which wasn't true. We had gone to spend the day at Cascade Lake and stopped at a restaurant on the way home. We were having so much fun talking and laughing that we lost track of time."

"I remember that trip," Mark said. "We all got home late that night."

"Exactly." She took a tissue from her coat pocket. "I tried to explain to him that we had just lost track of time, but he was convinced I was out misbehaving, and he said I would bring shame on him with my actions. I tried to explain that I'd done nothing but swim and spend time with *mei freinden* all day. He refused to believe me, and it was the last straw. I couldn't take the accusations and the criticism anymore, and it pushed me over the edge. I packed up my things and left after my parents went to bed that night."

"So for your whole life, he's made you think you're not worthy of his love. Or anyone's."

She nodded and tried to clear her throat past a swelling lump of anguish.

Mark halted the horse at a red light and turned toward her. "Were you really going to leave me?"

She nodded.

"Why?" The pain in his eyes was like a splinter in her heart.

"I can't live a lie anymore." Her voice was thin. "I can't stay in a pretend marriage. It's tearing me apart. You can have the *haus* and the business. I know besides not wanting to be shunned, they're the reason you married me."

After a moment he said, "Someone once told me there's more to life than owning a *haus*."

"Mark, I don't want to ruin your life anymore."

"You'd ruin my life if you and Ethan left me."

She bit back a sob as she stared at him. He turned toward the windshield and guided the horse through the intersection. Then they turned on the road that led to Laura's house.

When they reached the top of Laura's driveway, Allen came outside.

"Is everything all right?" he asked as he jogged down the steps.

Mark climbed out of the buggy. "Could we stay here tonight? I'll explain everything later, but we had to get out of the *daadihaus*."

"*Ya*, of course." Allen looked between them. "Let me help you with your horse and buggy."

Laura appeared on the porch, hugging a shawl to her middle. "What's going on?"

"They need a place to stay," Allen explained.

Laura waved them in. "Come inside out of the cold."

Priscilla leaned over the back of the buggy and nudged Ethan. "Ethan. Ethan, honey. I need you to wake up. You need to walk into *Aenti* Laura's *haus*, okay?"

Ethan rubbed his eyes as he sat up.

Priscilla grabbed the bag of clothes, and then she and Ethan climbed the steps and into Laura's house.

⌒⌢⌒

"I can't stay there," Mark said to his brother-in-law after telling him what Yonnie said to Priscilla. "It's too toxic for Priscilla and Ethan." He rubbed at the knots of tension in his neck. "I've never been so furious in my life."

"I can't believe how Yonnie talks to her." Allen shook his head as they stood in the office of his carriage business. "I would never speak to *mei dochder* that way."

"I know." Mark held up his hands. "I'm sorry to impose on you like this, but Jamie has a new *boppli*, and *mei dat* doesn't have room for us. Could we stay here until I find a *haus* to rent? I'll start looking tomorrow, and I'll see if I can work for *mei dat*. We'll be out of here before your new *boppli* is born."

"It's no problem." Allen shook his head. "You can stay here as long as you'd like." He pointed toward his shop, where he repaired and rebuilt buggies. "You can even work for me if you want to. My business is booming, and I can hardly keep up anymore."

"Danki." Mark started pacing as Yonnie's cruel tirade rang again in his mind. "I just can't get over the words he used toward her. Priscilla is *wunderbaar*, and she doesn't deserve to be spoken to like that." He stopped pacing and looked at Allen. "She said she wanted to leave me because she's ruining my life. I don't understand it. Why would she think that?"

"Did you ask her why?" Allen sat down on a stool.

Mark began to pace again. He felt as if his insides were tied up in knots. He shook his head, and then it hit him like a bolt of lightning. "I'm in love with her. The idea of her leaving me makes me physically ill."

Allen smiled. "It's been obvious to all of us that you two are in love. In fact, Laura and I were just discussing that on our way home from Jamie's *haus* tonight. I know the truth about why you married her. Laura told me."

"She did?"

"*Ya.* She was really upset when we left Jamie's *haus* earlier, and she needed someone to talk to. She told me everything during the ride home since Mollie was asleep in the back of the buggy. It really upset her when Priscilla cried while she held Alice. She said she hoped you and Priscilla would realize how much you love each other and work it out. I'm glad you finally realize you love Priscilla." Allen pointed toward the house. "Now you need to go tell her how you feel, and she'll realize that she doesn't need to leave you. In fact, she'll want to stay."

"*Danki* for letting us stay here," Priscilla said as she closed the door to the sewing room where Ethan was asleep on the sofa. "I appreciate it."

"Of course." Laura hugged her. "I'm so sorry your *dat* was cruel to you."

"*Danki.*" Priscilla took a deep breath. "I thought leaving Mark was the best solution, but Mark was the one who saved me. He got me away from *mei dat.*"

"So that's why you left when we were eighteen." Laura shook

her head. "Why didn't you tell Savilla and me what you were going through at home?"

Priscilla shrugged. "I guess I was embarrassed. I didn't want you to know since you and Savilla both had loving and supportive fathers."

Laura took Priscilla's hand and steered her to the spare room. "I set this room up for Cindy. She borrows Roy's horse and buggy to come visit me, and sometimes we talk late into the night. I ask her to stay instead of going home in the dark. This room will be perfect for you and Mark."

"Danki." Priscilla stared at the double bed, and her heart seemed to stutter before dropping to the pit of her stomach. There wasn't room on Ethan's sofa for her tonight. She and Mark would have to stay together for the first time since they were married.

Laura squeezed Priscilla's arm. "We'll talk more tomorrow, okay? You just get some rest." She started for the door and then turned and faced her. *"Mei bruder* loves you. Just give him a chance to tell you how he feels, okay?"

"Okay," Priscilla said, making a promise. She had to know if her friend was right.

Laura slipped out the door, and Priscilla sank onto the corner of the bed. She was confused but also relieved that Mark had taken her away from her father. Now she had to figure out what would happen next.

Soon after, she heard footsteps on the stairs and muffled voices in the hallway. Then a soft knock sounded on the door.

"Come in," she said as she stood.

Mark stepped into the room and closed the door behind him. He walked over to her, and his blue eyes glistened in the warm glow of the lantern on the dresser. "Can we talk?"

"Ya." The muscles in her shoulders tensed.

"Where were you going to go tonight?"

She shrugged. "I don't know. I went to see *mei mamm* to ask if I could borrow money from her. I wanted to find a little apartment to rent for Ethan and me. I thought I could get a job working as a waitress or seamstress and then I'd pay her back."

"What did I do to push you away?"

"You didn't push me away. You've been nothing but kind and supportive to Ethan and me." Her voice thinned. "But you deserve so much better than me. I'm damaged."

"No, you're not."

"I am." Fresh tears formed in her eyes. "And then when I held Alice tonight, I realized I can't stand to live in a loveless marriage. If I can't have a true marriage with you, then I'd rather be alone. It's torture to be with you but not have all of you, not have your whole heart."

"That's just it, Priscilla." He cupped her cheeks with his hands. "You do have my whole heart. I love you. I've loved you for months, but I didn't realize it right away. I didn't know what love was until I had a chance to get to know you."

The tears escaped down her cheeks.

"I love you too," she whispered. "I didn't know what love could be like before you. When I met Trent, I was looking for someone to love me, but that wasn't love. You make me feel strong and protected."

"Please don't leave me. I can't stand the idea of losing you and Ethan after all we've been through." His eyes searched hers. "I'll make things right. We'll find a *haus* to rent until I can build you one on *mei dat*'s farm. I'll work for *mei dat*. We'll make a life somehow. Give me a chance to show you."

"But what about *mei dat*'s land and his business?"

Mark shook his head. "None of that matters without you. I don't care where we live. I just want to be with you and Ethan. I want to be a family. God chose you for me, and God never makes mistakes. You're my life. You're my future."

He leaned down, and as his lips brushed hers, what felt like an electric current roared through her veins. She closed her eyes, and as she allowed his lips to explore hers, her entire body relaxed. He wrapped his arms around her, and she lost herself in the feel of his touch. This was what true love felt like.

When he pulled away, he rested his forehead against hers and looked into her eyes. "I've been dying to do that for months."

"For months?" she asked.

"*Ya.*" He grinned. "Ever since you said I had eager *maed* who followed me around."

They both laughed.

"Will you give me a chance to show you I can be a real husband?" he asked, his eyes pleading with hers.

"*Ya,*" she said. "I'm so grateful God sent me back here. I've been begging him to show me where I belonged, and he led me straight to you. I thought I had to leave this community to find happiness, but now I realize my heart has always been here. I'm supposed to be a member of the church, and I'm supposed to be your *fraa.* It doesn't matter where we live. I just want to be with you."

Mark wrapped his arms around her waist, and Priscilla's breath hitched in her lungs as his lips met hers again. She looped her arms around his neck and pulled him in closer. He deepened the kiss, and it lit a fire inside her, turning her bones to ash. She closed her eyes and savored the feel of his mouth against hers.

Yes. This is where I belong—here with Mark. This is my true home.

THIRTY

THE NEXT MORNING PRISCILLA CARRIED A PLAT-
ter to Laura's kitchen table and then sat down beside Mark. She
smiled at Ethan. He was sitting beside Mollie on the other side of
the table.

"I think that's everything," Laura said. "Let's pray."

They bowed their heads in silent prayer and then began filling their plates with eggs, bacon, home fried potatoes, and rolls.

"Have you given my idea any thought?" Allen asked Mark.

"What idea?" Laura divided a look between them.

"I asked Mark if he wanted to come work for me. You know
my business has been growing, and I could use a partner."

"Really?" Priscilla turned to Mark. "Are you going to do it?"

"I'll think about it." Mark picked up a piece of bacon. "I appreciate the offer, but right now I need to find a *haus*."

"No, you don't." Laura shook her head. "We have plenty of
room here. We'll put a twin-size bed in the sewing room for Ethan.
Mollie has her own room, and we have room for the *boppli*."

"*Mei schweschder.*" Mollie sat up straight and lifted her chin.
"I know she's a girl."

Priscilla grinned as she turned to Laura. "Are you having
a girl?"

"I don't know." Laura shrugged. "I guess we'll see."

A knock sounded on the back door, and Allen rose. "Are you expecting anyone?"

"No." Laura shook her head.

Allen disappeared into the mudroom while everyone continued to eat. He returned a few moments later with Priscilla's father walking behind him.

Priscilla swallowed a gasp. She looked at Mark, whose face had transformed into a deep frown.

"Yonnie," Mark said as he stood. "What are you doing here?"

"I want to talk to you and Priscilla. Please." *Dat* held up his hand. "I'm here to apologize."

Laura gestured toward the family room. "Why don't you go in there so you have some privacy?"

Mark looked at Priscilla as if asking permission, and she nodded. "Okay."

Priscilla stood, and Mark threaded his fingers with hers. The simple gesture of affection filled her with strength as she walked with Mark into the family room.

"What do you want to say?" Mark stood in front of her father with his head held high.

"I want to apologize . . . for everything."

Priscilla blinked and then shook her head. This was too good to be true.

"Why the sudden change in your demeanor?" Mark asked.

Dat's expression clouded. "After you left last night, I remembered a Scripture verse the bishop gave a sermon on recently. It's Colossians 3:12. 'Therefore, as God's chosen people, holy and dearly loved, clothe yourselves with compassion, kindness, humility, gentleness and patience.' I couldn't get it out of my head last night."

Priscilla's eyes watered as Mark gave her hand a gentle squeeze.

"Edna made me realize how terrible I've been all these years. She's been trying to tell me since Priscilla was a little girl, but I never listened." His dark eyes filled with tears. "*Mei dat* was tough on *mei bruders* and me. I always resented how he treated me, but I realize now I've become just as terrible as he was—if not worse."

He turned toward Priscilla. "You told me you thought I was disappointed in you because you weren't a *bu*. And now you might think I was hard on you because *mei daed* was hard on me. But the truth is when we learned your mother and I couldn't have more *kinner*, I was hard on you for one reason: to prove I could raise my only *kind* to be the model community member *mei daed* never thought I was. In the end, I was wrong, so very wrong."

He peered into Priscilla's eyes with a look of contrition she'd never seen.

"I've always been too tough on you, Priscilla. I realize now that I wasn't loving. I never guided you. I only criticized you. I wasn't the *daed* you needed or deserved, and I'm so very truly sorry. If only I could go back in time and fix everything, but I know I can't. I'm sorry. I was wrong. I pushed you away eight years ago, and last night I did it again. I was wrong to call you that cruel name. Please forgive me and come back to the farm. You belong there, and you've earned my horse business. I want to give it to family, and you're my only family."

"I forgive you," she said, her voice stronger than she'd hoped. "But it's too late for you to apologize. I can't go back there. I've moved on, and you should too. Mark and I have decided to find a *haus* to rent, or we might stay here. He's thinking about working with Allen."

With one hand still entwined with Mark's, she placed her other hand on his forearm. Her husband's strength gave her courage and kept her from breaking apart.

"Please." *Dat* looked between them. "I want you to come back. I will do better. I will be the *daed* you deserve and the *daadi* Ethan deserves."

"You say that now," Mark began, "but how do we know you won't lose your temper and begin to call Priscilla cruel names again? The name you called her should never be used to describe someone's *dochder*. It was inexcusable. Priscilla doesn't deserve to be treated that way, and you're not the example I want for Ethan."

"You're right." *Dat* nodded, his expression forlorn. "But I promise I'll do better. I will think before I speak."

Mark turned to Priscilla. "What do you want?"

"I don't want to go back there, but I want you to be *froh*," she said. "Do you want my father's business? Do you want to live on the farm?"

"I've already told you I don't care where we live as long as I have you and Ethan with me."

"Let's stick with our plan." She gave his hand a gentle squeeze.

"Fine." Mark looked over at *Dat*. "I can't take the chance of your verbally abusing Priscilla any longer. We're going to stay here."

Dat's eyes misted over. "You won't come back home?"

Mark shook his head and then nodded toward the doorway. "I think you should leave now."

Dat hesitated and then gave a curt nod before walking out of the house.

Priscilla looked up at Mark as panic stirred in her belly. "What did we just do?"

The look in Mark's eyes comforted her as he touched her cheek. "We stood up for what was right. When I married you, I promised to protect you and Ethan, and that's just what I plan to do." He leaned down and brushed his lips against hers. "Let's go finish our breakfast, and then I'll talk to Allen about working for him."

As Mark steered her back into the kitchen, a calmness settled over Priscilla. She suddenly knew to the very depth of her being that somehow everything would turn out just fine as long as she and Ethan had Mark by their side.

"Mamm!" Priscilla hurried over to her mother a week later as she gathered with the other women in the Bontrager family's kitchen before the church service. "How are you?"

"I'm fine." *Mamm*'s eyes sparkled with tears as she pulled her into her arms for a hug. "How are you?"

"We're doing okay." Priscilla nodded. "Mark is working for Allen, and we'll look for a *haus* to rent unless we decide to stay at Laura and Allen's for now."

"How are things between you and Mark?"

Priscilla tried in vain to suppress a smile. "Really *gut*. I've never been so *froh* in my life. He loves me, and he's such a *gut* father to Ethan."

"I'm so glad. I knew it would work out between you two. I could see how much he loved you before you realized it." *Mamm* dabbed her eyes with a tissue she took from her apron. "How's Ethan?"

Priscilla shrugged. "He's doing well. He and Mollie get along great, but he misses you and *Dat*."

"We miss all three of you. Our home feels so empty and incomplete without you and your family. I keep expecting Ethan to walk into the kitchen and tell me about his day at school." *Mamm* wiped away an errant tear, and an intense sympathy for her mother caught Priscilla off guard. She hadn't realized just how much the result of *Dat*'s hateful words had changed her world.

"Your *dat* feels terrible about what he said. I've been telling him for years that he was too critical of you, and that he said things that were cruel. He finally realizes how wrong he was."

Mamm cleared her throat. "Would you consider coming home? Your *dat* and I want you and Ethan to come back. We miss you so much." She folded her hands as if she were praying. "Your *dat* has promised me that if you come back, he'll do his best to make you feel welcome. He'll show you that he regrets all the years he hurt you. He'll make up for it."

Priscilla swallowed back a knot of emotion that threatened to choke her. "I appreciate all you said to him and how you finally made him realize how wrong he was. But Mark won't take the chance that *Dat* will hurt me again. He also doesn't want Ethan to hear *Dat*'s cruel words."

"I understand." *Mamm* paused. "But we also need you. Your *dat* is getting older, and he can't handle the work on his own. He wants to hire someone, but he'd rather have Mark. He really admires Mark, and he wants to leave the farm to Ethan and the rest of your *kinner* if you and Mark have more."

"I don't know what to say." Priscilla shook her head. "Mark doesn't want to come back."

"Why don't you think about it?" *Mamm* touched Priscilla's arm. "Tell Mark your *dat* needs his help, and he's willing to do whatever it takes to get all of you back home with us on the farm."

"All right. I'll talk to Mark tonight," Priscilla said, willing to make the promise.

Later that evening Priscilla climbed into bed beside Mark. She snuggled down under the covers, and Mark wrapped his arms around her and pulled her close.

"Are you going to tell me what's been on your mind all afternoon? Or do I have to guess?" Mark's voice in her ear sent a shiver dancing down her back.

"Why don't you guess?" She grinned.

"Let's see," he began. "You're wondering how you managed to snag yourself such a handsome husband."

She laughed. "Not even close."

"Okay. You're trying to figure out the best gift to get me for Christmas."

She chuckled. "Nope. That's not it either."

"All right. I give up." He released her, and she turned toward him. The soft yellow glow of the lantern complemented his chiseled face.

"It's actually serious."

"Uh-oh." His smile faded. "What is it?"

"I talked to *mei mamm* today before church. She wants us to come back to the farm."

His handsome face clouded. "No."

"Just listen for a minute." She sat up, leaning her back against the headboard. "She said *mei dat* wants us back. He needs your help with the farm. He also wants to leave the farm to Ethan and any *kinner* we might have in the future."

Mark propped himself up with a pillow. "What do you want to do?"

She shook her head as confusion filled her. "I don't know. Part of me wants to go back. Laura is going to have her *boppli* anytime now, and they don't need extra people in their *haus*."

"We're not homeless, Priscilla, and we're not destitute. I'll eventually find us another place to live. I have money in the bank. I've been saving for years."

"I know that." She touched his cheek, enjoying the scratchy feel of his beard. "What do you want?"

Mark looked across the room as if the dresser held all the answers. "I like working with Allen, but I do miss the horses."

"Really?"

He nodded as he faced her once again. "I enjoyed the work. I never knew how much I could enjoy training horses until I went to work with your *dat*."

"So you like working there more than you like working for Allen?"

"*Ya*, I do." His expression became fierce. "But I won't allow him to hurt you ever again."

"I know that." She touched his cheek again as affection overwhelmed her. "But what if we went back on our terms?"

"What do you mean?"

"What if we told him we'll come back only on certain conditions?"

"I'm listening."

"We just need to decide what we want." She touched his shoulder. "What will it take to get you back there?"

Mark rubbed his beard. "I would want to earn a salary, and then I'll build our *haus* when we're ready. It will be our *haus*, and I'll pay for it. I don't want your *dat* to foot the bill, and I don't want him to have a hold on us. I'll earn my way on that farm. I'm not going there to get anything for free."

"I understand."

"And your *dat* has to prove to me that he can treat you with respect. If he says one thing out of turn, we're gone." He snapped his fingers. "Does that sound *gut*?"

"Ya." She rubbed his shoulder. "Do you want to talk to my parents tomorrow while Ethan is in school?"

"If that's what you want, then *ya.*"

"Okay. It's settled, then." She smiled.

"Gut." Mark grabbed her by the waist, and she squealed as he pulled her over to him. "Come here, *mei fraa.*" He grinned before kissing her.

She relaxed against him as she lost herself in the feel of his lips, and bliss bubbled through her veins.

_____ ❧ _____

Priscilla stood beside Mark on her parents' front porch the following morning. The door opened, and her mother gave a little squeal as she opened it wide.

"Priscilla. Mark." *Mamm* gestured for them to come in. "I'm so *froh* to see you."

"It's nice to see you too," Mark said as they stepped inside the house. "Is Yonnie home?"

"Ya, we were just having *kaffi* in the kitchen," *Mamm* said. "Hang up your coats and come join us."

Priscilla looked up at Mark, and he gave her a reassuring smile as they hung their coats on the pegs by the front door. Then they followed *Mamm* into the kitchen.

"Priscilla." *Dat's* expression brightened as he looked up at her. "Mark. *Wie geht's?"*

"We were wondering if we could talk to you," Mark said.

"Please have a seat." *Dat* gestured to the chairs across from him.

"Would you like some *kaffi*?" *Mamm* offered.

"Ya, please," Mark said. *"Danki."*

"I'll help you serve it." Priscilla took mugs from the cabinet and set them on the table. Mark sat down across from *Dat*.

"What do you want to discuss?" *Dat's* expression seemed hopeful.

"Edna told Priscilla you still want us to move back to the farm," Mark began. "She said you want me to work for you, and you want to leave the farm to Ethan and any *kinner* we might have."

"That's true." *Dat* fingered his beard. "I really need your help. I can't run this farm by myself, and you're the best farmhand I've ever had. Besides that, you're family now." He looked up at Priscilla. "And I miss all of you. I especially miss having *mei gross-sohn* around."

Priscilla's hands trembled as she poured coffee into Mark's mug. Why did her father always know how to get right to her heart, no matter how much he'd hurt her in the past?

When she handed Mark his mug, he touched her arm and gave her a tender smile. The simple gesture calmed her, and her hands stopped shaking.

Crossing to the counter again, Priscilla filled a mug for herself and then sat down beside Mark. Her mother sat down across from her.

"What do you say?" *Dat* asked Mark. "Will you come back?"

"We will." Mark looked at Priscilla once again. "But only under certain conditions."

"Okay." *Dat's* expression brightened. "What are your conditions?"

"I want to earn a salary," Mark said. "We'll live in the *daadihaus* until I have enough money to build a *haus*."

"No, I can build you one," *Dat* said. "I have plenty of money."

"No." Mark's voice was even but firm. "I want to earn our *haus* and build it with my own money. I don't want anything for free. I'll save enough to build the *haus* Priscilla wants." He glanced at her. "I want *mei fraa* to be *froh*."

Priscilla gave him a little smile, and then she and her mother shared a smile.

Mark faced her father again. "And you have to treat Priscilla with respect. I won't allow you to hurt her anymore, and I want you to be a *gut* role model for Ethan. You have to earn back our trust. I won't permit you to insult or criticize Priscilla at all. If you do, we'll leave again. I'll find a *haus* to rent and go back to working for Allen or *mei dat*."

Dat nodded. "I understand, and I'll prove myself to you. I'll do anything to have you come back. I don't want to lose my family again. You're all important to me."

Mark looked at Priscilla. "Does that all sound *gut* to you?"

Priscilla nodded. *"Ya."*

Dat met her gaze, and his eyes glimmered with tears. *"Danki* for forgiving me and giving me another chance. I won't let you down."

Tears stung her own eyes as she silently asked God to guide her father's heart toward her.

Mark looped his arm around Priscilla's shoulders and gave her a little squeeze before looking at her father again. "When do you want us to come back?"

"How about today?" *Dat* asked.

Mamm clapped. "I'm so *froh*. I'll have my family back together."

Priscilla smiled. "Ethan is going to be so excited." She squeezed Mark's hand.

While she knew her relationship with her father would never be perfect after the way he'd treated her, for the first time in a long time, her heart was filled with hope.

—⟨⟩⟨⟩—

"So Mollie was right," Priscilla said as she held her newborn niece against her chest a week later. She moved the rocking chair in Florence's family room back and forth. "She knew she was going to have a baby *schweschder*."

"I know." Laura laughed. "She predicted I would have a girl, and I did."

Cindy smiled as she touched Catherine's little fingers. "I can't get over how tiny she is."

"She looks like an angel," Sarah Jane chimed in.

"I know." Priscilla looked down at her. "That little nose and that thick, dark-brown hair. She's so *schee*, and I love her name. Catherine Savilla Lambert is beautiful."

Laura smiled. "Mollie insisted we name her after her other *mamm*, as she calls Savilla. It seemed fitting that we remember Savilla this way."

"*Ya*, I agree." Happy tears gathered in Priscilla's eyes. "She's just perfect."

"You'll be next," Laura said with a smile. "I can feel it."

"I hope so." Priscilla bit her lower lip as heat infused her cheeks. Her marriage had been just about perfect the past couple of weeks, and she couldn't have been any happier. Their relationship had grown deeper and more meaningful since they'd stayed at Laura's house. Priscilla could feel Mark's love surrounding her and making her more courageous every day. She had the marriage she'd always wanted. God had truly blessed her the day she became Mark's wife.

They'd also settled into a comfortable routine on her father's farm during the past week. *Dat* had been respectful and kind to her, and they'd had a few meaningful talks. She was hesitant to trust him after the lifetime of hurt he'd subjected her to, but she allowed herself to remain hopeful that someday she and her father could grow closer.

She touched Catherine's little fingers, and her heart fluttered. She and Mark had so much to look forward to as a couple. She looked forward to the day she and Mark would have a child together. She was certain it would happen in God's perfect timing.

"May I have a turn to hold her?" Cindy held up her arms.

"Of course." Priscilla passed the baby over to Cindy and then stood so she could take the rocking chair.

"Are you ready to go?" Mark appeared in the doorway with Ethan by his side. "It's getting late."

"*Ya.*" Priscilla stood, and she and Mark both said good night to the sisters. She followed Mark and Ethan into the kitchen, where they said good-bye to the rest of the family. Then she walked with Mark and Ethan out into the cold so they could start their journey home.

"This is perfect," Mark said as Priscilla snuggled up next to him in front of the fire in the *daadihaus* later that evening. "Hot chocolate, a warm fire, and *mei schee fraa*."

"You say that to all the *maed*." Priscilla looked up at him and pulled the quilt over her lap. Then she smiled at the hearth, admiring the pinecones, evergreen branches, and candles she'd used to decorate it for Christmas.

"Are you calling me a user again?" he said, grinning.

"Well, you know what they say. If the shoe fits . . ." She laughed, and then she took a sip of hot chocolate before setting her mug on the coffee table and snuggling closer to Mark. "I can't believe how adorable our two new nieces are. Do you think we'll have a girl someday?"

"We can hope." He kissed her forehead. "How many *kinner* do you want?"

"I don't know. Maybe six?"

"Six?" He cringed, and she laughed. "How about two more?"

"Or three." She touched his bearded chin. "You have three biological siblings."

"*Ya*, I sure do." He pulled her closer and wrapped his arms around her shoulders. "I don't care how many we have as long as I'm with you."

"I feel the same way." She leaned against him and relished the sound of his heartbeat.

"I have something for you. I know it's not Christmas yet, but I can't wait to give it to you." He reached under the sofa, pulling up a large piece of flat wood. "I've been working on this for a while. I used to tinker with it before we moved in with Laura and Allen, before going to sleep." He handed it to her. "Here."

"Oh my goodness!" Priscilla gaped as she ran her fingers over the carving that was a perfect representation of their little house. He'd even included her small garden with the happy flowers. Tears filled her eyes at the love and tenderness he'd carved into the wood for her. "Mark. This is exquisite."

"You think so?" He frowned. "It's not perfect, but I'll get better as I work on more carvings." He smiled at her. "I wanted to use the tools you gave me to make you something special. We'll always have this as a memory of our first *haus*."

"I love it." She touched his cheek. "*Danki.*"

"*Gern gschehne.*" He threaded his fingers with hers. "This way you'll always remember where we started out."

"I love our little *haus*. I just want to stay here in front of the hearth with you." She looked up at him. "Do you think we should build a hearth in our new *haus*?"

"Why not? It's going to be our *haus*, right? We should have what we want."

"That's true."

"Like I said before, I just want to make *mei fraa froh. Ich liebe dich*," Mark whispered against her hair.

"I love you too."

Mark brushed his lips against hers, sending happiness buzzing through her like a honeybee. She smiled against his mouth and silently thanked God for giving her true love and happiness. Her most fervent prayers had been answered. She could hardly wait to see what tomorrow would bring.

DISCUSSION QUESTIONS

1. When Priscilla left the community eight years earlier, she believed she'd never go back. By the end of the book, she realizes the Amish community is her true home. What do you think caused her to change her point of view throughout the story?

2. Franey is jealous when she learns Mark is going to marry Priscilla. She's so upset that she says cruel things about Priscilla. Have you ever been jealous of a friend? If so, did that jealousy cause you to say things that weren't true? Did you regret what you said, and did you ask for forgiveness? Share this with the group.

3. Laura confides in Priscilla that she experienced miscarriages early in her marriage. She also shares with Mark that she is nervous about her pregnancy because of her past losses. Could you relate to Laura and her experience? Share this with the group.

4. Priscilla believes she's damaged and unworthy of love. Think of a time when you felt lost and alone. Where did you find your strength? What Bible verses helped?

5. At the start of the book, Mark doesn't believe he'll ever want to get married and have children. His dream of owning his own home on his father's farm is enough for him. However,

he changes as the story progresses. What do you think caused him to change his point of view about his future?

6. Yonnie has always been hard on Priscilla, believing his tough parenting style was permissible. He discovers the error of his ways at the end of the story. What made him realize he'd been wrong and ask for forgiveness? How have you felt convicted of a wrongdoing?

7. By the end of the book, Mark realizes he's fallen in love with Priscilla. What do you think helped him realize how strong his feelings for her were?

8. Which character can you identify with the most? Which character seemed to carry the most emotional stake in the story? Was it Priscilla, Ethan, Mark, or someone else?

9. What role did Ethan play in Mark and Priscilla's relationship? Did he help strengthen their marriage?

10. What did you know about the Amish before reading this book? What did you learn?

ACKNOWLEDGMENTS

As always, I'm thankful for my loving family, including my mother, Lola Goebelbecker; my husband, Joe; and my sons, Zac and Matt. I'm blessed to have such an awesome and amazing family who puts up with me when I'm stressed out on a book deadline.

Special thanks to my mother and my dear friend Becky Biddy, who graciously read the draft of this book to check for typos. Becky—I'm sure you ran out of a few dispensers of tape flags on this one! Also, thank you, Becky, for your daily notes of encouragement. Your friendship is a blessing!

I'm also grateful to my special Amish friend, who patiently answers my endless stream of questions.

Thank you to my wonderful church family at Morning Star Lutheran in Matthews, North Carolina, for your encouragement, prayers, love, and friendship. You all mean so much to my family and me.

Thank you to Zac Weikal and the fabulous members of my Bakery Bunch! I'm so thankful for your friendship and your excitement about my books. You all are amazing!

To my agent, Natasha Kern—I can't thank you enough for your guidance, advice, and friendship. You are a tremendous blessing in my life.

Thank you to my amazing editor, Jocelyn Bailey, for your friendship and guidance. I appreciate how you push me to dig deeper with each book and improve my writing. I've learned so much from you, and I look forward to our future projects together. I also cherish our fun emails and text messages. You are a delight!

I'm grateful to editor Jean Bloom, who helped me polish and refine the story. Jean, you are a master at connecting the dots and filling in the gaps. I'm so thankful that we can continue to work together!

Thank you to Janet Jeter for help with the twin research. You're so blessed to not only have a twin brother but also another set of twins in your family! Thank you for giving me pointers on Laura and Mark's connection. I'm so grateful to have you as one of my work buddies.

I also would like to thank Kristen Golden for tirelessly working to promote my books. I'm grateful to each and every person at HarperCollins Christian Publishing who helped make this book a reality.

To my readers—thank you for choosing my novels. My books are a blessing in my life for many reasons, including the special friendships I've formed with my readers. Thank you for your email messages, Facebook notes, and letters.

Thank you most of all to God—for giving me the inspiration and the words to glorify You. I'm grateful and humbled You've chosen this path for me.

The Kauffman

Amish Bakery Series

ABOUT THE AUTHOR

 AMY CLIPSTON IS THE AWARD-WINNING
and bestselling author of the Amish Heirloom
series and the Kauffman Amish Bakery series.
She has sold more than one million books.
Her novels have hit multiple bestseller lists
including CBD, CBA, and ECPA. Amy holds
a degree in communications from Virginia Wesleyan University
and works full-time for the City of Charlotte, NC. Amy lives in
North Carolina with her husband, two sons, mom, and three
spoiled-rotten cats.

Visit her online at amyclipston.com
Facebook: AmyClipstonBooks
Twitter: @AmyClipston
Instagram: @amy_clipston